Advances in Distributed Computing and Intelligent Data Analytics

nova
science publishers
New York

Advances in Distributed Computing and Intelligent Data Analytics

Soumi Dutta
Vinod Kumar Shukla
Shruti Nagpal
and
Niranjanamurthy M
Editors

Industry 4.0 and Intelligent Business Analytics for Healthcare

nova
science publishers
New York

https://doi.org/10.52305/MWCH6764

Library of Congress Cataloging-in-Publication Data

ISBN: 978-1-68507-602-3

Published by Nova Science Publishers, Inc. † New York

Contents

Preface ix

Part I. Industry 4.0 and Healthcare 1

Chapter 1 **Human Computer Interface Trends in Healthcare: Industry 4.0 View** 3
Simra Fathima Nazim, Vinod Kumar Shukla and Komal Saxena

Chapter 2 **Role of Urban Control Centers for City Planning and Monitoring in a Pandemic Outbreak** 15
Shaurya Gupta, Sonali Vyas and Kanta Prasad Sharma

Chapter 3 **Industry 4.0 for Promoting Health Inclusion in Emerging Markets: A Systematic Study of Narayana Healthcare, India** 29
Sana Moid, Nitin Shankar and Fatima Beena

Chapter 4 **Bitcoin Mining and Its Utility in the Healthcare Sector** 49
Farhana Hussain Altaf Hussain, Vinod Kumar Shukla, Leena Wanganoo and Amit Verma

Chapter 5 **Vocational Training and Integrative Technology in Neurodiverse Workforce** 71
Sonakshi Ruhela, Mark Eugine Francisco and Hibah Shata

Chapter 6 **Use of Some Standard Mathematical Models in Physiology and Pathology** 91
Saktipada Nanda and Sibashis Nanda

Chapter 7 **Training Healthcare Professionals in Artificial Intelligence Augmented Services** 117
Yasmeen Shamsi Rizvi and Sufian Zaheer

Part 2. Artificial Intelligence and Machine Learning in Healthcare 135

Chapter 8 **Healthcare Sector and Use of Artificial Intelligence Technology in Modern Times** 137
Kush Kalra and Pradeep Kulshrestha

Chapter 9 **Prediction of Cardiovascular Diseases Using Data Mining - Machine Learning and Deep Learning System** 145
Aiman Siraj, Vinod Kumar Shukla and Sonia Saini

Chapter 10 **Artificially Intelligent Queueing Modeling Approach to Analyzing and Improving Health Care Systems** 171
S. S. Mishra, Carol Hargreaves, S. Ahmad Ali and Sandeep Rawat

Chapter 11 **Clientele Perception and Trust on Artificial Intelligence Integrated Health Services** 189
Andre Magpantay

Chapter 12 **Leveraging Deep Learning: Early Detection and Prediction of Brain Disorders** 215
Maha Waheed Shahzad, Aiman Siraj, Aradhana Balodi Bhardwaj and Vinod Kumar Shukla

Part 3. COVID-19, Healthcare and Technology 239

Chapter 13 **COVID-19 Pandemic: Recovery and Death Ratio Analysis Based on Latitude Using Correlation and ANOVA** 241
Rinkal Sardhara and Shanti Verma

Chapter 14 **Pillars of a Corruption Free Economically Strong Healthcare Industry during COVID-19: Artificial Intelligence and Global Connectivity** 253
Kamakshi Mehta, Shikha Sharma and Vinod Kumar Shukla

Chapter 15 **Analyzing COVID-19 and Other Pandemics through Human-Computer Interaction** 271
Dulini Ratnayake, Vinod Kumar Shukla and Ruchika Bathla

Chapter 16 **Electronic Health Records and Challenges in Human Computer Interaction** 285
Pooja Lohit, Vinod Kumar Shukla and Anjuli Chaubey

Chapter 17 **A Novel Model to Anticipate Transparency in COVID-19 Records of India Using Blockchain** 299
Shanti Verma and Rinkal Sardhara

Chapter 18 **Applications and Implementation of Contactless Hand Sanitizer Using Proximity Sensor** 309
Syeda Fizza Nuzhat Zaidi, Vinod Kumar Shukla, Ashok Chopra and Archana Singh

About the Editors 323

About the Contributors 327

Index 347

Preface

In today's world, there is nothing permanent except change. We have seen the advent of the Fourth Industrial Revolution or Industry 4.0 over the last couple of years. Now is a perfect time to think about Industry 4.0 technology and leverage its advantages for the benefit of mankind. It cannot prevent the onset of pandemics; however, it can help and has helped prevent spread, educate, warn, and empower those on the ground to be aware of the situation, and noticeably lessen the impact. Industry 4.0 can fulfill the requirements of customized facemasks, gloves, and collect information for healthcare systems for proper controlling and treating of COVID-19 patients.

Major technologies of Industry 4.0 are required to solve the problems of this virus. It is useful to provide day-to-day updates of an infected patient, area-wise, age-wise and state-wise with proper surveillance systems. We also believe that the proper implementation of these technologies would help to enhance education and communication regarding public health. These Industry 4.0 technologies could provide a lot of innovative ideas and solutions for fighting local and global medical emergencies.

Today, we need to focus on technologies like mobile, cloud, analytics, robotics, AI/ML, 4G/5G, and high-speed internet; it has become possible to test several innovative approaches to pandemic response. The objective of this book is to bring together leading academic scientists, research scholars and professionals to exchange and share their experiences and research results in Industry 4.0 and Intelligent Business Analytics.

This research-oriented book will provide a common platform to all researchers in this domain. It covers different verticals of industry and academics, which is an added advantage of this book.

Part I. Industry 4.0 and Healthcare

Chapter 1

Human Computer Interface Trends in Healthcare: Industry 4.0 View

Simra Fathima Nazim[1], Vinod Kumar Shukla[2,*] and Komal Saxena[3]

[1,2] Department of Engineering and Architecture,
Amity University, Dubai, UAE
[3] Amity Institute of Information Technology, Amity University, Noida, India

Abstract

Interaction between humans and computers has become a part of our daily lives. From mobile phones to every other technology we deal with, direct interaction with computers plays a vital role. HCI is the study of the design and usability of software and technology, and its application and use in healthcare are not new. As the healthcare community evolves in the era of industry 4.0, its reliance on the latest technology keeps increasing. Every human will deal with healthcare facilities, and HCI trends have to look after making purposeful and empowered design and technology for both the patient and medical professionals. In a healthcare environment, devices have to be designed so that every patient can use them. This may include people with disabilities and medical professionals, and developing appropriate HCI becomes essential.

Keywords: Human Computer Interface (HCI), Industry 4.0, healthcare, technology

[*] Corresponding Author's Email: vinodkumarshukla@gmail.com.

In: Industry 4.0 and Intelligent Business Analytics for Healthcare
Editors: Soumi Dutta, Vinod Kumar Shukla, Shruti Nagpal et al.
ISBN: 978-1-68507-602-3

Introduction

Industry 4.0 includes virtualization concepts, decentralization, service orientation, modularity, real-time capabilities, and interoperability [1]. Based on industry 4.0, health 4.0 was derived for the health system. The aim of this is to manage diseases more appropriately by collecting information in real-time from patients and taking proper steps and requirements by using an algorithm that can also help predict the patients' conditions. This would help medical professionals to take care of the current state of the patients, and based on the prediction, many of the side effects of diseases can be eliminated. The fourth revolution would help the medical field design and implement various tools and technologies advancing the current state of the medical field in lesser time. Industry 4.0 will help reach these goals using different technologies: additive manufacturing, big data, sensors, artificial intelligence, holography, robotics, and the internet. The medical field can help achieve vast and maximized productivity, reduction in time and cost of implementation, use and analyze medical records/ data of patients to make use in different technologies, digitally store the recorded data and predict the condition of disease, reduce paperwork, enhance managements of tooling and materials used, use a centralized info system for the entire system, by using stored info it can detect new diseases possible to occur in a patient, store data in CAD file and reduce stock, detect data and find relative info, and use smart components to make customized implants for patients [2]. The human-machine interface plays a vital role in the technologies of industry 4.0. The HCI/ HMI designers must consider integrating all the technologies while designing for the healthcare system. The design should be able to interface with the existing objects as well as the new ones. It should be fit for every age group and for people who are good with technology and unfamiliar. As the world moves towards the fourth industrial revolution and its application in the medical field, it will have to consider every type of human, all age groups, patient types, profession, and satisfy all. The human-machine interface is the way to connect the technology with humans, and their satisfaction is the priority [1]. The fourth revolution is for faster technology along with satisfying customer demands. This era of technology has made humans expect more and more, making them dependent on tech. This chapter will look into the evolution of the industries, the fourth industrial revolution in healthcare in detail, its technologies, and how it affects human interaction with machines.

Human Computer Interaction

Human-computer interaction (HCI) is the study of design. It is a multidisciplinary field dealing with two aspects: an academic discipline that is studying how people interact with technology or computers and how it can be made better because nowadays everything has the involvement of computers. Second, a design discipline, which is designing interventions for systems involving people and technology. The former is about to set up the technology for the people to interact, and the latter is how to design that technology, and both are the major parts of HCI. The many branches which get influenced by HCI are visualization, computer-supported cooperative work, which is about how people work together with computers and their technologies, ubiquitous computing, and e-learning. The 'use' words of HCI are:

- *Useful*: Functional, does things
- *Usable*: Easy to do things, does the right things, enjoyable, user experience
- *Used*: Attractive, available, and acceptable to organization

Industry 1.0 to 3.0 in Healthcare: The old healthcare system or Health 1.0 was dominated by paper records, experiments, and practices with a fixed set of rules and no experimental. The entire era involved human work, from processing the entries to post-treatment operations. The result was hectic and required human efforts to keep track of all records of patients (Figure1.1). The work ethic of industry 1.0 led to the idea of involving industry 2.0 in the healthcare system. Industry 3.0 faced a drastic change as more robots were involved in performing tasks instead of humans. It was the era of computers and automation. The systems had human interaction but were limited, and a lot of work was done by machines [3].

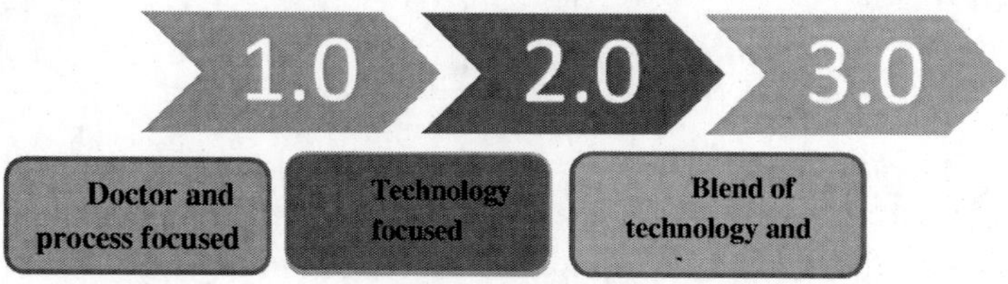

Figure 1.1. Healthcare and Industry 1.0, 2.0 and 3.0.

This era had a goal to improve access to information related to health through the means of the web. These resources facilitated the patients with an understanding of their issues and provided self-management and preventative care. All the data was accessed through the web, and the goal was to achieve digital healing and use social media to offer support, validation, and assurance. Through these facilities, patients were able to gain acceptance and understanding of the best health options.

Industry 4.0 in Healthcare: Industry 4.0 provides the medical field with new capabilities that are personalized for patient care (Figure 1.2). It has patient specific devices giving positive impact on the health of the patients.

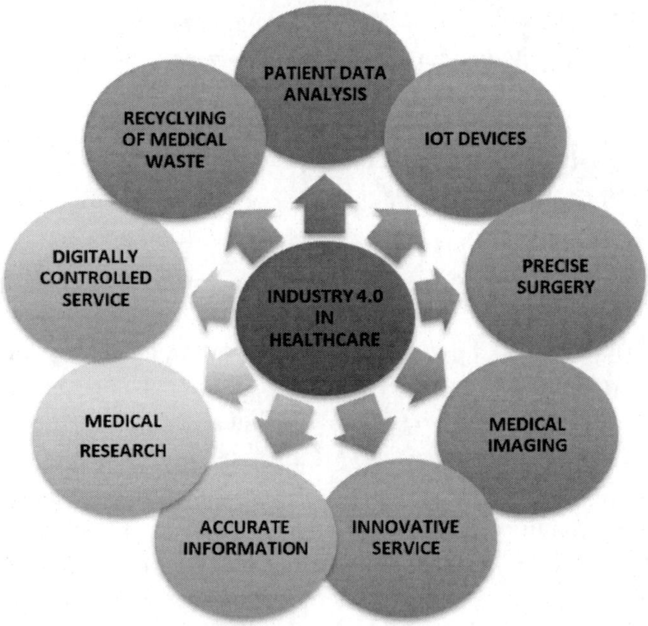

Figure 1.2. Industry 4.0 is based on the cyber-physical systems and Internet- of - Services.

Core Components of Industry 4.0

Cyber-Physical systems: These systems help the industry to connect the virtual and physical systems. It is a combination of internet services and ledgers which means anything that connects computation with biological processes. The calculations and vice versa govern the physical processes. The estimates are affected using physical process control, feedback loops, etc. Some of the advantages of CPS include the transparency that it creates between the two working worlds; it gives the ability of surveillance and control in the systems. It uses several sensors, actuators, and management to communicate between the cyber networks, namely the intelligent controllers and the physical network, which includes manufacturing infrastructure [4].

Internet of Things (IoT): This technology helps to have access to real time data from anywhere. It helps to coordinate between customer, supplier and company [4].

Internet- of – Service (IOS): These are the software-based services through the internet which allow users from private sectors to connect with companies and help develop value added services. Similar ideas are the service-oriented architecture (SOA), business process outsourcing *(BPO), and Software as a Service (SaaS) [4].*

Smart factory: This is the result of connecting IOS and IoT through cyber and physical networks. It helps to reduce human work and responsibilities of workers. It helps a cost-effective manufacturing with high flexibility and reduced complexity [4].

Core Principles of Industry 4.0

Virtualization: It is a concept of simulating data in a virtual simulation to reduce equipment use, minimize downtime, and help in complex situations. It helps to see the process virtually and then perform in real life, reducing costs and time of testing. Augmented reality is a new concept used that helps in monitoring. These concepts help to know what the human and machines are doing [4].

Interoperability: This is the fundamental principle of the fourth revolution. The ability to make machines and systems communicate with one another, coordinate their functions and access data is called interoperability. It helps to gain real-time information that allows humans and machines in decision-making and continues operations smoothly and uninterruptedly. Its integration with IoT will help industry 4.0 to achieve the above results [4].

Real-Time capabilities: With the integration of virtualization and interoperability, we can obtain information in real-time and take decisions appropriately. It helps to enhance the current functions and optimize the results of operations [4].

Decentralization: Centralized structures do not allow many scalabilities; once the system reaches its maximum capacity, no alternations can be made, and hence it becomes hard to respond to fluctuations. In a Decentralized system, logic nodes are used. The data is shared among all nodes to help enhance functions and operations intelligently. It improves coordination among all subsystems for complicated tasks [4].

Modularity: modular systems will have companies to respond quickly to demand fluctuation and ensure security.

Drivers and Challenges for Healthcare 4.0

The first driver is the IT department that will integrate EMRs and make them portable. The second is the interest of people in having practical knowledge and being informed, and this helps in expecting better health services where the frontline workers themselves- physicians, surgeons, and the whole hospital who realize that the latest technology used in the industry 4.0 incorporated healthcare system is more sophisticated and helpful in enhancing the efficiency of the whole system. The third favor is focusing on the disease and prevention and not just patient-centered treatments [4]. This system will look into the patient and consider the family history, lifestyle, and other factors that can affect the patient and help predict diseases. The last factor is the advancement of data and how data can be accessed from anywhere with high-speed data connectivity, and everyone can use Health 4.0.

Challenges in implementing information technologies in Healthcare: Integrating IT technologies and healthcare is possible when there is a comfortable fit between the IT and clinical processes. The most important factor affecting this is the mismatch of technology capabilities in addressing work processes within healthcare services. The HCI issues here begin with making the users comfortable with the new technologies of industry 4.0. Every user, be it patients or healthcare professionals, should follow the trend once the technologies are integrated into the system. Hence it poses a significant challenge for the HCI designers to make sure the technologies are understandable, easy to use, and valuable. As an HCI designers, we would need to look into every part of the technology requiring human-machine interaction and make most of it as the aim of industry 4.0 is to satisfy customer needs. Hence, integrating the IT technologies and making use of it entirely in the healthcare system is a challenge.

Approach: Technologies of Industry 4.0 in Healthcare

Internet of things (IOT): To define, IoT is creating an intelligent environment where data is shared among all devices through sensing technologies and cloud computing. Sensing devices are connected. The IoT has been used in the medical system for a long time namely to track and trace objects and people, collecting data and information record of the patients and staff data and use machines and sensors for specific tasks such as temperature, etc., the application can be clinical care and remote care [5]. The former is focusing on individual patients, i.e., using sensors to know real time information about patient's health conditions such as heat rate blood pressure, etc., by using these, it saves a lot of time for the medical profession and these data can be reached to them immediately and actions are taken precisely. The user can also view such information to be aware. The interaction between machines and humans has increased because of IoT in the healthcare system. It has optimized how everyone can be mindful of their medical conditions just a click away. Many devices for smart healthcare are also being used and in progress, making use of the IoT concept, some of which are the Google device health application and AliveCor Heart Monitor, and Viatom Checkme. The remote control is the IoT solution that allows the doctor and medical professionals to wirelessly access the patient's data. It provides access to the complete medical information profile, which helps recommend and make appropriate treatment decisions [5].

IoT and HCI relation should be more than just how the technologies are evolving for the people; the designers should look into the interconnectivity of different systems and make users engage in those systems, making it easier to deal with problems. So far, research has been technology-focused, and now it should be made user-focused. It is essential to make people the center of designing the technologies and not just emerging the technology [6]. Industry 4.0 will help achieve this by focusing more on user satisfaction, making IoT devices more user-friendly, with more interaction, and help solve issues. Healthcare systems have multiple devices connected to sharing information and records, and thus, implementing IoT to ease these activities will help healthcare professionals and patients.

Big data Analytics: Nowadays, the amount of data is increasing because of real-time data from different devices, and handling such a massive amount of data using the traditional way is difficult. Big data refers to this vast amount of data that needs to be adequately analyzed to give good outcomes and results [5]. The definition includes 3V, Volume, Variety, and Velocity. Volume is the huge amount; velocity is how fast the data is produced, and variety is the data collected. Health care professionals can now easily use big data analytics to retrieve, store, distribute and analyze the huge amount of data collected in the healthcare system [5]. It helps to understand the data quickly and gives insights allowing better decision-making, help to save and prevent diseases. The application of big data analytics in healthcare helps to bring optimal solutions. Some of the challenges of applying big data in healthcare are privacy, confidentiality, and organization change management. UI designers should be able to make big data usable. Data is received from thousands of sensors and streams and are put up to analyze and conclude; HCI designers should help make valuable insights of such large amounts of data. Healthcare data analysts help gather data from different sources and means and improve the healthcare organization in terms of care, lower cost, and patient experience [7]. Data analysts are becoming very important in this era as there is a lot of data available, and interpreting and analyzing is necessary to make important decisions in an organization. They help in making hospital executives understand the impact of the data collected from the hospitals. They collect data from the electronic health record, billing claims, cost reports, and patient satisfaction surveys and analyze them to better place the organization. There are many user interactions challenges that data analysts face. Data analysis's main steps are acquiring data, choosing architecture, shaping data into architecture, code/debug, and reflecting [8]. HCI designers should look into the challenges related to each step of data analysis. Under acquiring data, users face problems in finding where the data came from, as the data is acquired from different sources, in different formats, and from different parts of the organization. HCI designers should make data clear to the data analysts as to where the source is so that the further steps become easier. Choosing architecture, the analysts have to decide which platform to use for the analysis and how long the job is for. They might be used to a particular type of environment, and once new kind of data comes in; they will have to face the working environment for the analysis. Thus, HCI designers should make it easier for a user to decide the platform. Analysts find it hard to estimate effects of the different platform that suits their work and the time required to do so [8]. While sharping data for architecture, analysts have to move files back and forward, making it a painful task. While writing the code, the analyst should focus on the nature of computation instead of figuring out where the data is being processed. Lastly, while debugging and iteration, analysts believe that visualization plays a critical role; thus being able to visualize large data sets should be made simple. The data is sensitive to the user and must be used correctly.

Blockchain Technology: A lot of information and data needs to be moved in the healthcare system networks, and blockchain helps to do so while dealing with multiple parties involved in the network. Humans would require access to this information from anywhere at any time, and hence distributed databases helps in managing the data [9]. Maintain a lot of data, especially old data, can cost a lot which is now reduced using blockchain. Another contribution is the use of counterfeit medical products, which was a big issue in the medical field. Blockchain has a great application in the healthcare system, mainly electronic records, monitoring multiple devices, storing insurance information, and improving mobile health apps [10]. The HCI designers look into how easily the professional can access these data at any time needed. Some of the challenges in implementing blockchain in the healthcare system are security, scalability, and legality. The main focus an individual would have in healthcare systems is data security and data ownership. Blockchain technologies focus on designing for privacy and trust and designing blockchain interaction to ensure users with confidence that their data is secure and safe from intruders [11]. Mobile apps and remote health monitoring are some of the new technologies in healthcare and blockchain that keep improving security and quality as the information is sensitive and private [10]. Patients might access different healthcare facilities and hospitals, and blockchain can help retrieve data from different hospitals and help access and share data. HCI designers need to make data sharing and to store easily, thus making it user-friendly and trustworthy.

- Process to transform medical information to Blockchain: There are various steps are involved while processing the medical information with the help of Blockchain. These steps are illustrated with the following diagram Figure 1.3 (A) and (B). This explains the process from patient registration with connecting all medical history with connecting clinical data with Blockchain technology.

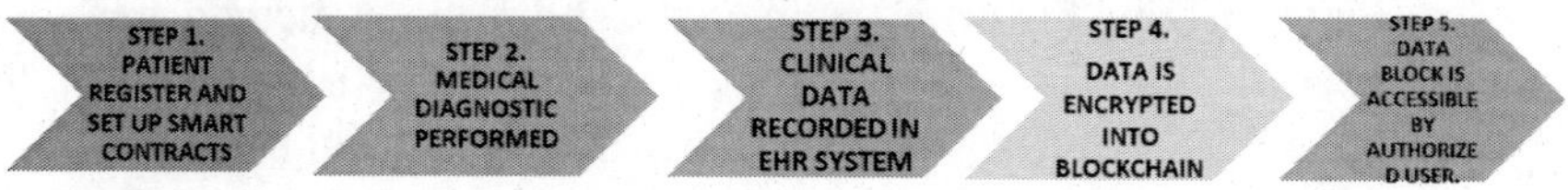

Figure 1.3. (A). Flow of patient information.

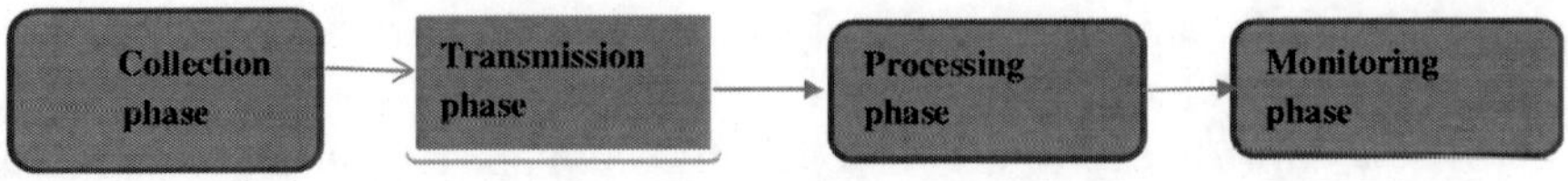

Figure 1.3. (B). Information processing and its Flow.

Artificial Intelligence (AI): AI is the computer field that helps make smart or intelligent computers that understand the data feed into them and help predict things. AI in healthcare can help analyze the patient records and make predictions that would help n prevention of diseases by taking precautions. AI helps to decide links between prevention or treatment approaches [12]. It will allow for improved care, diagnosis, and interpretation of data. Human-computer interaction can help validate the solutions provided by AI. All medical professionals should be able to use the trending AI application in healthcare, making it easier to make decisions. The machines and devices should be designed so that the AI helps enhance medical research and testing instead of replacing humans from the medical field [13]. It is more than just an interaction between a computer and a human; it works towards solving medical issues by teaming humans and machines, making them collaborative partners to enhance the results. HCI helps in making AI usable and useful to medical professionals and patients. The professionals should be able to learn it quickly and apply it immediately. One of the challenges of the HCI methods in AI is the focus on visuals designs. The focus should be made smart, rather than just on making it visually appealing. Designers should include functionalities giving more importance to smart functions such as voice input and smart search, which helps in reducing steps and repeating activities and makes more intuitive UIs. HCI and AI professionals can create designs and training models rather than consider the design a separate technical issue. HCI designers and the community should work more often on human-machine teaming, enhancements of methods, and increase their influence and knowledge in the Artificial intelligence department, which would help more cooperation of the two fields [13].

Optimization, Simulation and Predictive Analytics: In the healthcare industry, decision-making has always been a big part of supplying allocation solutions and analyzing big data. Applying the optimization method helps deal with location selection and management of capacity for both hospitals and the suppliers of the healthcare system. Service planning in healthcare is essential to provide adequate service. [14]. It helps in determining figuring out future demands for services Healthcare management and logistics are essential as well for scheduling and allocation of resources. Predictive analytics will help detect early signs of patient deterioration, identify at-risk patients in their homes to prevent hospital readmissions, and prevent avoidable downtime of medical equipment [15]. All of these decisions can be easily made using optimization, simulation, and predictive analytics.

Conclusion

The human-computer interface has gone through many advancements from the beginning of technology. The fourth revolution of the industry will make a significant change in how we use technology, and its impact on the healthcare system will advance all current treatment methods. Human-computer interaction is expected to increase in the coming year and will make all industry work easier. From big data, blockchain, artificial intelligence, the Internet of Things, and optimization, the healthcare professional will take care of patients more professionally, more accessible with real-time data. They will be able to predict and find solutions beforehand before the patient's medical condition worsens. As an HCI designer, keeping these technologies in mind and focusing on people's satisfaction is very important. Designing devices and internet platforms customized for the healthcare system will remove the barrier that keeps the medical industry from opting for industry 4.0.

In this chapter, we looked into the evolution of industries, their application in healthcare, industry 4.0 and its core components and principles, and the different technologies that are used in the medical field. We have represented how the human-computer interaction is affected by these technologies and how the future medical system will look one all healthcare systems will integrate these technologies in their current work system. We are moving towards an era of the latest technologies that help us solve all possible problems and satisfy customers.

References

[1] Stowers Kimberly, M., & Mustapha Mouloua. (2018, June 29). *Human Computer Interaction Trends in Healthcare: An Update.*

[2] Bologva, E., Prokusheva, D., Krikunov, A., Zvartau, N., & Kovalchuk, S. (2016, October 04). Human-Computer Interaction in Electronic Medical Records: From the *Perspectives of Physicians and Data Scientists.*

[3] Richard E. Crandall. (2017, September/October). *Industry 1.0 to 4.0: The Evolution of Smart Factories*: APICS Magazine.

[4] Chanchaichujit Janya, Albert Tan, Fanwen Meng, & Sarayoot Eaimkhong. (2019, August 7). *Healthcare 4.0 Next Generation Processes with the Latest Technologies.*

[5] Chanchaichujit, J., Tan, A., Meng, F., & Eaimkhong, S. (2019, January 01). Internet of Things (IoT) and Big Data Analytics in Healthcare.

[6] Lynch Koreshoff Treffyn, Toni Robertson, & Tuck Wah Leong. (2013, November). Internet of Things: *A review of literature and products.*

[7] Team, U. (2017, October 30). *What Is a Healthcare Data Analyst? How Do You Become One?*

[8] Fisher, Danyel Rob DeLine, Mary Czerwinski, & Steven Drucker. (2012, May/June). *Interactions with Big Data Analytic*s.

[9] Chanchaichujit, J., Tan, A., Meng, F., & Eaimkhong, S. (2019, January 01*).* *Blockchain Technology in Healthcare*.

[10] Chen, H., Jarrell, J., Carpenter, K., Cohen, D., & Huang, X. (2019, August 8). *Blockchain in Healthcare: A Patient-Centered Model*.

[11] Elsden Chris, Bettina Nissen, Karim Jabbar, Reem Talhouk, Caitlin Lustig, Paul Dunphy, . . . John Vines. (2018, April). HCI for *Blockchain: Studying, Designing, Critiquing and Envisioning Distributed Ledger Technologies*.

[12] Chanchaichujit, J., Tan, A., Meng, F., & Eaimkhong, S. (2019, January 01). *Application of Artificial Intelligence in Heal*thcare.

[13] Xu, W. (2019, july-august 4). *Toward Human-Centered Ai: A Perspective from Human-Computer Interaction. 3.*

[14] Chanchaichujit, J., Tan, A., Meng, F., & Eaimkhong, S. (2019, January 01). *Optimization, Simulation and Predictive Analytics in Healthcare.*

[15] Philips. (2020, June 12). *Predictive analytics in healthcare: Three real-world examples.*

Chapter 2

Role of Urban Control Centers for City Planning and Monitoring in a Pandemic Outbreak

Shaurya Gupta[1,*], **Sonali Vyas**[1,*] **and Kanta Prasad Sharma**[2,†]

[1]School of Computer Science, UPES Dehradun, Uttarakhand, India
[2]University Institute of Computing, Chandigarh University, Mohali, Chandigarh, India

Abstract

The whole world is struggling with the staggering consequences of the pandemic COVID -19. Governments and organizations worldwide are discussing how novel and innovative technologies can be used to eliminate the effects of the pandemic and how the coming pandemics can be averted or contained. Among the proposed solutions, the advancement of additional competent and comprehensive smart city initiatives will improve the way critical data is retrieved, managed, stored and distributed in a pandemic by reducing the implementation time for dangerous activities. The best response to a pandemic is to use various technological solutions that can eventually be deployed in an integrated manner, exploring numerous options. Therefore, this article discusses possible solutions, including contemporary approaches that are practical and helpful in developing novel health-oriented smart cities. The pandemic COVID -19 is forcing new ways for city governments to

* Corresponding Author's E-mail: shaurya55@gmail.com.
* Corresponding Author's E-mail: vyas.sonali86@gmail.com.
† Corresponding Author's E-mail: tokpsharma@gmail.com.

In: Industry 4.0 and Intelligent Business Analytics for Healthcare
Editors: Soumi Dutta, Vinod Kumar Shukla, Shruti Nagpal et al.
ISBN: 978-1-68507-602-3

manage public health emergencies and protect city residents. To this end, urban control centres play an essential role in the surveillance and management of the city's dynamics. The urban monitoring centre identifies irregularities and takes care of them. It also ensures that any disturbances or problems in the city are either appropriately rectified or immediately addressed so that the city returns to its normal operations as soon as possible.

Keywords: COVID-19, pandemic, health emergencies, urban administration, urban control centers

Introduction

The severe impact of the COVID -19 endemic will almost certainly change health and fitness management in the coming years. The rapid and uncontrolled spread of the SARS-CoV-2 virus among citizens worldwide requires effective management to be proactive at all times [1]. This leads to a synchronized decision that must be followed by strict action by public organizations and the government. It also necessitates the need for digital integration of cities [2]. Smart metropolises should be equipped with the best means to counter such endemics [3].

Moreover, increasing urbanization leads to efficient energy management in various areas [4]. Many communicable diseases can occur in densely populated areas, spreading rapidly. Human traffic in large cities can significantly increase diseases and disease symptoms like influenza [5]. The highly communicable diseases can occur at any time and take the form of a pandemic. Information management plays a crucial role in minimizing the impact of an impending pandemic. Early diagnosis and appropriate hygiene are the most important measures to combat an epidemic.

Consequently, communities should be efficient enough to quickly detect possible outbreaks of new or already known diseases and share sensitive information to make decisions more quickly [6]. Every day, extensive data is delivered from various sources such as cars, traffic lights, and surveillance cameras that must be directly linked to a city's digital framework [7]. The final enormous integration of an urban data highway will create a new path for a digital civilization [8]. COVID -19 pandemic has severely affected the entire earth with massive casualties, and finally, conclusions should be drawn for future actions. Figures 1 and 2 show the outrageous preliminary status of the spread of the virus. The contemporary lifestyle of people living in densely populated cities leads to the outbreak of an infectious disease that can lead to a pandemic [9, 10]. The article addresses the current expansions that are causing city governments to gear up to fight the next pandemic and the development of technologies and implementation of advanced methods related to the smart city's paradigm.

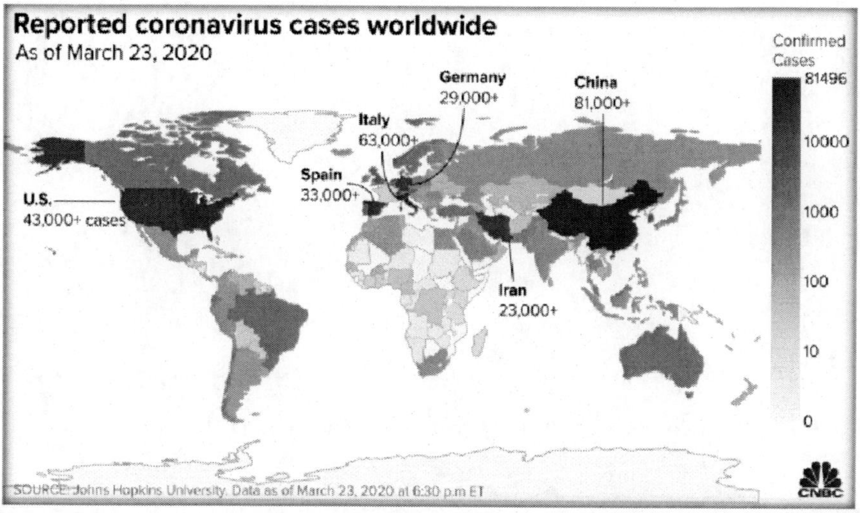

Source: https://coronavirus.jhu.edu/map.html [15].

Figure 1. COVID-19 total number of cases per million as on 23 March 2020.

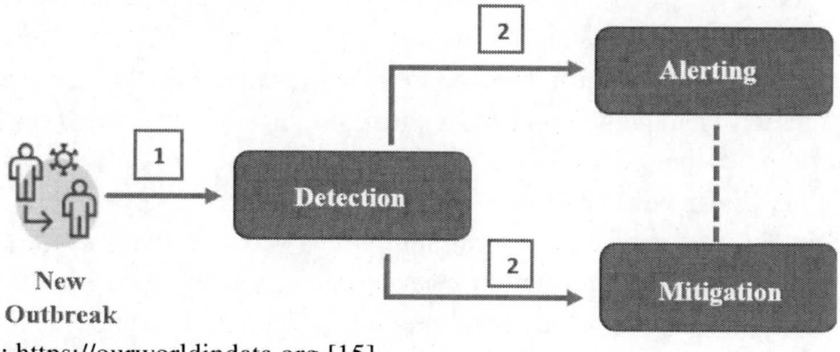

Source: https://ourworldindata.org [15].

Figure 2. COVID-19 total number of cases per million as on December 4, 2020.

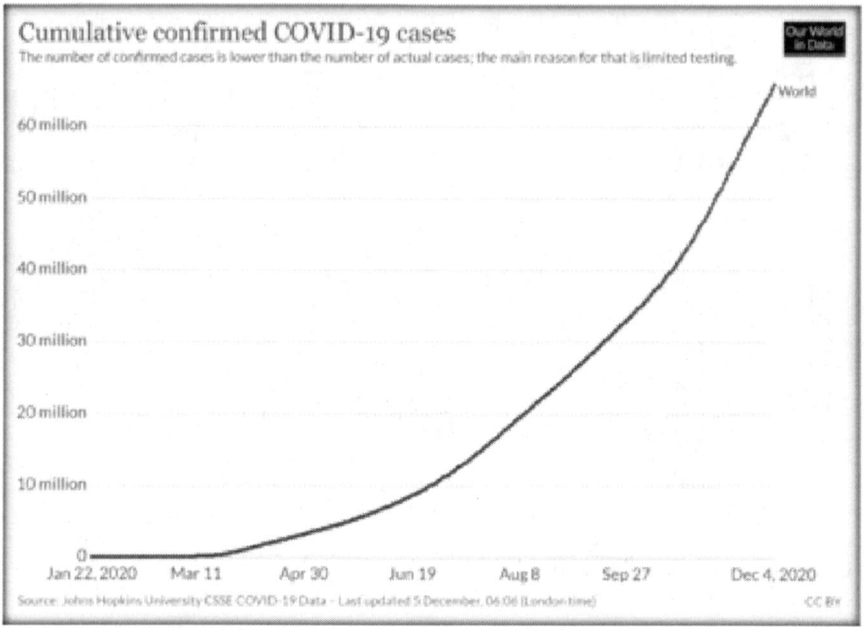

Figure 3. Epidemic outbreak detection, alerting, mitigation [15].

Emergency-Prone Atmosphere of Cities

Although an infectious disease outbreak is called endemic or pandemic when it has spread to numerous cities in different countries, it is considered a global pandemic, as shown in Figure 3. The pandemic COVID -19 started in Wuhan, a city in China, and over time spread rapidly to many cities in the world such as Milan (Italy) and New York (USA), resulting in numerous deaths, which in turn prompted the government to impose the practice of lockdown and quarantine. Coronavirus was transmitted by people handling their pets or cattle [11, 12]. The threat of a new pandemic will always be there in the present scenario. It depends entirely on the management or administration of the city whether it can handle a sudden potential outbreak or not [13, 14]. The management of an emergency or a potential outbreak in a city can be based on the following factors:

- *Detection:* an emergency or outbreak is detected when there is a sudden change in the usual behaviour or functioning of the various components. For example, if a fire breaks out in a particular region, the temperature increases along with the smoke. If there is an outbreak of disease, the number of requests for medical assistance in a city or a particular region of the city will increase abnormally [15, 16].

- *Alerting:* Once an emergency is detected, an alerting mechanism must be put in place, which may include sending alerts in the form of emails or SMSs in addition to TV. For effective and efficient alerting, sirens or illuminated signs can be placed in different city regions to indicate difficult areas to avoid [17].
- *Mitigation:* Specific measures need to be taken in case of a potential outbreak because they must be mitigated effectively once an emergency is detected. As in the case of a fire, timely mitigation would require the dispatch of fire trucks and traffic management to ensure that fire trucks are provided with clear routes to avoid delays in reaching sensitive locations [18].

However, the concept of alerting and mitigation are very different mechanisms, but the future or novel pandemics would require the more stringent concept of disaster management [13, 14]. Figure 3 explains the distribution of a possible outbreak using three abstract measures. The information gathered in the detection phase is critical in addressing an outbreak in its initial phase. Later, the alerting and containment measures are implemented independently to contain the spread of the detected pathogens. It was also found that alerting and containment are independent concepts when considering a smart city [19]. These units exchange data with each other and inform the metropolis's inhabitants accordingly. After detection, mitigation and alerting go hand in hand because alerting involves informing the citizens and the metropolitan government of appropriate actions with specific messages.

In contrast, mitigation involves delineating outbreak areas and tracking possible infected residents. In an airborne disease, metropolitan areas with inadequate sanitation and high population density will be exposed to the rapid spread of the disease. Data collected during an ongoing pandemic can be incorporated into the cyber-physical data infrastructure to enable a rapid response to a potential outbreak.

Metropolitan Data Management for Improved Responsivity

Managing a large city is a challenging task for running city services and infrastructure without irregularities and unforeseen events. Overseeing the overall management of the city involves managing public transport, electricity supply and waste disposal and requires a strict schedule of planning control. In a city scenario, some unforeseen events can cause service disruptions. Factors such as the magnitude of the threat, the severity of the impact, and the vulnerability of a region, can lead to a chaotic situation when the safety of citizens is considered. In emergencies, the public administration should ensure that the impact of such events does not lead to major destruction of urban dynamics in terms of citizens' lives. To manage such situations in an urban scenario, information should reach the public or the city administrator as early as possible to take the necessary actions. The response capability is a combination of responses and includes the response time to requests from the public by urban specialists [20]. Municipal command and control centres (CCCs) are important for municipal governments. They are considered an essential measure when considering a smart city scenario [21]. They are also referred to as operations centres. They are responsible for aggregating existing geolocated data, including data compiled by sensors and observation cameras distributed throughout the city in a real-time environment. These data are stored, managed and analyzed by specific platforms responsible for producing charts and maps. They also contain indicators of irregularities that support the city administration. The visualization tools with the appropriate capabilities and decision making in case of irregularities prove faster and more reliable. Metropolitan CCCs support consultants from different areas of public administration by integrating processes and system groups. And, finally, providing active support for substructure engagement.

COVID-19 Endemic Perspective

Many variants of coronavirus such as SARS-Cov-2 are responsible for causing the communicable disease COVID -19. In 2019, it began spreading from Wuhan, China; its high transmission rate spread rapidly. It also expanded from an epidemic to a massive pandemic in less than two months. Infection with the virus caused an extraordinarily high mortality rate among people, which led to fears among experts and the general public. It caused numerous psycho-sociological effects in different parts of society. In urban areas, it led to numerous infections and deaths, increasing uncontrollably in several countries. The major cities are more affected by the pandemic and depend on the urban structure of a particular city. It may have different consequences. Therefore, authorities at different levels of public administration need to identify and track down the residents of a city to protect them, especially in urban areas where population density and the likelihood of physical exchanges are relatively high. COVID -19 pandemic showed significant health problems compared to other pandemics worldwide. This pandemic emergency has gone through the cycles of urban disasters with catastrophic complications and affected the local dynamics on an enormous scale [22]. In a pandemic situation, there are several aspects of uncertainty, shifting threat, meeting deadlines, and population behaviour towards the management and treatment of a pandemic. See Table 1 next to COVID -19 to assess each aspect of outdated crises.

Table 1. Customary tragedies vs. COVID-19 pandemic

Customary Tragedies	COVID-19 Pandemic
Punctual complications	Large scale implications
Momentaneous impact	Lasting impact
Evident and undeniable information	Uncertainty and misinformation
Recovery Timeline reasonably defined	Unpredictability of recovery timeline
Event is visible	Invisibility of the threat

Given the general conditions of any emergency, metropolitan areas are highly dependent on data to understand the multi-faceted state of the pandemic situation and validate outcomes based on specific measures.

Decision-Making Data during a Pandemic

In pandemic situations, the voluminous data from different sources must be brought together in one place. Moreover, in the case of urban dynamics, configurations change radically for the duration of a pandemic, requiring authorities to redefine their regularity indicators from time to time. This unified data is essential for managing the determination to create important facilities for the development of the community and for developing specific regulations for mass gatherings of people. Keeping citizens informed with regular warnings facilitated through various media is also necessary. It is important to classify vulnerable zones and monitor them from time to time. City governments need to develop and implement a crisis management strategy framework [22]. Disruptions in the provision of vital facilities should be addressed within a specified time without interruption. In a complex pandemic scenario, a collaboration between municipal organizations and different health facilities is crucial to achieving the set objectives.

Processing of Massive Data

In smart cities, vast amounts of data are generated every second, so highly efficient algorithms are needed to transform data into useful information. In order to obtain historical data of cities and their inhabitants, it is essential to edit and process the statistical data. Nowadays, the concept of Big Data and Data Science has become very useful in research and is being used by various companies for business intelligence [23]. With the development of data processing algorithms, many opportunities have opened up for burgeoning smart cities projects such as healthcare and public administration [24]. Lack of planning, management, and support in healthcare poses a critical challenge for pandemic situations. AI algorithms have become an excellent tool for predicting and containing viral outbreaks. Neural networks also prove useful in predicting confirmed SARS-CoV-2 cases in many scenarios [25]. In the neural network prediction model, different variables are considered inputs for a city, such as population density, temperature etc. Along with artificial intelligence, machine learning techniques are also a powerful tool to combat such pandemics to predict new cases [26]. Deep learning advances provide excellent results in tracking the COVID -19 outbreak and its rate of spread. Moreover, this outbreak has helped to provide important data for training and evaluating the efficiency of neural networks. Research in AI algorithms and models is essentially expected to screen and evaluate humans to assess the spread of infection [27]. AI has also helped detect the spread of Fake News on social media in such a pandemic. The spread of Fake news can lead to the posting of false news on social media, which can hinder regular management. Therefore, AI systems are very important in condemning such kinds of reports or posts [28, 29]. A health-oriented smart city needs to detect, mitigate, and avoid fake news. In summary, the effectiveness of AI-based prediction and detection tactics depends entirely on the available data. Historical outbreak data related to Ebola, SARS-COV, etc., can help train AI-based models.

Consequently, we can conclude that the most critical and reliable factor for developing highly efficient smart cities is data from various sources and the training of AI models. The most important activity after detecting an outbreak is the implementation of alerting and containment processes. These processes need to be implemented so that they have a high impact. Various resources can be hired to contain the impact whenever an infectious disease outbreak is detected. Smart cities must have well-organized strategies to contain the outbreak to minimize the mortality rate and reduce the number of new cases. In such an adverse pandemic, the need for critical resources for smart city development becomes a challenge. Various cases of alerting and containment approaches for detecting the outbreak are discussed below:

- *Smart hospitals and health systems:* In terms of pandemic preparedness, it is a challenge for a smart city to incorporate smart healthcare solutions. In the initial phase of the outbreak and uncontrolled pandemic, hospitals should handle the large amount of big data generated by various data generators of a smart city such as sensors and actuators [30, 31]. The availability of hospital beds, medical staff and drugs, and medical kits must be buffered. As envisioned in future research [32, 33], smart healthcare systems should be integral to future smart communities or cities.
- *Smart traffic management:* The movement of citizens in large communities can also increase infectious diseases. To mitigate and prevent the impact of the outbreak, a smart transportation system can be helpful [34]. Affected regions can be easily isolated, or passenger traffic can be quickly stopped if a pandemic alert is triggered. Once the cyber-physical integration of cities is perfectly implemented, various new innovative ideas can emerge, such as self-driving cars that facilitate the transportation of infected people or healthcare workers. This may minimize the likelihood of novel infections. The precise tuning of automatic facilities requires a complete insight into a perfect urban metropolis.
- *Intelligent Repeat Groups:* Public hygiene, preventive seclusion, and tracking of likely ill individuals are just a few essential responses, including public health workers, transportation representatives, police, and special intelligent response teams that should be formed to deal with pandemic situations [35]. In addition, various emerging technologies and development platforms play an important role in containment. As in China and many other countries, drones and

robots have been used as smart tools to monitor and warn populations of quarantine orders, provide essential supplies, disinfect public transportation, and decontaminate specific regions of a city by releasing chemicals or disinfectant sprays. In smart cities, such initiatives should be fully implemented as they prove helpful in taking remedial action without delay.

- *Innovative research:* Whenever a virus is detected, the right pathogen associated with its RNA detection should be revealed immediately to enable medical tests to treat infected individuals. Therefore, researchers need to work extremely hard to develop medicines and vaccines to fight the pathogen, save lives, and possibly curb its spread. Scientific laboratories should get various information from major cities to get an insight into the spread of the pathogen under study in different regions of the world. This will help provide clues on the methods to deal with the new pathogen. In addition, technical facilities should consider the amenities of cities by quickly informing the population about preventive measures against the outbreak of the disease.
- *Alerting and notification:* In times of crisis, the public must be notified and alerted using text messages that vary depending on the recipient. It is important that alerts spread to the public [36]. Several avenues can also be used to transmit vital information to people's mobile devices.

Smart City Future Innitiatives

A city becomes "smart" when it harnesses new technologies such as Big Data, IoT, AI, etc., to create a livable and sustainable environment. Innovative technologies are renewing the urban face of cities by compiling and collecting data from a city's potential resources. This makes it possible to make quick decisions, automate processes, and estimate and consider the future course of events. This also leads to improved cities in terms of efficient waste management, smart transportation and providing basic amenities to the population. It can be seen that most cities are using smart metropolis ideas in addition to smart technological capabilities to introduce innovative methods for healthcare to address the epidemic COVID -19 [37]. Nowadays, cities are silently transforming in many ways, such as retrieving important data from websites to complex data sharing, which is of great benefit to health workers in their daily work. By and large, cities that collaborate and partner more are better able to combat epidemics than they were in the past. However, many promising initiatives are emerging over time, primarily focused on using Big Data analytics and AI to better contain and assess infectious disease growth rates and quarantine people during a pandemic. Forward-looking research initiatives need to use intelligent pedagogy and technologies to improve the day-to-day processes of city design and planning and the multiple communication techniques between citizens. The biggest concern is that such technologies must be smart enough to protect and support people. Cities must have a broad vision for the future of their society and seek solutions to achieve that vision [38]. As cities try to overcome such pandemics, there are various ways to accelerate improving infrastructure, transportation, and healthcare systems for a better future.

Conclusion

The pandemic COVID -19 affected almost every continent and severely impacted our lives. Although the exact death toll is unknown, it is still uncertain how much we will have to deal with this outbreak. Therefore, we should be ready to face the coming situation with improved reasonable means. An important component in predicting an epidemic is based entirely on data analysis. This is done by using data sets from various sources. Any spike or spike in data values is tracked by various specialised data sources that are an indispensable part of big cities. To create truly smart cities, the government must take the necessary steps to implement them. Finally, pandemics are tangible, and experts or researchers worldwide expect them to worsen over time. So, preparedness for this is critical, and governments need to get serious about it. However, structuring efficient and well-organised smart metropolises can meaningfully contribute to an improved and immediate response to epidemic outbreaks, which is very important for saving lives.

References

[1] Shafique, Laiba, Awais Ihsan, and Qingyou Liu. "Evolutionary trajectory for the emergence of novel coronavirus SARS-CoV-2." *Pathogens* 9, no. 3 (2020): 240.

[2] Allam, Zaheer, and David S. Jones. "On the coronavirus (COVID-19) outbreak and the smart city network: universal data sharing standards coupled with artificial

intelligence (AI) to benefit urban health monitoring and management." In *Healthcare,* vol. 8, no. 1, p. 46. Multidisciplinary Digital Publishing Institute, 2020.

[3] Trencher, Gregory, and Andrew Karvonen. "Stretching "smart": Advancing health and well-being through the smart city agenda." *Local Environment* 24, no. 7 (2019): 610-627.

[4] Silva, Bhagya Nathali, Murad Khan, and Kijun Han. "Towards sustainable smart cities: A review of trends, architectures, components, and open challenges in smart cities." *Sustainable Cities and Society* 38 (2018): 697-713.

[5] Budd, Lucy, Morag Bell, and Tim Brown. "Of plagues, planes and politics: controlling the global spread of infectious diseases by air." *Political Geography* 28, no. 7 (2009): 426-435.

[6] Chamoso, Pablo, Alfonso González-Briones, Fernando De La Prieta, Ganesh Kumar Venyagamoorthy, and Juan M. Corchado. "Smart city as a distributed platform: Toward a system for citizen-oriented management." *Computer communications* 152 (2020): 323-332.

[7] Costa, Daniel G., and Felipe P. de Oliveira. "A prioritization approach for optimization of multiple concurrent sensing applications in smart cities." *Future Generation Computer Systems* 108 (2020): 228-243.

[8] Dufva, Tomi, and Mikko Dufva. "Grasping the future of the digital society." *Futures* 107 (2019): 17-28.

[9] Ali, S. Harris, and Roger Keil. "Global cities and the spread of infectious disease: the case of severe acute respiratory syndrome (SARS) in Toronto, Canada." *Urban Studies* 43, no. 3 (2006): 491-509.

[10] Garon, Jack E., Shan-Ching Ying, Susan Monahan, Robert Humrickhouse, and Dianne Hunter. "The novel H1N1 outbreak: lessons learned." *Laboratory Medicine* 41, no. 1 (2010): 11-15.

[11] Short, Kirsty R., Mathilde Richard, Josanne H. Verhagen, Debby van Riel, Eefje JA Schrauwen, Judith MA van den Brand, Benjamin Mänz, Rogier Bodewes, and Sander Herfst. "One health, multiple challenges: the inter-species transmission of influenza A virus." *One health* 1 (2015): 1-13.

[12] Rabi, Firas A., Mazhar S. Al Zoubi, Ghena A. Kasasbeh, Dunia M. Salameh, and Amjad D. Al-Nasser. "SARS-CoV-2 and coronavirus disease 2019: what we know so far." *Pathogens* 9, no. 3 (2020): 231.

[13] Astarita, Vittorio, Vincenzo Pasquale Giofrè, Giuseppe Guido, Giulio Stefano, and Alessandro Vital. "Mobile computing for disaster emergency management: empirical requirements analysis for a cooperative crowdsourced system for emergency management operation." *Smart Cities* 3, no. 1 (2020): 31-47.

[14] Soyata, Tolga, Hadi Habibzadeh, Chinwe Ekenna, Brian Nussbaum, and Jose Lozano. "Smart city in crisis: Technology and policy concerns." *Sustainable Cities and Society* 50 (2019): 101566.

[15] Nikolay, Birgit, Henrik Salje, Katharine Sturm-Ramirez, Eduardo Azziz-Baumgartner, Nusrat Homaira, Makhdum Ahmed, A. Danielle Iuliano et al.

"Evaluating hospital-based surveillance for outbreak detection in Bangladesh: analysis of healthcare utilization data." *PLoS medicine* 14, no. 1 (2017): e1002218.

[16] Xu, Boyi, Ling Li, Daiping Hu, Bin Wu, Congcong Ye, and Hongming Cai. "Healthcare data analysis system for regional medical union in smart city." *Journal of Management Analytics* 5, no. 4 (2018): 334-349.

[17] Bernard, Eddie, and Vasily Titov. "Evolution of tsunami warning systems and products." *Philosophical Transactions of the Royal Society A: Mathematical, Physical and Engineering Sciences* 373, no. 2053 (2015): 20140371.

[18] Samuel, Carlos, and Laura K. Siebeneck. "Roles revealed: An examination of the adopted roles of emergency managers in hazard mitigation planning and strategy implementation." *International Journal of Disaster Risk Reduction* 39 (2019): 101145.

[19] Costa, Daniel G., and João Paulo J. Peixoto. "COVID-19 pandemic: a review of smart cities initiatives to face new outbreaks." *IET Smart Cities* 2, no. 2 (2020): 64-73.

[20] Goldsmith, Stephen, and Susan Crawford. *The responsive city: Engaging communities through data-smart governance.* John Wiley & Sons, 2014.

[21] Hojda, Alexandre, and Pedro Reis Martins. "Communication as a Tool for Expanding Social Participation: The Case of the Rio Operations Center." In *Lifelong Learning and Education in Healthy and Sustainable Cities,* pp. 521-537. Springer, Cham, 2018.

[22] Muse, Larissa Paredes, Pedro Reis Martins, Alexandre Hojda, P. A. D. Abreu, and P. C. D. Almeida. "The role of Urban Control and Command Centers in the face of COVID-19: The case of COR in Rio de Janeiro, Brazil." In *IEEE Int. Smart Cities Conf.,* ISC2. 2020.

[23] Erevelles, Sunil, Nobuyuki Fukawa, and Linda Swayne. "Big Data consumer analytics and the transformation of marketing." *Journal of business research* 69, no. 2 (2016): 897-904.

[24] Archenaa, J., and EA Mary Anita. "A survey of big data analytics in healthcare and government." *Procedia Computer Science* 50 (2015): 408-413.

[25] Pirouz, Behrouz, Sina Shaffiee Haghshenas, Sami Shaffiee Haghshenas, and Patrizia Piro. "Investigating a serious challenge in the sustainable development process: analysis of confirmed cases of COVID-19 (new type of coronavirus) through a binary classification using artificial intelligence and regression analysis." *Sustainability* 12, no. 6 (2020): 2427.

[26] Rees, E. E., V. Ng, P. Gachon, A. Mawudeku, D. McKenney, J. Pedlar, D. Yemshanov, J. Parmely, and J. Knox. "Early detection and prediction of infectious disease outbreaks." *CCDR* 45 (2019): 5.

[27] Mohsin, Mohamad Farhan Mohamad, Azuraliza Abu Bakar, and Abdul Razak Hamdan. "Outbreak detection model based on danger theory." *Applied soft computing* 24 (2014): 612-622.

[28] Vafeiadis, Michail, Denise S. Bortree, Christen Buckley, Pratiti Diddi, and Anli Xiao. "Refuting fake news on social media: nonprofits, crisis response strategies and issue involvement." *Journal of Product & Brand Management* (2019).

[29] O'Connor, Cathal, and Michelle Murphy. "Going viral: doctors must tackle fake news in the covid-19 pandemic." *BMJ* 369, no. 10.1136 (2020).

[30] Boulos, Maged N. Kamel, and Najeeb M. Al-Shorbaji. "*On the Internet of Things, smart cities and the WHO Healthy Cities.*" (2014): 1-6.

[31] Kang, Seungjin, Hyunyoung Baek, Eunja Jung, Hee Hwang, and Sooyoung Yoo. "Survey on the demand for adoption of Internet of Things (IoT)-based services in hospitals: Investigation of nurses' perception in a tertiary university hospital." *Applied Nursing Research* 47 (2019): 18-23.

[32] Cook, Diane J., Glen Duncan, Gina Sprint, and Roschelle L. Fritz. "Using smart city technology to make healthcare smarter." *Proceedings of the IEEE 106,* no. 4 (2018): 708-722.

[33] Trayush, T., R. Bathla, S. Saini and V. K. Shukla, "IoT in Healthcare: Challenges, Benefits, Applications, and Opportunities," *2021 International Conference on Advance Computing and Innovative Technologies in Engineering (ICACITE)*, 2021, pp. 107-111, doi: 10.1109/ICACITE51222.2021.9404583.

[34] Hansain, S., D. Gaur and V. K. Shukla, "Impact of Emerging Technologies on Future Mobility in Smart Cities by 2030," *2021 9th International Conference on Reliability, Infocom Technologies and Optimization (Trends and Future Directions) (ICRITO),* 2021, pp. 1-8, doi: 10.1109/ICRITO51393.2021.9596095.

[35] Liu, Wei, Xiao-Guang Yue, and Paul B. Tchounwou. "*Response to the COVID-19 epidemic: the Chinese experience and implications for other countries*." (2020): 2304.

[36] Fakhfakh, Faten, Mohamed Tounsi, and Mohamed Mosbah. "A comprehensive survey on broadcasting emergency messages." In 2019 15th International Wireless Communications & Mobile Computing Conference (IWCMC), pp. 1983-1988. *IEEE*, 2019.

[37] Pramanik, Md Ileas, Raymond YK Lau, Haluk Demirkan, and Md Abul Kalam Azad. "Smart health: Big data enabled health paradigm within smart cities." *Expert Systems with Applications* 87 (2017): 370-383.

[38] Gupta, Shaurya, and Sonali Vyas. "IoT in Green Engineering Transformation for Smart Cities." *Smart IoT for Research and Industry* (2021): 121.

Chapter 3

Industry 4.0 for Promoting Health Inclusion in Emerging Markets: A Systematic Study of Narayana Healthcare, India

Sana Moid[1,*], Nitin Shankar[1,†] and Fatima Beena[2,‡]
[1]Amity Business School, Amity University Uttar Pradesh, Lucknow Campus, India
[2]American College of Dubai, UAE

Abstract

Industry 4.0 promises to bridge need, resource varied necessities, and the health care sector requirements. Hence, there is an urgent need to understand how Industry 4.0 can be a valuable model for fulfilling various requirements of the health care sector using different and emerging technologies for providing affordable services, specifically in the perspective of an emerging market economy. The objective of this chapter is to comprehend the applicability of Industry 4.0 in the health care sector through the case analysis of Narayana Health City Bengaluru, India, and to do the mapping to recognize the domains of Industry 4.0 explored and implemented by them for providing affordable medical care, timely diagnosis and for remote diagnosis enabling more and more patients to be covered thereby promoting health inclusion for all. Various published sources in the form of research papers based on Industry 4.0 for the health care sector were studied to identify applications and future research direction. The study is primarily based on secondary data, explicitly using the interview insights given by Dr Devi Shetty to Prof Tarun Khanna, Harvard Business School, in 2017. Industry 4.0 has a

* Corresponding Author's Email: sanamoid14@gmail.com.
† Corresponding Author's Email: nitinshankar19@gmail.com.
‡ Corresponding Author's Email: fatimabeena@gmail.com.

In: Industry 4.0 and Intelligent Business Analytics for Healthcare
Editors: Soumi Dutta, Vinod Kumar Shukla, Shruti Nagpal et al.
ISBN: 978-1-68507-602-3

unique methodology for generating new concepts and undertaking its applicability in the health care sector through proper integration of emergent technologies like Artificial Intelligence or Big Data Analytics, smart machines, and software. Narayana Health City has given an entirely new dimension of providing affordable critical and specialized health care services to even remote areas. Using safe and fortified medical-grade networks with immersive visual experiences, they can virtualize every scarce resource that includes medical force, right from surgeons to paramedics to staff, and provide continuous access of specialist consultants remotely and have the facility of telemedicine. The hospital has touched upon some of the dimensions of Health 4.0 like precise surgery, digitally controlled devices, telemedicine for remote healthcare, resulting in better services for patients at an affordable cost. However, specific dimensions like Robotic surgery, Use of Artificial Intelligence and Big Data Analytics, etc., are still to be explored, leaving ample further research.

Keywords: Health 4.0, Industry 4.0, health care, emerging technologies, Narayana Health, health inclusion

Introduction

The world has witnessed multiple transformations in recent years, changing how one lives their life. Breakthrough events like Industrial Revolution (IR), World War, Great Depression, Computerization & Information Technology, and off late Industry 4.0 have transformed things for good. Industry 4.0 is the consequence of the advent of recent technologies like the Internet of Things, Cloud Computing, Artificial Intelligence (AI), cognitive computing, etc. Integrating these technologies into our lives has opened the way for a new and better lifestyle, making lives easier, faster, and affordable.

As one of the most noteworthy landmarks in history, the Industrial Revolution has impacted all aspects of life in its unique manner. Technological progressions and industrialization eventually gave birth to exceedingly mechanized and robust manufacturing processes that ultimately started the evolution of assembly lines and factory systems [1].

The first Industrial Revolution representing Industry 1.0 started in the eighteenth century and progressed up to the mid-and late 19th century and gave the power of mechanization and steam to the world. Towards the end of the 19th century and up until the beginning of the 20th century, the second industrial revolution introduced mass production on a large scale; this was possible due to electricity usage. This also meant the death knell for small and individual producers. This was characterized by bulk production and the use of electricity. In the last decade of the 20th-century production systems, planning and resourcing became computer efficient, accurate, and adaptable to various scenarios with the power of computers marking the dawn of a new chapter, i.e., Industry 3.0.

Figure 3.1. Transition from Industry 1.0 to Industry 4.0.

Further, this laid the stepping stone for revolution 4.0. The 21st century ushered Industry 4.0, promising meaningful and seamless marriage of hardware and software. Emergent technologies like Big Data, Blockchain, AI and IOT, etc., pledges to ensure the abundance of potential envisaged from industry 4.0 is realized. Simply observing the transition from Industry 1.0 to Industry 4.0 (Figure 3.1) echoes a change similar to hunting homo sapiens to thinking modern human beings.

The healthcare industry falls in the extreme complex category of VUCA world. The long and never-ending queue at the OPD of a hospital and the delay in the discharge and reimbursement process of the patient shows how indistinct the entire healthcare operation is. After a successful diagnosis and treatment of a specific disease, the prognosis remains uncertain. The volatility of the outcome has what made this industry unique.

Health Care 1.0 to Health Care 4.0

As reflected in a study by Zhong et al., Healthcare systems and manufacturing systems share various standard features. [2] Just as manufacturing or any other industry sector, the health care sector has also witnessed an enduring chronicle of evolutions, revolutions, and transformations. Health Care 1.0 represented the essential patient-doctor direct interaction where the patient would pay a visit to the clinic and meet the doctor and other associates of the team. Through in-person consultation and diagnosis, the medical practitioner would provide a line of treatment to treat a disease. Due to significant and transformative development in health, life science, and technology, various new medical equipment's and devices were invented, developed and tested and are progressively being used while providing health care delivery like imaging test equipment, monitoring devices, and surgical and life support devices are widely used in medical fraternity and institutes for diagnosis, monitoring, and recovery. This development of protocols and procedures was a hallmark of Health care 2.0. The next decade saw the efficient record-keeping of medical records for developing, fine-tuning, and testing new protocols. Testing efficacy and understanding of the established protocols in the different regions also evolved, riding on the revolution in the IT-sphere, resulting in 3.0. Further advancements in telecommunication devices and bandwidth enabled swift and efficient adoption of Tele-OPD's and consultation (Figure 3.2).

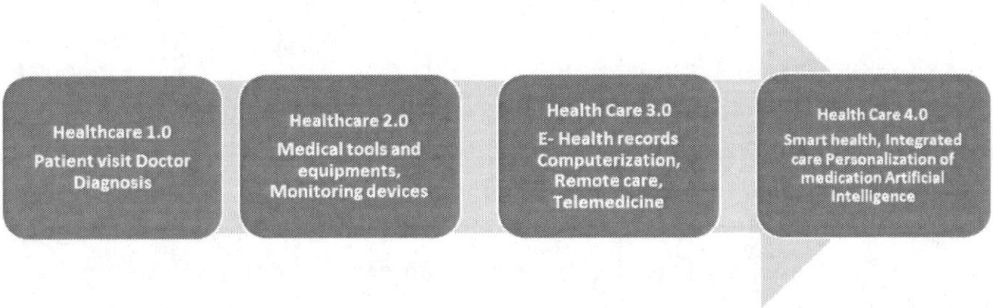

Figure 3.2. Transition from Health Care 1.0 to Health Care 4.0.

The current COVID-19 pandemic amplified the demand for telehealth and virtual visits, paving the way to remote diagnosis. These have steered various revolutionary transformations in health care delivery resulting in Health Care 3.0. The health care domain picked many clues from factory management systems to smoothly run their operations like colour-coding the patient's wrist bands with their levels like pre-operative post-operative, ICU, etc. With the advent of emerging tech in wearable devices, these bands can become monitoring devices too. Real-time data flowing in interventions and timely treatment will become a reality, improve success rates, and reduce mortalities. This is just one of the possibilities emerging technologies are promising to deliver. These healthcare 4.0 technologies have the stability, expanse, and accuracy to bring medical services to the doorstep at affordable rates (Figure 3.3).

The two major features of Health Care 4.0 thus can be presented as:

- *Smartness:* Application of AI techniques to improve seamless communication between stakeholders (medical fraternity, patient's) for achieving customized and patient-centred smart health care management leading to timely diagnosis and correct line of treatment.

- *Prediction analysis:* Healthcare 4.0 can synthesize tetra bytes of data in seconds, mining relevant data matching the symptoms with existing data and suggesting the diagnosis (even the rarest of symptoms will not go unseen) and a further line of treatment and the results obtained will further strengthen and accuracy. Empowered decision making is what HC 4.0 promises to deliver [3, 4, 5].

How do you intend to solve the problem affecting a massive chunk of the community with institutional void like money, institution, human resources, regulatory infrastructure, etc., and over and above lack of credibility adding to the situation? Each of these institutional voids represents an opportunity for an Entrepreneur to fill these voids and develop an affordable, innovative solution for a problem that has ever existed and felt but not yet resolved.

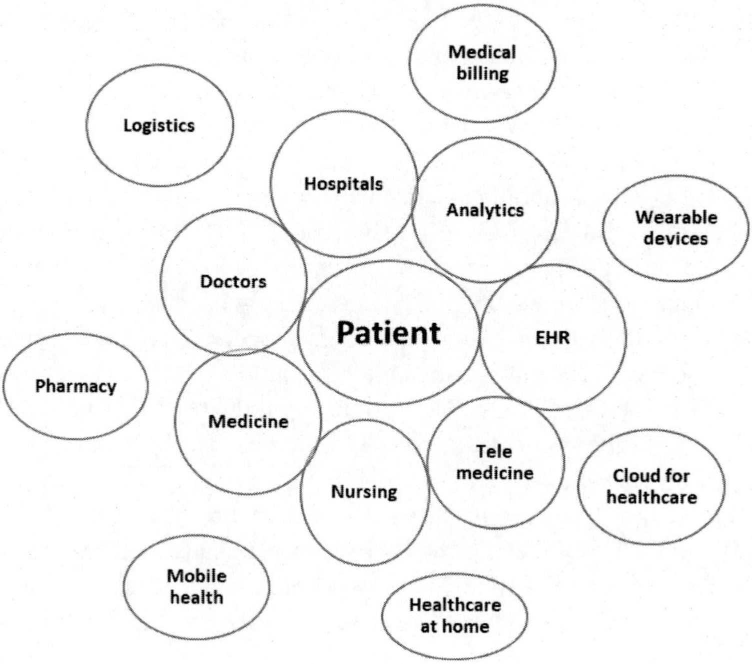

Figure 3.3. Interconnections in Health Care 4.0.

Information credibility is a significant void that we might struggle with today about institutional voids. *How to ensure that the basic sterilization requirements are met, ensure that doctor who is approached is a well-trained specialist, and provide that medicine/drugs being sold in the market are not pirated.* Such issues like ensuring credibility in the sanctity of transaction, information on the quality of providers, recourse mechanism, quality of facility, medicines, equipment, etc., wrestle emerging economies a lot more than the developed economies.

The problem revolves around ensuring credibility in ensuring the sanctity of a transaction. Institutional void is not just about credibility issues, but it's also about inclusion, health inclusion specifically where everyone has got equal access to all the health care facilities that they require, it's about the affordability of these services by all. Around two million heart surgeries are required to be done every year, but on average, all hospitals put together could perform about 1,50,000 surgeries barely. Rest who could not afford it would perish, and a significant chunk of such population is young male earning members. So there was a desperate need to provide an affordable solution to a problem faced by most of the country's population.

What are some of the critical interventions within hospitals required: the way surgeries are done, the way patient is treated, aftercare service for the patient, insurance cover? A CABG (Coronary artery bypass surgery) surgery-coronary artery bypass graft at Narayana Health is around $2000 compared to a similar surgery in the USA that costs around $100,000. It makes us think about the principal drivers that have contributed to lowering that cost.

This gap has inspired Dr. Shetty in creating what stands today as one of India's largest multispecialty hospital chains, encompassing thirty-one tertiary hospitals across nineteen cities of India. By building HC 3.0 and embracing HC 4.0, Narayana Health City has optimized productivity and minimized the cost. This has further enabled a multifold increase in NH's capacity to treat and offerings as well.

This chapter talks about the transformation brought in the health care industry by Dr Devi Shetty, whose work in Narayana Health care made it possible to deliver affordable solutions to one of the most acute problems faced by Indians: heart disease. The chapter has tried to map Industry 4.0 for the healthcare sector with the business model dimension and services of Narayana Healthcare to identify the further scope of implementation of those aspects of Industry 4.0, which is still not covered.

Literature Review

Industrial 4.0 utility in HC 4.0 and its tremendous impact was recorded in 2017 by Thuemmler and Bai. These have ushered significant change in the existing healthcare system, making it fluid and adaptive, resulting in some innovations like virtual and Tele-OPDs [6].

Chawla and Davis 2013 created a basis where Big data analytics can be used for patient-centric outcomes to reduce readmission rates [7]. Jee and Kim conducted a study to explore big data applications for reshaping the healthcare sector and presenting diverse possibilities and issues created by Big Data. It was concluded in the study that data security has emerged out as one of the major challenges which needs to be incorporated in the structure while planning that integration [8].

It can be inferred that Industry 4.0 applications are being used in the healthcare sector, leading to Health 4.0. However, in India, the picture is bleak as only a few sizeable super-speciality healthcare chains have adopted the model and do not touch all the dimensions. Initial capital investments often deter stakeholders from adopting technology even at losing out unchartered territories, whose shores will be unlocked using technology. Further, the most significant deterrent is the training of people on the new systems and the gestation period required for it [9].

Manufacturing implants and other patient-specific medical devices are a tricky and costly affair for any manufacturer because every patient's requirement may differ from each other. Industry 4.0 utilization of smart machines can overcome this challenge of customization [10].

Whether production of medical equipment or implants, customization of the same as per case the specific requirement is a task that pushes the prices. Moreover, this requirement of customization can be easily fulfilled by Industry 4.0 through mechatronics, robotics, and AI. Implants are customized via algorithms as per case-specific individual requirements. Further, the intelligent manufacturing system fulfils the requirement of customization in the medical field as per specifications Industry 4.0 provides through Health 4.0 offers extensive opportunities for enhancing digital manufacturing and efficiently solving all the critical issues and problems (Figure 3.4).

Industry 4.0 has been improved the record-keeping of patient records, laboratory identification leaps, and bound, making the health care sector truly digital [11, 12, 13]. This revolution in the health care sector has been evolving the manufacturing and designing of surgical tools and devices by introducing smart technology fit [14, 15].

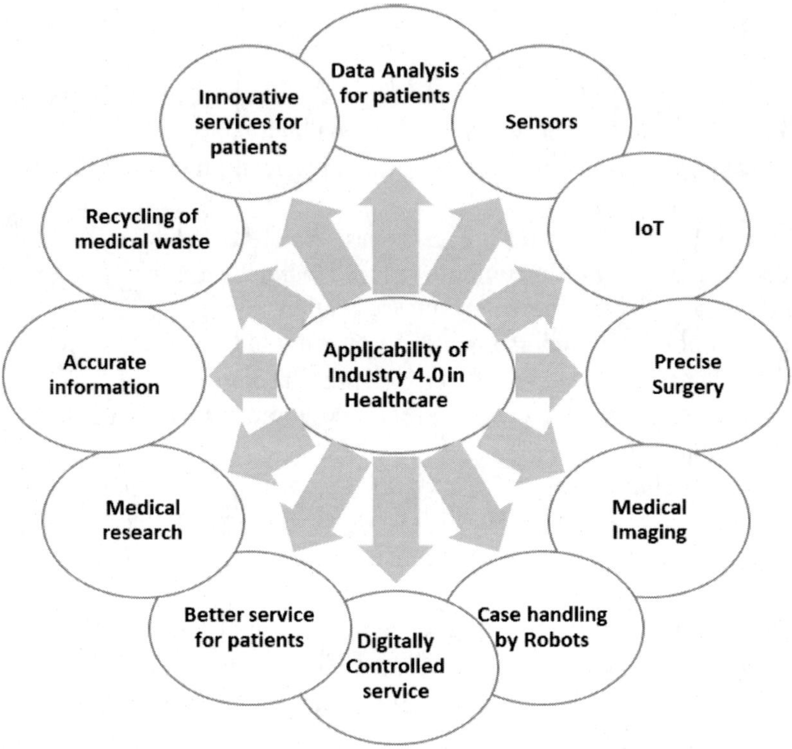

Source: Javaid et al. 2019.

Figure 3.4. Application of Industry 4.0 in Health Care.

One of the major requirements of the health care sector is the customization of implants and small implants; Industry 4.0 has an immense impact in meeting this requirement in quick turnaround time maintaining high quality [16, 17]. Smart medical components can communicate with monitoring systems and remote physicians using IoT. [18, 19].

Industry 4.0 in the health care sector provides hospitals with complete monitoring solutions of the entire process, patient monitoring, increasing quality of medical treatment, and optimizing monitoring cost [11, 20, 21]. This has led the health care sector to transfer the benefits to patients by providing them with cost-effective treatment packages, customized implants, etc. [12, 22]. Industry 4.0 has ensured reliable, real-time data ushering in a new era in research and development in the healthcare sector. [16, 23].

Technology Integration in Health Care Sector in the Frame Work of Industry 4.0

Figure 3.5 represents the varied possibilities and tremendous opportunity that Healthcare 4.0 bring to the table. Nowadays, Drones are used frequently for dropping medical supplies. Who would have thought that the pandemic would become the perfect foil for integrating these technologies in every day delivery models? Look at clogged-up roads of a developing country like India during peak office hours, now think of a scenario where there is an emergency requirement of blood for a patient, and the blood bank is at some distance. This would sink the strongest hearts, add drone service to this scenario, and save lives. IoMT (Internet of medical things) integration with wearable devices can revolutionize remote monitoring, especially for older people who may not afford the visits or movement could be a challenge for them too. The information flow within the stakeholders can make the diagnosis precise and the line of treatment more effective at the desired pace, which is often missing.

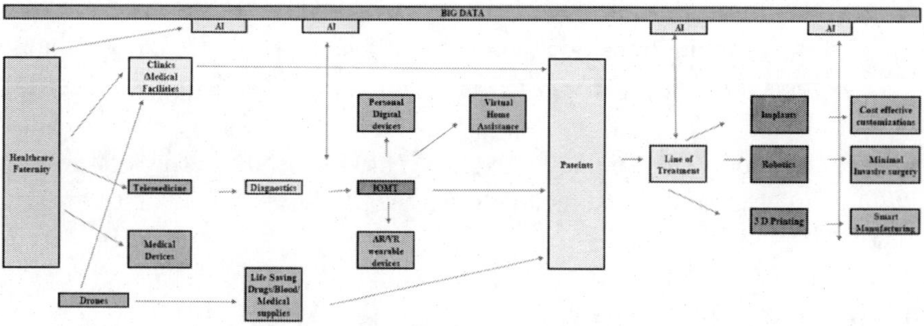

Source: Authors compilation.

Figure 3.5. Technology and healthcare Integration.

Research Gap and Objectives of the Chapter

In the medical field, customization or patient-centric services, reduced lead time, and other critical surgical supplies are critical issues that cannot be solved solely through traditional technologies alone. It is required to have an adaptive and responsive system incorporated into Healthcare 4.0 to meet the desired required quality. This revolution is vital for emerging markets like India. It is essential to provide accessible and affordable Health Care services to the last man in the country's last mile. Studies conducted earlier have not addressed this issue of emerging markets; hence, the present chapter attempts to understand how the implementation of Health 4.0 in a specialized care hospital can effectively help promote health inclusion.

The chapter will analyze the role of intelligent policy like Industry 4.0 in developing countries to make further tertiary care available to everybody, thus leading to health inclusion. It will address the issues that need to be addressed, such as what it would take to fix the problems with primary healthcare in India, the major roadblocks. The reasons why Dr Shetty, a social entrepreneur, was able to reduce the cost of CABG surgery by almost half in the last two decades, and how the special insurance policy developed for patients in collaboration with the state government has resulted in health inclusion. Objectives of the chapter are as mentioned below:

- To analyze the role of Industry 4.0 in the healthcare sector, taking the case of Narayana Healthcare (NH) to further the vision of making tertiary care available to everybody for the promotion of Health Inclusion.
- To study the transition pattern from Health 1.0 to Health 4.0 and its impact on medical service management in an emerging market like India.
- To deeply investigate the working model of Narayana Healthcare in order to understand its alignment with Industry 4.0.

Business Model Filling the Institutional Voids

Dr Devi Shetty had to be an entrepreneur first and be a Doctor, healer, or Heart Surgeon. Transportation provided by the medical bus has made it possible to visit the remote areas of Bangalore and bring the patients to the hospital, thus removing the problem of accessibility for those who cannot travel to the hospital. It is essential to have medical outreach to educate people on what is happening in the hospital, which is part of entrepreneurship. The concept of telemedicine started in a much more local setting that represents entrepreneurship in many different alternative ways. It was required to create a protocol to train the lesser trained general physicians, nurses, and attendants to know what questions are supposed to be asked to understand the requirements of a heart patient requiring cardiac surgery.

Another way through which telemedicine represents Entrepreneurship is dealing with the state. The government's resources are probably underutilized as the situation is unclear to them regarding the utilization of extra resources to improve healthcare infrastructure. The hospital has used the spare satellite capacity for telemedicine. That is what entrepreneurship is all about, working with people who do not see things as entrepreneurs but are then persuaded to see things in your way? About 45% of Dr Devi Shetty's patients pay an amount of even less than $ 3000 for operative intervention. 'Yeshasvini,' another initiative by Dr Devi Shetty in association with the Karnataka State Government in 2002, a micro-insurance plan that reimburses NH about the US $ 1200 covered approximately 30% of these patients.

The health Insurance Plan provided by Dr Shetty is one of its kind in India. It started when there was hardly any health Insurance in the Indian market. The insurer will pay a minimal amount like 10 cents in a month, and an equal matching contribution will be paid by the State Government, making it equal to around $1 a year and thus accumulating the amount to a considerable corpus by the time the person needs tertiary healthcare services. This is what an entrepreneur can do to society. It brought a wave of reform in Health Insurance in the Indian market.

Patients who are not covered by any insurance scheme or could not afford any are given concessions basis their economic condition, borne by NH's charitable trust, individual donors, other charitable agencies or the Hospitable itself as per the case, procedure, and time. Further to increase NH's penetration in rural areas, both brick and click model. i.e., rural clinics and Tele-OPD is adopted. Analyzing the model, one can say that this is not what a cardiac surgeon must do. Providing medical education, medical outreach, telemedicine is not what a cardiac surgeon would be doing. However, thinking practically in a developing economy with so many institutional voids, the ultimate care facility could not reach them. All these voids prevent the transacting partner from getting together. Devi's health city acts as a credibility enhancer, thus reassuring that all sorts of transactions are reliable, reproducible, and reassuring credibility in every aspect of tertiary health care facilities.

- *Profitability:* The managing team at NH have a unique style of evaluating accounting ledgers daily and scrutinizing income statements closely to assess daily profitability; this process, in return, allows them to have real-time information regarding their concessional margins, which can be passed on to their patients in need without compromising on their margins and sustainability. NH has been a well-managed, profitable entity with a proven track record from the onset. This can be well understood by just a look at the NH's stakeholders too from niche corridors of financial world Pine Bridge investment, and JP Morgan holds 12.5%, Biocon's Pharma queen Kiran Mazumdar-Shaw holds 2.5%, and the remainder of the stake is entrusted with dynamic Dr Shetty and his family. Shetty has shown how to run a profitable social enterprise without compromising any stakeholder's (Doctor's, Inventor's, and Patient's) interest.

- *Innovations in Operations:* One of the innovations done when D Shetty set up NH in 2001 was how doctors are remunerated. Classically, cardiac surgeons are remunerated surgery-wise, representing a substantial percentage of a hospital's overall expenses. Dr Shetty asked his surgeons and NH's staff to work for set remunerations; this was in no ways lower to what they take home under normal circumstances remuneration, but he wanted the doctors to perform more surgeries that will eventually bring down the cost per procedure as per the concept of economies of scale. This approach has been one of the core savings areas at Narayana Hrudayalaya.

In the initial days of NH, patients came because of Dr Shetty's skill and reputation. Though the significant draw, NH's Bangalore camps record 2500 OPD's daily, proving the savings on their bill. The economies of scale helped NH increase backend bargaining power with bulk orders for their daily hospital requirements. NH started to save nearly 40% by importing FCL's of surgical gloves from Malaysia. NH has progressed to digital X-ray technology, thus saving on the recurring cost. NH's strategy to optimize asset utilization (MRI, CT's) for 14 hours from the usual 8 hours helped them in two ways dispersing the patient is over longer periods, with discounts offered during evening hours and passing the benefits of economies of scale to patient's NH strategic alliance with vendors also reaped benefits with huge capital cost savings on equipment. Vendors like that of Blood gas analysis were shown the platform NH is for showcasing their products and making money of consumables used in their equipment and their philosophy, keeping the interest of all stakeholders.

Implementation of Industry 4.0 for Health Inclusion

Challenges arising from global warming and its effect on the environment: Integration of machines in our everyday life makes it easy day by day, reducing physical activities and giving rise to lifestyle diseases like diabetes, hypertension, etc.

1.4 billion population, millions of Primary and Tertiary medical centres (including private setups), billions of files spread over thousands of kilometres across India. The path to the moon is known. The way to these files is unknown. Further, the cost of maintaining these records is unsustainable, and additionally, when required, it is a challenge to retrieve data. HC 4.0 has the capability and capacity to tackle both of the difficulties above with a solution like a cloud space, Big Data Mining, and AI. This can exponentially increase medical fraternity efforts to change the course from a fee and face-based approach to a holistic wellness approach by being preemptive in diagnosis.

At NH, virtual and online platforms treatments are offered to around 3,000 patients. They have 55,000 diabetic patients who are being treated in the out-group. The health care industry is trying to structure its data systems; however, their inhibition or lack of funds to move away from legacy software hinders the emerging tech from delivering at its full potential.

In 2016, Narayana Healthcare announced its alliance with Cisco for delivering reasonably priced speciality healthcare services remotely through Cisco's Virtual Expertise Digital solution. The partnership enabled NH to offer diagnostic facilities for super-specialized procedures to a high-quality, high-value patient experience in Oncology, neurology, etc., to patients from nook and corner of the country at affordable costs. Access to primary Healthcare is a challenge that looms large around most of the country. With the advent of technology interventions available to fill this gap, Healthcare institutions embark on the journey to embrace this transition. In the present times, what is required is to create agile and adds value to patient care.

Cisco's adoption of virtual systems gave fuel to NH's dream of increasing their reach multifold in rural and urban setups. The digitized platforms helped execute advanced specialized procedures, thus increasing the accessibility and affordability of their services. Cisco has also implemented modifications for NH infrastructure, empowering healthcare distribution at district centres and multi-speciality hospitals of Narayana across the country, constructing a truly enhanced mobile and digital hospital experience, thus promoting health inclusion. The Cisco Virtual Expertise Digital solution has helped connect patients with NH doyens aptly and proficiently, irrespective of remoteness.

The Digital experience brings voice, video, and data to the patients regardless of remoteness and validates how telehealth and sensors within health care devices can produce fresh opportunities for innovation.

Real-time data transmission via Telemetry (with two-way video call) of a patient's symptoms, vitals, and history transcends into seamless analytics, resulting in precise diagnosis creation and treatment. A thorough 'clinical examination' and review of all examinations are now possible in a faultless mode with the choice of recording the entire interaction, which could be later accessed. It has enabled medics from NH to perform critical diagnostics like Diacom viewing and detecting Thrombolysis in cardiac care. This partnership has helped NH empower their care teams to help offer greater preemptive and predictive maintenance for their patients.

The high levels of encryptions make the Cisco Virtual Expertise Digital solution secure and safe, protecting patient data confidentiality and privacy, ensuring no leakage or theft of data during data transmission and usage.

Scale Driven Model: The Road Ahead

NH has achieved cost leadership in its segment and domain, a feature that has been made possible through process innovation. The conclusion is that the health care industry requires more intervention in process innovation than just product innovation. Over the years, NH Bangalore that Dr Shetty opened in 2001 grew to one thousand beds; the facility has progressed to cutting-edge technology and surgeons successfully executing some 30 surgeries per day which is the maximum cardiac operations done by any hospital in India. This, coupled with an impressive 2.5% mortality rate and hospital-acquired infection rate of 2.8 per 1000 ICU days, is per global gold standard. In the local setting of Bangalore and India, the business model of Narayana Hrudalaya has gained wide acceptance as one can walk in the city and see that patients are primarily from India and Bangalore with adjoining areas specifically. The same model was seen with disbelief leading to scepticism with grudging acceptance. In addition to patients from India, patients come from Africa, New York. They are insured and are from War-Torn countries through charitable bodies for free service, Middle East and Pakistan. There is Visa Hotline for fast-tracking contentious cases so that hospitals can talk and provide medical visas.

The next part of the transition would be when the rest of the world would come and see the model. What is required to involve more and more such entrepreneurs who could replicate the same model of providing tertiary care in either the rest of the world or India with different disease treatments? Telemedicine could prove to be a helping aid for places like Adis, where they have state-of-the-art Hospitals but no professionally trained doctors as they decamp for lucrative greener pastures once they get their complete training. So with prior appointments, Doctors from Narayana Hrudalaya could be available on call to give the advice required by the hospital on the other side. It is lovely to see that scale-driven cardiac tertiary care has been successfully replicated in a place like Adis. The idea of breaking the health care service in bits and pieces and diagnosing it has helped in spreading, and this was the real essence of Narayana Health city to make affordable tertiary care available to all so that the surgeon gets to focus on the most critical part and other parts of the services are outsourced to other people whose skills are less scarce.

It's crucial to analyze the model used by Narayana Health City as several people require cardiac care for a place like India, where males specifically are predominantly more prone to this issue than too at an early age. So with issues of institutional voids in the form of lack of proper health care facility, lack of credibility, and affordability issues, it is interesting to see how all this works. A model is required to effectively provide high-quality medical services to a vast chunk every day. You need to treat many patients with high quality and low price points and provide affordable cardiac care for India and the world. Turning scale into cost advantage is the critical insight. Scale matters because it leads to the amortization of fixed costs. In this case, the number of patients attended or operated on leads to easy amortization of the fixed cost of equipment, thus lowering the cost of surgery performed per patient.

The scale has given the benefit of opportunities for negotiation with the suppliers of the related equipment. A Health Care facility coming up in a semi-urban space of an emerging market might not sound like an attractive deal for providers, but the huge chunk of clientele to be served every day makes it one of the most attractive options to capitalize on. So the scale effect amortizes fixed costs, provides more opportunities for negotiation, lowers the prices for medical consumables and assembly line operations.

The pricing strategy adopted for CABG Surgery at Narayana is another crucial aspect where patients choose to pay for the surgery depending upon their affordability. Some patients can for the breakeven price of a particular surgery, they have the option to pay for a list price of the surgery that allows for a modest profit, then is the option for paying what is known as Karuna Hridaya Package, which is paying below the breakeven cost, and even if the patient cannot pay in all these options, then there are surgeries for free. Around

65% of the patients pay above the breakeven price, creating a surplus for those who cannot afford it. So there is a robust accounting control system that ensures you manage a cash reservoir that should maintain sufficient liquidity. So there is an algorithm that works to allocate care facilities depending upon the criticality of the cases. The trick is to run the Stochastic Optimization Model that ensures you have sufficient cash to run the operations smoothly and make sure you do not have too much cash, which means that you are not treating enough poor patients to fulfil your vision. A very accurate understanding of the financial health of the enterprise is required.

The business model truly represents a mélange of making profits for the service of the society that represents a mix of profit and charity. Every patient coming contributes to the surgeon's knowledge, contributing to the amortization of fixed costs, lowering the per-unit costs, and improving the quality of care.

It is possible that not every tertiary care can be broken down into bits and pieces, so what is required is to see where this focus factory can be applied where the Scale model can work. What is needed to find areas where the scale model can work? Entrepreneurship, Experimentation, and Iteration: This model is required to work in any geography or other areas of problems. The accelerator effect has been working, leading to a chain of development. Entrepreneurship, Experimentation and Iteration have worked for this model, which can be replicated to other categories or geographical locations.

Conclusion and Recommendations

Health Care 4.0 has provided numerous opportunities and challenges for reengineering health care systems. For the deriving benefit of the opportunities and addressing the challenges of achieving smart and connected health care, it is highly recommended to focus on patients, caregivers, and health care professionals. On comparing the evolution of Industry 1.0 to 4.0 and Health Care 1.0 to 4.0, it is visible that new technologies, equipment, and data are being developed, utilized, and implemented in both domains.

The pandemic has fast-tracked many technologies into commercialization and mass usage; society has embraced technology faster than people who developed, even though it applies to the health care sector. The technology which has been lying around unutilized is of high utility. The time is ripe, lockdowns and restrictions have put most medical institutes to develop Tele-OPDs and virtual monitoring systems; however, these utilize most of the

Health Care 3.0. The transition to embracing Health Care 4.0 has still to happen. IT innovators are in prolonged discussions with the medical fraternity working on APIs to bridge the gap and visible opportunity gap.

Health Care 4.0 can increase the quality of outcomes from

- Affordable options
- Enhanced doctor's satisfaction
- Enhanced experience of patient's
- Holistic wellness.

These four are inter-wined and form the centrepiece of Health Care. 4.0. Health Care 4.0 needs to concentrate on these vital outcomes to balance the positive and negative dependence of the aims and integrate them systematically [24]. For a developing country like India, health inclusion is imperative for the growth and wellness of the country, and NH has shown that path to achieve it. HC 4.0 can be the real game-changer with its endless capabilities. Once integrated with current systems, solutions for the poor and those at remote locations would be more possible.

Data analytics and artificial intelligence are not novel concepts, and NH has presented very one with an efficient working model by utilizing the same. Algorithms incorporated with AI have made sense of mines of already available Big data. From keeping patient records digitally to customization of treatment, every operation has been made seamless, accurate, and within no time. Hospitals, clinics, doctors, and healthcare workers get patient data in different forms like health records, medical history, laboratory reports, text messages, phone conversations, etc. Structuring it according to the requirements and finding insights from it has been developed by smart data scientists. Moreover, a patient visiting a hospital does not have to stand in a queue for long hours.

Narayana Health has redefined how super-speciality healthcare protocols and delivery models. Operating on extremely safe medical-grade platforms with immersive visual experiences, they can virtualize scarce resources, including NH surgeons, NH paramedics, and staff deliver entree to specialist consultants remotely. The hospital has touched upon some of the dimensions of Health 4.0 like precise surgery, digitally controlled devices, telemedicine for remote healthcare resulting in better services for patients at affordable costs. However, specific dimensions like Robotic surgery, Use of Artificial Intelligence and Big Data Analytics, etc., are still to be explored, leaving ample further research.

References

[1] Kamble SS, Gunasekaran A, Sharma R (2018) Analysis of the drivingand dependence power of barriers to adopt industry 4.0 in Indian manufacturing industry. *ComputInd* 101:107–119.

[2] Zhong, X., Lee, H. K., & Li, J. (2017). From production systems to health care delivery systems: A retrospective look on similarities, difficulties and opportunities. *International Journal of Production Research*, 55(14), 4212–4227. https://doi.org/10.1080/00207543.2016.1277276.

[3] Kansagara, D., Englander, H., Salanitro, A., Kagen, D., Theobald, C., Freeman, M., &Kripalani, S. (2011). Risk prediction models for hospitalreadmission: A systematic review. *JAMA*, 306(15), 1688–1698. https://doi.org/10.1001/jama.2011.1515.

[4] Damen, J. A., Hooft, L., Schuit, E., Debray, T. P., Collins, G. S., Tzoulaki, I., Lassale, C. M., Siontis, G. C., Chiocchia, V., Roberts, C., &Schl€ussel, M. M. (2016). Prediction models for cardiovascular disease risk in the general population: *Systematic review*. *BMJ*, 353, i2416.

[5] Wynants, L., Van Calster, B., Bonten, M. M., Collins, G. S., Debray, T. P., De Vos, M., Haller, M. C., Heinze, G., Moons, K. G., Riley, R. D., &Schuit, E. (2020). Prediction models for diagnosis and prognosis of covid-19 infection: *Systematic review and critical appraisal. BMJ*, 369, m1328.

[6] Thuemmler C, Bai C (2017) *Health 4.0: how virtualization and big dataare revolutionizing healthcare*. Springer, New York.

[7] Chawla NV, Davis DA (2013), Bringing big data to personalized healthcare: a patient-centered framework. *J Gen Intern Med* 28:660–665.

[8] Jee K, Kim G-H (2013) Potentiality of big data in the medical sector: focus on how to reshape the healthcare system. *Healthcare Informatics Research* 19:79–85.

[9] Kagermann H (2015) Change through digitization—value creation in theage of industry 4.0. In*: Management of permanent change. Springer*, Wiesbaden, pp 23–45.

[10] Javaid M, Haleem A (2019), *Industry 4.0 applications in medical field: A brief review, Current Medicine Research and Practice*, https://doi.org/10.1016/j.cmrp.2019.04.001.

[11] Lobo FA. *Industry 4.0: Redefining Manufacturing of Future Medical Devices. ECN*; 2017. https://www.ecnmag.com/article/2017/10/industry-40-redefining-manufacturing-future-medical-devices.

[12] Wang S, Wan J, Zhang D, Li D, Zhang C. Towards smart factory for Industry 4.0: a self-organised multi-agent system with big data-based feedback and coordination. *Compu tNetw*. 2016;101:158e168.

[13] Kilic T. Digital hospital; an example of best practice. *Int J Health Sci Res Policy*. 2016;1(1):52e58.

[14] Filipe L, Fdez-Riverola F, Costa N, Pereira A (2015) Wireless body areanetworks for healthcare applications: *Protocol stackreview International Journal of Distributed Sensor Networks* 11:213705.

[15] Zhong TY, Xu X, Klotz E, Newman ST. Intelligent manufacturing in the context of industry 4.0: a review. *Engineering*. 2017;3:616e630.

[16] Javaid M, Haleem A. Additive manufacturing applications in medical cases: a literature-based review. *Alexandria J Med*. 2018;54(4):411e422.

[17] Stock T, Seliger G. Opportunities of sustainable manufacturing in industry 4.0. *Procedia CIRP*. 2016;40:536e541.

[18] Aceto G, Persico V, Pescape A. The role of Information and communication technologies in healthcare: taxonomies, perspectives, and challenges. *J Netw Comput Appl*. 2018. https://doi.org/10.1016/j.jnca. 2018.02.008.

[19] Jee K, Kim GH. Potentiality of big data in the medical sector: focus on how to reshape the healthcare system. *Healthc Inform Res*. 2013; 19(2):79e85.

[20] Liu YK, Xu X. Industry 4.0 and cloud manufacturing: a comparative analysis. *J Manuf Sci Eng*. 2017;139(3):1e8.

[21] Javaid M, Haleem A. 4D printing applications in medical field: a brief review. *Clin Epidemiol Global Health*. 2018. https://doi.org/10.1016/ j.cegh.2018.09.007. [In press].

[22] Kotevski A, Koceska N, Koceski S. E-health monitoring system. In: *International Conference on Applied Internet and Information Technologies*. 2016. https://doi.org/10.20544/AIIT2016.32.

[23] Bahga A, Madisetti VK. A cloud-based approach for interoperable electronic health records (EHR's). *IEEE J Biomed Health Inf.* 2013;17(5): 894e906.

[24] Jingshan Li & Pascale Carayon (2021): Health Care 4.0: A vision for smart and connected health care, *IISE Transactions on Healthcare Systems Engineering*, doi:10.1080/24725579.2021.1884627.

Chapter 4

Bitcoin Mining and Its Utility in the Healthcare Sector

Farhana Hussain Altaf Hussain[1], Vinod Kumar Shukla[1], Leena Wanganoo[2] and Amit Verma[3,*]

[1]Department of Engineering and Architecture,
Amity University, Dubai, UAE
[2]Research Scholar, University of Petroleum and Energy Studies,
Dehradun, India
[3]HTMi Switzerland Dubai, UAE

Abstract

The World Health Organization (WHO) has set a total digitalization of healthcare by 2030, focusing on health data collection, analysis, and communication. It has been highlighted that disaggregated data will receive considerably more attention; hence, improving health information systems is crucial. (WHO report, 2016). In recent years, public health has slowly paced towards digital change. Traditional paper files are replaced with electronic records providing the same information in a digital format in terms of clinical record management. The present state of healthcare information systems is highly fragmented. While many sources create increased volumes of personal healthcare data – from physicians to pharmacies, laboratories to hospitals, and even our mobile phones and smart devices – the information is almost always isolated within data silos – segregated and inaccessible from outside the confines of the data silos.

* Corresponding Author's Email: amitlko22@gmail.com.

In: Industry 4.0 and Intelligent Business Analytics for Healthcare
Editors: Soumi Dutta, Vinod Kumar Shukla, Shruti Nagpal et al.
ISBN: 978-1-68507-602-3

The chapter attempts to review software and the algorithm of Bitcoin Mining, Bitcoin currency, and its processes used in the Healthcare Sector. The Healthcare industry above is a complicated real-time network of several participative nodes of industry such as physicians, pathologists, pharmacists, medical suppliers, surgeons and patients. Bitcoin Mining is a speed game between people or companies that excavates with different computational forces to understand the numerical problems, provide proof of work, expand their answer, and understand the Bitcoin hubs. Healthcare is one of the industries where the implementation of Blockchain can rapidly enhance the quality of service to the patient and integrate reliable real-time details to healthcare providers. Today, everyone is very much aware of bitcoin and the profit of mining bitcoin. It is very competitive to mine profitability as you can only get rewards if you arrive at the right answer before any other miners. Further detailed understanding of how the mining works, what is needed, its benefits, how secure the network is, etc. are discussed throughout the chapter to understand Bitcoin mining better.

Keywords: healthcare, smart contract, bitcoin mining, decentralized distributed ledger

Introduction

The term "digitalized clinical records" should be accurately known, as there is a general understanding of the difference between electronic patient records and electronic medical records (E.H.R.s). The E.M.R. is a set of data of the patient's medical and treatment history to let practitioners keep the record and monitor several parameters. However, it cannot be shared unless the results are physically produced on paper. At the same time, the E.H.R. is significant in sharing the data with all the stakeholders, including the patient, and supporting each practitioner, making it a live-action set of information. The majority of relevant information in healthcare is disjointed and disconnected from other systems and beneficiaries. With the implementation of emerging technologies such as Blockchain, the healthcare sector can integrate the entire chain. This will enhance the processes between the patient, healthcare practitioners and supply chain network with secure data transfer, including the utilization and consumption of supplies, patient history and diagnostic reports between stakeholders. The financial transactional data, as well as patient's medical data transaction, is enabled through Blockchain. In this technology, the financial transaction is conducted with the help of Cryptocurrency/Bitcoin.

On the other hand, Cryptos provide a token of confidence between transacting parties because they are more than just a financial vehicle.

The term currency is familiar to almost everyone, and computerized mining has translated it into Bitcoin's latest trendy and electronic currency. Any currency (bill/Coin/notes) accepted in any country is due to the popular trend of acceptance and the conformity and acceptance of the central government and public thereof to the printed piece of paper. Similarly, in the computerized network, the acceptance or the conformity of purchase provides it equal value to the currency despite no central governance linked to the bitcoin opposite to any other regular currency based on the network and blockchain assurances.

The creation of a popular cryptocurrency named "Bitcoin" began in 2008. Transferred via the computer, it is created with the core concept to eliminate expense, reliance, and delays caused by the banks in completing the transaction. Bitcoin is the most secure and reliable private cryptocurrency-based underlying technology (Blockchain) [1]. The first Bitcoin transaction was initiated in May 2010 by Mr Lazlo to purchase two pizzas by offering 10,000 bitcoins worth $41 in 2010 [2].

Bitcoin

Bitcoin began as a free computer program venture and a paper published by Satoshi Nakamoto in 2009. Nakamoto, who appears to have been made to convey Bitcoin to this world, designed a framework of online value exchange that supports promising Internet money. Bitcoin is the decentralized progressed cash, computerized currency, or coins that any user may send through the Internet for purchase or exchange. Contrast with distinctive choices; bitcoins have various favourable circumstances. Bitcoin mining is highly accepted in the current market and many bitcoin users/miners.

In today's environment, medical and technological breakthroughs have a tremendous impact on population health management. Transactions are completed utilizing the Internet without the need and involvement of a bank or clearinghouse. It implies that each country can utilize the currency with much lower expenses and no necessities or arbitrary limits [2]. The process of storing, accounting, retaining, authenticating, and transmitting blockchain data is based on a distributed system structure that demonstrates trust relationships among distributed nodes using pure mathematical methods rather than central institutions, leading to a decentralized trusted distributed system [3]. The ability to collect data for one patient, compounded by the many more whom opt-in, can change the way individuals manage their health [4].

Innovative technologies such as Blockchain and cryptocurrency, on the other hand, offer data ownership transparency and allow each stakeholder greater involvement and responsibility in healthcare distribution and management. The concept of an encrypted public ledger between medical agencies, patients, and networks owned and mined promises a bright future. Medical chain, one of the London-based enthusiasts of the electronic health record industry, enables its healthcare providers to secure the data and pay consultation fees through med tokens.

Conceptual Model for Bitcoin Mining in Healthcare

The data in healthcare become lifesaving or always threatening with its available resources to the practitioners and consultants. Few innovative software companies have led it to support the healthcare providers such as Avaneer, Professional Credential Exchange, etc. to secure the smart contracts between the patient and doctors, availability of real-time data, etc. Robomodo offers a single point of contact by linking chatbots, telemedicine sessions and wearable diagnostic tools to enhance efficiency. The below model (Figure 4.1) is a simplified representation of the blockchain-based health care industry contracting, recording and transfer along with its benefits such as payments initiation through Bitcoin, real-time sharing, verified invoicing security and transparency.

Based on extensive literature review, the stepwise approach of the Bitcoin mining process is illustrated, and its algorithm is explained below:

The Bitcoin Blockchain

Blockchain has dramatically transformed the healthcare industry and has impacted a large population. This has entirely revived the industry's capabilities and devised away from multiple issues of the healthcare industry such as rising operations cost, data infringements, and ineffective systems. Estonia has effectively moved to 99% of digital prescriptions since 2012. Akiri, one of the established healthcare network operators from Foster City,

California states data is the lifeblood of industry leverages blockchain principles to secure the data.

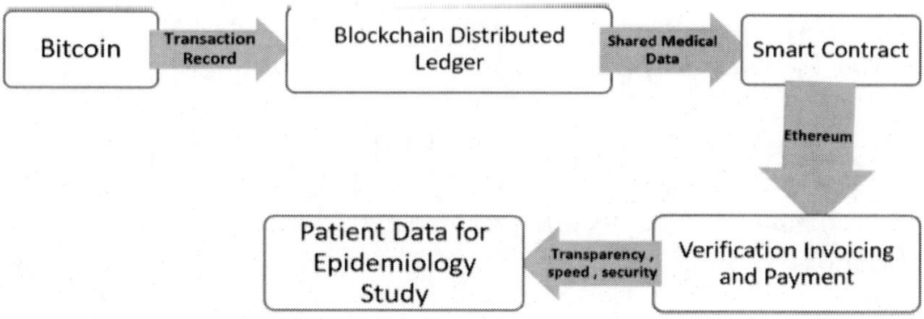

(Source: Author's Interpretation)

Figure 4.1. Conceptual Model for the study.

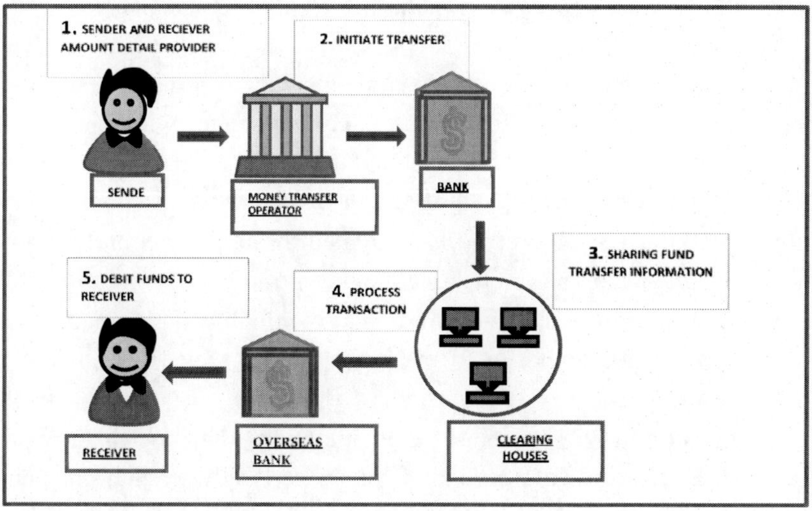

Figure 4.2. Traditional transaction chart.

Bitcoin provides seamless payment of the cryptocurrencies, security and protection of your transaction and related data due to the secured algorithms used and the rewards of huge profits. A blockchain is the number of blocks that are linked to each other like a chain. Every individual block in the Blockchain holds a compilation of data. Blockchain is a distributed record, which signifies that a copy of the file or document circulates over the network among all partners in the network. Every companion holds a replica of the whole record or ledger. On regular bank transactions (Figure 4.2) transfer of money from one account to another, the record for such transactions and their details are secured for record keeping of the senders and the receivers account statement time of transaction amount, etc.

This data can tamper, and it can be easily manipulated. Blockchain is beneficial to secure such possibilities with its secure digital network using cryptography [5]. BurstIQ's platform, another software company from Colorado, maintains a massive amount of healthcare data following Health Insurance Portability and Accountability Act (HIPAA) compliance depending on Blockchain to share store and securely restrict prescription drugs' exploitation.

Attributes of Blockchain

The attributes of the Blockchain are discussed in detail as under.

- **Peer-to-peer:** There is no central authority to manage or manipulate the transaction. All members communicate with one another straightforwardly. This enables the data exchange to be made straightforwardly with third-parties involvement called Peer to Peer.
- **Distributed:** The record is circulated through the complete system, making changing or updating the data not relatively smooth.
- **Cryptographically Secured:** Cryptography is applied for the surveillance authority to make the record sealed, in other words, tamper-proof.
- **Include only:** Data must be combined for the Blockchain with the time-consecutive procedure. This property advises that once data is combined with the Blockchain, it is hard to change it and be addressed as essentially unchanged. We can say it has: "The privilege to be overlooked or right to deletion".
- **Consensus:** It gives Blockchain the ability to update the record using agreement techniques in this quality. It is because of this that it has decentralization potential. Any central authority or force does not update the record. Alternatively, any modification to the Blockchain is vetted against strict criteria set down by the blockchain obligation and only added on the Blockchain once an agreement has been reached [18].

How Blockchain Works

Alongside using blockchain technology, the medical supply chain is also equally impacted and has been vigorously manned by pharmaceuticals and supply chain companies such as Embleema, Chronicled, etc. Where Chronicled optimizes to eradicate drug trafficking, Embleema uses blockchain technology to fast-track drug development.

A node or hub initiates a transaction by constructing and later digitally marking it with its private key (made by cryptography). A transaction can describe multiple steps in a blockchain. This is usually a data structure representing a transaction of significant value between clients on the blockchain network. Transaction data structure generally consists of considerable value, important guidelines, source and targeted addresses, and other approved data.

Peers have propagated a transaction that confirms and validates the transaction based on predetermined criteria by applying a Gossip protocol flooding code. Typically, to verify the transaction, more than one node is needed. Once the transaction is verified, it is added to a chain distributed throughout the network. The payment is verified at this level.

In this process, when there is a new creation of a block, it gets transformed into a part of the ledger, and then the next new block binds itself to the last updated block cryptographically. This connection is a point of hash. Here the transaction gains its second confirmation, and the block gains its first confirmation. Each time a new block is produced, transactions are reconfirmed. This can take up to six confirmations in the network to consider the final transaction [6], [7], [8].

Bitcoin Mining

The "bitcoin mining" result is twofold. First, as computers solve complex math problems on the Bitcoin network, they generate new Bitcoin, which gets added to the Blockchain ("bitcoin" usually appears without capitalization when referring to the individual coins themselves), not unlike a mining operation extracts gold from the ground. Second, Bitcoin miners make the Bitcoin payment network trustworthy and secure by addressing computational math problems and confirming transaction information.

This decentralized processing means that there is no central authority that regulates bitcoin. Instead, Bitcoin is upheld by many computers across the world called "nodes". This computer network serves the same operation as the Federal Reserve, Visa, and Mastercard yet with crucial contrasts. Each node stores the transaction information of the previous transaction and carries the encrypted values, which help to check its validity throughout the chain. Nevertheless, unlike the involvement of central authorities in any other monetary exchange, Bitcoin nodes are scattered all over the world and record transaction data in a public list that anyone can access.

When somebody makes a buy or deal utilizing bitcoin, it is considered "exchange." Any transaction made, whether online or in-store, is recorded in banks or any point-of-sale services. Bitcoin excavators accomplish a similar impact without these foundations by clustering transactions together in "squares" and adding them to an open record called the "blockchain." Nodes at that point keep up records of those squares to be checked into what is to come. Once Bitcoin miners add a new block of transactions to the Blockchain, part of their job is to ensure the accuracy of those transactions. Earlier mining bitcoin and producing hashes were easily accomplished by simply using desktop computers.

Bitcoin Operational Framework

A patient's journey in a healthcare system revolves around his profile from doctors/consultants, nurses, physicians, pharmacies, labs, insurance providers, and technicians in its shortest tenure. The processes can be understood through the comprehension of a network framework. A network is a web with different hubs (clients), and connections are also known as (exchanges) between these hubs. As a network, the Bitcoin Network's motive is to empower clients to send tokens to one another (bitcoins). This is an amalgamation of software and network technologies where several cash trades exist, and a user can purchase and offer bitcoin for dollars, euros, and more. The bitcoin is put away in a digital wallet on a user's computer or versatile gadget. Sending, exchanging, and receiving bitcoins is as simple as sending an e-mail, and users can buy anything against the exchange of bitcoins [9].

The bitcoin network is verified by miners and is compensated with recently produced bitcoins for confirming transactions. After transactions are verified, they are recorded in a transparent public record. Bitcoin opens up an entire modern platform for development. The software is open-source, and anyone can audit the code. Bitcoin is changing funds in the same behaviour as the Internet has changed publishing. This becomes crucial when it is related to critical health conditions, diagnosis, treatment, and surgical interventions in a complicated chronic ailment. The data is not only been transferred and updated at several touchpoints; however, the real-time developments must be administered in time to the right section of the chain.

Bitcoin is decentralized, and there is not one computer that holds the ledger. This means that in bitcoins, every computer that takes an interest within the framework is also keeping a copy of the record, making cryptocurrency usage safer through Blockchain technology. To hack the record, a hacker may have to take down several computers keeping duplicate records and updating them continuously; this reduces the possibility of hacking the network to the least [10].

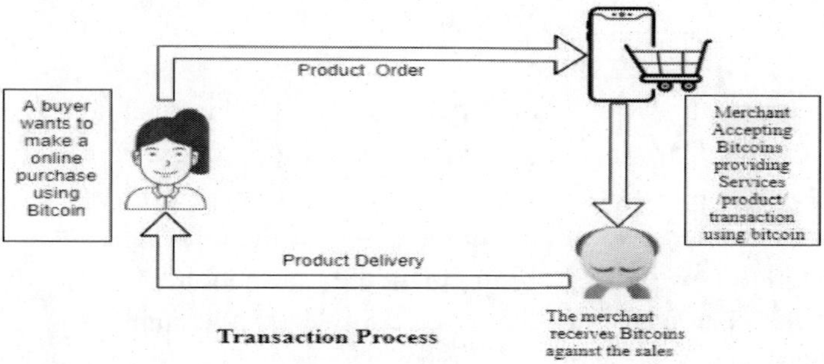

Figure 4.3a. Bitocin based transaction process.

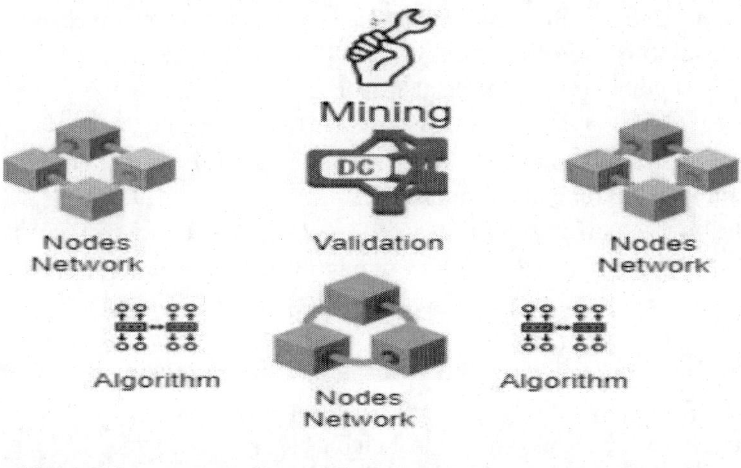

Figure 4.3b. Mining – transaction verification process.

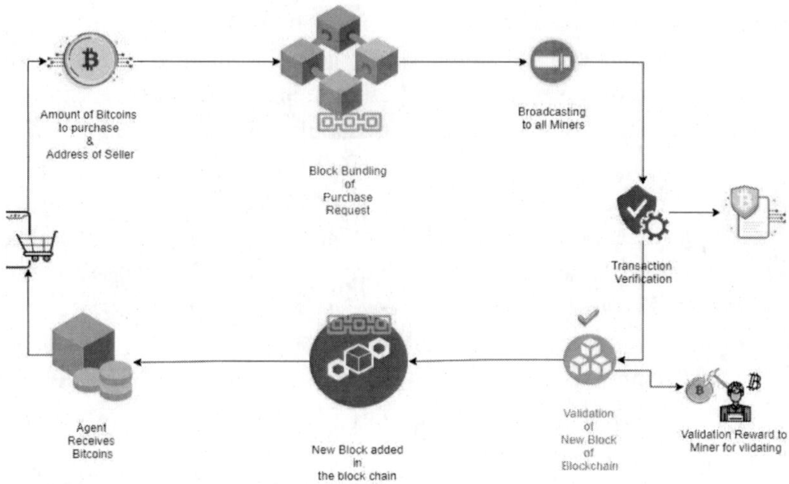

Figure 4.3c. Bitcoin purchase transaction.

The transaction generation results from buyer wish to do a bitcoin transaction online through a merchant providing services/product/ transaction using bitcoin as illustrated in the above figure (Figure 4.3a). The stated amount of bitcoin is required to initiate the action, and the merchant's address needs to be generated by the user willing to do the transaction.

Mining is a set of processes performed by the miner to validate the algorithm through the network's nodes. The bitcoin mining is depicted in the figure (Figure 4.3b). Mining is a set of processes performed by the miners to validate the algorithm through the nodes on the network. For every new block validation, the first miner who has verified the transaction receives the reward. At the same time, the new block is added to the Blockchain, which in turn provides Bitcoins to the merchant who is providing the online product. For example, UAE's private healthcare provider has also adapted Estonia's proven cyber security company for 'Keyless Signature Infrastructure' KSI by a California based company -Guradtime.

The bitcoin purchase initiates a process usually not seen by the users. It is a back-end where on each online purchase, the number of bitcoins to be purchased along with the seller's address is coded into block budling of each purchase request (Figure 4.3c). This turns to the block bundling of the purchase request and starts broadcasting to all miners the possibility of verifying the transaction and receiving bitcoins as a reward. After the transaction verification, a new blockchain block is validated, leading to the generation of a new block in the chain, resulting in the agent's delivery of bitcoins. Data storage is equally an important aspect, and blockchain has shown reformational development in the industry. Factom, an Austin based Software Company, produces storage products using blockchain technology for the healthcare industry.

How to Start Bitcoin Mining?

Mining, as stated in creating bitcoins by becoming a node inside the peer-to-peer system, requires the basic setup of bitcoin mining hardware and internet connection. It was possible to mine with just one P.C. or fast video processor card during the inception of bitcoin. However, today it is only possible with Custom Bitcoin ASIC chips that offer execution up to 100 times the capacity of a more established system to establish a node [11]. Bitcoin mining with anything less will consume more in power than one will probably gain. It is fundamental to mine bitcoins with the best bitcoin digging machine constructed explicitly for that reason [12].

How does Bitcoin Mining Works?

Once starting bitcoin, one can search those numerous online systems that list out the most up-to-date Bitcoin transactions occurring continuously—allying with a Bitcoin client and approving transactions by examining data blocks, often known as hashes. Communication is carried out through networks known as hubs or nodes, essentially information blocks. Furthermore, because the data is encoded, a miner must double-check his replies [13].

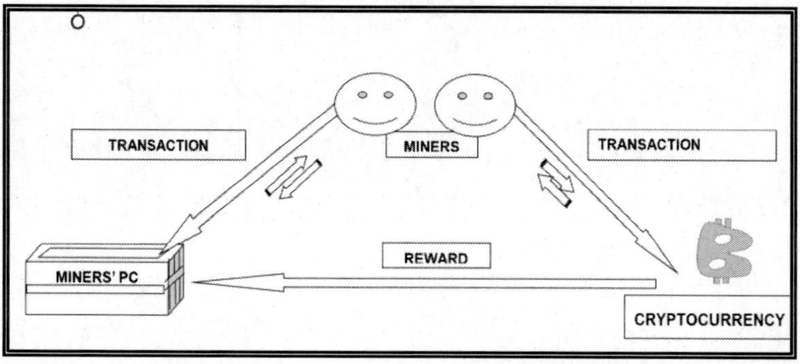

Figure 4.4. Process of mining.

As depicted in Figure 4.4, when the nodes get verified, a transaction ends fruitful, and the miner is compensated with some Bitcoins. To put it plainly, you are going about as a bank assistant, alongside numerous other bank assistants meeting on the web.

Hashing

Hash is a mathematical system that takes the input of any size and returns the output of a fixed length after operating on it. In other words, it is a cryptographical algorithm that results from fixed-sized outputs called the hash. Hash is a one-way function due to this unique property; it is impossible to derive the generated hash. Every time a different input is run to the hash function, the output results in a completely different hash [14].

The hash is an algorithm used to secure the Blockchain and write new transactions during the mining process in bitcoin. They have a fixed string size depending on their function type, which are 16-bit, 128-bit, 256-bit. However, in bitcoin's Blockchain, SHA-256 is used and not the others as the collision resistance break after several hashes [15].

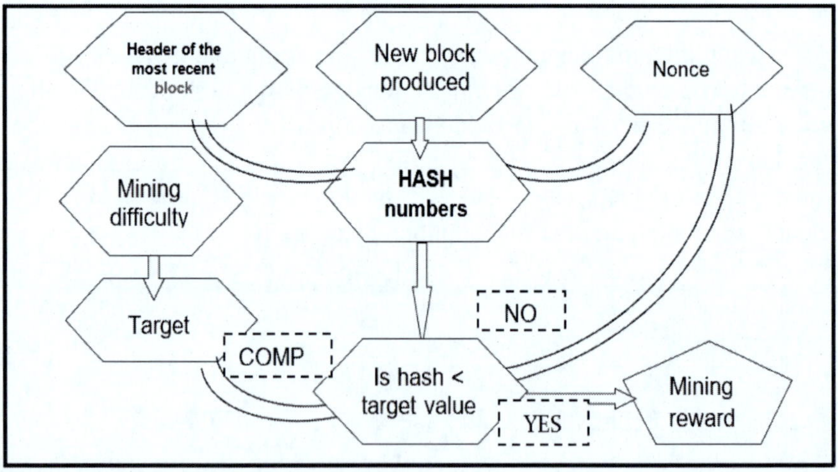

Figure 4.5. Generation of a Bit coin process.

Cryptographic hash functions need to have specific properties to be secure; these properties are:

- **Deterministic:** Despite the number of times you dissect through a specific input through a hash function, you may still get the same result/output. This is extremely important as it would be very difficult to keep track of the input if the hashes are different every time it runs through the hash function.
- **Quick computation:** in bitcoin mining, the competition is quite significant to compete fast; it is very important to mine quickly. Hence to mine quickly, the hash function needs to return the hash output fast enough else the system will not be efficient.
- **Small changes** in the input of transaction change the output: this is a critical step in the function as every time the input is changed, even if that is one letter or number, the output is completely changed in the block.
- **Collision resistance:** each input will have a specific hash to prevent the collision.

Each time a block is received in bitcoin mining, it gets hashed and afterwards combined to the Blockchain. The block is only added if the hash is less than the goal of complexity. Once it is added to the Blockchain, it is known by everyone in the network. Figure (Figure 4.5) emphasises the process of generation of bitcoin. It indicates the hash value's Hash number and mining difficulty process compared with the target value. Unless the target value is not achieved, the mining reward is not received.

Bitcoin Mining Hardware

Initially, Bitcoin's inventor expected Bitcoin to be mined on CPUs (your workstation or personal computer). Bitcoin mining hardware was made exclusively to explain Bitcoin blocks and solve Bitcoin blocks a lot faster and utilize less power than more traditional hardware for bitcoin mining such as CPUs, GPUs, or FPGAs. Bitcoin ASIC technology continues getting quicker, progressively proficient, and increasingly profitable, pushing the cutoff points of what makes the best Bitcoin mining hardware [16].

Some Bitcoin miners' hardware is listed under:

- Antminer S9 – Hash power:14.0 TH/s,
- Antminer R4–Hash power-8.6 TH/s,
- Antminer 17Pro – Hash power: 62 T.H./s
- EBITS E12+ – Hash power: 50 TH/s,
- Terminator T3 – Hash power: 43 TH/s [16].

Selecting Best Bitcoin Miners

The few important factors to be considered before purchasing Bitcoin mining ASIC are-

- *Hash power:* This is the unit of power the miner needs to take care of the mining math issue. It essentially measures how many numbers of estimates the miners can make every second.
- *Efficiency:* One need to purchase the most proficient bitcoin mining hardware possible. Since miner utilizes much power, you need to purchase one that converts energy or electricity into bitcoins.
- *Cost:* Modest mining hardware will mine fewer bitcoins, which is why proficiency and power utilization are essential. The quickest and more effective mining hardware is going to cost more [22].

Bitcoin Mining Software

The software for bitcoin mining handles the mining procedure of receiving all the completed mining work done by the hardware as it is required to be transferred to the bitcoin network. Table 1 represents the bitcoin software and its compatible operating system, and Table 2 represents the pros and cons of bitcoin mining software. It also tracks the miners' input/output and displays statistics: miners speed, hash-rate, etc. Therefore, the software should be:

- Easy to user interface.
- Power saving mode.
- Supporting the mining pool.

- Quick in sharing submission
- Able to choose the highest frequency rate for hashes

Uses of bitcoin software:

- For a solo miner, the miner is aligned to the Blockchain with the help of mining software.
- For the pool miners, it helps to link you to your mining pool.
- For cloud miners, mining software is not required.

Table 1. Bitcoin mining software and compatible operating system

Types of mining software	Windows	Linux	Mac OS X
BTCMiner	YES	-	YES
CGMiner	YES	YES	YES
BFGMiner	YES	YES	YES
EasyMiner	YES	YES	YES
RPC	-	-	YES
Multiminer	YES	YES	YES

Source: [17] - Daniel Phillips (2021).

Table 2. Pros and cons of bitcoin mining software

Types	Pros	Cons
CGminer	It supports GPU, FPGA, ASIC	Its textual interface.
BFGminer	It's considered a very powerful miner as its performance is very high due to the large number of features it provides and supports advanced users. Switching between pools are easy.	It does not support GPUs. Limited emphasis on manufactures done by ASIC devices.
Easyminer	Supports G.U.I.	Installing windows triggers A.V.
R.P.C.	It supports pool mining and logging, also provides tons of various features	Management is conducted exclusively via the command line.
Awesome miner	It is convenient and provides a multifunctional graphic interface. It can mine the available and expensive cryptocurrencies.	Large software products cost more.

Crypto Mining 102: Algorithms. [18] (2019).

Not to forget, Bitcoin mining software requires a bitcoin wallet as your software will require a Bitcoin address to send you the rewards and payouts that you will receive after mining.

Hashing Algorithms

The algorithms are the accurate flame thrower in the cryptography toolbox. The one-way functionality distinguishes hashing algorithms: one can get the output/result from the input but not the other way around. Furthermore, an exact input constructs or discovers the precise output. For various cryptographic types of money, different hashing methods are used [19] [20].

Various Types of Algorithms

SHA-256 and Scrypt are the most commonly employed to authenticate transaction data blocks. The primary differences between them stem from the following relationship: the more significant the mining difficulty, the higher the hash rate required. Hence, the higher the cost of successful Bitcoin mining. The common sense items of a couple of hashing algorithms can be characterized as per the result below.

- **SHA-256:** It is a part of cryptographic functions most commonly used in bitcoin mining. It stands for "secure hash set of codes/algorithm". It was the first to be utilized in the digital currency world. Understanding in regards to mining is a calculation process that is executed to ensure whether the data in the block has been altered from its initial state. This procedure prevents tracing back to the initial data as it is encrypted, hence secure. In simple words, this algorithm is not that complex; thus, it does not require a lot of resources to execute this function. The reason why this function can be implemented easily is that it uses logical and arithmetic operations.
- **SCRYPT:** It was developed to fight the "centralization of computing power" risks. Its function is to reduce the efficiency of logic circuits typical of ASICs. It is a multi-level code set (algorithm): it initiates with converting information through the SHA-256. The next step is

to utilize the elements of the SALSA algorithm (the Stochastic Approach for Link-Structure Analysis), to utter hash generation. It is utilized by many other algorithms, like LiteCoin, DogeCoin, MonaCoin, etc. In contrast to SHA-256, the plus point of scrypt is that it is a quicker mining algorithm as it can also use a smaller variety of the hash size if a miner specifies it to do so. For scrypt algorithm, the least amount of time utilized to execute a block of data entirely is just thirty seconds. Regardless, there is a betrayal side which is the vulnerability of the transaction security while other blocks are operating or proceeding.

- **XII:** X11 is a substitute hashing algorithm that is utilized for cryptocurrencies like Dash. Its' aim is to be exceptionally productive on the CPUs and the GPUs. As the name recommends, it utilizes a blend of eleven unique encryption algorithm. It could be debatable that X11 is progressively challenging and less subject to ASIC structures that reduce mining expense. However, both works to verify their particular blockchains. Regrettably, the X11 was not passing the ASIC Proof; it took a couple of months for the first ASICs to be accessible for this algorithm. There are very few technical details regarding X11 functions, except the 11-hashing algorithm. An elevated level of security can be accomplished while keeping up a proficiency 30% higher than the SHA-256 only when these hash functions are combined.
- **ETHASH:** This algorithm was made as a function to achieve the Proof of Work of the Ethereum blockchain. The two standard cryptographic functions are blended by these algorithms: the SHA-3 and the KECCAK algorithms. The function that is resulted in this algorithm is resistant to ASICs but yet quick enough to confirm and execute. It is no longer profitable to mine the algorithm with the CPU, as it has efficiency issues. On the other hand, GPUs are the ideal alternative and generally need 1-2 G.B. of RAM on each GPU utilized. To mine with GPU, one should download Ethminer, which works with some other Ethhash-based cryptocurrency. Ethash depends on an aimlessly developed dataset known as D.A.G. (Directed Acyclic Graph) and which after every 30,000 blocks is

refreshed, the size of the D.A.G. expands after every 30,000 blocks (right now at 3.01 GB) [21].

Table 3, explains the benefits of the several discussed algorithms with their limitation or obstacles for Sha 256, Scrypt Etshah, and XII.

Nevertheless, the determination and perseverance of the blockchain industry have not allowed these barriers to halt them. Bitcoin is a word with dual meaning, an innovative technique of disbursement network, and the first digital currency of the electronic era that is widely used worldwide without any centralized authority. Bitcoins are digital coins, which can be generated, transferred, or exchanged on the internet network for mining, transfer, or purchase without the bank's involvement or any clearinghouse. The digitally integrated transaction allows smooth, faster, cheaper, and borderless transfer of information from sender to receiver without the hurdles of documentation and banking. Bitcoin mining is the procedure to add exchange records into the record blockchain of previous period exchanges for Bitcoin's people group. The transaction is validated with the help of the science of mining.

Table 3. Advantages and disadvantages of algorithms of hashing algorithm

Algorithm	Advantage	Disadvantages
Sha256	It is secured due to the prevention of tracing back to the initial data as it is encrypted. It encodes right into a 256-bit code.	
XII	It utilizes a blend of eleven unique encryption algorithm. It aims to be productive on the CPUs as well as the GPUs. Can get proficiency 30% higher than the great SHA-256 only when all hash functions are combined.	All 7 algorithms need to be combined with being better than SHA 256
Scrypt	It reduces the efficiency of logic circuits of ASICs It sets multi-levels of code (algorithm): converts data through the SHA-256 second, it utilizes the elements of the SALSA algorithm.	Vulnerability of the transaction security
Ethash	It is resistant to ASICs but yet quick enough to confirm and execute.	Mining with CPU has efficiency issues.

Conclusion

The impact of technology is not limited to the business and security of data; however, it may also assist in the surveillance of the epidemic outbreak and monitoring. Moreover, DNA analysis and genomes engineering is actively administered by a few leaders in the industry, which will securely facilitate buying, selling, storage, and searching of genetic information. Bitcoin has effectively converted the transaction business by achieving higher value, recognition, and supporters worldwide. The chapter will provide the appropriate data for understanding the basic procedure, reasons to mine, and processes with its optimum details of the growing confidence worldwide.

The Healthcare sector is sensitive to the information; hence, owing to the close linkage of Blockchain with Bitcoin and cryptocurrency, the adoption of technology can leverage to respond to the patient's trust, credibility, security, and privacy. Miners (network participants with many Bitcoin processing capacities) compete to validate transactions by solving complicated programmed challenges. Bitcoin mining verifies the block, changes it, and then timestamps it in chronological order, allowing each member to show who owns what at any given time. The above conceptual model will help the healthcare sector visibility patients' records, payments, smart contracts, and data protection. The data can be transferred between the participants without any time lag and alteration. Hence, Bitcoin mining is an important tool for the future of the healthcare sector.

References

[1] Pearl, R. (2018, April 10). Blockchain, Bitcoin and the Electronic Health Record. *Forbes*. https://www.forbes.com/sites/ robertpearl/2018/04/10/ blockchain-bitcoin-ehr/?sh=6f6e63fb79e7.

[2] Agrawal, H. (2020, August 21). 9 Interesting Bitcoin Facts Every Bitcoin Owner Should Know. *CoinSutra–Bitcoin Community*. https://coinsutra.com/bitcoin-facts/.

[3] Sun, J., Ren, L., Wang, S. & Yao, X. (2020). A blockchain-based framework for electronic medical records sharing with fine-grained access control. *PLOS ONE*, *15*(10), e0239946. https://doi.org/ 10.1371/journal.pone.0239946.

[4] Omnicomp Health Group. (2018). *Cryptocurrency-in-Healthcare*. https://www.omnicomhealthgroup.com/pdfs/Cryptocurrency-in-Healthcare.pdf.

[5] Vujičić, D., Jagodić, D. & Ranđić, S. (2018). "Blockchain technology, bitcoin, and Ethereum: A brief overview," *2018 17th International Symposium INFOTEH-JAHORINA (INFOTEH)*, pp. 1-6, doi: 10.1109/INFOTEH.2018.8345547.

[6] *What The Hell Is Blockchain And What Does It Mean For Healthcare And Pharma?* (2018, August 8). The Medical Futurist. https://medicalfuturist.com/what-the-hell-is-blockchain-what-does-it-mean-for-healthcare-and-pharma/.

[7] O'Dwyer, K. J. & Malone, D. (2014). "Bitcoin mining and its energy footprint," 25th I.E.T. *Irish Signals & Systems Conference 2014 and 2014 China-Ireland International Conference on Information and Communications Technologies (ISSC 2014/CIICT 2014)*, pp. 280-285, doi: 10.1049/cp.2014.0699.

[8] Mastering Bitcoin: Programming the Open Blockchain, by Andreas M. Antonopoulos (2nd edition, 2017).

[9] Carnegie Mellon University, & D.R.S. (2018). *Introduction to Bitcoin Mining*. http://euro.ecom.cmu.edu/resources/ elibrary/epay/ IntroductiontoBitcoinMiningSterry.pdf.

[10] How Bitcoin Mining Works. (2018). https://www.bitcoinmining.com/.

[11] Bitcoin Mining Guide - Getting started with Bitcoin mining. (2018). https://www.Bitcoinmining.Com. https:// www.bitcoinmining.com/getting-started/#hbmw.

[12] Ankalkoti, P. & Santhosh, S. G. (2017). A Relative Study on Bitcoin Mining. *Imperial journal of interdisciplinary research, 3*.

[13] Verduyn, M. C. (2009). *Bitcoin and Beyond Cryptocurrencies, Blockchains, and Global Governance*. Taylor & Francis.

[14] By reading this article, you're mining bitcoins. (2019). *By Reading This Article, You're Mining Bitcoins.* https://qz.com/154877/by-reading-this-page-you-are-mining-bitcoins/.

[15] Chapter 8. Mining and Consensus. (2018). Mining and Consensus. https://www.oreilly.com/library/view/mastering-bitcoin/9781491902639/ch08.html.

[16] Taylor, M. (2017). *The Evolution of Bitcoin Hardware*. Blockchain Technology in Finance. https://michaeltaylor.org/papers/Taylor_Bitcoin_IEEE_ Computer_ 2017.pdf.

[17] Phillips, D. (2021). *How to Mine Bitcoin: Beginner's Guide (2021)*. Decrypt.Co. https://decrypt.co/49448/how-to-mine-bitcoin.

[18] Crypto Mining 102: Algorithms. (2018). *Coin360*. https://coin360.com/news/ crypto-mining-102-algorithms

[19] Kizhner, N. (2021). *Cryptocurrency for Dummies: Bitcoin and Beyond.* Https://Www.Naomikizhner.Com/. https://www.naomikizhner.com/bitcoin-and-beyond/.

[20] Vujičić, D., Jagodić, D. & Ranđić, S. (2018). "Blockchain technology, bitcoin, and Ethereum: A brief overview," *2018 17th International Symposium INFOTEH-JAHORINA (INFOTEH)*, pp. 1-6, doi: 10.1109/INFOTEH.2018.8345547.

[21] Mining & Common Mining Hashing Algorithms Explained – Cryptomorrow – Cryptocurrency, Bitcoin, Ethereum. (2019*). OTCPM24*. https://otcpm24.com/2019/ 05/11/mining-common-mining-hashing-algorithms-explained-cryptomorrow-cryptocurrency-bitcoin-ethereum/.

[22] *BitWats release Most Profitable ASIC Miners*. (2021). Global News Wire. https://www.globenewswire.com/news-release/2021/ 04/21/2214523/0/en/BitWats-release-Most-Profitable-ASIC-Miners.html.

Chapter 5

Vocational Training and Integrative Technology in Neurodiverse Workforce

Sonakshi Ruhela*, Mark Eugine Francisco† and Hibah Shata‡
Amity University Dubai, UAE
Maharat Learning Centre Dubai, UAE

Abstract

Neurodiversity is in individuals with neurological conditions like Autism Spectrum Disorder, Attention Deficit Hyperactive Disorder, and Dyslexia that possess special pattern recognition, memory, organization, and numerical and verbal ability. Autism, as the traditional psychological theories suggest, focuses on perceptual and sensory processing deficits only; however, the recent domain-specific social cognitive theories propose a primary and detailed psychological impairment of social cognition about employability. It is seen that the Neurodiverse population suffers from an immense struggle with suitable employment opportunities. This trend is changing with considerate interest in industry readiness programs, specific life skills, and cognitive, technical training. The chapter discusses vocational training and integrative technology measures that can create employability skills in the neurodiverse population. This chapter adopts a secondary research method to highlight neurodiversity, technological aids, reforms, and occupational opportunities.

* Corresponding Author's Email: sruhela@amityuniversity.ae.
† Corresponding Author's Email: markeugine_francisco@yahoo.com.
‡ Corresponding Author's Email: ceo@maharatgcc.com.

In: Industry 4.0 and Intelligent Business Analytics for Healthcare
Editors: Soumi Dutta, Vinod Kumar Shukla, Shruti Nagpal et al.
ISBN: 978-1-68507-602-3

The extensive literature study advocates the need to transition to vocational training and skill acquisition from primary education and invest in integrative technologies for individuals with autism, thereby creating possibilities for future employment. It also highlights that an increasing number of companies, such as SAP, Ernst and Young, Hewlett-Packard Enterprise, and Microsoft, have revisited and transformed the HR practices to accommodate neurodiverse talent pools. Furthermore, these organizations have significantly improved productivity, quality improvement, and increased employee engagement.

Keywords: vocational training, neurodiverse, Industry 4.0, inclusion, learning technologies

Introduction

Everyone experiences the world differently, and these contrasts are inherent to our neurological system. It is the distinct way our brains are wired to process and respond to any information. *Neurodiversity* refers to neurological differences that may possess a common thread, such as attention deficit disorder (ADD), Autism spectrum disorder (ASD), attention deficit disorder with hyperactivity (ADHD), and dyslexia. Literally, in Neurodiversity, people tend to think quite differently.

Australian sociologist Judy Singer in the year 1988 wisely coined the term Neurodiversity [1]; however, it was Harvey Blume who popularized the word in an article in The Atlantic in the year 1998 [2]. However, the term has only come into common use in the last few years. Academicians, researchers and professionals today highly regard Neurodiversity emphasizing that it possesses a very buoyant, positive and liberal approach to mental disability. Neurodiversity is more accommodative and includes people who have different styles of thinking and processing. It emphasized recognizing the unique skills and talents that can be integrated to work on complex tasks and problems. Neurodiversity believes that those individuals who learn, think or process any information differently are not necessarily handicapped.

In an article in 2017 on 'Neurodiversity as a Competitive Advantage' at Harvard Business Review, the researchers highlighted that Neurodiversity also comprises less commonly known neurological conditions such as dyspraxia, dyslexia or dyscalculia [3]. Dyscalculia is usually known as difficulty in learning or understanding math and other number-related symbols, dysgraphia, difficulty writing or transcribing words on paper, and hypergraphia, a compulsion to write constantly poetry, lists, diaries etc.

Therefore, Neurodiversity can be defined as the diversity of human brains and minds as the immeasurable variation in neurocognitive functioning within the human race. Alongside, neurodivergent entails brain functioning in such a way that deviates significantly from the predominant societal standards of "normal." Likewise, a group of people is neurodiverse or "different" if one or more group members differ significantly from other members, especially in their neurocognitive functioning.

Theoretical Background

The Neurodiversity Movement (NDM) concentrates on a strengths-based approach with two significant entitlements. Mainly, nonconformities from the customary neurotypical brain result in contradictory behavioural patterns that are natural discrepancies, not disorders or illnesses. Secondly, supporting a logical outlook, if neurological differences are merely varying, then the group of neurodiverse people deserves to be treated the same way as neurotypical people.

The Neurodiversity Movement originated from the Autistic Rights Movement in the 1990s. Judy Singer, an Autistic Australian sociologist (1998), coined the term, and since then, the emphasis on working within the neurodiversity model has expanded beyond autism, encompassing other classifications of neurodivergence [1]. Also, the paradigm has gradually gained footholds in different realms of scholarship, literature, and journals.

The Neurodiversity Paradigm

This paradigm is a specific standpoint on neurodiversity – an active approach that eventually simmers down to the following fundamental principles:

- Neurodiversity is a natural and worthwhile form of human diversity.
- There is no specific validity or sound judgment on whether a person has a 'normal brain' or 'healthy' form of neurocognitive functioning. Most of them are residual rules, culturally constructed beliefs, invisible and intangible rules.

- The manifestation of underlying social forces regarding neurodiversity is similar to the other systems of human diversity, such as diversity of ethnicity, culture, and gender. These dynamics wherein diversity is embraced usually act as a foundation of creative and extraordinary potential.

Principles

Neurodiversity is predominantly observed as a necessary form of human diversity, detesting the stereotypical idea that there are only healthy and unhealthy and normal and abnormal individuals. It also proposes that grouping neurodivergence features such as autism or bipolarity as pathological (aiming at medically treating it) has no scientific basis and gives an impression of social and cultural prejudice that desires to label and oppressing the individuals. The social underpinnings around neurodiversity are similar to other forms of human diversity and comprise unequal social power distribution.

In Practice

Psychotherapists who work with the neurodiverse workforce often refuse to label it clinically pathological or medically unfit. Instead, the attempt is to train or coach behaviours that eventually find their way into harmonious living with their natural neurological conditions and help them to heal from a sense of internalized oppression.

Classification and Development of Neurodiverse Population

Autism Spectrum Disorder

Autism Spectrum Disorder is a neurological condition that influences individuals' ability to communicate and interact with other people. They displayed restrictive and repetitive behaviours, different ways of thinking, and social communication constraints. In DSM V, ASD is categorized as a neurodevelopmental disorder whose onset is in the developmental period. It is typically manifest at an early stage of an individual's life characterized by developmental delays that produce social communication and social interaction impairments. They are excessively dependent on routines (follows schedules and step-by-step procedures) and extremely sensitive to changes in the environment (such as noise, the colour of the wall, people) which may result in inappropriate and challenging behaviour (interrupting a conversation, running over the places, throw things). Due to these exceptional attributes, individuals with ASD limit or impair everyday functioning. The severity of the condition varies on the onset of the disability, early intervention, developmental level, and chronological age.

Figure 5.1 illustrates how each individual with ASD differs from one another as it encompasses various characteristics that vary in severity. Some individuals may display a high-level intense focus and interests and can communicate well. Some may exhibit great difficulty in communication and are very sensitive to the stimulus in the environment.

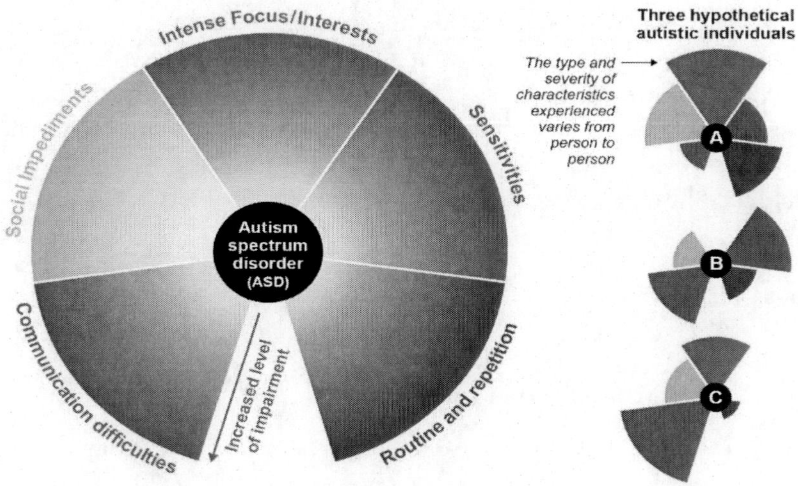

Figure 5.1. Characteristics of Autism Spectrum Disorder [4].

Diagnosing children with ASD is difficult since no existing medical test is specialized for it, and no cure now. According to the Centers for Disease Control and Prevention (2020), about 1 in 52 children were diagnosed with ASD, four times prevalent among boys than girls. Nowadays, many individuals with ASD break the stigma of the condition by speaking, expressing, and living in the typical community rather than the four corners of the classroom or centre [5]. However, most of them live dependently with their family and cannot find a full-time job.

Authors [6] revealed that 94.1% of the gathered ASD population had been employed, by which 22.4% worked from teaching, education, health, and social sector, followed by 19.3% working from corporate organizations, accounting, legal, and administrative sectors. The researchers concluded that late diagnosis of ASD could be why this neurodiverse workforce is primarily unemployed and underestimated.

Attention Deficit Hyperactivity Disorder (ADHD)

Attention Deficit Hyperactivity Disorder is a neurodevelopmental disorder that involves a specific part of the brain that controls impulses and self-regulation. They are characterized to display persistent patterns of inattention, which make an individual finish the task on time, and hyperactivity-impulsivity, which results in saying or doing something without proper thinking. Since attention is at stake, they are energetic but with poor concentration, leading to being absent-minded and easily distracting. Since these negative traits exist, individuals with ADHD encountered academic challenges and affected their employability. Figure 5.2 illustrates the age diagnosis of people with ADHD.

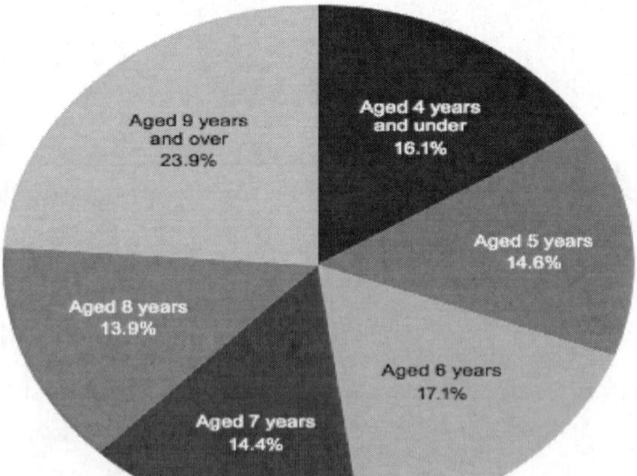

Figure 5.2. Age Diagnosis of Attention Deficit Hyperactivity Disorder [7].

According to [8], one-third of the individuals with ADHD cases were diagnosed before the age of six, emphasizing the importance of early diagnosis and intervention. Young adults and adults with ADHD are less likely to finish high school or even acquire a college degree. It is caused by the inability to manage a bulk of workloads, disorganization, struggling to follow directions, and committing careless errors. They received a stigma of being sporadic and disorganized in the job and difficulty maintaining a relationship with colleagues because of temper and self-regulation. As they face various work conflicts such as delay, high error rate, and inability to change, companies still believe that their creativeness and energy are required in any form of job.

Applied Integrative Technology for Neurodiverse Individuals

The endless discoveries transform various disciplines and industries into a new perspective of living in the contemporary world. The advancement of technology continuously generates new innovative technologies that provide life comfortability and temporary solutions in the recent issues. Blended technology for people with neuro-diverse disabilities emerges purposively to assist an individual in developing specific skills such as independence, life skills, and skill acquisition by simulating the real-world scenario. Schools, healthcare centres, and private sectors integrate assistive technologies into curriculum and programs to address these individual needs. It is a growing trend and promising digital solution that transfers target knowledge and skills to individuals with less social pressure, constraints, and anxiety in a fun way of learning facilitated by trained teachers and therapists. These technologies are in the form of external assistive device equipment, instrument, and software and application platform.

Integrative technology for people with neuro-diverse disabilities varies in form, administration, and target goal. Several traditional assistive technologies improve knowledge and skill acquisition and reduce challenging behaviour among these individuals. Walky-Talky for speech recognition, Text-to-Speech to enhance communication skills, and Nuts and Bolts to minimize fidgeting and increase attention are examples of assistive technology used in previous years. The new millennium caused the progression of technology and brought artificial intelligence to life. Educational application platforms, tablet-based learning, and virtual reality-based interventions mark a new trend of integrative technologies for neuro-diverse individuals.

These technologies are computer-based and aim to simulate real-world scenarios, imitate human behaviours, and produce sensory activities that help neurodiverse individuals. It demonstrated virtual environments, presented avatars, basic instructions, and various activities and settings. Generally, it aids individuals to learn to acquire skills as follows:

- Knowledge (Example: fine motor skills, do's and do not, and social norms)
- Life skills (Example: communication skills, socialization, and self-regulation)
- Practicing independence (Example: toilet training, crossing the road, and attending an interview).

By providing the individuals with a simulation, they can experience a depth of social engagement and eventually a smooth transition to employment.

- *The Serious Game – Guess the Emotion*- a computerized emotional training intended for children with ASD to improve content-dependent body emotional expressiveness [9]. The children were trained to recognize and imitate full-body movements relevant to acquiring information about other people's feelings. The findings suggest that body postures and gestures are more likely to transmit social information than facial expression because they involve eye-to-eye contact, which children with neuro-diverse disabilities, especially ASD, lack. In teaching a child these skills, authors [10] suggested six essential factors in designing various integrative technology-based interventions: matching, recognizing, observing, understanding, generalizing, and mimicking, which was drawn from Kolb's experiential learning model and Piaget's cognitive model. Additionally, a study [11] claimed that this game is a powerful tool for educational purposes in teaching an individual to express and recognize emotions and body movements.
- *Virtual Reality-based* – Teaching a specific subject – In music education, authors discovered that categorizing the tasks from the simple to complex tasks can help individuals learn easier than regular teaching strategies [12]. Behaviour analysts or software developers

should design a virtual reality-based game-like learning environment (VRGLE) in such a way that it meets an equilibrium on content-gameplay and intuitive game control in teaching Mathematics [13]. Experiential learning, especially in Science, is necessary for each school, requiring laboratory tools and machines. A study [14] revealed that schools should invest in virtual reality-based simulations of scientific experiments and observations where it delivers a high user experience and are found to be more enjoyable and engaging.

- *Face Say*– Computer-based social skills training program consists of three different computer activities with animated photos of real persons. Amazing Gazing, Band-Aid Clinic, and Follow the Leader are interactive activities that allow the children to respond appropriately to social situations. Author [15] provided an insight on the benefits of using interactive computer-based games to enhance specific social skills of neurodiversity. The game can decrease negative behaviours and become more assertive, responsible, and self-controlled with family members. Computer-based interventions are widespread and valuable tools in improving an individual's social skills [16]. Additionally, the author's explained [17] associated Face Say as an intervention in improving affect recognition, mentalizing, and social skills as it changes the individual's cognitive and social skills.
- *An XR – AI (*extended reality – artificial intelligence) based Assistive Technology Platform helps users with neurodevelopmental disorders like ASD improve social, cognitive, and self-care skills. A study [18] employed seven scenarios using Auticare, such as (a) ball pecking and targeting, (b) colour identification, memorizing and matching, (c) instruction based fruit groupings, (d) traffic light learning, road crossing, and vehicle interaction, (e) supermarket shopping, (f) restroom training, and (g) alphabet interaction. The seven learning virtual environments were designed to train children with ASD to enhance critical behaviours to facilitate their maturity and holistic development. After the intervention, they displayed low mood swings, temper tantrums, and were proactive. With the help of VR therapy sessions, the trained children were observed to be less anxious

when in closed and narrow spaces and showed positive changes in the three targeted skills. Auticare is user-friendly and was perceived well by the participants. They prefer and enjoy the virtual reality training session than the regular therapy sessions as no participant dropped the entire session.

- *Cave Automatic Virtual Environment (CAVE)* - A VR-based intervention tool based on extensible 3D Graphics (X3D), simulates real-life scenarios. Most neuro-diverse individuals have social deficits by which social pressures and lack of non-verbal recognition can provoke their behaviours. This tool aims to repeat specific social interactions through a scenario-driven system without any feeling of constraint. The tool enables the users to act as normally as possible with less pressure in selecting a seat and participating in a group discussion. It also focuses on simulating real-life scenarios, ease of interaction, and immediate feedback from the interaction. In using CAVE, [19] emphasized the need to know the level of students' knowledge about virtual reality so that the facilitator can adjust the activities according to the level of mastery and its objectives.

Skill Acquisition, Life Skills, and Independency for Neurodiverse Workforce

Skill Acquisition

Acquiring a new skill and knowledge is one of the fundamentals that an intervention aims to achieve from individuals with neuro-diverse disabilities. Developing their fine motor skills, such as gripping and holding, is a prerequisite to a more difficult task. Academe and private centres incorporate applied behaviour analysis as an intervention to teach a child a new skill. They are implementing the principles of reinforcement, punishment, and extinction to strengthen and maintain the acquired skill. Skills required constant training to entirely execute it from the classroom to the real world. However, it is observed that intervention in skill acquisition to neurodiversity lacks specifically in pursuing higher education to employment.

The neurodiverse workforce received stigma, discrimination, and challenges to employment in the modern workplace [20]. They should be taught the skill set required in the contemporary working environment and maintain them. Being sensitive during the recruitment process is essential for the neurodiverse workforce to learn. Confidently expressing self and displaying more assertive body gestures could help the individuals get hired. There is a lack of specific literature about training programs for neurodiverse young adults who pursue a college education [21]. They are missing some practical skills and important traits to successfully fulfil their job in the future.

Life Skills

These skills enable an individual in neurodiversity to adapt and deal with every challenge in life effectively and positively. The main objective of life skills is to survive the social demands and overcome stress and anxiety. According to [22], to successfully teach individuals various life skills, they should gain perceptual experience, appreciative experience, and creative experience. These experiences allow them to understand life and eventually facilitate them to vocational training.

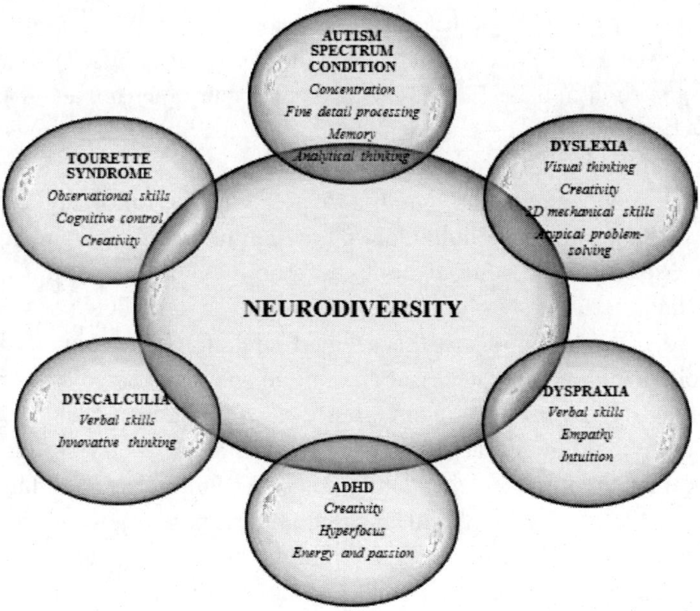

Figure 5.3. Neurodiversity in terms of strengths [26].

Companies struggle to hire, develop, and retain a neurodiverse workforce because of social deficient, emotion regulation, and adjustment skills [23]. However, [24] revealed that companies should invest in management training for these workforces, which provides a high level of support and helps them adjust to the company culture. Also, [25] encouraged the companies not to overlook these individuals as they display a different spectrum of the working environment. They are recognized to possess positive attitudes, creativity, and lateral thinking. Due to these remarkable traits, the neurodiverse workforce begins to recognize in the market. Figure 5.3 represents the benefits of neurodiversity in the workplace by specifying the unique strengths of each neurodiverse individual.

Independency

Building independence for neuro-diverse individuals might be a challenging process. Still, with proper training and maintenance, these individuals will eventually increase their confidence and realize their ability to do things independently. They should learn how to control their own lives considering social sensitivity and responsibility as community members. Training them how to use the toilet alone impacts when they grow as adults. Teaching them to cross the road and be familiar with signals can obey universal laws and norms. Also, practising communication and social skills with them will enable them to attend an employment interview confidently. Teaching an individual how to be independent early in life matters in the following years. The disability compromises an individual's functioning and development through different aspects. Most neurodiversity does not have the opportunity to enter higher education and, worst end up unemployed and dependent on their parents. Author's [28] suggests that a solid foundation of learning during early childhood development is necessary among the neurodiverse workforce.

Figure 5.4 represents the integrative technologies, which focused on neurodiverse children's teaching related to skill acquisition, basic life skills, and training to do things independently. These technologies can be the solution to break the curve of unemployment and underestimation of neurodiversity as a workforce. In an elevated level of training, these technologies can equip young adults with the necessary skills and knowledge to find a job, attend an interview, get hired, and retain the employer. Many companies have started including neurodiversity in the workforce. Author's [24] developed a neurodiversity-smart HR framework that establishes an inclusive workforce.

The neurodiverse workforce might be the potential solution to various organizational issues that need to be considered and thought of by renowned companies globally. Since integrating technology have an extraordinary impact on teaching a child the necessary skill, this intervention might also work with young adults and adults.

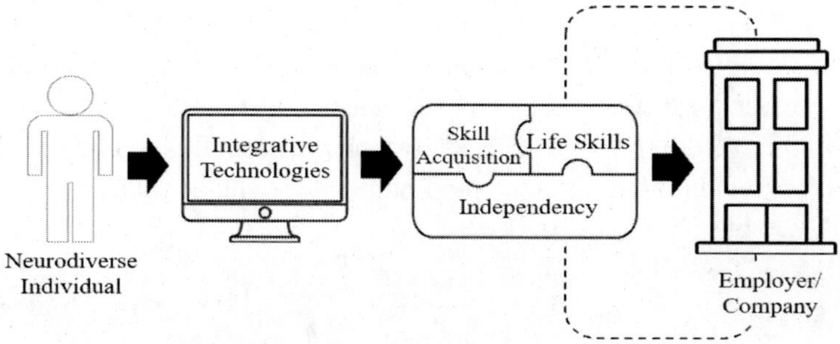

Figure 5.4. Utilization of integrative technology to train neurodiverse workforce with skill acquisition, life skills, and independency.

The Neurodiverse Workforce

Several neurodevelopmental conditions such as ASD and dyslexia possess extraordinary and exceptional skills that reach the extremes. However, people often see them struggle to meet the standards their respective employers seek. Several highly renowned companies such as Microsoft, SAP, Hewlett-Packard Enterprise have brought in significant reformations in their HR processes to include and access neurodiverse talent. As a result of integrating contemporary HR practices, these companies have gained productivity, quality improvement, encouraged innovative capabilities and increased employee engagement.

Neurodiversity at Workplace

In the emergence of Industry 4.0, various industry sectors have started to accommodate the neurodiverse workforce in the talent pool. Some are SAP, Microsoft, Ernst and Young, Goldman Sachs, DXC Technology, IBM, Ford, and JPMorgan Chase. Ernst and Young have been forefronts in supporting people with disabilities to the mainstream in the workplace. Talent acquisition is crucial in selecting a perfect candidate for a suitable position. A company should have a firm and well-structured recruitment process and a well-trained team. The recruitment team must be unbiased, open-minded, set aside negative assumptions and judgment, and consider the changes the neurodiverse workforce can bring to the organization.

The neurodiverse workforce might lack specific skills necessary in workgroup dynamics and customer services, but they possess incredible creativity, productivity, and critical thinking. This workforce is one of the missing pieces to innovate corporate businesses and change unhealthy organizational culture. Once each company integrates this initiative, they can bring tolerance, build acceptance, and break the social stigma.

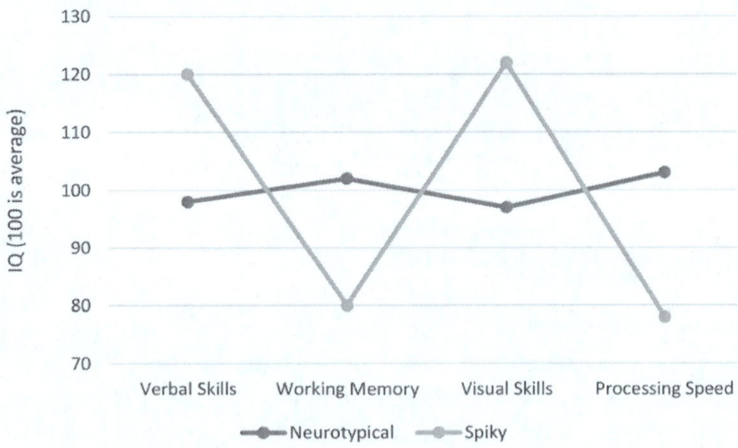

Figure 5.5. Spikey profile of neurodiverse talent [28].

Neurotypical individuals have equipped with skillsets that neurodiverse individuals lack. However, their skills are considered ‘spikey profile’ (see Figure 5.5), which means they possess specific ways of thinking, perception, and information analysis. They exceed the limit in comparison to neurotypical individuals. Focusing on their exceptionality and emphasizing what they can do in the workplace is fundamental in aligning their roles in the organization.

Strength-Based Approach

A strength-based approach for a neurodiverse workforce is an effective strategy to value their unique characteristics, personal resources, capacity, knowledge, skills, and strengths. Strength pertains to neurodiverse individuals' skills in dealing with life's adversity while meeting their needs and reaching their expected outcomes. The approach emphasizes support systems such as working environment, colleagues' social networks, and organizational accommodation to the neurodiverse workforce. Those elements, if working together, can lead to a positive outcome that draws on the individual's work productivity and success. In general, most individuals with autism spectrum disorder (ASD) display strengths in attention to detail, being mindful about a routine, good memory, innovative thinking, dedicated, and loyal employees.

However, in 2019, 90% of individuals with ASD were either underemployed or unemployed because organizations are unaware of the benefits and capabilities this workforce can bring and eventually change the industries [29]. If the strength-based approach is well implemented in an organization, it enables self-esteem and self-determination among the neurodiverse workforce and improves employee performance and productivity. Empowering them with consistent encouragement and reducing workplace barriers could build a foundation of tolerance and inclusion in the organization. Also, during the hiring process, the recruitment team should look after what the candidate can offer instead of focusing on their disability. The movement towards a more healthy and positive workplace by integrating a strength-based approach will reduce social stigma towards the neurodiverse workforce and easier access to employment. This approach also proves that it is not the individual who is disabled. It is the society that disables the people.

Challenges Around Neurodiversity and Work

Employers' lack of confidence, support, and accommodation towards neurodiverse workforce – Lack of confidence from employers may result from unknowing benefits of people with disabilities. However, work accommodation and training are perceived as additional funding and costly investment to train and retain disabled people in employment. The disability pay gap is another concern of the neurodiverse workforce. They are receiving lesser compensation than neurotypical people due to their disability. As a result, their morale, motivation, and determination to look for a job or stay in the job are sceptical, leading to the prevalence of unemployment among disabled people. They are twice more likely to leave work and thrice less likely to move into employment.

Stereotyping is one big challenge in recruiting and selection process among the neurodiverse workforce. Autistic people are well diverse kind. However, about 16% of people with autism in the United Kingdom are employed, which signifies that multifaceted challenges exist and that the idea of neurodiversity is not applicable across different companies [30]. In dyslexia, despite its number, very few employers are modifying recruitment to avoid excluding them. They do not know that they are losing a huge potential of talent. Although dyslexia is a reading and writing deficiency, social and environmental factors impair confidence and self-esteem in adulthood. Considering the existence of assistive technologies for spelling and grammar, the corporate world is still reluctant to accommodate dyslexic people.

Recruiting for Neurodiversity

Employment starts from the recruitment process. It ensures that only shortlisted candidates who have ticked, if not all, most of the boxes will be allowed to continue their job application. Qualifications, job requirements, and job descriptions are the typical subheadings in any job postings, which will dictate who will interview and meet the recruiter. In this stage, the modification of the recruitment process is required because of the initial screening itself. Recruiters are indirectly discouraging disabled people from applying.

In today's time, modifying recruitment processes to exclude neurodiverse talent is necessary. This involves restructuring the job description, selecting a well-diverse recruitment team, and setting qualifications to encourage everyone to apply for a job posting. The next stage is the interview. The interview is a challenging and crucial part of the recruitment process, especially among the neurodiverse workforce. For example, people with ASD exhibit poor eye-to-eye contact, lousy body language, and deficit social skills. This basic observation may be one of the factors that deter the next stage of recruitment.

However, interviews should not focus only on what the eye can see. Recruiters are encouraged to test neurodiverse candidates' memory recall, performance during the interview, and knowledge on the job, predicting later job performance. Therefore, different assessment styles should be explored, and interviewers should be as unbiased, objective, and non-judgmental as possible before rejecting someone on first impressions. Once employed, neurodiverse individuals should have received equal access to support and accommodation, career development, and high-quality jobs. The responsibility is on employers to make sensible adjustments such as providing assistive technologies such as required software, additional screens for sensitive vision, or conducive office spaces designed for their needs. Those peculiar needs of the neurodiverse workforce in the working environment are appreciated by the community and break the traditional workforce.

Therefore, even if already hired, the organization should increase the retention rate and reduce the attrition rate among the neurodiverse workforce. As a form of motivation and encouragement to the neurodiverse workforce, providing constructive feedback, handling change sensitively, and social support are beneficial to achieving its goals and individual needs.

References

[1] Doyle N. (2020). Neurodiversity at work: a biopsychosocial model and the impact on working adults. *British medical bulletin*, *135*(1), 108–125. https://doi.org/10.1093/bmb/ldaa021.

[2] *AMA J Ethics.* 2015;17(4):348-352. doi: 10.1001/journalofethics. 2015.17.4.msoc1-1504.

[3] Austin, R. D., & Pisano, G. P. (2017). Neurodiversity as a competitive advantage. *Harvard Business Review*, *95*(3), 96-103.

[4] First, Michael B. MD Diagnostic and Statistical Manual of Mental Disorders, 5th Edition, and Clinical Utility, *The Journal of Nervous and Mental Disease:* September 2013 - Volume 201 - Issue 9 - p 727-729. doi: 10.1097/NMD.0b013e3182a2168a.

[5] *Centers for Disease Control and Prevention, Autism Spectrum Disorder* (ASD), [Online Accessed on May 2021] https://www.cdc. gov/ncbddd/autism/addm-community-report/index.html.

[6] Frank, F., Jablotschkin, M., Arthen, T., Riedel, A., Fangmeier, T., Holzel, L., and Elst, L. *Education and employment Status of Adults with Autism Spectrum Disorder in Germany – a cross sectional survey*, 18.

[7] Visser, S. N., Zablotsky, B., Holbrook, J. R., Danielson, M. L., & Bitsko, R. H. (2015). Diagnostic experiences of children with attention-deficit/hyperactivity disorder. *National health statistics reports*, (81), 1-7.

[8] Visser, S., Zablotsky, B., and Danielson, M. (2015). Diagnostic Experiences of Children with Attention-Deficit/Hyperactivity Disorder. *National Health Statistics Report*, No. 81.

[9] Piana, S., C. Malagoli, M. C. Usai and A. Camurri, "Effects of Computerized Emotional Training on Children with High Functioning Autism," in *IEEE Transactions on Affective Computing*, doi: 10.1109/TAFFC.2019.2916023.

[10] Park, J., Abirachel, B., and Zhang, Y. (2012). A Framework for Designing Assistive Technologies for Teaching Children with Autism Spectrum Disorder's emotions. *CHI: Conference on Human Factors in Computing Systems*, 2423 – 2428.

[11] Schrader, C., Brich, J., Frommel, J., Riemer, V., and Rogers, K. (2017). Rising the Challenge: An Emotion Driven Approach Toward Adaptive Serious Game. *Serious Game and Edutainment Applications*, 3 – 28.

[12] Shahab, M., Taheri, A., Mokhtari, M., Shariati, A., Heidari, R., Meghdari, A., and Alemi, M. (2020). Utilizing social virtual reality robot (V2R) for music education to children with high functioning autism. *Education and Information Technologies*.

[13] Xu, X. and Ke, F. (2016). Designing a Virtual Reality Based, Gamelike Math Learning Environment. *American Journal of Distance Education*, 30 (1), 27 – 38.

[14] Bogusevschi, D., Muntean, C., and Muntean, G. (2020). Teaching and Learning Physics using 3D Environment: A Case study of Combined Virtual Reality and Virtual Laboratory in Secondary School. *Journal of Computers in Mathematics and Science Technology*, 39 (1), 5 – 18.

[15] Hopkins I., Gower, M., Perez, T., Smith, D., Amthor, F., Wimsatt, F. C., and Biasini, F. (2011). Avatar Assistant: Improving Social Skills in Students with an ASD through a Computer-Based Intervention. *Journal of Autism and Developmental Disorders*, 41, 1543 – 1555.

[16] Kaur, K., and Pany, S. (2017). Computer-based Intervention for Autism Spectrum Disorder Children and Their Social Skills: A Meta-analysis. *Scholarly Research Journal for Humanity Science and English Language*, 4 (23), 6056 – 6071.

[17] Rice, L. M., Wall, C. A., Fogel, A., and Shic, F. (2015). Computer-Assisted Face Processing Instruction Improves Emotion Regulation, Mentalizing, and Social Skills in students with ASD. *Journal of Autism and Developmental Disorders*, 45, 2176 – 2186.

[18] Sathrayanarayanan, A. R., Chandra, B., Bose, J., and Leghu, M. (2020). Virtual Reality Therapy for High Functional Autism Spectrum Disorder in Improving Social, Cognitive, and Self Care Skills Using Auticare. *International Research Journal of Modernization in Engineering Technology and Science*, 2 (8).

[19] Sivy, M., Sobota, B., Korecko, S., and Hudak, M. (2019). Virtualized Collaborative Learning Environment in the Process of Teaching People with Disabilities. *17th International Conference on Emerging eLearning Technologies and Applications*.

[20] Patton, E. (2019). Autism, Attributions and Accommodations: Overcoming barriers and integrating a neurodiverse workforce. *Personnel Review*, 48 (4), 915 – 934.

[21] Zeedyk, S., Tipton, L. A., and Blacher, J. (2014). Educational Supports for High Functioning Youth with ASD: The Postsecondary Pathway to College. *Focus on Autism and Other Developmental Disabilities*, 1 – 12.

[22] Jaya, H., Haryoko, S., Sahanuddin, Suhaeb, S., Sabran, and Mantasia. (2018). Life Skills Education for Children with Special Needs in order to facilitate Vocational Skills. *Journal of Physics: Conference Series*, 1028.

[23] Morris, M. R., Begel, A., and Wiedermann, B. (2015). Understanding the Challenges Faced by Neurodiverse Software Engineering Employees: Towards a More Inclusive and Productive Technical Workforce. *17th International ACM SIGACCESS Conference on Computers and Accessibility*, 173 – 184.

[24] Rao, B., and Polepeddi, J. (2019). Neurodiverse Workforce: Inclusive Employment as an HR Strategy. *Strategic HR Review*, 18 (5), 204 – 209.

[25] Brinzea, V. M. (2019). Encouraging Neurodiversity in the Evolving Workforce – The Next Frontier to a diverse workplace. *Science Bulletin – Economic Sciences*, 18, 13 – 25.

[26] Brînzea, V. (2019). Encouraging Neurodiversity In The Evolving Workforce – The Next Frontier To A Diverse Workplace. *Scientific Bulletin – Economic Sciences, 18*, 13-25.

[27] Quinn, M. (2016). Promoting Independence among Children with Disabilities at the Mulwakee Center for Independence (MCFI). *Journal of Child and Developmental Disorders*, 2 (3).

[28] Nancy Doyle, Neurodiversity at work: a biopsychosocial model and the impact on working adults, *British Medical Bulletin*, Volume 135, Issue 1, September 2020, Pages 108–125, https://doi.org/10. 1093/bmb/ldaa021.

[29] United Nations, "*Department of Economic and Social Affairs Disability*," [Online Accessed on May 2021] https://www.un.org/ development/desa/disabilities/ resources/factsheet-on-persons-with-disabilities/disability-and-employment.html.

[30] Learning Disability Today, "*Government pledges to monitor autism employment gap - for the first time*," [Online Accessed on May 2021] https://www.learningdisabilitytoday.co.uk/government-pledges-to-monitor-autism-employment-gap-for-the-first-time.

Chapter 6

Use of Some Standard Mathematical Models in Physiology and Pathology

Saktipada Nanda[1,*] and Sibashis Nanda[2,†]
[1]IEM, Salt Lake, Kolkata, West Bengal, India
[2]Learnikx Education, Sydney, Australia

"Mathematics is a more powerful instrument of knowledge than any other that has been bequeathed to us by human agency" - Descartes'

Abstract

Most of the physical phenomena in the actual world exhibit non-linear character. In recent years, significant advances have occurred in the design, construction, and development of mathematical/analytical models for the solution of these physical problems. If appropriate initial and boundary condition(s) are associated with the models, the whole system generates a mathematical problem. In this way, a mathematical model establishes a relationship between mathematics and the rest of the world (the physical world). Analytical models are developed (or modified) based on mathematical concepts and using mathematical languages and symbolism. The three major advantages of using mathematical tools over others in modelling are:

- Mathematics can provide well-ordered rules for manipulation - essential in modelling
- Mathematics gives unique result for an investigation

* Corresponding Author's Email: saktipada.nanda@iemcal.com.
† Founder and CEO; Corresponding Author's Email: sibashis_nanda@learnikx.com.au.

In: Industry 4.0 and Intelligent Business Analytics for Healthcare
Editors: Soumi Dutta, Vinod Kumar Shukla, Shruti Nagpal et al.
ISBN: 978-1-68507-602-3

- Mathematics is capable of proving general results from which the results for particular cases may be deduced assigning appropriate values to the parameters (in the admissible range) involved in the investigation.

Information about the physical system represented by the model is estimated qualitatively and quantitatively by solving the mathematical problem by applying the best possible mathematical technique. The selection of appropriate mathematical methods for the solution will depend on the purpose for which the model may be applied for investigation. The models are validated by comparing the analytical results of the mathematical problem with the behavior exhibited by the physical problem. If the two do not match, the model is modified by including more parameters or leading to rejection of the model. As the physical models are based on experimental investigation, so they are superior to the mathematical models constructed on the theoretical investigation. But a mathematical model has the advantage of studying the role of key parameters controlling the system within a short period. Mathematical modeling is essential in studying human physiological problems (brain injury, blood flow, population growth, and spread of COVID-19 etc) where experimental investigations cannot be performed to obtain adequate data. So, improved mathematical models are developed (sometimes old models are modified) using suitable symbolism to define the operation of a physical system.

As most of the phenomena in the physical world cannot be described by mathematical objects (due to their non-linear character), mathematicians and scientists throughout the globe are continuously developing and modifying mathematical models to solve the practical problems effectively in the domain of physical science, bio-science, social science, medicine, statistics, management, engineering, and technology. They are extensively utilized in making predictions when a particular parameter is varied in a range. The models play a convincing role in health science not only in the prediction of occurrence of critical health irregularities but they may reduce the risk in the treatment of fatal diseases like cardiovascular and neurological dysfunctions, brain injury due to vehicular accidents and soccer games, novel coronavirus infection, absorption of medicine in the human metabolic system leading to morbidity and even death. Our best endeavours is to construct some sophisticated mathematical models for the following types of problems:

- in the study of Brain Injury Problems
- in the study of Blood Flow through an Atherosclerotic (diseased) Arterial Segment
- in Decaying of the absorption of a medicine in human rheological system

- in estimating the spread of a disease (COVID 19) growing or decaying exponentially
- in estimating the population growth in the coming years.

We sincerely believe that the book chapter will throw light on the latest developments in the field of mathematical modelling and thus reinforce and solidify the understanding of this ever expanding domain.

Keywords: mathematical models, brain injury, arterial segment, human rheological system, rheological parameters, non-newtonian fluid model, COVID 19

Introduction

"A good theory (or model) should be as simple as possible, but not simpler" - Einstein

Before presenting a chapter on 'Mathematical Modelling,' it seems relevant to present a clear and distinct idea about the purpose of the project. As most of the physical phenomena in the actual world exhibit non-linearity, their solution seems challenging to academicians and engineers. Therefore, for evaluating a phenomenon in the real world, they use the best capability and technique to design the problem to exhibit the physical system or phenomena's nearly exact behavior. Models are developed to capture the problem and to explore the best possible solution to it.

- What are models and how they function to analyze and find a suitable solution of a health care problem?
- Models describe our beliefs about how the world functions.
- What are the purpose behind the construction of models (physical or analytical)?

The basic idea behind the design, construction, development, and modification of models is manipulating the physical world to determine our objectives in the best possible way. These models are capable of describing our beliefs on the functioning of the physical world. As most of the physical phenomena in the actual world exhibit non-linear character, available mathematical tools fail to provide techniques for the clear and unique solution of the problems. Some integrated approach is necessary to acquire scientific knowledge about the natural world.

Mathematical models are developed using suitable symbolism to define the operation of a physical system. Researchers usually develop three kinds of models-experimental, numerical, and mathematical (or analytical), depending upon the nature of the problem and purpose of investigation. We exclude 'simulation models as they are based on computer simulation very less on the actual mathematical background. The physical models based on the experimental investigation are superior to analytical models based on the theoretical study. As the topic is multidisciplinary so it is a collaborative learning tool from different strata of investigations.

But mathematical models have some distinct advantages over the others.

1. In mathematical models the beliefs on the functioning of the real world are expressed in the artistic language of mathematics.
2. Mathematics is a language that is precise, unambiguous and accurate. It can provide formulas to present our ideas and assumptions.
3. It can describe accurately a set of well-defined rules for the solution.
4. Mathematics is capable of proving general results from which the results for particular cases may be deduced assigning appropriate values to the parameters (in the admissible range) involved in the investigation.
5. The formula and results on mathematics invented and accumulated over time and are readily available for further use. /Delete 'and'
6. The knowledge may be applied in solving complicated real world problems.
7. The results of the analytical study may be refined through the inclusion of more parameters or exclusion of some irrelevant ones.
8. It has the capability to have some intelligent guess about the results of the problem under consideration.
9. It may test the generated potential solutions among different design choices and choose finally the solution that best fits the requirements of the real world problem.
10. It may provide scope for better design and analysis of a problem.
11. Mathematical models based on system of differential equations (ordinary or partial) may provide a comprehensive mechanism for presenting the output of the analysis.

12. After the invention of high speed computers, numerical calculations involved in the investigation can be performed in seconds with high degree of accuracy.
13. Many of the shortcomings of the mathematical models observed at the stages of analyzing and testing may be overcome by returning to the designing stage.

Thus, mathematical modeling becomes essential in cases where experimental investigations are difficult to carry out to obtain adequate data. It is a reality that no human being will allow to conduct experiments on any of his organs. Also, the human organic system is much superior to other animals, and consequently, the data available from sub-primates cannot be effectively accepted for the human organic system. So the best possible technique of investigating these problems is based on the construction of analytical models (sometimes modification of existing models) covering the affected state of the human metabolic system. If a real-life problem involves a variation of one or more physical and (or) rheological parameters in some acceptable range, analytical modeling is a must for investigating the problem.

The construction and analysis of different mathematical models in health science, precisely brain injury and blood flow are being extensively used in predicting the occurrence of various diseases and the treatment of the diseases [1]. Creating an appropriate mathematical model, physiologists, biochemists and engineers use their knowledge of science (both physical and biological) to explore the best possible solutions to a real-life problem. Real-world problems of engineering, scientific and industrial relevance are studied through the appropriate mathematical models. Engineers and technologists design models for their products based on their knowledge of mathematics.

In the realm of medical and physiological sciences, mathematical models are growing day by day on account of various reasons discussed earlier. So, more and more sophisticated analytical models are extensively used to study the mechanics of the function of the human cranial system and blood flow as they may provide a better perception of the critical parameters controlling the system. Also, the output of the dissertation may add some additional input in the health sector and may improve human activity. This dissertation introduces solving various problems in the natural world generated from physiological and engineering applications.

This book chapter will present the general idea of modeling with mathematics as a tool and how real-life problems are modeled to extract a feasible solution. Models may not be unique for a problem, so the model choice is an important task and involves sound knowledge about the information expected. If multiple reasonable models exist for one problem, then the results are tested for ensuring the performance and the model that best meets the requirements is selected.

Objective of Mathematical Modelling

It may be defined as a skillful art of converting a problem from application domain to simple but deterministic mathematical formulations. The results extracted from the solution of the problem may lead to decision-making. It may be a guidance for further investigations of the problem after the inclusion of some additional information that was not known and not included in the original investigation. Based on mathematical concepts and using mathematical languages and symbolism, analytical models are constructed (or modified) for the generation of some inference on real-world non-linear problems. Engineers and professionals apply their knowledge of science and mathematics to find suitable solutions to some real-life problems. Developing an appropriate mathematical model for the problem, they analyze, solve and test the solution's applicability. When the study led to multiple reasonable solutions, they apply different design choices to extract the best possible solution to the problem under consideration.

We believe that knowledge of science and mathematics may be applied to find solutions (or, at least, have an intelligent guess) to an endless number of problems generated in different areas creating appropriate mathematical models. This book chapter covers the following areas where specific information are collected by formulating some problems of health science - brain injury, blood flow, decaying of the absorption of medicine in the human rheological system, forecasting population growth, estimating the spread of COVID 19 by the effective use of mathematical structures. The motivation behind the analysis is to extract some results about the too complicated system of the universe. An attempt is made to apply theoretical knowledge of Mathematics to the solution of some challenging application-oriented problems - the role of mathematics for tomorrow's technology. Also, it may offer a balance of theory and practice, which is intellectually inspiring. So, our journey begins with the use of knowledge of science and mathematics and our previous experience to develop mathematical models, extract some information (solution/s), test the potential solutions, and finally accept the solution that best fits the requirements of the problem. Sometimes stochastic analysis may be required to come to a valid conclusion. The design of mathematical models in health science is a collaborative measure of the surgeons, physiologists, hematologists, engineers, and mathematicians. So, mathematical modeling has multidisciplinary applications in almost all domains of science, engineering, and technology. The purpose of the discussion is not to confuse the new environment but to present the fundamental principles and techniques of mathematical modeling in a simple and easily understandable manner. Further study is suggested for a detailed understanding of highly mathematical aspects related to the study.

Role of Mathematical Models in the Study of Brain Injury Problems

After World War II, it was common to observe that cranio-cerebral trauma is the single major cause of death due to accidents on the road or in fast games. Many mathematicians, physicists, and medical professionals have contributed their experimental and theoretical research works in diagnosing and treating such trauma.

Mathematical models gives confidence in the study of injury of the human cranial system due to the following reasons:

- Brain damage cannot be macroscopic-ally detectable and so its presence is to be speculated from physiological and neurological malfunction.
- It is not possible to conduct experiments (analytical or experimental) on human head.
- No human being will voluntarily allow investigation on any part of the cranial vault.
- As human head is much superior to other animals so the results of the experiments done on the inferior animals fail to explain the potential injury mechanism of the human head subjected to any kind of severe direct impact or an impulsive load on the head or rotation of the head.
- The properties exhibited by a living being stops just after the brain death.
- The geometry of the cranial vault does not resemble to any standard geometric structure.

- Surgical sources of human specimens are rare and produce a limited amount of specimen.
- No two persons can be found whose brain geometry and mechanism are exactly similar.

These shortages are bound to persist shortly. So, for studies about the mechanics of the human cranial system, mathematical modelling has proved to be quite important and relevant. It will enhance our ability to sound judgment on the risk of morbidity due to head trauma. Mathematicians and physiologists are developing sophisticated mathematical models to deal with a few problems related to brain injury mechanisms that are believed to be of much interest to researchers working in this domain. Also, the construction and analysis of mathematical models and design of the protective instruments for cranial vault can proceed to a more sophisticated level.

In most of the analytical studies associated with brain trauma, the spherical geometry and the layered structure of the cranial vault are considered. The investigations are made through the consideration of elastic or viscoelastic behaviour of the skull/brain tissues.

The two main hypotheses of brain damage introduced in the study are

- *Rotational hypothesis:* Development of high shear stress in brain tissues due to a sudden rotational acceleration of considerable magnitude leading to rupture of the tethering cerebral blood vessels.
- *Cavitation hypothesis:* Following a direct impact with a projectile or an impulsive load on the head, cavity is formed on the cranium.

Based on the experimental and theoretical research works on cause and remedies of brain damage contributed by the mathematicians, physicists and medical professionals some of the models of the human head proposed in the investigation of Brain-injury problems are:

Model I: Mathematical Model of Brain Injury Problem When the Cranium Is Subjected to an Angular Acceleration

High shear strains may develop due to rotational acceleration of the head (a very common phenomenon in soccer games or vehicular accidents), leading to the break of harmony of the blood vessels. Author's proposed to estimate the outcome of rotational acceleration on the occurrence of concussion due to celebrity using simple geometric (spherical) structure, viscoelastic behavior of the brain tissues, and some input angular acceleration [2]. Due to rotational accelerations, the distortion of brain tissues occurs, and if the distortion crosses a critical value, traumatic brain injury originates. In the analytical model, the outermost case representing the human skull is a rigid spherical shell, the cerebrospinal fluid (CSF) between the skull and the gray matter to be inviscid and compressible viscoelastic characteristics of the brain tissue occupying the central position was incorporated. In the beginning, the potential solution of the problem is sought, incorporating the elastic nature of the brain tissues (Figure 6.1). Considering the brain tissues as elastic, the elastic solution of the problem was generated in the Laplace Transform space. As Laplace inversion in closed form could not be done due to the complexity of the solution in the transformed space so numerical inversion was carried out following Bellman, R et al. (1966) [3] and then Bland's 'correspondence principle' (1960) [4] was applied to study the viscoelastic characteristics of the brain tissues. The objective of the investigation is a prediction of the threshold of cerebral concussion for human beings. The results were compared with Bycroft (1973) [5], who did not incorporate the presence of CSF in the model. Nanda, S. P. et al. (2017) [6, 17] presented an estimate of the qualitative and quantitative role of the various rheological and physical parameters on shear stress and strain generated in the gray matter (brain). Shear stress plays an important role in the study of traumatic brain injury.

In spherical co-ordinates system ((r, θ, ρ) , the equation of motion of the brain and the cerebrospinal fluid are governed by the pair of partial differential equations

$$\frac{\rho_1}{\mu_1}\frac{\partial^2 w}{\partial t^2} = \frac{1}{r}\left(r\frac{\partial^2 w}{\partial r^2} + 2\frac{\partial w}{\partial r} + \frac{1}{r}\frac{\partial^2 w}{\partial \theta^2} - \frac{w}{r}\frac{1}{\sin^2\theta} + \frac{\cot\theta}{r}\frac{\partial w}{\partial \theta} \right) \tag{1}$$

$$\frac{1}{c_2^{\,2}}\frac{\partial^2 \phi_1}{\partial t^2} = \frac{1}{r^2}\frac{\partial}{\partial r}\left(r^2\frac{\partial \phi_1}{\partial r} \right) + \frac{1}{r^2 \sin\theta}\frac{\partial}{\partial \theta}\left(\sin\theta \frac{\partial \phi_1}{\partial \theta} \right) \tag{2}$$

where W: shear displacement of a point (r, θ) of the brain

ϕ_1 : Velocity potential for CSF

(ρ_1, ρ_2): Densities of the brain and the CSF

(a, b) : External and internal radii of the spherical shell

c_2 : Velocity of propagation of pressure waves in the CSF

μ_1 : Shear modulus of the brain

μ_2 : Viscosity coefficient of the CSF

$\tau_{r\theta}$: Shear stress

[Due to the axisymmetric nature of the problem, the equations are independent of the azimuthal displacement]

The system is subjected to the following boundary conditions:

(1) The head is subjected to an input angular acceleration

$$\ddot{\phi} = \begin{cases} B \sin \Omega t, & 0 < t < \pi / \Omega \\ 0, & t > \pi / \Omega \end{cases}$$

, Ω is the angular frequency at $r = a$ (outermost surface)

(2) $\dfrac{\partial w}{\partial t} = \dfrac{1}{r} \dfrac{\partial \phi_1}{\partial \theta}$ at $r = b$ (interface between the brain and the CSF)

and

(3) $\tau_{r\theta}^{\ br} = \tau_{r\theta}^{\ CSF}$

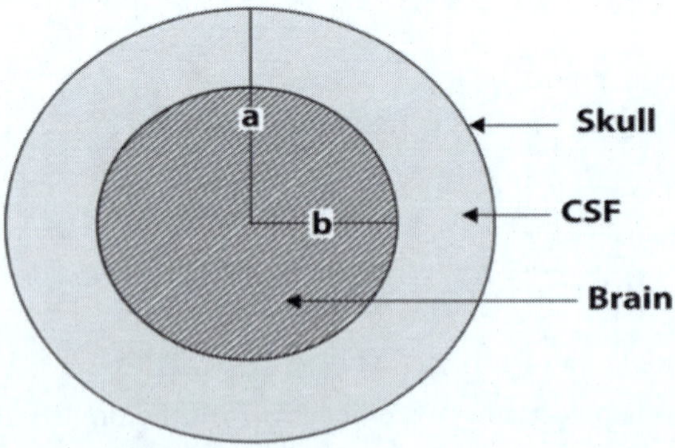

Figure 6.1. Simplified model of the composite structure of the Brain, the CSF and the Skull.

For the quantitative estimation of shear stress and shear strain developed in the brain due to the input angular acceleration, the values of different physical constants are collected from standard literature as

$$a = 0.0774m \quad b = 0.0762m \quad \rho_1 = 0.9774 \times 10^3\, kg/m^3 \quad \rho_2 = 0.998 \times 10^3\, kg/m^3$$
$$c_2 = 145.03\; m/s \quad \mu_2 = 8.98\; kg/ms$$

The improved numerical solution was sought by developing computer codes and the graphs are plotted using MATLAB 8.5. Figure 6.2 presents some specific information on the tolerance curve for cerebral concussion using the value $\theta = \pi/2$. T he results extracted from the mathematical model is exhibited through the graph. For a particular value of $\Omega = 40\; rad/s$, the optimum value of the angular acceleration predicted for loss of consciousness is $1.6 \times 10^3\; rad/s^2$ at around 6 ms. In a similar study, Bycroft (1973) [4] obtained that severe concussion occurs around 20 ms when the angular acceleration (Ω) reaches the critical value $3.5 \times 10^3\; rad/s^2$.

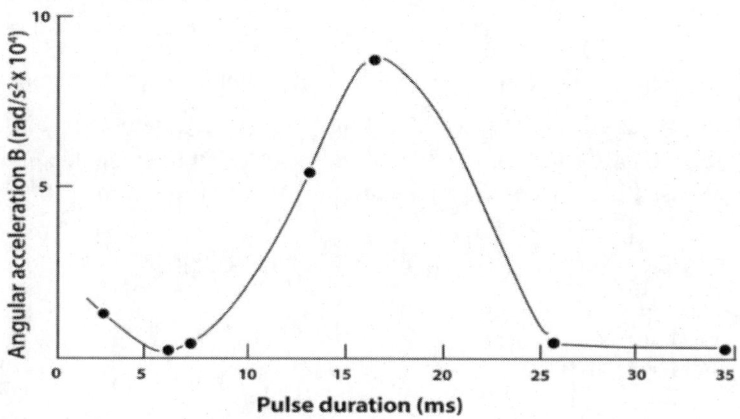

Figure 6.2. Threshold of cerebral concussion.

The variation in value is due to non-consideration of the presence of CSF in the skull-brain system. The findings of the improved model is acceptable to the surgeons working in the frontier of treatment. Thus the model seems to be more efficient in describing the overall profile in the investigation of the problems. The output might have applications in the design and construction of protective systems like helmets, air cushion bags for human head. If standardized helmets are worn the injury of the brain in professional American-style soccer may be partially or completely eliminated.

More refined results may be obtained if damping behavior of the brain tissues is given due consideration in the model.

Model 2: Mathematical Model of Brain Injury Problem When the Outermost Surface of the Cranium Is Subjected to a Time-Dependent Impulsive Force

In most of the mathematical models presented to study the cause and remedies of the brain dysfunction, the porosity of the cranial bone were ignored. The study of the anatomy and physiology of the controlling organ of the human body confirms the presence of a porous layer (called diploe) situated between the inner and outer tables of the vault. The layer consists of enumerable number of cavities (pores) filled by organic fluids. Potential solutions with specific information were procured by Nanda and Basu Mallik [8, 9] through the inclusion of the porous layer in the models created for the purpose (Figure 6.3).

If $\vec{u} = (u_r, u_\theta, 0)$ and $\vec{U} = (U_r, U_\theta, 0)$ represent the displacement vectors of the solid and the fluid media respectively then the constitutive equations of equilibrium for the solid-fluid material in the displacement form were expressed in terms of the two partial differential equations [10]

$$G\nabla^2\vec{u} + (P - G + Q)\, grad\, e + (Q + R)\, grad\, \varepsilon = 0 \quad (3)$$

$$grad(Qe + R\varepsilon) = b_1 \frac{\partial}{\partial t}(\vec{U} - \vec{u}) \cdot \quad (4)$$

where λ, G, Q, R are the four elastic constants, $P = \lambda + 2G$, b_1 is the Darcy's constant, and ∇^2 represents the Laplacian in the (r, θ, ϕ) system.

Due the axisymmetric nature of the problem the azimuthal displacements $u_\phi = 0, U_\phi = 0$ as they are independent of the angle ϕ.

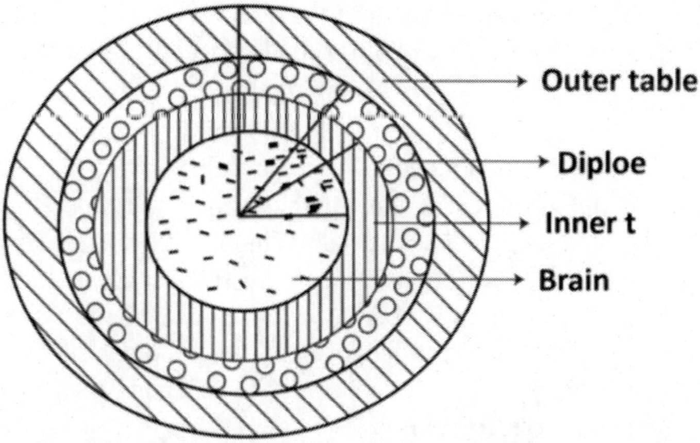

Figure 6.3. Schematic representation of the layered structure of the cranium with porous layer.

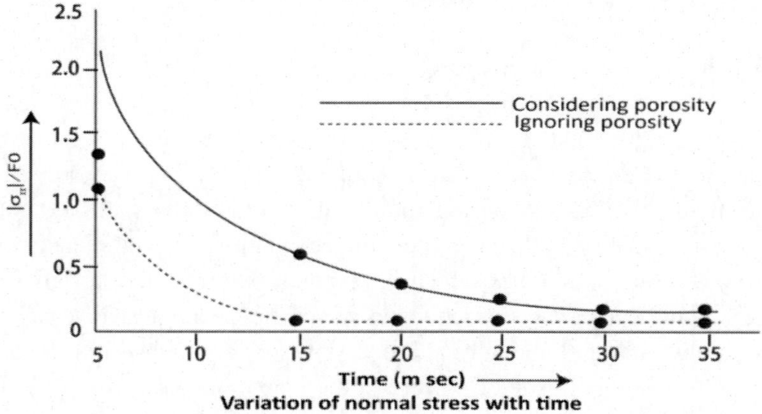

Figure 6.4. Non dimensional value of Normal stress.

The outermost surface of the whole system was subjected to a harmonically time dependent force $F(\theta)e^{i\omega t}, t > 0$ and the continuity of the stress and strains at the interface were given due consideration in the analysis. The applicability of the model was validated through the analysis of the quantitative output of the investigation. The values of different parameters and physical constants were collected from standard literature and computer codes were developed.

The non-dimensional value of the normal stress $\left(\frac{|\sigma_{rr}|}{F_0}\right)$ generated in the brain with time are exhibited in the Figure 6. 4.

Impact load $F(\theta) = F_0$= constant.

Comparing the results (with and without porosity), it is observed that the value of the normal stress is remarkably high with the consideration of porosity. It gradually diminishes as time progresses and its variation becomes negligible after a certain interval of time. So the mathematical model serves the object of improving our knowledge about the working of the system. The objective of the analysis is to use the knowledge for creating secured and well protective system for the cranium.

Role of Mathematical Models in the Study of Blood Flow Through an Atherosclerotic Arterial Segment

A study report aimed at investigating models to estimate cardiovascular disease risks, published by WHO in September, 2019, estimated the proportion of individuals in the age group 40 - 64 years has more than 20% risk of CVD (Carotid Circulatory Disorders) attack. [11] The survey was conducted in 79 mostly low and middle income countries throughout the globe. An unusual growth developed in the inner side of human artery is medically termed as *stenosis* which is responsible for many cardiovascular problems. The immediate consequence of the hematological disease is the increased obstruction to the normal blood flow leading to insufficient flow of blood to various organs and/or rupture of the artery. Anyone may be a victim of the disease unless precaution is taken in life style (lack of physical exercise, consumption of alcohols, taking fatty diets etc.). The elderly people with high blood sugar and pressures are the soft target of the disease and has a high risk for survival. So, more and more experimental and analytical investigations are necessary to study the effect of high concentration of stresses in the arteries/veins that is responsible for the genesis and growth of the disease. The knowledge of science and mathematics may be used to develop an appropriate mathematical model of the problem and then exploring potential solution of it. Finally the output may be analyzed by varying the values of the physical and rheological parameters in some admissible range. Mathematical models were developed to study the blood flow irregularities in the human arterial chain considering the rheological character of blood together with the geometry of the stenotic growth.

In most of the studies on blood streaming through the arteries constricted due to some abnormal growth within, mathematical models are developed paying due attention to the following fluid model for blood, geometrical shape of the artery and growth and the physical behavior exhibited by blood in the inner lining of the artery.

- Blood is represented by some non-Newtonian fluid (that do not follow Newton's law of viscosity) model. In most of the investigations, the accepted non-Newtonian fluid models are Herschel-Bulkley, Casson, Two-phase, Bingham Plastic, Power law. In some previous investigations the Newtonian fluid model was considered to represent blood. Experimental investigations on the rheological behavior of streaming blood confirm that it is a suspension of erythrocytes in plasma and so may be better represented by a non-Newtonian fluid model. The equations governing the flow of fluid in the models are available.
- The stenotic geometry are polynomial, exponential or smooth cosine. Each has its mathematical expression.
- The artery is a long cylindrical tube and the axis is taken as z-axis. The length of the tube (artery) is assumed to be large enough compared to the diameter, so that the end effects may be neglected.
- The slip (velocity discontinuity at the wall of the artery) or no slip boundary conditions are imposed depending upon the requirements of the investigation.

In concurrence with the logic given for developing analytical models to study blood flow irregularities in stenotic region, the rheological and physical nature of the blood together with the geometry of the stenosis were modeled mathematically by the researchers. The investigations on the circulation of blood in the human arterial chain made by the hematologists agreed that malfunctioning of the system is due to the change of dynamic nature of blood, pressure distribution and the flow resistance (impedance) occurring as a consequence. So, sophisticated and analytical models were devised on characteristics of blood and the stenotic geometry to explore modern approach on the cause and remedy of the hematological diseases. The studies are based on different fluid model for blood (Newtonian or non-Newtonian) and various geometry for the growth. The construction of analytical models for the analysis of multiple and /or overlapping stenosis manifested in the human artery is a complicated task and so deserves special attention. It is a collaborative activity of the physiologists, hematologists, physicists, engineers and the mathematicians. Plenty of analytical models and illustrations are available in standard literature. Still solutions in the exact form are not easy to get and some shortages bound to exist in the near future.

Some of the intellectually stimulating models of human narrow artery/vein constricted due to unnatural growths covered in the analysis of hematological problems are introduced:

Model 3: Mathematical Model of Multiple Stenoses in the Human Artery Taking H-B Model for Blood

A mathematical model was designed by Basu Mallik & Nanda [12] to estimate the change in flow behaviour of blood streaming through a long but narrow arterial segment having multiple stenosis (Figure 6.5). The axi symmetric flow through an artery with circular cross section were included in the investigation. Blood exhibits non-Newtonian behaviour as it is a suspension of erythrocytes in plasma and may be better represented by Herschel-Bulkley (H-B) fluid model when flowing through a long tube of diameter 0.095 mm or less. The smooth cosine model of the growth manifested was given due consideration in the analysis. The expressions for fluid velocity, plug flow velocity, flow rate and the shear stress have been derived numerically and their variation with change in the value of the parameters were presented through graphs for a standard measurement of the power index parameter (n = 0.75).

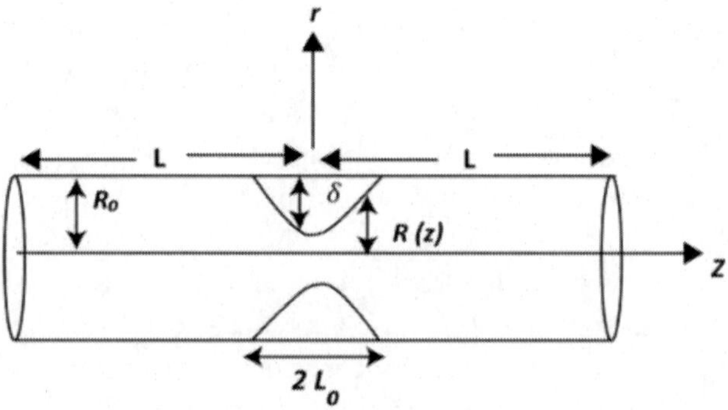

Figure 6.5. Geometry of the artery with multiple stenosis.

The constitutive equation describing H-B fluid

$$-\frac{du}{dr} = f(\tau) = \begin{cases} \frac{1}{k}(\tau - \tau_0)^n, \tau \geq \tau_0 \\ 0, \qquad elsewhere \end{cases} \tag{5}$$

where u: axial velocity of blood τ_0 : yield stress n: flow behaviour index of blood k : viscosity coefficient of blood- the parameters n and k account for non-Newtonian effects. The smooth cosine geometry of the growth was mathematically represented by the smooth cosine model:

$$\frac{R}{R_0} = \begin{cases} 1 - \frac{\delta}{2R_0}\left[1 + \cos\frac{2\pi}{L_0}\left(z - d - \frac{L_0}{2}\right)\right], d \leq z \leq L_0 + d \\ 1, otherwise \end{cases} \tag{6}$$

where

R, R_0 : radius of the obstructed and unobstructed artery, L_0, d = stenosis length and location δ : maximum height of the growth z : measured along the axis of the artery.

The system was subjected to the boundary conditions

$u = u_s \; at \; r = R(z)$ (slip condition)

(2) τ is finite at $r = 0$ (regularity condition)

(3) $\frac{du}{dr} = 0$ at $r = 0$

The formulated problem was solved and information for the following blood components - fluid velocity, plug flow velocity, flow rate and the shear stress were obtained in closed mode from the analysis. The extracted expressions were computed numerically and graphical representations of the variation of the physical quantities with change in the value of the parameters were presented through graphs. It might provide a perception about the genesis and growth of the disease. The corresponding results for Newtonian model of blood were generated as a special case by the variation of rheological parameters in the specific range. This model had the capability to overcome many of the shortcomings of the previous investigations.

Model 4: Mathematical Model of Multiple and Overlapped Stenoses in the Human Artery Taking Bingham Plastic Fluid Model for Blood

Nanda et al. (2017a) [7] designed and presented an improved mathematical model to investigate the result of obstruction in the human artery due to the presence of radially non-symmetric (but axially symmetric), multiple and overlapped stenosis (Figure 6.6). The non-Newtonian nature of blood was characterized by Bingham plastic fluid model and the stenotic geometry was represented by a polynomial expression that best fits its asymmetric-overlapping shape.

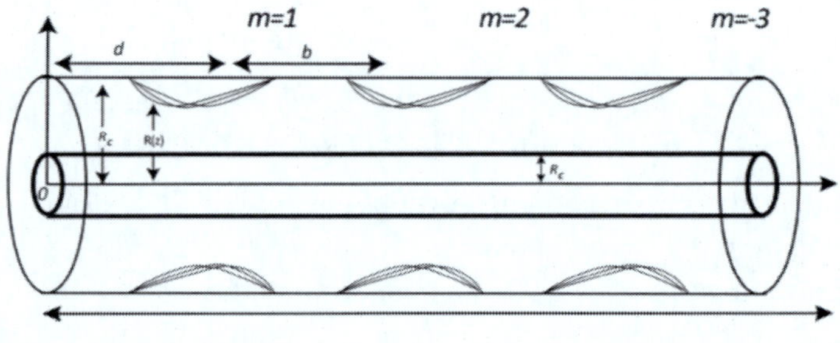

Figure 6.6. Geometry of axially symmetric but radially non-symmetric multiple stenosis.

The fluid-flow equation for Bingham plastic fluid model:

$$\dot{\beta} = f(\tau) = -\frac{du}{dr} = \begin{cases} \dfrac{\tau - \tau_0}{\mu}, \tau > \tau_0 \\ 0, \quad \tau \le \tau_0 \end{cases} \tag{7}$$

where τ_0 is the shear at the wall when $r = 0$ and μ is the viscosity coefficient of blood. The geometry of the stenosis shape was represented by the polynomial model as

$$\frac{R}{R_0} = \begin{cases} 1-\varepsilon\left[L_0^{\,s-1}\{\gamma z - md - (m-1)L_0\} - \{\lambda z - md - (m-1)L_0\}^s\right] m(d+L_0) - L_0 \le \gamma z \le m(d+L_0) \\ 1, \, otherwise \end{cases} \tag{8}$$

where R, R_0 : Tube radius with and without stenosis, L_0, d - stenosis length and location m = stenosis number, $s(\geq 2)$ = stenosis shape parameter and $\varepsilon = \frac{\delta}{R_0} \cdot \frac{s}{L_0^{\,s}(s-1)}$ z : measured along the axis of the artery.

The problem was solved considering the boundary conditions

(1) $u = 0$ at $r = R$ (no slip condition)
(2) τ is finite at $r = 0$ (regularity condition)

It was difficult to extract the potential solution of the analysis with some extended ideas in quantitative form but computations and graph plotting with MATLAB 7.0 made the task easier. The stenosis height and parameters were seen to have substantial effect in the generation of shear stress in the stenotic region. The results were in close agreement with the physical condition of the problem. The results were in close agreement with those obtained in a separate study by Nanda et al. (2017b) [13] where the flow was considered through an elastic cylindrical tube and the blood was represented by power law fluid model.

Model 5: Mathematical Model for Population Growth in India Using ODE

A population is said to follow exponential growth model if it increases at a rate proportional to the number or quantity present at that instant.

Mathematically, if y be the measure of the population at an instant t then the model is represented by the ODE $\frac{dy}{dt} = ky$ - (9)where the constant of proportionality $k(>0)$ is termed as relative growth rate. The solution of the differential equation (ix) is $y(t) = ce^{kt}$ (10) the constant of integration c is determined in terms of an initial or boundary condition consistent with the physical nature of the problem. How to determine the positive unknown k, the relative growth rate? As the growth rate is not known then it is to be calculated from the given data.

The population of India in 2016 and 2018 are respectively 132.45 and 135.26 (in crores) [Source: World Bank, United States Census Bureau]. So, the population has increased from 132.45 to 135.26 over a period of 2 years.

Plugging the data $y = 135.26,\ c = 132.45,\ t = 2$ in the equation (10)

$135.26 = 132.45 \times e^{k.2} \Rightarrow e^{2k} = 1.02 \Rightarrow k = 0.011 = 1.1\%$

The equation (x) becomes

$$y(t) = ce^{0.011t} \tag{11}$$

What are the estimated population in 2020 and 2022? (Table 1).

Taking 2018 as the base year when $t = 0$, the estimates of the population (in crores) of 2020 and 2022 are $y(2)$ & $y(4)$ obtained as $135.26e^{0.022}$ and $135.26e^{0.44} = 138.27$ & 141.35 respectively.

Table 1. Population growth and estimation (2016-2022)

Year	**Population (in crores)**
2016	132.45
2018	135.26
2020	138.27
2022	141.35

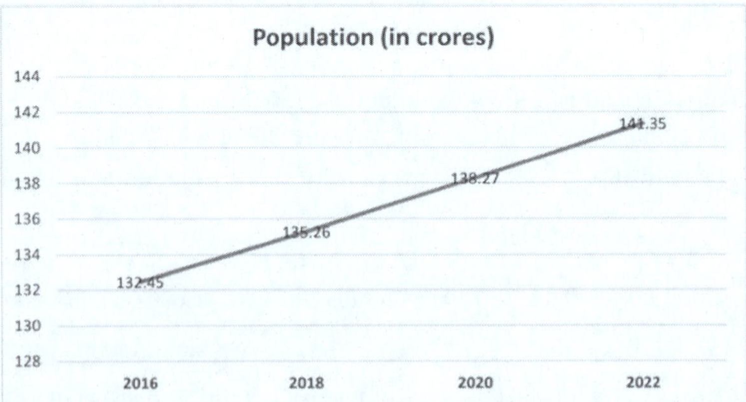

Figure 6.7. Growth of population in India (2016-2022).

So, the growth of population (Figure 6.7) in India is showing an exponential trend.

Model 6: Mathematical Model for Decaying of the Absorption of a Medicine in Human Rheological System with ODE

A population follows exponential decay model if it decreases at a rate proportional to the number or quantity present at that instant. We will frequently use the term *population* meaning human population, plants, bacteria present in a system. Mathematically, if $y(t)$ be the measure of the population at an instant t then the model is represented by the ODE

$$\frac{dy(t)}{dt} = -ky \cdot \tag{12}$$

where relative decay rate is represented by the constant of proportionality $= -k(< 0)$. The solution of the differential equation (12) is

$$y(t) = ce^{-kt} \tag{13}$$

the constant of integration C is determined in terms of an initial or boundary condition consistent with the physical nature of the problem. A simple example of decay model designed by ODE is the absorption of a medicine injected in the blood stream of a patient. Medical research has established that more medicine is present in the rheological system faster will be the absorption. Absorption is faster means the total quantity of medicine present in the system will tend to decrease. Now a reasonable mathematical model defined by an ODE will be designed to fit the problem. Let $y(t)$ represents the amount of medicine present in the system at an instant t. Then the rate of decrease of the medicine due to the absorption $-\frac{dy}{dt}$ will be proportional to the amount of the drug $y(t)$ present at that instant. In the mathematical language it generates the relation $-\frac{dy}{dt} \propto y(t) \Rightarrow \frac{dy}{dt} = -ky, k(> 0)$ is the constant of proportionality. The value of k will be dependent on the medicine composition and is generated through experiment. The mathematical tool (an ODE) explored is exactly same as the relation (12)

Model 7: Mathematical Model for the Spread of a Disease Growing or Decaying Exponentially

The design and construction of mathematical models play a key role in the analysis of the problems involving rates of change which are modeled with ordinary differential equations of first order. Here population means patients to whom a drug is administered or decay of a radioactive substance due to emission etc. It is observed that many of the physical or social phenomena involve rates of change so the natural choice for mathematical modeling of them are differential equations of first order.

We attempt to predict the spread of a certain disease in a population of L individuals. At any instant the rate will depend on the two factors which are apparently conflicting:

- The number of individuals already affected at that instant that 111will definitely enhance the trend.
- The number of individuals who are not affected at that instant that may be a reason for a diminishing trend.

Let the number individuals in the population L affected by the disease at an instant t is $y(t)$. So the number of unaffected individuals in the population at that instant is $L-y$ which decreases with the increase of affected individuals y. The rate of increase $\frac{dy(t)}{dt}$ will depend on the the two conflicting components y and $L-y$ which are mutually dependent. Initially the number of affected individuals is known as y_0, then the problem is subjected to the initial condition $y(0)=y_0$.

If the problem is fitted to a mathematical model then the model will be governed by the following first order ordinary differential equation as an initial value problem:

$$\frac{dy(t)}{dt} = ky(L - y), y(0) = y_0 \tag{14}$$

where $k(> 0)$ is the constant of proportionality that depends on that specific disease and may be obtained through some experimental measure.

In the simplified form the differential equation of (14) becomes

$$\frac{dy}{dt} - kLy = -ky^2 \tag{15}$$

which can be written in the form $\frac{1}{L}\left\{\frac{1}{y} + \frac{1}{L-y}\right\}dy = kdt$

Integrating, the solution is obtained in the form

$$\frac{y}{L-y} = ce^{Lkt}, y(0) = y_0 \tag{16}$$

The particular solution of the initial value problem is

$$\frac{y}{L-y} = \frac{y_0}{L-y_0}e^{Lkt} \Rightarrow \frac{L}{y} = 1 + \frac{L-y_0}{y_0}e^{-Lkt} \tag{17}$$

The mathematical model offers an exponential growth or decay model as the rate of growth or decay is directly proportional to the population. Apart from analytical analysis, the model may be validated by fitting a data set on COVID 19 active cases in India. In mid 2020, the approximate population of India is 13800 *lakhs* Total COVID - 19 cases reported in India on the three days of the year 2020 (in *lakhs* – Table 2):

Table 2. COVID-19 Cases in three days (Nov- 1, 2 and 3)

Day	**Cases (in *lakhs*)**
November 1	82.29322
November 3	83.12947
November 5	84.11034

Source: Worldometer's COVID - 19 data.

As the rate of growth (k) is not known so its value is calculated by using the data for NOV 1 and NOV 3. Time is considered in day.

$$L = 13800, y = 83.12947, y_0 = 82.29322, t = 2$$

Applying the values in (17), we get the growth rate as $k = 3.68 \times 10^{-7}$ In order to estimate the number of active cases for NOV 5, 2020 the values are taken for the constants and parameters as $L = 13800, y_0 = 83.12947, t = 2, k = 3.68 \times 10^{-7}, y = ?$ where y denotes the estimated number of active cases on NOV 5. Equation (17) computes $y = 84.070$ which almost follows the result of the given data set. The essence of the investigation in the present scenario is to present the variation of the physical quantities with change in the value of the parameters.

Conclusion

The book chapter presents 'Role of Mathematical Models in predicting and exploring different scenarios.' But due to the restriction of pages, it could not accommodate more that have their domain of applications. An attempt is made to design and develop a few mathematical models to analyze and find a suitable solution. In most cases, multiple reasonable models can be developed for a problem. We believe that all information can not be extracted from one model, and so the choice of the shape of a model will depend upon the need and wants of the stage. We believe that the discussion will provide some relevant information that will be used in the future development of the topics.

The discussion may be concluded by the wilful message of Jesus:

> "Ask, and you will receive. Search, and you will find. Knock, and the door will be opened for you."

References

[1] Nanda Saktipada et al. (2020), Head Injury Needs Life Saving Care - *JMSCM*, Vol 1(2), pp. 218 -224.

[2] Bland, D. R. (1960). *The Theory of Linear Viscosity*, Pergamon Press.

[3] Bellman, R., Kolaba, R. E. and Lockett, J. A. (1966). *Numerical Inversion of the Laplace Transform,* American Elsevier Pub. Co.

[4] Goldsmith, W. (1972). *Biomechanics, its foundations and Objectives*, Prentice Hall, 585 – 634.

[5] G. N. Bycroft, *J. Biomech.* 6, 487495 (1973).

[6] Nanda, Saktipada, Nanda Sibashis et al. (2017): An analytical study on Brain Injury due to an input rotational acceleration on skull- brain system of the human head, *JCBPS,* Vol. 7, pp 038-046.

[7] Nanda, Saktipada et al. (2017a). A study on Bingham Plastic Characteristics of blood flow through multiple overlapped stenosed arteries- Saudi *J. of Eng. and Tech.,* Vol. 2(9), 349-357.

[8] Nanda, Saktipada & Basu Mallik, B. (2011). Effect of Axi-symmetric External Load on the Stress-field generated in a Poroelastic Spherical Shell - *Int. J. of Civil Eng*., Vol 1(1), pp 7-16.

[9] Basu Mallik & Nanda (2011). Effectiveness of American football helmets in Mild Traumatic *Brain Injury* (MTBI)- IEMCON organized by IEM in collaboration with IEEE (conference paper).

[10] Biot, M. A., (1956). *J. Appl. Mech*., *Trans ASME,* Vol 23, pp 91-96.

[11] United Nations. Transforming our world: the 2030 agenda for sustainable, development. 2015. https://www.un.org/ga/search/view_doc.asp?symbol=A/RES/70/1&Lang=E (accessed July 26, 2019).

[12] Basu Mallik, B, Nanda, Saktipada (2012), A Mathematical Analysis of Blood Flow through Stenosed Arteries: A non-Newtonian Model - *IEM Int. J. of Mgt. & Tech.* Vol 2 (1), pp 69-16.

[13] Nanda, Saktipada et al., (2017b), Study on the effect of non-Newtonian nature of blood flowing through an elastic artery with slip condition. *J. of Che. Bio. and Phy. Sc*. (JCBPS, Sec C), Vol 7(4), pp. 934-942.

Chapter 7

Training Healthcare Professionals in Artificial Intelligence Augmented Services

Yasmeen Shamsi Rizvi[1,*] and Sufian Zaheer[2]

[1]Jamia Millia Islamia, New Delhi, India
[2]Vardhman Mahavir Medical College, New Delhi, India

Abstract

It has been estimated by the World Health Organization (WHO) that by 2030, the world will face a scarcity of approximately 18 million healthcare professionals (HCP). There are millions of people with deficient access to medical specialty care in the US alone, and this demand is escalating. There is thus an urgent need to address the problem of an overburdened health system. The adoption and scaling up of artificial intelligence (AI) may help alleviate the shortage of human resources. AI has transformed the healthcare sector and its impact can be seen in many areas of healthcare function. Administrative tasks that occupy considerable time of a HCP are steamlined with the help of AI. It is predicted that AI may also make clinical decisions in the near future. AI reduces error due to human fatigue, brings down medical expenses, supports and replaces labor-intensive tasks, minimizes invasive surgeries, and decreases mortality rates. However, there is an urgent need for the upskilling of healthcare professionals as medical education, even now is largely based on traditional curricula. AI and Machine Learning, along with other relevant technologies will be able to penetrate healthcare services, leading to skilful medicine-machine interaction. As technologies need to be rapidly adopted for a healthier world, it is thus important to study the critical need for new skills in HCPs.

[*] Corresponding Author's Email: yasmeenrizvi44@yahoo.com.

In: Industry 4.0 and Intelligent Business Analytics for Healthcare
Editors: Soumi Dutta, Vinod Kumar Shukla, Shruti Nagpal et al.
ISBN: 978-1-68507-602-3

Keywords: artificial intelligence, AI literacy, digital healthcare, AI training, medical education, soft-skills training, healthcare professional

Introduction

> "We can only see a short distance ahead, but we can see plenty there that needs to be done"- Alan Turing (1950)

The medical profession in the future will be characterized by remote consultation/treatment, information from multiple data sources, applications of artificial intelligence (AI), and, most importantly, the adept handling of medicine and machine interface. As witnessed during the COVID-19 pandemic, an overburdened health system is a global problem. The World Health Organization has estimated that by 2030, the world will have scarcity of approximately 18 million health care workers including doctors and other allied health care workers. There are millions of people with deficient access to medical specialty care in the US alone, and this demand is escalating. There is thus an urgent need to address the problem of an overburdened health system. Given the dire situation, healthcare systems need to adapt and scale up AI-based medical practice as it may help alleviate the shortage of human resources. To perform in the future scenario of AI-based medical procedures, the healthcare professionals (HCP) must possess knowledge of their fields of medicine and have the ability to work on data platforms to improve patient care. The question therefore is, 'are our HCPs ready for the future?'

The Need for Artificial Intelligence in Medical Practice

Artificial Intelligence (AI) is the ability of computers to mimic higher cognitive processes of humans, such as the ability to reason, perceive, generalize and learn experientially. In 1950, the British Mathematician Dr. Alan Turing, a man ahead of his time, had famously said [1], "I propose to ask the question, can machines think"? Those were the times when computing had just begun. Since then, over the last 70 years, there has been a massive transformation of computing abilities; around the world, AI has transformed industries and is poised to radically change the field of the healthcare sector [2]. AI today is based on years of research and has many important applications in many fields. It has moved from being a topic of science fiction to becoming part of scientific publications [3]. The developments in AI technology currently indicate that it will have a great impact on all fields of human knowledge and activity. For instance, AI is now quickly fitting into routine healthcare settings making patient management easy. Integrating knowledge and clinical skills of healthcare professionals with the efficient information processing power of deep structured learning algorithms and advanced neural networks has produced promising and impressive results.

AI is thought to provide instant relief to a multitude of challenges being faced by healthcare ecosystems globally, such as lack of healthcare professionals, aging and burnout of physicians, and higher demand for chronic disease management. WHO (World Health Organization) estimated that there would be a needs-based shortage of 18 million healthcare providers by 2030, mostly in developing and underdeveloped countries [4]. Most countries, including developed nations, have limitations in developing, utilizing, and upskill their existing and potential manpower. There is an increasing demand for a better organized and universally available healthcare system as the aging population is increasing. It is predicted that by 2030, the population above the age of 65 years would double, which in turn would result in a higher demand for the management of age-related chronic problems and diseases. Because of the shortage of skilled healthcare professionals, such a situation might result in almost a crisis in the healthcare sector. Providing access to universal healthcare worldwide may thus become a major challenge; however, this predicted problem can be resolved by applying AI and machine learning in healthcare processes, resulting in even more reliable diagnosis, surgery, and other interventions. Training medical students and practitioners, administrative staff, and data analysts is the way forward for averting the foreseen healthcare crisis.

New Frontiers in Artificial Intelligence Augmented Healthcare

AI has opened up new frontiers for precise, personalized diagnostics and better treatment. The present fourth industrial revolution that the world is experiencing has hugely impacted all sectors of the economy and has led to transformations in the healthcare sector. It is thus important that healthcare decision-makers quickly decide upon how to adopt AI technologies within their organizations. AI in healthcare is expected to provide potential solutions in the fields of preventive & social medicine and advanced diagnostics and enhance physicians' capacity to treat more patients. With AI methods and their tools, it is easy for healthcare providers to sift through large amounts of data, confirm very quickly suspected infections, chronic diseases, and cancers, prognosticate the disease, and tailor specific therapeutic requirements. AI makes it possible to predict the unique problems in a large group population and also aids in identifying specific needs.

According to experts in this field, Artificial intelligence represents an approaching revolution that will bring about revolutionary changes and improvements in the quality of patient care. Procedures would be safer, faster, and cheaper with less dependence on manpower. Some of the common use scenarios of AI in the medical profession as depicted in Figure 7.1, are as following:

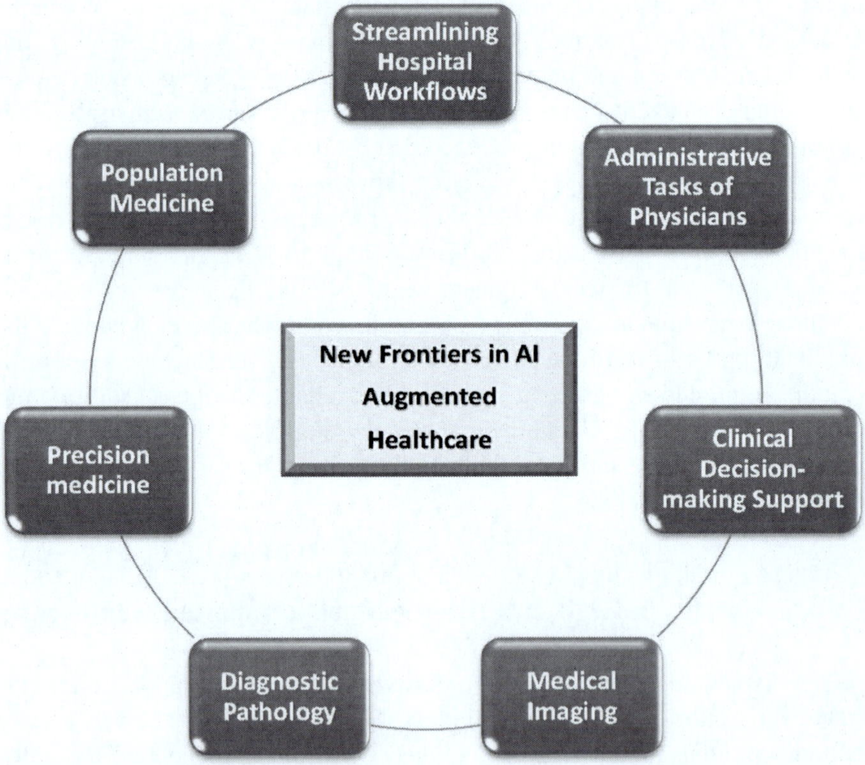

Figure 7.1. AI in Healthcare-New Frontiers.

Streamlining Hospital Workflows

AI can help physicians and other HCWs become more efficient in scheduling their daily work and selecting appropriate diagnostic tests and treatments. For example, AI-equipped voice-to-text transcription can greatly shorten the time utilized in everyday routine tasks in healthcare facilities, such as entering/updating data inpatient records and prescribing appropriate radiological imaging and diagnostic tests.

Administrative Tasks of Physicians

It is a very common observation that doctors cannot devote adequate time to their patients due to administrative engagements. Daily routine tasks such as compiling clinical notes, updating patients' medical records, and putting chronological information in patients' case sheets, out-patient and inpatient forms are very time-consuming. The developments in AI can take care of these important administrative processes, and physicians can spend the saved time examining patients, analyzing diagnostic reports, giving advice for healthy lifestyle choices and preventive measures. For instance, in an AI scenario, when a patient reaches a hospital for a check-up, the physician greets him/her along with his virtual allied health care assistant, who takes notes from the discussion between the doctor and patient and creates an electronic medical record from the relevant information provided by the patient. The doctor can then instantly consult her/his tablet that has access to AI-enabled tools and a large database of thousands of similar patients with their medical history, symptoms, and clinical presentations. A doctor can then make quick and accurate decisions regarding radiological and pathological examinations that a patient may require. As the digital processes lead to saving of precious time, the patient may hence be able to discuss his specific lifestyle concerns with his physician, who may suggest to her/him a personalized care plan. "Ping, An" Good Doctor's AI-assisted hospital consultation system, has developed a unique machine that can access pulse and record heart rate [5]. This system can reduce the frequency of patients' visits to the hospital and medical drug stores by doing quick precursory check-ups and advise prescriptions only when required. This innovation would help China cope with the shortage of China's healthcare professionals.

Clinical Decision-Making Support

AI can help physicians and caregivers integrate electronic medical records with other patients' data, such as radiological images and diagnostic test results, to make patient care more efficient and the delivery of appropriate therapies easier. It will also encourage doctors to treat an increasing number of patients with age-related chronic diseases cost-effectively by providing AI-driven clinical algorithms and support systems [6]. In 2016, New York University Langone medical center launched a "predictive analytics" unit at their Center for Healthcare Innovation and Delivery Science using data and algorithms and modeling them to look into methods and ways of decreasing unnecessary hospital admissions. They have hypothesized several models, and currently, their model in operation includes how to predict behaviour of patients who do not visit the hospital at their scheduled appointments and identifying patients who do not have electronic health records of their active disease. The unit was also successful in making models and devices that can anticipate and prevent disease onset, alarm the doctors about patients who have increased risk of a particular disease, decrease hospital admissions and shorten stays, and reduce chances of a person suffering from the particular disease for which she/he is at increased risk. Likewise, in 2017, IBM's AI-powered "Watson" gave very high hopes to oncologists to better diagnose and manage patients suffering from cancer. Physicians of the future will have to hone their skills and competencies so that they can more efficiently organize data and manage patients by using tools that are AI-enabled.

Medical Imaging

Machine learning (ML) was used in diagnostic imaging as early as the beginning of the 1980s [7]. Without using specific programming, ML learns patterns from data and helps in computing algorithms to perform particular tasks in radiology. With AI, radiologists can use automated image analysis to cut short time in diagnosis and determine more precise extent and stage of disease, all of which greatly enhance patient management. This does not mean that machines are going to replace the radiologists who review medical images to identify the source and extent of problems; rather, the AI systems will aid the clinicians by flagging issues that need to be looked at with more precision [7]. For example, using AI-based algorithms in reviewing the medical images of trauma patients would help identify all the injuries and their effect on underlying tissues with great accuracy that would result in better patient outcomes. AI-based algorithms can easily detect a subtle alteration in images. AI-equipped tools and machines are more likely to identify minor and hairline fractures that can be very easily missed on standard images.

Deep learning (DL), a class of ML methods, can lead to major improvements in how complex tasks in imaging are handled traditionally. These traditional procedures are time-consuming and require skilled manpower. An end-to-end approach can be applied by DL, delivering a wholesome functional solution. For example, machines have been taught to read retinal scans (for example, Google's DeepMind), and their reports are as competitive and accurate if not better than an experienced junior doctor.

Diagnostic Pathology

The two key elements of pathology specialty, namely, image and data analysis, are pertinent to AI, ML, and DL. As most of the final diagnosis is made by pathologists, they are also known as "The Doctor's doctor." The important aim of AI in pathology is to design innovative image analysis tools and systems which can be helpful for diagnostic support or to help in understanding the pathophysiology of diseases in a novel way. In addition to those achieved by pathologists by extensively using unbiased image-based algorithms [8]. Some of the areas where early and encouraging the use of AI has been done include tumor detection, automated tumor grading, immunohistochemistry scoring, blood test analysis, and predicting mutation status, although it is still very early to draw any specific and concrete conclusions [9]. The common use of digital imaging in pathology practice, particularly in high throughput scanning devices and whole slide imaging technology, produces high-quality diagnostic images.

Precision Medicine

Traditionally, healthcare facilities have concentrated on generalized solutions that can help in managing a large number of sick people with similar signs and symptoms. Modern AI-augmented healthcare will enable physicians to analyze enormous amounts of data to appropriately indicate ideal treatment for a specific patient. For example, AI-enabled machines can help to sift through thousands of mutations in a cancer patient to zero in on mutations that have triggered cancer growth. Capabilities like these will enable a selection of specific and targeted therapies instead of the less effective traditional generalized approach in treating cancer patients [10].

Precision medicine is "a rapidly emerging new approach for diagnosis and management including treatment and preventive measures that consider lifestyle, dietary habits, differences of genes and environmental factors for each person" [11]. This approach will help physicians, researchers, and pharmaceutical companies to cater to the therapeutic and preventive needs of a particular group of patients with a specific disease more precisely and accurately and avoid generalized strategies. The purpose of "precision medicine" is to use large multivariable and multidimensional databank that identify subtle differences in genes and their phenotypic expressions, tailor diagnostic modalities, therapeutic requirement needs, preventive measures, and predict prognosis [12]. This offers health care providers a unique opportunity to plan early interventions and therapy accurately— whether treatment or preventative—for every patient individually [13].

Population Medicine

AI allows healthcare and public health organizations to integrate and analyze large volumes of healthcare data to identify more effective disease prevention methods for groups of people. With capabilities like deep learning (DL), AI is uniquely capable of identifying the patterns and trends in disparate datasets to help physicians and policymakers understand the needs of a population [14]. In July 2019, the Geisinger health system announced that it would help artificial intelligence identify patients who are predisposed to chronic disease and provide them preventive advice and care at the population level [15]. This would immensely help people who carry a significant risk of developing a high-burden disease.

Legal and Ethical Challenges

Besides learning the skills of AI-augmented healthcare, it is also important for HCPs to understand and address the ethical and legal issues associated with it. An important question that needs to be addressed is, "how do we ensure that AI algorithms are of high quality and that they are safe for the patients?" This is an important concern since users cannot provide a logical explanation for how a given output is reached by a specific algorithm [16]. Implicating liabilities to AI algorithms is challenging because, as authors [17] explained, the "focus of laws and the base on which legal doctrines are erected is human conduct". Hence, the application of legalities on "the conduct of AI may not stand valid in a court of law." A very challenging solution had been proposed by David Vladeck, who stated that if some injury or mishappening occurs due to AI algorithms, then all parties that were involved in the working and implementation of the algorithm should together take responsibility instead of blaming a specific entity. Another reasonable solution is that just like physicians get themselves insured against lawsuits, AI machines in the future may need to be insured against lawsuits during the course of delivery of healthcare services.

A Need to 'Reboot' Medical Education

Authors [18] stated that perhaps medical education had reached another 'Flexnerian moment. 'A century ago, Abraham Flexner had studied the status of medical education in U.S. and its impact on medical practice. His report about the 'lack of modern science in medicine' had led to the closure of 50 percent of medical schools in the U.S. With the un-doubtable advantages of AI based medical practice, the question that arises is, are our HCPs trained to be able to use the information and intelligence tools? Because medical education still follows the traditional system in most parts of the world [19] [20] [21] [22] [23], the answer to the question is 'perhaps not'! [24] reported that medical students needed to be upskilled to leverage health care information technology (HCIT); however, the curriculum and pedagogy are inadequate. A study conducted in the year 2018 among medical students in Germany found "that 68 percent were not aware of the specific technologies and methods being used in radiology AI" [25]. [26] reported that medical schools should include courses in computer education to facilitate computing collaborations for the development of technology in healthcare. Apart from technical training, soft-skills training for a physician in areas such as emotional intelligence, leadership and communication will also become very important for handling patients in the AI era as these skills are not easy for machines to take [19] [21] [23] [27].

There is a need felt to bring in transformative changes, or in other words, a 'reboot' of medical education is required, for HCPs to cope with the quantum leaps in technological advancements. Contemporary medical training needs to focus on imparting knowledge, skills, and ability that will help align humans and machines. There is no doubt that expertise in medical sciences and its clinical application lies and should continue to lie at the core of medical education. However, the modern curriculum should also train HCPs to offer treatment with cutting-edge precision in a data-driven environment where human intelligence can leverage artificial intelligence. Training in information technology, ML, robotics, and soft skills should be integrated into modern medical education. Physicians in the future will need to possess a repertoire of skills to leverage AI in Healthcare. Besides mastering medical science subjects, they would also need to know subjects such as Mathematics, Statistics, Computer Programming, fundamentals of AI and ML, and ethical-legal issues related to it [28].

Between the years 2000 to 2015, 15 national reports had highlighted the need for reforms in American medical education [29]. A joint report by the European Union's EIT Health discussed how AI could lead to improvement in healthcare processes and outcomes. It also reported that AI could enhance the efficiency of care delivery by HCPs and improve healthcare systems to provide services to a larger population. Authors [30] reported that "The most critical challenge is how we can transform the health care data into additional values for precision medicine, preventive medicine, and predictive modeling". Training in areas of healthcare data capturing and processing is thus very critical for HCPs belonging to the present and future 'big data era. Learners, thus, not only need to have basic knowledge of how data is "aggregated, analyzed, and ultimately personalized in health care delivery through artificial intelligence applications" but should also know how to manage applications embedded in either decision support software (DSS), robots or even social media apps [21]. Researchers have also reported the need to have AI augmented self-learning platforms and the integration of ML courses with clinical courses [22] [31]. It is thus concluded from the review of literature, that curriculum reforms are the need of the hour to equip medical students and practicing HCPs with the necessary skills to utilize the vast possibilities offered by intelligence tools and information platforms.

According to Han et al. [32], medical education needs to become aligned with the radical changes in healthcare technologies and suitably train students in a computer-networked world. Doctors go through extensive periods of exhaustive training and examinations before they can become licensed physicians [32]. Over the last couple of decades, there have been major medical training and teaching changes in terms of training and teaching; however, medical education even today follows the traditional curriculum and examination patterns. The key skills that these curricula focus on are similar in most countries, although the duration of training differs between countries [33]. There is less time invested in training medical students or residents to integrate AI and healthcare, process digital healthcare submissions, and familiarize them with telemedicine [23]. The 2018 meeting of the American Medical Association (AMA) indicated positive changes in medical education with the adoption of AMA's first policy on augmented intelligence. A move that encouraged teachers and research scientists to study how AI could be integrated with medical education [34].

Another very important aspect of resident and physician training, which is currently lacking in medical education in many colleges, is working with electronic health records (EHRs). EHRs are a storehouse of very precious information but are currently only being used in many countries as a replacement for pen and paper writing. It has many benefits, such as saving time, enhancing patient safety, and implementation of AI in the healthcare sector. Getting trained in how to input unbiased and relevant data into EHR is essential towards the building of algorithms for AI and ML. However, given the challenges of implementing electronic patient records, there is a need to understand physicians' inhibitions and appreciate the need for the successful integration of these technologies in their daily practice. The medical curriculum and CME's of undergraduate medical students, resident doctors, and physicians currently do not include training on the use of EHR's. Introductory courses on the maintenance of EHRs may be introduced at the beginning of clinical training.

AI in Medical Education: A Snapshot

Several institutes and universities have initiated the integration of AI in healthcare. Some of these are collaborative projects involving medical students/resident doctors and data experts to create healthcare technologies, summer courses for medical students, assignments based on solving healthcare problems with ML knowledge, and introductory courses in ML for undergraduate medical students. For example, at the Dell Medical School, the University of Texas, training in soft skills has been added to the curriculum, while activity in basic sciences has been reduced [35]. The Illinois Model for Medical Education at 'The Carle Illinois College of Medicine in Urbana Champaign' boasts of being a pathbreaker in the field of undergraduate medical education. Their program focuses on four areas spanning four years of medical education, namely, "basic sciences, clinical sciences, engineering and innovation, and medical humanities" [36]. Several institutions that have initiated studies in AI-supported medical education have been listed in Table 1. Continuing education programs/conferences/events based on AI-supported healthcare subjects have been organized by top global medical schools and societies such as Massachusetts Medical Society, Radiological Society of North America, Mayo Clinic, University of Pittsburgh School of Medicine, National Academy of Medicine (NAM), and Healthcare Information and Management Systems Society.

Table 1. Artificial Intelligence in Medical Education

S. No.	Institutions
1.	The Xiangya Hospital, Central South University, Changsha, China, Laboratory in health information technology
2.	Proposed satellite life sciences campus of Indian Institute of Technology, Delhi in Jajjhar (Haryana) in association with All India Institute of Medical Sciences (AIIMS), New Delhi
3.	emlyon business school, France, Health Management and Data Intelligence (PG Course)
4.	Johns Hopkins University, The Machine Learning and Healthcare Lab, Biomedical Engineering department
5.	The Human Diagnosis Project, a partnership of the American Medical Association, the American Board of Medical Specialities, and multiple academic centers
6.	The Carle Illinois College of Medicine in Urbana Champaign, the first engineering-based college of medicine.
7.	Harvard Medical School, Department of Biomedical Informatics
8.	Duke Institute for Health Innovation, Incubator for health technology innovation
9.	The Sharon Lund Medical Intelligence and Innovation Institute (MI3) at Children's Hospital of Orange County (CHOC)
10.	Massachusetts Institute of Technology, The College of Artificial Intelligence
11.	University of Florida, Radiology Department
12.	New York University (NYU) Langone Health, Center for Healthcare Innovation & Delivery Science.
13.	Stanford University Center for Artificial Intelligence in Medicine and Imaging
14.	Stanford school of Medicine, Center for Professional Development
15.	University of Virginia, Center for Engineering in Medicine
16.	The Michener Institute of Education at UHN, Canada
17.	University of Toronto's elective, Computing for Medicine certificate course.

Tighter Integration of Medical Education

Training of existing medical teaching faculty and practicing specialists in AI applications in healthcare and soft skills are important requirements for the future workforce. Besides bringing reforms in medical college/school subjects curricula, the entire medical education field needs to have an integrated focus towards skill-building in AI-augmented healthcare across all stages of education. Courses in pre-medical, UG, PG, Super specialization, and continuing education need a tighter integration. A systematic approach towards educating medical students throughout their journey was suggested by [22]. Based on our review of the literature, some stage-wise recommendations have been listed in Table 2.

Table 2. Stage-wise recommendations for medical education

S. No.	Stage	Recommendations
1.	Class 12 pre-medical course	Courses in Statistics, Mathematics, Soft Skills, and Computer programming along with traditional subjects; Student group projects based on AI in healthcare
2.	Medical College Entrance Examinations	Questions in Mathematics, Statistics, Programming and Soft Skills along with Traditional Subjects
3.	Undergraduate Medical Students	Knowledge about medical data sets, electronics health records (EHR); Fundamentals of AI and ML; Basic soft skills courses in Emotional Intelligence, Communication and Leadership
4.	Post-graduate Medical Students/ Residents	Super-specializations such as AI Augmented Radiology, or Pathology, etc. Collaborative projects with AI scientists; Clinical application of AI in patient care, ethico-legal issues concerning AI in healthcare
5.	Licensing Examinations	Questions on AI in healthcare. EHR, Soft Skills, ethico-legal issues concerning AI in healthcare
6.	Practicing Doctors	Mandatory requirement to earn credits through AI in healthcare courses, Soft-skills courses and participation in AI in healthcare conferences, ethico-legal issues concerning AI in healthcare
7.	Medical College Faculty	Mandatory requirement to be certified in AI in healthcare courses and Soft Skills courses; Mandatory participation in AI in healthcare conferences

Mitigating Apprehension

One of the first misconceptions that need to be alleviated from the minds of healthcare stakeholders is that AI is a "job-killer" or that it intends to replace human physicians with robot equivalents. It is essential to do so, as it will help create interest, garner support from HCPs towards the positive progression of the field of AI, and also lead to openness towards getting trained in the required skills. For HCPs across many countries, AI-augmented healthcare is a radically different way of doing their current job, and it should prove to be a better way. It is an augmentation to the clinical skill or judgemental power like a pathologist or radiologist, who reviews hundreds of images daily and makes very important and critical decisions about each one. AI is not expected to take over that process but is expected to enhance and streamline workflow and provide additional guidance to make a good radiologist/ pathologist into a better radiologist/ pathologist. For instance, pathologists have used AI to reduce errors in detecting cancerous lymph nodes (from 3.4% to 0.5%) [37]. By helping identify high-risk patients, AI can assist surgeons and radiologists in reducing the rate of breast-conserving surgery by 30% in patients whose biopsies were initially considered high-risk lesions but were ultimately found to be non-cancerous after surgical removal. AI can help predict surgical site infections (SSI) by building models that incorporate multiple data sources such as diagnostic reports and prescriptions, thus, helping inpatient care in a big way [38]. AI can also provide support during surgery by enabling the surgeon to look for bleeders. Thus, AI and ML in healthcare can catch critical issues that may otherwise fall through the crack and so would enhance the work of HCPs rather than replace him or them; it is a safety net that would support HCPs, and hence would be welcomed by them.

Conclusion

For the better care of patients, HCPs need to possess the skills to leverage the benefits of AI technology. Working with AI systems in healthcare that support clinical decision-making will be a critical requirement in the future. Healthcare systems worldwide need to adapt and scale up AI-based medical practice as it would help alleviate the shortage of human resources. AI-augmented healthcare systems can significantly reduce the pressure on healthcare systems across the world. The new frontiers opened by AI in healthcare will greatly benefit the world population. Physicians in the future will thus need to possess a repertoire of skills to leverage AI in healthcare. HCPs must possess knowledge of their fields of medicine and the ability to work on data platforms to improve patient care. At present, HCPs are not equipped to leverage the benefits provided by AI technologies. That is mainly because medical education systems, worldwide, still mostly focus on traditional subjects and pedagogy for training future practitioners.

As medical students are not exposed to the integration of AI technology with medical practice during their course of study, this gap in training results in a workforce unable to bring about a skilful interaction between artificial and human intelligence.

Besides developing technical knowledge, HCPs need to be made aware of the ethical-legal implications of the use of AI in healthcare. They should also be trained in social skills as machines will not be able to learn easily, competencies such as leadership, emotional intelligence, and communication. Curriculum and pedagogy reforms are hence the need of the hour so that medical students and practicing HCPs are equipped with the necessary skills to utilize the vast possibilities offered by intelligence tools and information platforms. Though several institutes and universities have initiated the integration of AI in healthcare, such initiatives collectively can be described as nascent. The huge gap that still exists needs to be addressed through reforms in medical education and pedagogy and tighter integration between all stages of education of HCPs. Courses in pre-medical, UG, PG, super-specialization, and continuing education need to be integrated to focus on skill-building in AI-augmented healthcare across all stages of education. Before policy-makers consider implementing the recommendations stated in this study, it is very important to study the apprehensions that may be in HCPs and find ways to alleviate them as it would lead to support from HCPs towards the positive progression of the field of AI in healthcare.

References

[1] Turing, A. M. (1950). *Computing Machinery and Intelligence, Mind*, Volume LIX, Issue 236, October, Pages 433–460, https://doi.org/10.1093/mind/LIX.236.433.

[2] West, D. M. & Allen, J. R. (2018). *How artificial intelligence is transforming the world*. From: https://www.brookings.edu/ research/how-artificial-intelligence-is-transforming-the-world/ [accessed 2021-02-14].

[3] Lewis-Kraus G. (2016). The Great AI Awakening. *New York Times*.

[4] WHO (2019). *Health workforce*. Accessed on 09 February 2021. who.int/health-topics/health-workforce.

[5] Hariman, Keith, Antonio Ventriglio. & Dinesh Bhugra. (2019). "The future of digital psychiatry." *Current psychiatry reports*, 21.9 1-8.

[6] Barrett, M., Boyne, J., Brandts, J., et al. (2019). "Artificial intelligence supported patient self-care in chronic heart failure: a paradigm shift from reactive to predictive, preventive and personalised care". *The EPMA journal*, *10*(4), 445–464. doi.org/10.1007/s13167-019-00188-9.

[7] Hosny, A., Parmar, C., Quackenbush, J., et al. (2018). "Artificial intelligence in radiology". *Nat Rev Cancer.*, *18*, 500–10.

[8] Aeffner, F., Zarella, M. D., Buchbinder, N., et al. (2019). Introduction to Digital Image Analysis in Whole-slide Imaging: A White Paper from the Digital Pathology Association. *Journal of pathology informatics*, *10*, 9. https://doi.org/ 10.4103/jpi.jpi_82_18

[9] Serag, A., Ion-Margineanu, A., Hammad Qureshi, A., et al. (2019). "Translational AI and Deep Learning in Diagnostic Pathology" *Frontiers in Medicine.*, *6*, A185. doi.org/10.3389/fmed.00185

[10] Nagarajan, N., Yapp, E., Le, N., et al. (2019). Application of Computational Biology and Artificial Intelligence Technologies in Cancer Precision Drug Discovery. *BioMed research international*, Vol *2019*, 1-15. doi.org/10.1155/2019/8427042

[11] Bertalan Masko. (2017) "The role of artificial intelligence in precision medicine". *Expert review of Precision medicine and drug development.*, *2*(5), 239-241.

[12] Bodein, A., Chapleur, O., Droit, A. & Lê Cao, K. A. (2019). A Generic Multivariate Framework for the Integration of Microbiome Longitudinal Studies with Other Data Types. *Frontiers in genetics.*, *10*, 963. doi.org/10.3389/fgene.2019.00963.

[13] Kermany, D. S., et al. (2018) "Identifying medical diagnoses and treatable diseases by image-based deep learning". *Cell.*, *172*, 1122–1131.

[14] Alotaibi, Sultan Refa. (2020). "Applications of artificial intelligence and big data analytics in m-health: a healthcare system perspective." *Journal of Healthcare Engineering*, *2020*.

[15] Mikhailov, D. & Perrin, N. (2019). Why we can't leave AI in the hands of Big Tech [Internet]. *The Guardian*. 2019 [cited 11 January 2019]. Available from: https://www.theguardian.com/ science/2017/nov/03/why-we-cant-leave-ai-in-the-hands-of-big-tech.

[16] Sullivan, H. R. & Schweikart, S. J. (2019). "Are Current Tort Liability Doctrines Adequate for Addressing Injury Caused by AI?" *AMA Journal of Ethics.*, *21*, (2), E160-166.

[17] Bathae, Y. (2018). "The artificial intelligence black box and the failure of intent and causation". *Harv J Law Technol.*, *31*(2), 889-938.

[18] Masys, D. R., Jarvik, G. P., Abernethy, N. F., Anderson, N. R., Papanicolaou, G. J., Paltoo, D. N., Hoffman, M. A., Kohane, I. S. & Levy, H. P. Technical desiderata for the integration of genomic data into Electronic Health Records. *J Biomed Inform.*, 2012 Jun, 45(3), 419-22. doi: 10.1016/j.jbi.2011.12.005. Epub 2011 Dec 27. PMID: 22223081; PMCID: PMC3328607.

[19] Imran, N. & Jawaid, M. (2020). Artificial intelligence in medical education: Are we ready for it? *Pak J Med Sci.*, 2020, *36*(5), 857-859. doi.org /10.12669/pjms .36.5.30.

[20] Wartman, S. A. & Combs, C. D. (2019). Medical Education Must Move From the Information Age to the Age of Artificial Intelligence, *AMA J Ethics*, Feb 1, *21*(2), E146-152. doi: 10.1001/amajethics.2019.146.

[21] Wartman, S. A. & Combs, C. D. (2019). Reimagining medical education in the age of AI. *AMA J Ethics.*, 2019, *21*(2), E146-E152.

[22] Kolachalama, V. B. & Garg, P. S. (2018). Machine learning and medical education. *NPJ Digit Med*, *1*, 54.

[23] Paranjape, K., Schinkel, M., Nannan Panday, R., Car, J. & Nanayakkara, P. (2019). Introducing Artificial Intelligence Training in Medical Education. *JMIR Med Educ*, 5(2), e16048. doi: 10.2196/16048PMID: 31793895PMCID: 6918207.

[24] Wald, Hedy, S., George, Paul, Reis, Shmuel P. & Taylor, Julie Scott (2014). Electronic Health Record Training in Undergraduate Medical Education, *Academic Medicine*, March - Volume *89* - Issue 3, p 380-386 doi: 10.1097/ ACM.0000000000000131.

[25] Pinto dos Santos, D., Giese, D., Brodehl, S., et al. (2018). Medical Students' Attitude towards Artificial Intelligence: A Multicentre Study. *Eur Radiol.*, July. Published ahead of print. doi: 10.1007/s00330-018-5601-1.

[26] Law, M., Veinot, P., Campbell, J., et al. (2018). Computing for Medicine: Can We prepare Medical Students for the Future? *Acad Med.*, November. Published ahead of print. doi: 10.1097/ACM.0000000000002521.

[27] World Economic Forum Report (2020). How do we upskill a billion people by 2030? Leadership and collaboration will be key. Retrieved from: https://www.weforum.org/agenda/2020/01/2025-leadership-collaboration-skills-training.

[28] Park, S. H., Do, K., Kim, S., Park, J. H. & Lim, Y. (2019). What should medical students know about artificial intelligence in medicine? *J Educ Eval Health Prof*, 16, 18 [FREE Full text] [doi: 10.3352/jeehp.2019.16.18] [Medline: 31319450].

[29] Beck, M. (2015). Innovation is sweeping through U.S. medical schools. Wall St J. February 16, https://www.wsj.com/articles/ innovation-is-sweeping-through-u-smedical- schools-1424145650. Accessed February 9, 2021.

[30] Yang, C. C. & Veltri, P. (2015). Intelligent healthcare informatics in big data era. *Artif Intell Med.*, *65*, 75–77. doi: 10.1016/j.artmed.2015.08.002.

[31] Beam, A. L. & Kohane, I. S. (2016). Translating artificial intelligence into clinical care. *JAMA*, *316*, 2368–2369.

[32] Han, Eui-Ryoung., et al. "Medical education trends for future physicians in the era of advanced technology and artificial intelligence: an integrative review." *BMC medical education*, *19*.1, (2019): 1-15.

[33] Weggemans, M. M., van Dijk, B., et al. (2017). "The postgraduate medical education pathway: an international comparison". *GMS J Med Educ.*, 34(5), Doc63.

[34] American Medical Association (2019). Augmented intelligence in health care, https://www.ama-assn.org/system/files/2019-01/augmented-intelligence-policy-report.pdf [accessed 2021-02-10]

[35] Johnston, S. C. (2018). Anticipating and training the physician of the future: the importance of caring in an age of artificial intelligence. *Acad Med*, 2018 Aug, *93*(8), 1105-1106. [doi: 10.1097/ACM.0000000000002175] [Medline: 29443717].

[36] The Carle Illinois College of Medicine (2021). *Paradigm-Shifting Curriculum: An innovative curriculum designed for innovative students*. Retreived from https://medicine.illinois.edu/education/ paradigm-shifting-curriculum/.

[37] Wang, D., Khosla, A., Gargeya, R., et al. (2016). "Deep learning for identifying metastatic breast cancer". arXiv:1606.05718.

[38] Soguero-Ruiz, C., Fei, W. M., Jenssen, R., et al. (2015). "Data-driven Temporal Prediction of Surgical Site Infection". *AMIA Annu Symp Proc.*, *2015*, 1164-1173.

Part 2. Artificial Intelligence and Machine Learning in Healthcare

Chapter 8

Healthcare Sector and Use of Artificial Intelligence Technology in Modern Times

Kush Kalra* **and Pradeep Kulshrestha**
Sharda University, India

Abstract

There has been an increase in the present days regarding the accumulated health information comprising medical, hereditary, and ecological data. Each day, healthcare experts, researchers and patients generate an enormous quantity of records from a range of machines. These comprise Health Records in Electronic Form and smartphone apps that keep an eye on patient wellbeing. Artificial Intelligence (AI) technologies using instrument education algorithms and computational command have the most superior capability to attain information and give an ideal result to the receiver. Everyday checks thereby help to make full-size information to identify a behavioural outline about fitness condition to estimate with uppermost numerical accuracy based on full-size data capturing and extensive scale samples. Artificial Intelligence thereby makes it clear to evaluate the nexus between avoidance and treatment and patient results in every diagnosis and treatment phase. Many hospitals are looking for AI solutions to sustain and execute operational schemes to enhance accuracy and price efficiency. For disabled patients and patient care, the use of robotics has been preferred. AI will engage increasingly over the subsequent times in the association between hospitals and patients, and it must be bound by core moral values and high regard for patients.

* Corresponding Author's Email: krrish.kush@gmail.com.

In: Industry 4.0 and Intelligent Business Analytics for Healthcare
Editors: Soumi Dutta, Vinod Kumar Shukla, Shruti Nagpal et al.
ISBN: 978-1-68507-602-3

Keywords: health, patient, disease, doctor, technology, science, etc.

Introduction

A limb of computer science, Artificial Intelligence (AI), is devoted to forming systems that execute works and that frequently need human intelligence, with diverse technological approaches. An enormous quantity of information can be reclaimed from electronic records, which could barely be scrutinized, investigated, or understood using traditional data-processing techniques. Extensive data comprise smart handsets appliances, social media, and uniform electronic well-being records [1]. The most appealing data types are the medicinal images, such as those acquired through x-ray and ultrasound tests with the elevated prospect for research and scientific applications amongst the fitness data. Radiologists, being the initiators of medicine, can now admit Artificial Intelligence as a fresh associate in their job, along with a possibility for an elevated responsibility of radiology in healthcare [2].

Drug innovation is a prolonged and expensive procedure, and therefore, any technology proficient in advancing the competence of drug growth is always desirable. Additionally, facilitating companies to process and examine a large quantity of post-market data can denote improved insight into original creative works in the actual scenario and advance information and exactness of treatment options. This technical progress may bring about necessary lawful and regulatory strategy confrontations given the segment is a highly synchronized view of the convergence of physical, biological and mathematical sciences. Artificial intelligence in the health sector uses various algorithms to estimate human cognition while analyzing complex medicinal information. Artificial Intelligence is the aptitude for algorithms to estimate conclusions based on structures with no straight human contribution.

Unprecedented access to healthcare: The ease of use of the web and a cultural want to self-regulate with many fitness concerns expand healthcare access. Amid increasing healthcare expenses and many fitness concerns, persons with the help of buyer electronics are executing extra medicinal actions independently.

For instance, for the discovery of cancer, there are quite a few applications available that allow a person to utilize their smartphone to identify a high likelihood of cancer merely by taking an image of the affected part [3]. UM-Skin CheckApp is a skin cancer discovery application invented at Michigan University and accessible at no cost to the general community [4]. Based on artificial intelligence ("AI"), these applications typically work on infrastructure, usually fixed to power superior computing apps, like those that can identify cancer.

In skin tumour/diseases diagnosis, Artificial Intelligence may be superior to your medical doctor at detecting skin cancer [5]. Artificial Intelligence has been placed to resolve the most complex health challenges due to its remarkable ability to recognize likelihood for relational data sets. Artificial Intelligence can drop treatment-at-home costs, improve lifetime value, and transform at-home care for adults [6]. Further, it (AI) can advance treatment processes for rural private clinics/hospitals, whose patients may not contact experts [7]. AI can also mechanize some healthcare responsibilities, releasing busy doctors to focus entirely on multifarious cases [8]. It can permit better value of life by providing relief to patients from time-consuming responsibilities, such as supervising diabetes.

Artificial Intelligence in Healthcare

In today's current scenario, healthcare has changed a lot from the past. In 1991, no one even knew about the World Wide Web but now, in 2019, Artificial Intelligence technology is impacting the lives of the human generation. With healthcare-related Artificial Intelligence predicted to be a $200 billion business by 2025, consumers are dying to get their hands on the latest healthcare applications and technology. Currently, AI healthcare is focusing more on patient outcomes and trying to reduce the cost of medicine. Patients suffer a lot from different kinds of diseases; many doctors are anxious that they are not well prepared to take care of these patients accurately. Therefore, the discoverers and innovators are trying to develop the friendliest patient approach.

Novel Artificial Intelligence technology assists in gathering statistics for scientific study using electronic wellbeing records from patients from corner to corner of the nation [9]. Based on patient evidence, there are programs for recognizing effective treatment. Data is necessary for a highly receptive Artificial Intelligence for knowledgeable medical choice. To lessen manual work and supply additional correct services to the patients, nurses and doctors have initiated accepting technology.

A) *Curing health diseases using artificial intelligence:* In the developing countries, there is also inequality between urban and rural health services, which these days has become a grave difficulty, of which the lack of capable healthcare givers is the main reason for the unavailability and inferiority of healthcare in a rural region. More and more people in rural areas are suffering from diseases that have not been noticed before. Through their findings, a few researchers have shown that the application of computers could hopefully get better healthcare results in rural areas of developing countries.

B) *Use of electronic health records in healthcare systems*: Electronic Health Records have brought planned modifications to the Healthcare Industry. Clinical documentation is one of the most critical areas where much time is invested but with the likelihood of voice acknowledgement also united with NLP, many attempts can be saved. These days, doctors do not even worry about cases where drug overdoses or any wrong combinations or allergies are given by chance.

C) *Use of virtual health assistance in healthcare systems*: Nowadays, health monitors have Artificial Intelligence included in them. Some of the techniques in which this can occur are:
   - Reminding patients to obtain their medicines at the chosen occasion, also when they are about to run out of medicines and order prescriptions.
   - Remind them of physician actions and administer bookings, allowing online communication with the physician.
   - It is also probable for patients to check medical websites and raise associated health queries.
   - Virtual Mode can by no means replace meeting the doctor physically, but they can at least help ease the pressure and doubts faced by the patient.

Intensive care units are the most intense parts of any hospital. It is a case of life and death and has lots of stress in that environment. As every moment is counted, patients are monitored 24/7 with an army of devices. It has highlighted AI-driven systems to monitor the patients in critical conditions in the ICU around the clock, where they mainly focused on monitoring movements. Researchers had installed some sensors in the patients' room over two months so that they could collect the information and its range about the movements. Algorithms were thereby designed to analyze the data collected and identify when the patient left their bed or returned. It was also able to detect whether the patient was out of his chair or not. AI here could also help the patients guide them when and what to do, especially in critical cases.

Consequence on Healthcare Professionals: Healthcare experts may believe that their independence and power is in danger of Artificial Intelligence confronting their proficiency. Healthcare professionals' moral responsibility towards individual patients might be affected by the utilization of Artificial Intelligence systems. These might be guided by benefits, such as price competence or broader community fitness concern. With the development of many novel technologies, the beginning of Artificial Intelligence is expected to mean the skills and expertise required of healthcare professionals will alter.

Artificial Intelligence could allow the mechanization of tasks that human beings have beforehand carried out in many fields. This could liberate health experts to use extra time engaging straightforwardly with patients. However, there are apprehensions that the opening of Artificial Intelligence systems might be used to rationalize the service of less-skilled employees [10]. This could be difficult if the technology stops working and employees cannot distinguish errors or take up essential responsibilities without computer supervision. A connected apprehension is that Artificial Intelligence could make healthcare experts satisfied and less likely to check outcomes and confront mistakes [11].

Conformity Concerns Occurring from Application of Artificial Intelligence to Medical Technologies

Health check machines and expertise used within the medicinal field frequently are highly controlled. Regulatory authorities aspire to ensure that products are secure and effective and that any data produced in association with the development of the products are precise and can be relied on to notify treatment options. Customers are also concerned that their data are proper compiled, analyzed, and used correctly. The ease of using computer resources combined with advancement in algorithm development currently allows Artificial Intelligence apps to be used in medicinal decision responsibilities with hopeful consequences [12]. Using the Artificial Intelligence method in radiology signifies a pertinent issue for study teams [13].

The extensive eagerness concerning the growth of software based on Artificial Intelligence in radiology is shown by the highly optimistic tendency of books/magazines in the last ten years. However, some moral disputes are clear-cut and need to be protected against. One of them is the apprehension that algorithms might reflect human beings' prejudice in result creation.

Application of AI in non-medical fields has been shown to make difficult results that replicate prejudices intrinsic in the data used to teach AI [14]. Also, Volkswagen's algorithm permits motor vehicles to circumvent emissions tests by dipping their nitrogen oxide release when used [15]. Private segment designers who make Artificial Intelligence algorithms for scientific utilization could focus on such programming to users toward clinical dealings that would produce enlarged earnings for their buyer. However, it will not essentially replicate improved care. These instances show the importance of grave guidelines and rule intervention about utilizing Artificial Intelligence.

Liability and Responsibility of Artificial Intelligence Medical Devices: There are additional legal repercussions of Artificial Intelligence and its use, whether in healthcare or elsewhere, along with the fundamental guideline and data protection. One of these is answerability. When perplexing issues are connected with pathologic entities, errors in Artificial Intelligence occur mainly in the preparation of data sets rather than an actual cypher of illness. When Artificial Intelligence devices decide, their choice is based on the composed data and the algorithms. [16]. Even if they imitate the human brain's neural system, Artificial Intelligence devices think differently than human beings. Better, they think more rapidly and precisely [17]. Humans are not capable of processing all of these and considering them to formulate a choice, and there is an enormous figure of possibility in each given situation.

While Artificial Intelligence systems can think about every possible scenario and every deliberation, humans consider what is in their brains [18]. Artificial intelligence is incredibly changeable and is designed to study from actual knowledge. Will the maker be neglectful for not having predicted what has been explained as unpredictable?

Conclusion

Over the subsequent years, AI will play an increasingly important role as the association between doctors and patients [19] grows. It will need to be bound by moral principles, such as beneficence and high opinion for patients [20]. We should remember that the radiologist is beyond just a predictor of reports only. The duty of a working radiologist also comprises stating of conclusions, education and a lot of additional duties that cannot be carried by computer programs [21]. One can dispute that Artificial Intelligence might, at least in the future, be able to do health sector/physicians jobs. However, human communication and understanding by a doctor and a patient stay an essential element and challenging too.

References

[1] Artificial intelligence in precision cardiovascular medicine, National Library of Medicine, https://pubmed.ncbi.nlm.nih.gov/28545640/ visited on 5th feb, 2021.

[2] https://www. medscape.com/viewarticle/863127, accessed on 10th Feb, 2021.

[3] Nicole Galan, How Effective Are Skin Cancer Apps for Early Detection?, Medicalnewstoday (2019), Accessed on: 24 May 2021, https://www. medicalnewstoday.com/articles/285751#popularskin-cancer-apps.

[4] Rogel Cancer Center, Michigan Medicine, UM SkinCheck App (2020), Accessed on: 24 May 2021, https://www.rogelcancercenter.org/skin-cancer/melanoma/ prevention/app.

[5] Gigen Mammoser, AI May Be Better at Detecting Skin Cancer Than Your Derm, *Healthline* (JUNE 11, 2018), Accessed on: 24 May 2021, https://www.healthline.com/ health-news/ai-may-be-better-at-detecting-skincancer-than-your-derm#1.

[6] Shourjya Sanyal, *How Is AI Revolutionizing Elderly Care*, FORBES (Oct. 31, 2018), Accessed on: 24 May 2021, https://www.forbes.com/sites/shourjyasanyal/ 2018/10/31/how-is-ai-revolutionizing-elderlycare/#61b5a 239e07d.

[7] Nicholson Price II W., Medical AI and Contextual Bias, HARV. J.L. & TECH 1, 18 (forthcoming, 2019). 8 Thomas Davenport & Ravi Kalakota, The Potential for Artificial Intelligence in Healthcare, 6 *Future Healthcare Journal* 94, 95-97 (2019).

[8] Kent, Jessica, Artificial Intelligence, Big Data to Improve Diabetes Management, *Health IT Analytics (Aug. 13, 2019),* Accessed on: 24 May 2021, https://healthitanalytics.com/news/artificial-intelligence-big-datato-improve-diabetes -management.

[9] *Use of Artificial Intelligence in Healthcare and Medicine,* https://healthitanalytics.com/news/top-12-ways-artificial-intelligence-will-impact-healthcare accessed on 11th feb, 2021.

[10] Rose, D., & Joshi, N. (2018). The Digital Doctor: Hope, Hype, and Harm at the Dawn of Medicine's Computer Age. *Annals of Emergency Medicine,* 71(1), 154-155.

[11] Lee, J. D., & Seppelt, B. D. (2006). Human factors and ergonomics in automation design. *Handbook of human factors and ergonomics, 3.*

[12] LeCun Y, Bengio Y, Hinton G (2015) Deep learning. Nature 521: 436–444.

[13] Erickson BJ, Korfiatis P, Akkus Z, Kline TL (2017) Machine learning for medical imaging. *Radiographic* 37:505–515.

[14] Char D S, Shah N H, Magnus D (2018) Implementing machine learning in health care - addressing ethical challenges. *N. Engl. J. Med.* 378:981– 983 Char D S, Shah N H, Magnus D (2018) Implementing machine learning in health care - addressing ethical challenges. *N. Engl. J. Med.* 378:981–983.

[15] Angwin J, Larson J, Mattu S, Kirchner L (2016) http://www.propublica. org/article/machine-bias-riskassessments-in-criminal-sentencing.

[16] Scherer M U, Regulating artificial intelligence systems: risks, challenges, competencies, and strategies. *Harv. JLTech.* 29:354–400 (2016).

[17] Castelvecchi D, Can we open the black box of AI? Nature 538:20–23 (2016).

[18] Mnih V, Kavukcuoglu K, Silver D et al, Human-level control through deep reinforcement learning. *Nature* 518:529–533 (2015).

[19] Thierer A, O'Sullivan A, Russel R, *Artificial intelligence and public policy.* Mercatus Research Paper (2017) https://www. mercatus.org/ system/files/ thierer-artificial-intelligence-policy-mrmercatus-v1.pdf.

[20] Char D S, Shah N H, Magnus D, Implementing machine learning in health care - addressing ethical challenges *N. Engl. J. Med.* 378:981–983 (2018).

[21] Russell S, Bohannon J, Artificial intelligence. Fears of an AI pioneer. *Science* 349:252. (2015).

Chapter 9

Prediction of Cardiovascular Diseases Using Data Mining - Machine Learning and Deep Learning System

Aiman Siraj[1,*], Vinod Kumar Shukla[2,†] and Sonia Saini[3,‡]

[1,2]Department of Engineering and Architecture, Amity University, Dubai, UAE

[3]Amity Institute of Information Technology, Amity University, India

Abstract

Inaccurate information is vulnerable. Whether it is in terms of data breaches or being inclined towards inconsistency, redundancy, data noise, and in worst cases missing chunks of data, leaks of data could violate people's privacy and are strictly forbidden by the law. Data can also be manipulated to harm people and can have hazardous outcomes. It is thus essential to make a system that makes it easier to classify data and perform operations simultaneously. So applying filters is essentially a need, but the job becomes more manageable if multiple filters are used. This system is designed to make the process of predicting heart disease easier. Data is manipulated and checked with the existing information learned by the system through both machine learning and deep learning.

* Corresponding Author's Email: aimansiraj84@gmail.com.

† Corresponding Author's Email: vinodkumarshukla@gmail.com.

‡ Corresponding Author's Email: ssani2@amity.edu.

In: Industry 4.0 and Intelligent Business Analytics for Healthcare

Editors: Soumi Dutta, Vinod Kumar Shukla, Shruti Nagpal et al.

ISBN: 978-1-68507-602-3

The data is then filtered through various algorithms, and the output is obtained. The naïve Bayes classification procedure plays a crucial role in developing this system. On the other hand, decision trees help infer a given problem statement and help make the right choice. Neural networks are also used for the same purpose as the above two and help make the correct decisional output. All of this is done systematically to balance data with the right resources. There is an alarming increase in heart diseases reported in a single year. Most of these are symptoms of strokes and shockingly consist of the youth. If a system can make an early prediction of this disease, it could increase the survival rate. There could also be situations where getting a medical diagnosis could not be possible. In these cases, this system can prove to be a great alternative. Getting a complete diagnosis done every time proves costly and takes much time. Some of the data used in the system are constant, so a heart patient can easily refer to his/her previous reports for the data. Other variables that change, like the beating heart rate, blood pressure, can be measured at home. Therefore, this system has proven to be dependable. It is also easy to use and gives quick results. This paper talks about the heart and its structure. It mentions the different types of heart-related diseases and the symptoms of being affected by them. The different procedures used are explained in a detailed manner. The objective and way the system has been used are explained in detail and the implementation of data learning and machine learning.

Keywords: artificial intelligence, data mining, decision trees, deep learning, machine learning, neural networks

Introduction

Health always remains one of our primary concerns as humans. It is almost inevitable to think about it. Heart diseases are one of the most dreaded diseases as they can take a toll on your life. The sooner the disease is predicted in a person, the higher are the chances of survival. One of the organs created and developed first in the embryo is the heart. This happens during the first three weeks where the embryo's size is as close to that of a kidney bean. The mass of a heart is approximately 300 grams in adults. Exercise is shown to increase in size and benefit it. There are many lifestyle factors and choices that significantly impact the heart. Be it food, alcohol or drug consumption, smoking, etc. This disease can first have mild symptoms or no symptoms at all. People do not realize that they are undergoing it unless they suffer from a heart stroke or any major symptom. Multiple methods and techniques are used to predict a heart disease depending on the case's complexity. Diagnosis of the person is made by a familiar cardiologist first, and then depending on the type of heart disease, a senior specialist doctor is recommended. The medical sector is one industry that collects enormous amounts of data every day. Hence sorting the data is very important. This can be done using machine learning algorithms. So the only possible solution would be to use the concept of data mining in our system. This particular field of technology has no end to it. It keeps on updating with time and brings in a variety of new algorithms and techniques to improve the predictive analysis and endless possibilities of concluding. This system works by combining multiple machine learning algorithms for a single purpose that predicts heart-related diseases. The naïve Bayes classification procedure plays a crucial role in developing this system. On the other hand, decision trees help infer a given problem statement and help make the right choice. Neural networks are also used for the same purpose as the others, predicting accurate results. The predicted earlier, the better we can prevent and ward it off. Getting a complete diagnosis done every time is not possible as it proves to be costly and takes much time. Depending on multiple factors, it is not easy to recognize what type of disease a person is diagnosed with. This is why it is to be understood that data mining plays a unique role in investigating these types of data. If a system can make an early prediction of this disease, it could increase the survival rate. In that case, the analysis of the patient can be done immediately, and the disease can be diagnosed; this would save many lives significantly. There could also be situations where getting a medical diagnosis could not be possible. In these cases, this system can prove to be a great alternative. It scans through vast amounts of scattered data, finds a relation between it to make it more sensible and efficient, and collects it as co-related information. It checks for redundancy, noise, and redundant data and provides a better set of data to work on. It also makes the whole process easier and faster, saving much time. Hence, it has a lot of future scopes and can be worked upon in numerous ways.

Literature Review

Heart

The heart is the most requisite organ in the human body. It is made up of muscles and does the job of pumping blood throughout the entire body. This liquid transports all kinds of nutrients and, most importantly, oxygen. Then the unwanted waste in blood like carbon dioxide is sent to the lungs. The size of this organ varies from person to person. It is said to be approximately like the fist and is located on the left side of the body. The positioning is betwixt both the lungs & in the chest's middle portion. It is an essential organ, and its health must be considered at all times as carelessness in these matters could lead to a deadly result [1].

It pumps this vital fluid with a consistent pattern which is decided with the help of special cells present in the SA (Sino-atrial) nodes. This fluid contains all types of nutrients and other minerals to be transported in the body. They are called pacemakers. The circulation is done by contracting its muscles, which results in a current which travels through the rest of its parts. The AV (Atrioventricular) node is responsible for the system of conductivity of a heart that causes this current and corresponds to all the functions in the upper portion of the heart. It is called the AV node because it comprises the area between ventricles and atria and conducts electricity [2].

On the right side, the blood contaminated with carbon dioxide enters from the atrium to the ventricle while going through venae cavae, which then goes to the pulmonary artery and flows to the lung. This is where oxygen is passed, and carbon dioxide is released. While on the left side of the heart, this newly oxygen-supplied blood circulates to the atrium and then to the ventricle. Which is then spread throughout the body after passing through the aorta, and the process continues. Hearts are legitimately one of the first organs formed in the human body and continue to play a vital role in survival. An average of 80 heartbeats is what is said to be found in adults while in a resting period in a single minute. During the 2010's it was found that one of the prevalent causes of death worldwide was heart disease. It accounted for up to 28% of fatalities. Cardiology is a vast subject and challenging to narrow down as there are many cardiovascular diseases. Cardiologists have to diagnose a patient's symptoms thoroughly every single time before arriving at conclusions [3].

Structure of the Heart

The mass of a heart is found to be approximately 300 grams in adults. Exercise is shown to increase the size and benefit it. This is probably why exercise is highly recommended to patients diagnosed with heart disease. Athletes and people who play sports, in general, are known to have good heart health, which is the result of their constant training. It is also known to boost the immune system [4].

Heart Wall

It has three layers: endo -, myo- and epicardium. The pericardium is a double membrane sac that surrounds the wall of the heart. Each of these layers like structure has different types of functions. The cardiac band has a very complex structure and is surrounded by collagen. This complexity is what makes pumping out blood more effective and uncomplicated. The three layers are mainly comprised of two different types of cells. One of which is pacemaking, which is responsible for the heart's electrical phenomena. The others are muscles, which helps in the flexibility of the organ. The cells of the four chambers are 97% constituted by these muscle cells. These cells are made up of special types of protein [4].

Chambers

The heart is divided into four chambers. Atria - comprises of two top chambers. The ventricle comprises two bottom chambers. A cardiac skeleton forms the structure. It has fibrous rings which serve as a base [5].

Valves

Consist of four valves. Their purpose is to separate each chamber. One lies between every atrioventricular path. There is one at the end of every ventricle. Every time the ventricle contracts, the valve is filled with blood [5].

Pericardium

It is a sac-like structure. It covers up the portion around the heart. The outward surface is rather strong and made of fibres. It has lubricant like fluids, which helps maintain the heart's position. It also has anti-infecting properties [6].

Left Heart and Right Heart

Each side contains two chambers, one of which is an Atria and a ventricle. A valve separates these. The right heart is what collects blood from the entire body. Vena cavae veins are responsible for transporting blood to the right heart. On the other end, Pulmonary veins are responsible for bringing in oxygen-rich blood to the left side of the heart. This blood is transferred back from the lungs. The left side of the heart is thicker than the right heart. It exerts more force to pump back the oxygen-rich blood back to the heart and then to the different parts of the body [7].

Blood Circulation and Nerve Supply of the Heart

Coronary circulation achieves several nutrients in the heart cells. It also supplies an adequate amount of oxygen. It is done to remove unwanted and excess substances in the blood. Arteries, veins, different nodes and other vessels participate in this circulation. The blood flow rate depends on how open the heart is. Coronary arteries supply blood to the different parts of the heart. A group of small lymph like branches lies below the base of each of the layers of the heart; these are called plexuses. The plexus is what characterizes the nervous system of the body. Nerves send different types of signals to the heart, initiating various processes. They have a deciding impact on a heart's beating rate. It also affects the way a heart contracts and retreats. There are cardiovascular pairs in the heart's centre, which are the origin of these nerve signals. On the other hand, the cardiac plexus is formed by the network of these particular nerves. One of these nerves is the vagus nerves. It is a long nerve that helps access the parasympathetic nervous system not just to the heart but also to a few other organs. This system helps conserve the heart's energy and slowdowns heart rate. Although the ventricles instead use the sympathetic system. This system keeps the heart prepared in case of any potential hazards [8].

Development of the Heart

One of the organs created and developed first in the embryo is the heart. This happens during the first three weeks where the embryo's size is as close to that of a kidney bean. As time progresses, the rest of the parts of the heart start taking shape. The heartbeat rate increases drastically from the fifth week to the ninth week of embryo development and then drops down to normal. However, no difference in the heartbeat has been noted based on gender before birth. Though in adults, females are known to have a faster heartbeat as their hearts are smaller in size when compared to men [9].

Types of Heart Diseases

These diseases are the reason for the majority of deaths globally. There are many reasons why one could be diagnosed with this disease. However, cases of older people diagnosed are generally higher in number. However, these are not infectious and are rarely passed down due to genetics. There is an alarming increase in heart diseases reported in a single year. Most of these are symptoms of strokes and shockingly consist of the youth. There are many lifestyle factors and choices that significantly impact the heart. Be it food, alcohol or drug consumption, smoking, etc. Food-related choices that people make in their daily lives have a huge impact on their heart health [10].

Cardiomyopathy affects the muscle area and causes it to change abnormally. It expands the surface and enlarges the muscle causing it to become more rigid. It forces it to stop functioning in the usual way [10].

Ischaemic

It is caused in the coronary artery. Fat like substance is covered around it. They block the passage of blood to and from the various parts of the body. This may result in aches in the heart. This could also result in an attack which would then be highly hazardous [10].

Valvular

This disease causes blood to flow in the opposite direction, which may be fatal to the body. It could also cause leaks in different areas of the body. It could also prevent the flow in the required direction; hence. As a result, many body parts would not receive blood. This would eventually lead to the whole body's system crashing [10].

Pericardial

Here, the sack-like structure whose position is around the heart gets swollen up, and in some worse cases, liquid might fill up in this sack. This causes the chest to ache badly, and the pain may get transferred to other parts of the body. The sack could then have a risk of being infected and could pose a problem for the rest of the organ. Although this can be cured in the early stages, it poses difficulties in breathing and can be lethal for health. An important thing to note is that it barely has any symptoms at first [11].

Congenital

This occurs naturally in a person's body. Some people are born with defects in their hearts. They are not standard and result in these types of heart disease. Some of which may be minor, while the others are extremely major. Some naturally have a depression formed in the organ, like a hole. That may cause a few problems but nothing that major. Some affect the vessels of the organ. The impure blood is sent back to the body instead without enriching it with oxygen in a few cases. Complexities arrive when the defects are known to impact multiple parts of the organ. If this is caused during birth, it may stay hidden for an extended period until it finally reveals itself in the later years when the body is fully developed [11].

Arrhythmias

As the name suggests, it is caused by anomalies in how a heartbeats. It is known to have a consistent rhythm. Although at often it might be disturbed by several factors. Eventually, this could lead to a stroke. The chest feels constricted here too. It can take place in different parts of the organ [11].

Failure

This is defined as the inability to pump out a sufficient amount of blood required for the body. At times, the chest may feel constricted, and breathing would become tougher with time. Most of the related heart diseases eventually end up with this. Usually, this would result in the death of the person [11].

Tools and Machines Used for Diagnosis

There are multiple methods and techniques used to predict a heart disease depending on the case's complexity. Diagnosis of the person is conducted by a standard cardiologist first, and then depending on the type of heart disease, a senior specialist doctor is recommended. These methods are used to investigate the defects, abnormalities and other conditions that could pose a problem on the well-being of a person [12].

General Examination

This is done by touching the chest using hands to check for the person's pulse. A stethoscope is also used to listen to the beating rate. It could also be used to check for other indications, such as preventing people's hands and legs to see any internal haemorrhages. The strength of the heartbeat and the way it beats is considered. Any sudden increase or decrease is noted down and checked for unusualities [13].

EchoCG

All normal hearts have two beats in the audible range. One is called "lub," and the other is called "dub." This particular rhythm is different in some hearts, where the sounds might split up into more than two sounds. This type of sound is called murmurs. These indicate that the heart is affected by some kind of disease. It also depends on the highest frequency made by these sounds and how audible they are based on their sound. Although some heart diseases can have a normally beating heart, this method would prove ineffective in these cases [13].

Imaging

These methods are used to see how the organ functions and its size and shape. It is done using multiple techniques, and each of them is assessed and noted down individually, which is then inferred to understand the condition of the heart. The heart is also put under a stress test and checked to respond to those conditions. If any unwanted fluid resides around the organ, we can find it using this particular method. We can also find if there is insufficient oxygen in the blood. If, in any case, the blood is flowing in the opposite direction, then we can immediately find it out [13].

Blood Test

These are key factors in determining a huge number of diseases. Usually, when a person meets with a gouge, the body releases troponin. This could then conclude whether a heart has failed to work or is there any chance of survival. However, the key problem is that it is not very specific. They're generally used to test a person's health and if there are any anomalies present. If there is any risk associated with the organ, it is quick to identify it as it shows abnormal values [13].

Electrocardiogram (ECG)

Several nodes are placed on the body that records how active the organ is electrical. These signals are then traced to check the physical health of the organ. Approximately ten leads are attached to the body, and then the signals are received, and the calculations are performed. In some instances, the heart disease is not detected initially, creating a testing environment. Here the heart is made to go through several abnormal situations where its reactions are then noted, and then observations are made accordingly. If the blood supplied or being given to the heart is not adequate, then this method is excellent at detecting it. Also, the heartbeats are carefully monitored, and their rhythm is analyzed. Sometimes patients are kept under observation for longer than a day. This is done to ensure that all the test results are very consistent and accurate and the details about the heart disease are measured precisely [13].

Symptoms, Causes and Factors Which Are Likely to Cause a Risk

Symptoms

They are nothing but indications of the happenings in the body and could point to the fact of whether a person has a particular disease or not. Here it is important to note that symptoms differ with different types of diseases and may also differ by the gender of the person.

Most of these symptoms would include changing heartbeat pattern, chest aches, discomfort in the chest area, breathing problems and difficulty, fever, nausea, pain in the nearby organs, slow or fast heartbeat, fainting and dizziness, rashes on the skin, or different spots present on the body, swelling of hands and feet, change in skin colour to pale blue or purple, and sudden decrease in weight and lightheadedness. If a person experiences any of these symptoms, they are likely associated with heart disease. Early identification of symptoms could aid the person's treatment, and not just that, they could be saved from undergoing high-end treatments in the future. Usually, patients cannot recognize the symptoms until they undergo a heart stroke, attack, or seizure. In such cases, immediate medical attention should be sought, and all required tests should be performed on the patient [14].

Causes

Like symptoms, causes too differ by the type of disease diagnosed with. There are several causes out of which the most common are unhealthy eating and obesity. Excessive amounts of fat in the body can clog arteries and eventually lead to a stroke. Another prevalent cause would be smoking, as it can cause fatality and damage many organs of the body. Some causes could be natural defects in the organ. They are consuming any form of drugs or alcoholic drinks. Excessively high or low blood pressure is a cause. Excessive consumption of sugar, which also leads to diabetes or low amounts of insulin in the body, could also invoke a stroke in the heart. Caffeine is also a rare cause. In some cases, over-consuming medicines which are prescribed could also prove to be a cause, such as defects in the heart, unhygienic conditions of the body, and infections caused by microorganisms in the body. A disorder in the cells or tissues of the body, drastic changes in the heart structure, which could be caused by ageing, and the list goes on are some of the common causes of experiencing a heart-related disease. Though some causes are still unknown to humankind [15].

Risk Factors

One of the most common risk factors would be the age of a person as the body gets weaker with age and is prone to more diseases, and not just that, the defence mechanism of the body also slows down as time passes by. The gender of a person is also likely to determine the outcome, as it is generally men who get affected by such a disease. However, women are also likely to experience after menopause. Genes and the medical history of ancestors also play a part. An unhealthy diet or a diet that lacks nutrition and smoking are also factors. Variation in a heartbeat and blood pressure and rise in cholesterol levels due to stress and inactivity of the body could also put the heart at risk. Besides these above situations, hygiene is also essential to prevent the heart from being put at risk [15].

Data Mining

It is the way to scan huge chunks of data to find connections, similarities, and repetitive patterns to come up with the most accurate prediction. This particular field of technology has no end to it. It keeps on updating with time and brings in a variety of new algorithms and techniques to improve the predictive analysis and endless possibilities of concluding. Since machines have been developing continuously for the past decades, many operating procedures have changed drastically and demanded the user learn its way of operation. The speed at which data is processed and stored has increased, so naturally, people's work is also different. It is thus essential to find new and improved methods to deal with data constantly [16].

Mining data has become a severe need as the amount of data collected every year becomes twice its size in the next three years. Hence, a system that sorts out relevant data and reduces redundancy is required to develop proper outcomes that are likely to happen. Also, repetitive data would cause much inconsistency during the processing period, which would then become a hassle for the users to then deal with [17].

Different survey questionnaires and several people's inputs are also considered before arriving at a final possible conclusion. Reasons behind past successful projects are deeply analyzed, and the reason for a project not meeting the expectations is also checked. So similar data is organized together and checked for anomalies. Then unknown possibilities are detected and recognized. Any loopholes in the system are detected. This is usually an automatic process and very rarely requires human intervention. It is motivated to find usefulness out of the data collected and make sense out of the data that creates some purpose. It is trying to sort out data intelligently so that there is more than just sorting done. So, the system can then improve accordingly based on these observations [18].

Machine Learning

It is how a machine educates itself about the procedures and happenings by the programs embedded within it and its surroundings and improves the overall user experience with time as it continuously collects and evaluates data regularly. So basically, constant repetitions and patterns in data are observed and noted down automatically in the system's database. Now, this information is used to improve. Future decisions such as a person's likes/dislikes are noted down, then the future recommendations are tuned in according to it, or a customer's shopping cart is analyzed. Similar products that could spike their interest are displayed to them. It could also be used in prediction analysis of data to see the probable outcome of the given input again to enhance the experience vividly and ensure that a user is satisfied with the result [25].

The machine itself does all this; there is no human involvement even in the complicated processes. This concept is derived from artificial intelligence systems and is frequently used with several data mining models. This is generally done with vast amounts of data and has a systematic analysis done regularly, and then the data is worked upon. The key solution here is that the machines can access the data by themselves and interact with the environment, which would be a new learning experience for them [26].

Data can be of numerous forms, and the system needs to be so adaptable that it can work accurately with all kinds of data. Words are considered data, and the meaning behind those repetitions of words is understood and considered. So then, the following actions that are taken by the system are adjusted based on the previous input. It is almost like a customized version based on the user's choice and also decided by it. It is also very fast as it keeps on updating data whilst processing it simultaneously and is pretty accurate for being so fast most of the time. Although you do need a reasonable amount of time to train your machines so that they are efficient in the long run [27]. The following are the five techniques used in the system that is created (Figure 9.1).

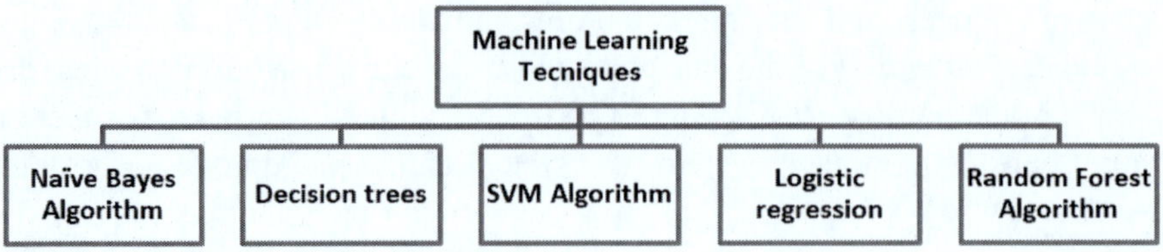

Figure 9.1. Machine learning technique.

Naïve Bayes Algorithm

It is how we can classify data that treats and analyzes each data module in an independent form. It is ideally thought to be different from the rest of the processes and considered a single independent working unit. This technique is generally used in the statistical analysis of extensive data in volume and is harder to sort with multiple classes [19].

Posterior, Likelihood, Prior, Normalizing constant

$$P(A \mid B) = \frac{P(B \mid A)P(A)}{P(B)}$$

$$P(B) = \sum_{Y} P(B \mid A)P(A)$$

Figure 9.2. Image depicting the Naïve Bayes algorithms and it's parameters (M. Wongker et al. 2019).

Here in Figure 9.2, 'P' indicates the probability of each event respectively. 'A' is the initial predictor value, and 'B' is the class value, also called the normalizing constant. The probability of A/B is being predicted, which is the posterior value or the predicted outcome/target. The probability of B/A denotes the likelihood of the event. 'A''s probability is the possible prior outcome of 'A'. Likewise, the probability of 'B' is the possible prior outcome of 'B'. ∑ 'y' is used to indicating the sum of all 'y' values of the dataset for which the probability is being calculated.

Now it is called "naïve" because such a prediction and assumption can never really be accurate, but the uniqueness of this concept is what makes it stand out and valuable. The concepts of probability and statistics are essential components of this algorithm. Although this algorithm is versatile, it is good with languages processed naturally. This whole process is generally speedy and saves much time. It is perfect for data that has been divided into multiple categories. This algorithm is definitely used whenever the concept of machine learning applies to any system. All the calculations are done all the problems to be solved are simplified to the greatest extent possible to maximize the predictions. Each type of data could probably require a different approach and is treated differently and in a unique manner [20].

Decision Trees

These are shaped like a tree and are used consistently in the decision-making process and are used to list all types of possible outcomes, consequences, and functions of a particular system. Usually, it is used with only such statements that have control of the program code and are bounded by a condition. Its working pattern and structure physically are very similar to that of the flowchart. Like any typical tree, it also has leaves, branches, and nodes, and each of them has a different function. The purpose of this model is to reach a conclusion or to solve the key problem [21].

One of the main reasons it is so popular is that it is straightforward to understand that even a person with no knowledge of the system would keep up with the work. Since all types of outcomes are predicted, it is elementary for people to understand the next possible best move or what could be fatal. Although it is tough to update the whole model from time to time, even if a small aspect changes, the whole model can be affected majorly, and if an unnoticeable change occurs, it could be concerning. They are really valuable as they can work well even with a small amount of data that is difficult to decipher. It has to be kept in mind that calculating every move and outcome can become challenging as the data gets more complex [22].

Support Vector Machine Algorithm

This algorithm uses the coordinate dimensions in order to classify data by using a method called "kernel trick." It is not a supervision-based algorithm to work freely without any human intervention. It manipulates data by creating a line between the two coordinates, identifying relations among the data depending on its type, and examining the hyper-planes [24].

Logistic Regression

There is a binary value in this type of classification where the whole system's output is statistically determined based on this value. This value is what the whole calculation and estimation depend on to yield maximum results. This intends to obtain high accuracy when binary values are used and help understand its core concept [22].

Random Forest Classifier Algorithm

This algorithm works on the concept of decision trees. It is like combining multiple trees to form a new structure to give better results than the standard algorithms. This can be used to solve complex problems and falls under the supervision of learning. It is basically like taking an average of all the possibilities and creating a mean value of the result. So the accuracy increases multiple times compared to a standard decision tree system [25].

Deep Learning

It is a part of machine learning but works with real-time data. Its function is very similar to that of a brain, and its job is to evaluate and analyze data for optimal output while making system-related decisions. This particular data would be the input whose output would be based on the choices made by the inputs given through machine learning. It is a way to check the accuracy of a system, and all of this data is collected without any human supervision. And this data is used to make patterns for the betterment of the system. This is also one of the core concepts of artificial intelligence. It usually is implemented with a network of system [28].

Also, a bonus is that since it precisely tries to replicate the processes of the brain, then it can manipulate all sorts of data like voice, text, objects, and different language identification. Any information fed into its database is the type of information that can be easily manipulated. As the world keeps on transforming into a more digital one, we see this particular concept grow deeper along with it, especially with big data. It is also really versatile as it is used in several industrial sectors [29].

The key factor here is being accurate. It has to be precise to give in such detailed and correct outputs as its aim is not just to meet the users' expectations but also to ensure that it accurately gets the job done. It is also really fast, so naturally, the technical components, processors, and other parts also have to be fast to ensure that the system works at its expected speed. The networks here are multi-layered hence why the system is referred to as "deep," which means that every layer is connected, yet the whole process is executed systematically. Also, another point to note is that as the data being worked on keeps on increasing the system's accuracy, it also increases simultaneously, which is why it is so popularly used [30].

Neural Networks

These consist of multiple algorithms that identify, detect and recognize multiple similarities and repetitions in data. It is very similar to how our brain works with, reacts, and processes information. Most people prefer using this decision model because the input keeps changing, and the values are comparatively different. This is one of the main reasons you will not have to design the entire system again. It quickly recognizes connections and patterns between vast chunks of data. It also works on the concept of regression, just as the Naïve Bayes algorithm does [23].

Like the neural network in the body, this also has the concept of nodes connected in several layers like patterns and are used for sending and receiving information. These are mainly used in deep learning and are a core subject. It works on the concept that it can produce some data as output by observing its surroundings and taking it as an input. So when the system is initially taught to configure data and manipulate values, there are sample random values given as input first, and then how the system reacts to the sample data given is checked. Hence, it's considered to be one of the reasons behind the success of artificial intelligence networks [24].

Proposed System through Machine Learning and Deep Learning

Our proposed system would consist of multiple machine learning algorithms to check the output of a given heart patient's details. If the patient is then diagnosed with heart disease depending on the outcome of these algorithms, then a deep learning-based ECG would be done. The classification and segmentation of images would be done in supervision using neural networks.

Software Requirements:

OS: Windows XP and above
Python IDE: python 3.x and above, Jupyter Notebook

Setup tools and pip to be installed for 3.6.x and above
Open source Python tools used are:

- *Numpy* is used to deal with array/matrices and makes it easier to manipulate them.
- *Pandas* is used to interpret and analyze data and provide high-quality performance.
- *Matplotlib. pyplot* – When used, it turns matplotlib into an interface like MATLAB and helps use those features. We are also using the inline feature so that the output is as desired.
- *Seaborn* – It is used to draw a graph and statistical outputs.
- *Warnings* – It is used to address any issues that may cause concern later. We are going to ignore such deprecations by filtering them.

Parameters Used to Achieve the Output

1. Gender of the person (binary value where 1 is male and 0 is female)
2. Age of the person (variable value)
3. A maximum heart rate that can be achieved either by exercise or induced professionally (variable value)
4. Heart rate as a normal or abnormal parameter (3 being normal and 6-7 being defective)
5. Fasting blood sugar of the person (usually greater than 120mg but again a variable value)
6. Resting blood pressure of the person which can be easily checked(variable value)
7. Cholesterol (serum – this checks of the presence certain elements in the body)

8. The type of chest pain a person suffers from (1 being a normal type of angina, 2 being abnormal, 3 being not angina and 4 being a pain that does not have any symptoms)
9. Angina (which is induced by exercise or other physical activities)
10. Number of vessels that are classified as major (Anywhere from 0-3)
11. ECG's resting values (variable 0-2)
12. ST depression which is the output of ECG (the variable value which can also be induced by physical activity)
13. Slope value of ST depression (1 being upwards, 2 being flat and 3 being downwards)

Machine Learning Application Results Explained with Sample Outputs

Data.shape – Basically prints out the number of attributes in terms of rows and columns describing the tabular structure of the data.

Data.isnull().sum() – Checks if the data value is null (to avoid any further computational problem).

data.shape	data.isnull().sum()	y = data["target"]
(332, 14)	age 0 sex 0 cp 0 trestbps 0 chol 0 fbs 0 restecg 0 thalach 0 exang 0 oldpeak 0 slope 0 ca 0 thal 0 target 0 dtype: int64	ax = sns.countplot(data["target"]) target_temp = data.target.value_counts() print(target_temp) 1 186 0 146 Name: target, dtype: int64
DataShape	Null Value check	Target Value check

The next step would be to assign the target value by some variable we are using **'y'** (Target value help us to understand the output). We can check the ratio of male and female patients.

```
countFemale = len(data[data.sex == 0])
countMale = len(data[data.sex == 1])
print("Percentage of Female Patients:{:.2f}%".format((countFemale)/(len(data.sex))*100))
print("Percentage of Male Patients:{:.2f}%".format((countMale)/(len(data.sex))*100))
```

```
Percentage of Female Patients:30.12%
Percentage of Male Patients:69.88%
```

We can also check the random 'n' rows using the head function. This helps us to check any part of the dataset for sampling (Figure 9.3).

```
data.head()
```

	age	sex	chest_pain_type	resting_blood_pressure	cholesterol	fasting_blood_sugar	rest_ecg	max_heart_rate_achieved	exercise_induced_angina	st_depression	st_slope	num_major_vessels	thalassemia	target
0	63	1	3	145	233	1	0	150	0	2.3	0	0	1	1
1	37	1	2	130	250	0	1	187	0	3.5	0	0	2	1
2	41	0	1	130	204	0	0	172	0	1.4	2	0	2	1
3	56	1	1	120	236	0	1	178	0	0.8	2	0	2	1
4	57	0	0	120	354	0	1	163	1	0.6	2	0	2	1

Figure 9.3. Dataset Sampling.

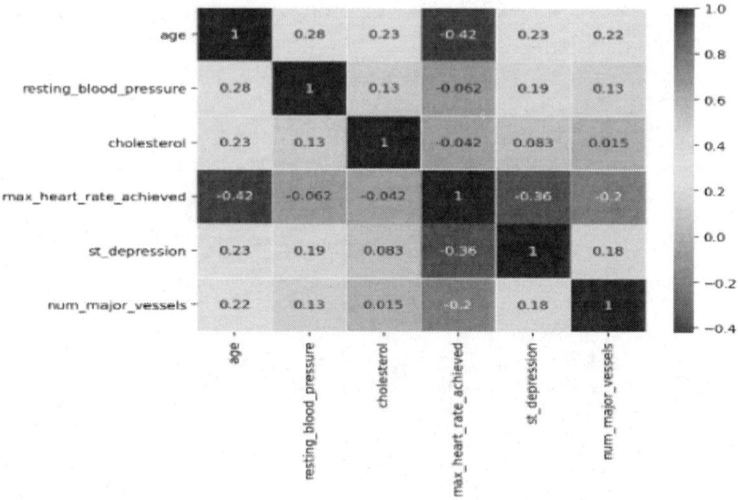

Figure 9.4. Correlation matrix.

We can also create a correlation matrix (Figure 9.4) to check the relation between the parameters and how they depend on each other. A correlation matrix is basically used to identify the relation between all coefficient values to check how they depend on each other and their impact on the dataset. Every cell in the matrix depicts a correlation with the other variable. It is used to present the data summary and serve as an input analytically and help diagnose the data in an advanced way.

We now have to split the data set into training and testing data to make the prediction process easier.

```
X = data.iloc[:, :-1].values
y = data.iloc[:, -1].values
```

```
from sklearn.model_selection import train_test_split
x_train, x_test, y_train, y_test = train_test_split(X,y,test_size = 0.2, random_state = 1)
```

```
from sklearn.preprocessing import StandardScaler
sc = StandardScaler()
x_train = sc.fit_transform(x_train)
x_test = sc.transform(x_test)
```

Now we will individually check the accuracy of each of the five algorithms and see which one yields to be the most accurate one.

```
from sklearn.metrics import classification_report
from sklearn.linear_model import LogisticRegression

m1 = LogisticRegression(random_state=1)
m1.fit(x_train, y_train)

y_p1 = m1.predict(x_test)
print(classification_report(y_test, y_p1))
```

```
              precision    recall  f1-score   support

           0       0.85      0.82      0.84        34
           1       0.82      0.85      0.84        33

    accuracy                           0.84        67
   macro avg       0.84      0.84      0.84        67
weighted avg       0.84      0.84      0.84        67
```

Logistic regression:
Accuracy 84%

```
from sklearn.metrics import classification_report
from sklearn.svm import SVC

m2 = SVC(random_state=1)
m2.fit(x_train, y_train)

y_p2 = m2.predict(x_test)
print(classification_report(y_test, y_p2))
```

```
              precision    recall  f1-score   support

           0       0.81      0.85      0.83        34
           1       0.84      0.79      0.81        33

    accuracy                           0.82        67
   macro avg       0.82      0.82      0.82        67
weighted avg       0.82      0.82      0.82        67
```

Support Vector Machine:
Accuracy 82%

```
from sklearn.metrics import classification_report
from sklearn.naive_bayes import GaussianNB

m3 = GaussianNB()
m3.fit(x_train, y_train)

y_p3 = m3.predict(x_test)
print(classification_report(y_test, y_p3))
```

```
              precision    recall  f1-score   support

           0       0.82      0.79      0.81        34
           1       0.79      0.82      0.81        33

    accuracy                           0.81        67
   macro avg       0.81      0.81      0.81        67
weighted avg       0.81      0.81      0.81        67
```

Naïve Bayes : Accuracy 81%

```
from sklearn.metrics import classification_report
from sklearn.tree import DecisionTreeClassifier

m4 = DecisionTreeClassifier(random_state=1)
m4.fit(x_train, y_train)

y_p4 = m4.predict(x_test)
print(classification_report(y_test, y_p4))
```

```
              precision    recall  f1-score   support

           0       0.68      0.76      0.72        34
           1       0.72      0.64      0.68        33

    accuracy                           0.70        67
   macro avg       0.70      0.70      0.70        67
weighted avg       0.70      0.70      0.70        67
```

Decision Trees : Accuracy 70%

Random Forest Classifier, which has the highest accuracy among the five algorithms which is 87%

```
from sklearn.metrics import classification_report
from sklearn.ensemble import RandomForestClassifier

m5 = RandomForestClassifier(random_state=1)
m5.fit(x_train, y_train)
y_p5 = m5.predict(x_test)
print(classification_report(y_test, y_p5))
```

```
              precision    recall  f1-score   support

           0       0.88      0.85      0.87        34
           1       0.85      0.88      0.87        33

    accuracy                           0.87        67
   macro avg       0.87      0.87      0.87        67
weighted avg       0.87      0.87      0.87        67
```

We can type in data to check if the algorithms can predict it. For the example, we are using the Random Forest Classifier to predict as it had the highest accuracy.

```
print(m5.predict(sc.transform([[44,1,0,112,290,0,0,153,0,0,2,1,2]])))
[0]
```

```
print(m5.predict(sc.transform([[20,1,2,110,230,1,1,140,1,2.2,2,0,2]])))
[1]
```

The result predicts the target value where 1 indicates a positive patient and 0 indicates a negative patient who does not have a heart disease.

ECG Deep Learning and Imaging

Once the machine learning output determines the result, the patient should undergo a deep learning-based electrocardiogram to obtain the heartbeat analysis. Then images should be taken and checked to examine the overall condition of the heart. Based on the imaging technique, which is done by using neural networks, images can then be classified. Then the seriousness of the case and the affected area can be determined according to the output. Once they are classified, these images can be segmented to retain their accuracy, and results are obtained. So overall this system will increase the survival rate of a heart patient by early and fast prediction.

Conclusion

This chapter talks about the importance of using machine learning and deep learning integrated systems in heart care. Living in an era where it is essential to take care of health as new diseases are found with coming time which is concerning but at the same time a wakeup call for everyone. This paper aims to create a system that could predict cardiovascular diseases in a short amount of time. It also suggests improvements that can be made in the future while keeping all inconsistencies in mind. It explains the functionalities of the heart, its components and the different types of heart diseases, and the factors which can cause it. The different procedures used are explained in a detailed manner. The objective and way the system has been used are explained in detail. Implementation of data learning and machine learning is given. It uses various algorithms to arrive at a single accurate conclusion. When discussing future scope, we can come up with similar ideas for an early prediction of other diseases. The complexity of those diseases can be worked upon using various machine learning algorithms. Such similar concepts can be used to predict other diseases such as neurological diseases. If we collect such data on a larger scale, we may flourish well in this field as the prediction process would become accurate as of time increases, saving many lives. There could also be situations where getting a medical diagnosis could not be possible. In these cases, this system can prove to be a great alternative. It scans through huge amounts of scattered data, finds a relation between it to make it more sensible and efficient, and collects it as co-related information. A key issue would be finding people with immense technical knowledge to update and additional features when required. We need to ensure that the person's health background is understood to achieve maximum success technically. We can surely hope for an increase in demand for machine learning and deep learning-based prediction models in the future. Furthermore, more facilities to solve any problems faced and ensure a safe, trustworthy experience for every user and improve accuracy with every use ensure correct results every time.

References

[1] Sowmiya, C., and P. Sumitra, "Analytical study of heart disease diagnosis using classification techniques," *INCOS*, Srivilliputhur, 2017.

[2] Satu, M. S., F. Tasnim, T. Akter and S. Halder, "Exploring Significant Heart Disease Factors based on Semi Supervised Learning Algorithms." *IC4ME2*, Rajshahi, 2018.

[3] Ed-Daoudy and K. Maalmi, "Real-time machine learning for early detection of heart disease using big data approach," *2019 International Conference on WITS*, Fez, Morocco, 2019.

[4] Khemphila and V. Boonjing, "Heart Disease Classification Using Neural Network and Feature Selection," *2011 21st International Conference on Systems Engineering*, Las Vegas, NV, 2011.

[5] Mendis S., Puska P., Norrving B. (2011). *Global Atlas on Cardiovascular Disease Prevention and Control.* World Health Organization in collaboration with the World Heart Federation and the World Stroke Organization.

[6] Fuster V., Kelly B. B. - Institute of Medicine of the National Academies (2010). "Epidemiology of Cardiovascular Disease." Promoting cardiovascular health in the developing world: a critical challenge to achieve global health. Washington, DC: National Academies Press.

[7] Mozaffarian D., Roger V. L., Benjamin E. J., Berry J. D., Borden W. B., et al. (January 2013). "Heart disease and stroke statistics -2013 update: a report from the American Heart Association."

[8] Chou R., Dana T., Blazina I., Daeges M., Jeanne T. L. (November 2016). "Statins for Prevention of Cardiovascular Disease in Adults: Evidence Report and Systematic Review for the US Preventive Services Task Force." JAMA.

[9] Purushottam, K. Saxena and R. Sharma, "Efficient heart disease prediction system using decision tree," *International Conference on Computing, Communication & Automation*, Noida, 2015.

[10] Kelly B. B., Fuster V. (2010). *Promoting Cardiovascular Health in the Developing World: A Critical Challenge to Achieve Global Health.* Washington, DC: National Academies Press.

[11] Bai W., Li J., Liu J. (October 2016). "Serum phosphorus, cardiovascular and all-cause mortality in the general population: A meta-analysis." Clinica Chimica Acta; *International Journal of Clinical Chemistry.*

[12] Olaniyi, E. O., O. K. Oyedotun, A. Helwan and K. Adnan, "Neural network diagnosis of heart disease," *2015 International Conference on Advances in Biomedical Engineering (ICABME)*, Beirut, 2015.

[13] Sudeshna, P., S. Bhanumathi and M. R. A. Hamlin, "Identifying symptoms and treatment for heart disease from biomedical literature using text data mining," *ICCPEIC*, Melmaruvathur, 2017.

[14] Yuliang, H., Q. Junxuan, W. Haibin and W. Xiubo, "Quantized analysis for heart valve disease based on cardiac sound characteristic waveform method," *ICSPS* Dalian, 2010.

[15] Eckel R. H., Cornier M. A. (August 2014). "Update on the NCEP ATP-III emerging cardio-metabolic risk factors." *BMC Medicine.*

[16] Ming, J., L. Zhang, J. Sun and Y. Zhang, "Analysis models of technical and economic data of mining enterprises based on big data analysis," *2018 ICCCBDA*, Chengdu, 2018.

[17] Talia, D., "Making knowledge discovery services scalable on clouds for big data mining," *2015 ICSDM*, Fuzhou, 2015.

[18] Bogorny, V., and S. Shekhar, "Spatial and Spatio-temporal Data Mining," *2010 IEEE International Conference on Data Mining*, Sydney, NSW, 2010.

[19] Wongkar, M., and A. Angdresey, "Sentiment Analysis Using Naive Bayes Algorithm Of The Data Crawler: Twitter," *2019 Fourth International Conference on Informatics and Computing (ICIC)*, Semarang, Indonesia, 2019.

[20] Tripathi, S. Yadav and R. Rajan, "Naive Bayes Classification Model for the Student Performance Prediction," *2019 2nd ICICICT*, Kannur, Kerala, India, 2019.

[21] Patil, S., and U. Kulkarni, "Accuracy Prediction for Distributed Decision Tree using Machine Learning approach," *2019 3rd International Conference ICOEI*, Tirunelveli, India, 2019.

[22] Gavankar, S. S., and S. D. Sawarkar, "Eager decision tree," *2017 2nd International Conference for Convergence in Technology (I2CT)*, Mumbai, 2017.

[23] Huang, Y., L. F. Capretz and D. Ho, "Neural Network Models for Stock Selection Based on Fundamental Analysis," *2019 IEEE Canadian Conference of Electrical and Computer Engineering (CCECE)*, Edmonton, AB, Canada, 2019.

[24] Liu, T., H. Mei, Q. Sun and H. Zhou, "Application of neural network in fault location of optical transport network," in *China Communications*, Oct. 2019.

[25] Ray, S., "A Quick Review of Machine Learning Algorithms," *International Conference COMITCon*, Faridabad, India, 2019.

[26] Katarya, R., and P. Srinivas, "Predicting Heart Disease at Early Stages using Machine Learning: A Survey," *ICESC*, Coimbatore, India, 2020.

[27] Gavhane, A., G. Kokkula, I. Pandya and K. Devadkar, "Prediction of Heart Disease Using Machine Learning," *2018 Second International Conference on Electronics, Communication and Aerospace Technology (ICECA)*, Coimbatore, 2018.

[28] Kaskavalci, H. C., and S. Gören, "A Deep Learning Based Distributed Smart Surveillance Architecture using Edge and Cloud Computing," *Deep-ML*, Istanbul, Turkey, 2019.

[29] Lee, K. B., "An Application of a Deep Learning Algorithm for Automatic Detection of Unexpected Accidents Under Bad CCTV Monitoring Conditions in Tunnels," *Deep-ML*, Istanbul, Turkey, 2019.

[30] Aksu, D., and M. Ali Aydin, "Detecting Port Scan Attempts with Comparative Analysis of Deep Learning and Support Vector Machine Algorithms," *IBIGDELFT*, ANKARA, Turkey, 2018.

Chapter 10

Artificially Intelligent Queueing Modeling Approach to Analyzing and Improving Health Care Systems

S. S. Mishra[1,*], Carol Hargreaves[2,†], S. Ahmad Ali[3,‡] and Sandeep Rawat[4,§]

[1]Dr. Rammanohar Lohia Avadh University,
Ayodhya, Uttar Pradesh, India
[2]National University of Singapore, Singapore
[3,4]Babu Banarsi Das University, Lucknow, Uttar Pradesh, India

Abstract

A wide variety of mathematical and computational techniques and programming are considered under operations research to deal with problems connected with applied science. One such technique is queueing theory, which can solve and analyze the waiting lines mathematically, such as an average number of customers waiting in the queue. Nowadays, queueing models are used to analyze and suggest congestion minimization in the service and optimize inappropriate delivery time in various airlines, banking, restaurants, health care systems, etc. Therefore, keeping in view the potential and versatility of queueing model, we intend to apply it in health care systems (HCSs) to

* Corresponding Author's E-mail: smssmishra5@gmail.com.
† Corresponding Author's E-mail: carol.hargreaves@nus.edu.sg.
‡ Corresponding Author's E-mail: ali.bbdu@gmail.com.
§ Corresponding Author's E-mail: sandeeprwt11@gmail.com.

In: Industry 4.0 and Intelligent Business Analytics for Healthcare
Editors: Soumi Dutta, Vinod Kumar Shukla, Shruti Nagpal et al.
ISBN: 978-1-68507-602-3

analyze and improve health care systems by evaluating its performance measures. Much less work has been undertaken and reported in this direction by using AI tempered queueing models. Now, it is a need of the hour to couple such methodology with HCSs to include the accuracy and precision in predicting its performance measures. In this light, to bridge this critical gap, the AI tempered queueing model is proposed to apply in the analysis of HCSs in the present proposal. Artificial intelligence and its techniques can easily handle the analysis of the health care system's performance appropriately as required by today's industry 4.0.

Keywords: artificial intelligence, queueing models, performance measures, health care system

Introduction

During World War II, the discipline of operations research came into existence when two power centres were clashing with their interests. Resources available for war were limited to afford the burden of war. Hence, mathematical sciences were born to deal with the crisis out of that situation. Thus, it proves that the science of operations research is undoubtedly meant to solve the crisis problem and provide the most relevant result that can best suit the given problem [1]. Since World War II, operations research has been used as a scientific discipline to analyze the performance measures of service-providing organizations. For this, we carry out various analytical procedures on how better decision-making in diverse applied systems can be ensured. Operations research has good routing of application in the healthcare system after the fifties [2, 3, 4, 5]. Nowadays, queueing models are used to analyze and suggest the congestion minimization in service-inefficiency, in the inappropriate delivery time for various applications such as airlines, banking, restaurants, healthcare systems, etc. It will also respond to Covid-19 like studying and improving with real data-driven analytics. Operations Research consists of a varied range of techniques and models that have potential to analyze the performance measures of the health care system and accordingly to suggest improvements by reorganizing its components involved in the organizations serving the society [6, 7, 8, 9]. Queueing models of operations research focus on evaluating various service providing models which are frequently used in improving the various service providing systems like telecommunications, banks, airlines and various healthcare systems [10, 11, 12, 13, 14, 15, 16, 17, 18, 19].

In this process, we will discuss various queuing models and their applications to the healthcare organization to analyze and suggest improving its quality and efficiency to meet the increased demands of patients. If we want to increase the efficiency of the healthcare systems, then it becomes imperative to subject it under the mathematical analysis of waiting line theory [20, 21, 22, 23, 24, 25, 26, 6, 28, 4]. An assessment of bed assignments of the healthcare system, including time utilization of doctors, waiting time of patients, and probability of a patient turning away from the system was proposed and discussed by [29, 30, 31].

So far, insufficient applications of queueing models in the fields of health care systems have been made. Hence, queueing models have good potential to deal with the rising cost of the healthcare system in the present scenario of increasing demands of health care of populations consisting of children and old ones [32, 33]. This is also because of inefficient delivery and infrastructure engaged in the healthcare systems. Inefficiency in each service provider brings the lousy name to not only the governance but also the health status of the society is also affected enormously [34, 35, 36, 37].

Therefore, by applying the queueing modelling approach, we can minimize the cost of the whole health care system, and inefficiencies can be identified and mathematically analyzed to improve the system. Presently, it is our experience that when we go to the service-providing health care system, a large queue of patients at various hospitals and clinics are seen [38, 30, 31]. In order to fairly tackle this situation, collected data inputs and simulation modelling coupled together can provide one of the trade-offs between the waiting time of the patients and the service times of doctors and other staff to use various appointment techniques in the different settings [39, 40]. A review of literature on the application of queueing theory and its model was presented and reviewed [41]. Similarly, a brief account of the use of queueing theory in health care system was suggested as multi-server queuing models to use in the application of health care situation [12, 32, 34, 42, 43, 44, 45].

Nevertheless, an interesting suggestion of how to use scheduling for departments in the hospital and phone calls was made for optimizing congestion of emergency department and its variability. This is also interesting to remark that a refused admission at the cardiac aid centre was discussed [46]. Queueing approach with evolutionary computation for improving hospital bed occupancy and resource utilization [39]. Moreover, some more researchers have done relevant research in the healthcare system, for example [47, 48, 49]. Patients' choice of healthcare systems depends on their satisfaction. How healthcare systems are rendering the services to the patient affects the factors of whether service of the healthcare system is given timely and efficiently; and whether it is patient-centred delivery of a quality healthcare system. Doctors as medical experts are the most prominent elements of the healthcare system who can analyze and improve the healthcare system by providing quality health services to the patients. Patient satisfaction about hospital services: a study from the outpatient department of tertiary care hospital is reported [50].

Traditionally, the healthcare system is a noble profession intended to render patients health care service to humanity which now has transformed into the health care industry. Gradually, the healthcare system has evolved over the years. Its profile is continuously changing after establishing nursing homes and hospitals in the corporate sectors, health insurance entry to pay a third party, and the online health care system available for the patients. The patient is supposed to be a customer of a healthcare system, and therefore, one can buy the services by paying the money. The patient has a certain right to get the service instead of paying the money, and thus, a patient can question the quality of health services. Under the pressing needs, corporate and government health services need a qualitative intervention to maintain the choice of healthcare services on the top priority [20].

Because of maintaining the quality of health services in various forms and considering the choice and satisfaction of the patients, the organizations dealing with healthcare services have to engage good professionals, including the doctors, paramedical and managers, etc. The reasonable price of health services, the good behaviour of the personnel, and a fewer complaints oriented system can lead to the choice of health care system for the patients. Doctors as medical experts of the healthcare organization are the system's backbone. If doctors are happy, the patients will also be happy, and hence doctors' environment of working culture must be ideal and patient-centred [26]. Doctors need to provide good timely, efficient, and well soothing services. Medical experts must listen to the patients, understand their problems, show courtesy, and talk face-to-face. A hospital or nursing home is a platform where doctors and patients meet together to discuss, identify and address patients' problems by having close interactions. Hospitals and nursing homes are found in several cities where they operate in local areas between minimal distances. Under this situation, it becomes difficult to choose the healthcare systems for their benefits and wellbeing [27].

The least work has been reported so far about the artificial intelligence (AI) tempered queueing model approach to the health care system to analyze it more systematically and appropriately to provide optimal and qualitative service by evaluating its performance measures. Here, we intend to identify the opportunities in the service improvement of health care systems engaged in human services. We wish to collect real-life data related to healthcare systems that provide services to the human population. In order to bridge this critical gap, AI tempered queueing model is proposed to apply in the analysis of HCS in the present work so that analysis of the performance of health care systems can be made in an appropriate and versatile manner as required by today's industry 4.0.

Model Assumptions

This chapter has following assumptions as:

1. The patients are feel-friendly with the organization system of the medical centre.
2. The arrival rate of the queuing patients and their service rates are compatible with the exponential distribution.
3. The system for the queue discipline follows the manner; when the first patient will go to the server, others will be ready for the service.
4. When we have a multi-channel queue, none of the servers or medical experts is idle.

Materials and Methods

Following basic useful material and relevant methods are used in this section.

Queueing Model

Here, we consider the Markovian queueing model. Both arrival and service follow Poisson probability law, and it has a single server with first come and first served discipline and infinite capacity. There are several operating characteristics or performance measures of the queuing model: traffic congestion, expected number of customers in queue and system, expected waiting time in queue and system, and service utilization factor or busy period (Figure 10.1).

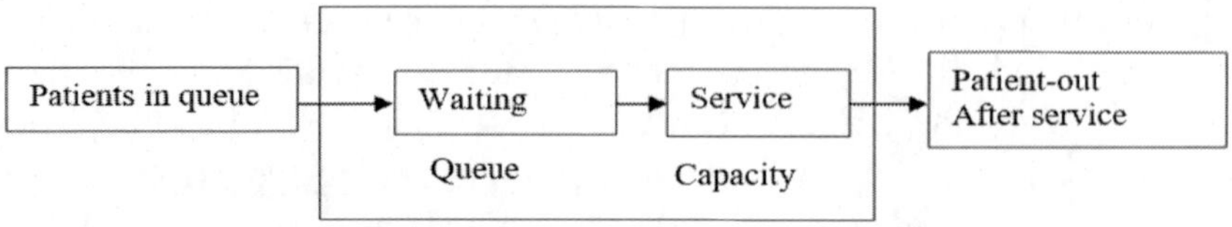

Figure 10.1. Basic Structure of Queue.

M/M/1 Model

The queueing model M/M/1 consists of the following salient features: (i) arrival obeys Poisson law, (ii) service time follows exponential, (iii) server is single, (iv) capacity is unlimited (v) discipline applied is first come and first served. System-state refers to the size of customers at a time in the system. It may be any non-negative integer number.

Single Server Queueing Model

In the single server queueing model, there is a single server as a medical expert with other related facilities that are important for the treatment services to the patients. It follows its suggested probability distributions and given rules of queueing discipline.

Multi-Server Queuing Model

In the multi-server queueing model, there consists of multi-server medical experts with other allied facilities, which are compulsory for rendering the treatment services to the patients. It follows its designated probability distributions and given rules of queueing discipline.

Service Time

The amount of time in which the service of a customer completes is defined as service time.

Busy Period

It is a period in which the server provides the service to customers.

Idle Period

The idle period of the server is a time duration in which the server is not engaged in service.

Artificial Intelligence

Artificial intelligence is defined as the science and engineering of producing intelligent machines [20]. Artificial Intelligence is the general name for modelling systems inspired by all living beings' behaviour in nature. This phenomenon has emerged in the 1950s and can be considered an interdisciplinary concept. The behaviour of artificial intelligence systems comes up in six different ways – control of a system, decision making, estimation, learning, problem-solving, optimization. Today's main artificial intelligence methods are; expert systems, fuzzy logic, genetic algorithms, and artificial neural networks. Expert systems are decision support systems based on specific expert opinions. It is usually used to make recommendations based on patient data in the healthcare sector. *Artificial neural networks* are a method that mimics the operation of the biological nervous system. Artificial neural networks are used in many applications, such as identifying and classifying previously unrecognized patterns in data in the health sector.

Artificial Neural Network Approach

This is a computational technique that is trained once it works like the human brain to function. This is also known as the nature-inspired or bio-inspired approach. ANN is a multilayer and multi-nodal mechanism that imitates the human brain's biological neurons. We connect these neurons by links. Dendrites, axons, synapses are essential elements that are believed to ensure the brain's functionality. It follows the connectionist approach deciphered by the interface of multi-disciplinary values such as artificial intelligence, cognitive psychology, neuroscience, philosophy of mind, etc. As per the latest MIT report, ANN (Figure 10.3) is among the top ten technologies in the world. The mathematical framework of ANN is given as under.

i. Neural inputs are denoted by x, and its bias is x0 = +/-1 (the computing process is affected by some neurons).
ii. Synaptic connection is denoted by weights w.
iii. Activation function (Figure 10.2) is given by y = sum (wx) + b, b is bias; y is an output. Y is also known as a result of ANN function, which is similar to the axon of a neuron.
iv. Activation furthers as ynext = f(y), y comes from (iii).
v. This output, through a synapse, becomes the input to the next layer.
vi. f(y) >= θ, y = 1, f(y) < θ, y = 0, θ is a threshold quantity.
vii. Here, at input f is "linear", & f is "nonlinear" at hidden linear and nonlinear both at the output layer.

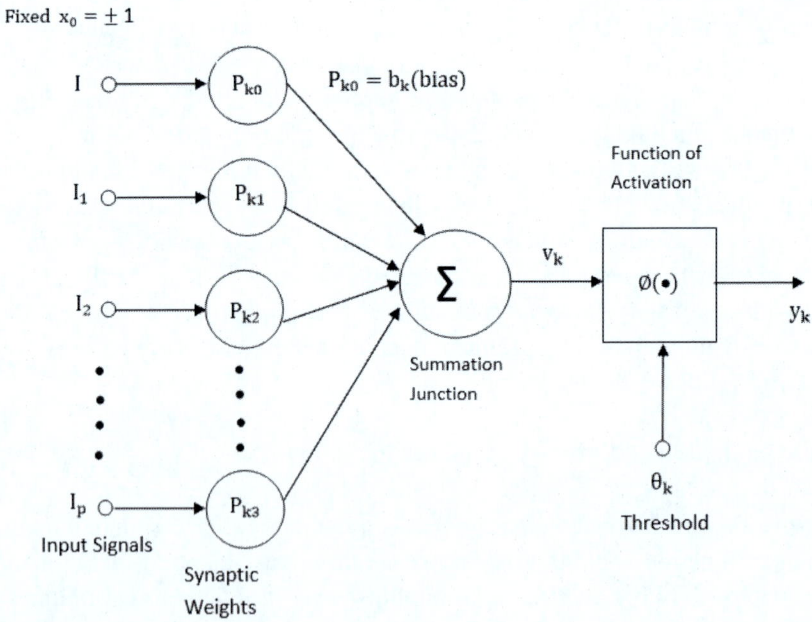

Figure 10.2. Description of Activation Function

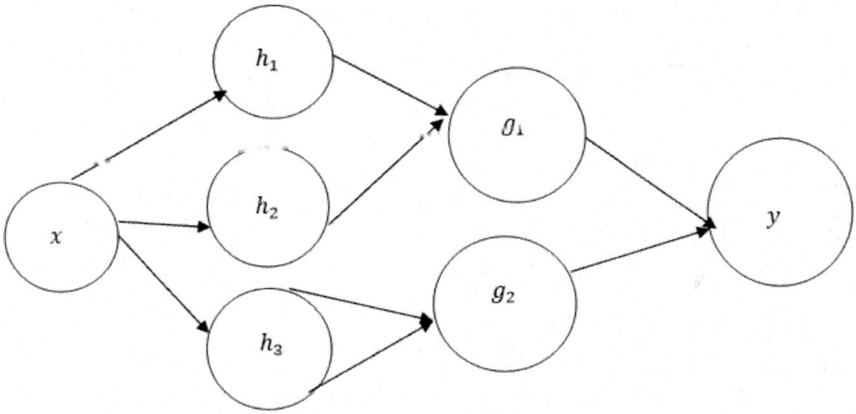

Figure 10.3. Architecture of ANN

Table 1. Choice-data of customers/patients

S. No.	Choice of customer/ Patient Yes/No	Capacity of queue/ system (25-100)	Service/treatmen t cost per unit (Rs. thousands) (10-30)	Waiting Line of customers/ patients (5-50)	Servers/medical experts (1-15)
1	No	75	17	19	5
2	Yes	55	15	9	2
3	Yes	40	19	19	5
4	Yes	55	24	11	8
5	No	70	25	19	5
6	Yes	40	20	30	9
7	Yes	70	15	30	8
8	No	80	22	10	3
9	Yes	65	16	40	11
10	No	50	14	40	12
11	No	75	18	20	4
12	Yes	55	16	10	3
13	Yes	40	20	20	6
14	Yes	55	25	12	9
15	No	70	26	20	6
16	Yes	40	21	31	10
17	Yes	70	16	31	9
18	No	80	23	11	4
19	Yes	65	17	41	12
20	No	55	15	41	13
21	No	75	19	21	5
22	Yes	55	17	11	4
23	Yes	40	21	21	7
24	Yes	55	26	13	10

Table 1. (Continued)

S. No.	Choice of customer/ Patient Yes/No	Capacity of queue/ system (25-100)	Service/treatment cost per unit (Rs. thousands) (10-30)	Waiting Line of customers/ patients (5-50)	Servers/medical experts (1-15)
25	No	70	27	21	7
26	Yes	75	17	19	5
27	Yes	55	15	9	2
28	No	40	19	19	5
29	Yes	55	24	11	8
30	No	70	25	19	5

Table 2. Normalized choice-data of customers/patients

S. No.	Choice	Capacity	Service Cost	Waiting Line	Servers
1	0	0.00000000	0.42857143	0.62500	0.54545455
2	1	0.68181818	0.07142857	0.62500	0.45454545
3	1	0.95454545	0.57142857	0.00000	0.00000000
4	1	0.59090909	0.14285714	0.93750	0.72727273
5	0	0.31818182	0.00000000	0.93750	0.81818182
6	1	0.86363636	0.28571429	0.31250	0.27272727
7	1	0.40909091	0.14285714	0.00000	0.00000000
8	0	0.04545455	0.42857143	0.31250	0.27272727
9	1	0.36363636	0.78571429	0.06250	0.54545455
10	0	0.72727273	0.85714286	0.31250	0.27272727
11	0	0.02272727	0.50000000	0.65625	0.63636364
12	1	0.70454545	0.14285714	0.65625	0.54545455
13	1	0.97727273	0.64285714	0.03125	0.09090909
14	1	0.61363636	0.21428571	0.96875	0.81818182
15	0	0.34090909	0.07142857	0.96875	0.90909091
16	1	0.88636364	0.35714286	0.34375	0.18181818
17	1	0.43181818	0.21428571	0.03125	0.09090909
18	0	0.06818182	0.50000000	0.34375	0.36363636
19	1	0.38636364	0.85714286	0.09375	0.63636364
20	0	0.75000000	0.92857143	0.34375	0.36363636
21	0	0.04545455	0.57142857	0.68750	0.72727273
22	1	0.72727273	0.21428571	0.68750	0.63636364
23	1	1.00000000	0.71428571	0.06250	0.18181818
24	1	0.63636364	0.28571429	1.00000	0.90909091
25	0	0.36363636	0.14285714	1.00000	1.00000000
26	1	0.90909091	0.42857143	0.37500	0.27272727
27	1	0.45454545	0.28571429	0.06250	0.18181818
28	0	0.09090909	0.57142857	0.37500	0.45454545
29	1	0.40909091	0.92857143	0.12500	0.72727273
30	0	0.77272727	1.00000000	0.37500	0.45454545

Queuing Model Analysis

The patient choice depends on characteristic variables of the health care system (Table 1). The capacity of the queuing model is equivalent to the capacity of service (treatment) providing health care system. Service cost of the queuing model refers to the average treatment cost in thousand rupees and waiting time refers to the waiting time of a patient waiting for his/her turn for treatment, in particular, health care system (any hospital or nursing home). Servers of the queuing model refer to doctors or medical experts engaged with a particular health care system. Using purposive sampling, patient-choice primary data has been collected from various health care systems (hospitals and nursing homes) of Ayodhya (Uttar Pradesh, India). The method of data collection was interview-quest (direct & indirect through localized inquiry) depending on four essential variables: the capacity of the system, average treatment cost for non-critical diseases (common diseases), and waiting for a line of patients, and several medical experts available with the particular organization. Their respective ranges are also given in individual columns (Table 2).

Supervised and Unsupervised Learning

Supervised Training

An external teacher or supervisor plays an essential role in providing input and matching output. Examples include decision trees and Naïve Bays etc. ANN is also an example of supervised learning, but it is to note here that it is also a case of unsupervised learning.

Unsupervised Training

No such pair of input and output is made available by an external teacher or supervisor in this training set. Examples include density estimation in statistics, clustering k means, dimensionality reduction methods such as component analysis and independent component analysis.

Training Set

Training set (Table 3) is a data set on which technique is trained to learn to adapt the decision making that can predict the result as intended by researchers.

Table 3. Training data set

S. No.	Choice	Capacity	Service Cost	Waiting Line	Servers
1	0	0.00000000	0.42857143	0.62500	0.54545455
2	1	0.68181818	0.07142857	0.62500	0.45454545
3	1	0.95454545	0.57142857	0.00000	0.00000000
4	1	0.59090909	0.14285714	0.93750	0.72727273
5	0	0.31818182	0.00000000	0.93750	0.81818182
6	1	0.86363636	0.28571429	0.31250	0.27272727
7	1	0.40909091	0.14285714	0.00000	0.00000000
8	0	0.04545455	0.42857143	0.31250	0.27272727
9	1	0.36363636	0.78571429	0.06250	0.54545455
10	0	0.72727273	0.85714286	0.31250	0.27272727
11	0	0.02272727	0.50000000	0.65625	0.63636364
12	1	0.70454545	0.14285714	0.65625	0.54545455
13	1	0.97727273	0.64285714	0.03125	0.09090909
14	1	0.61363636	0.21428571	0.96875	0.81818182
15	0	0.34090909	0.07142857	0.96875	0.90909091
16	1	0.88636364	0.35714286	0.34375	0.18181818
17	1	0.43181818	0.21428571	0.03125	0.09090909
18	0	0.06818182	0.50000000	0.34375	0.36363636
19	1	0.38636364	0.85714286	0.09375	0.63636364
20	0	0.75000000	0.92857143	0.34375	0.36363636

Test Set

It is a set of data set (Table 4) on which trained ANN is implemented to predict the result, which is further tested for its validation by applying a particular statistical technique that is popular for this validation (Figure 10.4).

Table 4. Item-wise details of ANN

S. No	Item	Value	S. No	Item	Value
1.	Error	0.0113648	10.	capacity.to.1layhid2	3.3317125
2.	Reached threshold	0.0078138	11.	sercost.to.1layhid2	-3.29086001
3.	steps	162.00000	12.	waitline.to.1layhid2	-2.72490112
4.	Intercept.to.1layhid1	0.2872926	13.	servers.to.1layhid2	2.069096353
5.	capacity.to.1layhid1	-4.560636	14.	Intercept.to.2layhid1	-0.1135797
6.	sercost.to.1layhid1	2.6017708	15.	1layhid1.to.2layhid1	7.17029216
7.	waitline.to.1layhid1	5.1726111	16.	1layhid2.to.2layhid1	-8.3325735
8.	servers.to.1layhid1	-3.5874590	17.	Intercept to choice	6.82293677
9.	Intercept.to.1layhid2	-0.1423771	18.	2layhid1.to.choice	-15.6212382

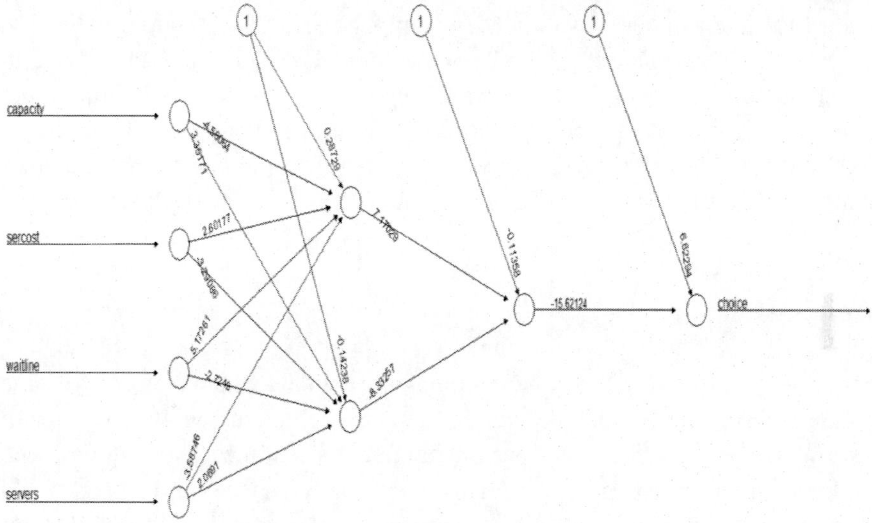

Figure 10.4. Actual Structure of ANN (Error: 0.011365 Steps: 162).

Prediction of Results

Using test set, we can predict results as represented in Table 5.

Table 5. Predicted results

S. No.	Choice of the patient	Actual Value	Predicted Value	S. No.	Choice of the patient	Actual Value	Predicted Value
1	No	0	0.0001574444	5	No	0	0.0001780392
2	Yes	1	0.9988942366	6	Yes	1	0.9988699712
3	Yes	1	0.9988641440	7	Yes	1	0.9989045705
4	Yes	1	0.9988512247	8	No	0	0.0001624484
5	Yes	1	0.9988877244	10	No	0	0.0001544251

Validation

Unless the queue model is validated, it cannot be recommended for application in various fields. Therefore, the present model is subjected to validation through fitting the general linear modelling for choice prediction through the popular parameter of coefficient of variation. It comes out to be 0.00579139479, which is relatively less than the standard one. Consequently, it authenticates the model for future use in various areas of applications.

Conclusion

Markovian queues are fundamental queueing models which reflect a volume about its application. Its derivation and mathematical analysis comprise several system performance measures, including health care, which has been undertaken here to predict health care performance and suggest an improvement. To date, ANN has been the most sought-after technique for classifying and predicting various performance measures of the queueing model. Tables 1-5 describe various data and results involved in the discussion of the model. Figure 10.1 to 10.4 presents clear pictures, including basic architecture, input-output drawn structure, and final parameters of the results. The coefficient of variation as an established rule of validation of the model has been used in this work. This can be served as a guiding and instructional framework for the application in various areas, including the health care system and other service-providing systems.

References

[1] Taha, H.A. (1987), *Operation research: an introduction* (Fourth Edition, Macmillan Publishing: New York).

[2] Kritchanchai, D. and Hoeur, S. (2018). Simulation modeling for facility allocation of outpatient department. *Int J Healthc Manag.* 2018; 11(3):193–201. Available from: https://doi.org/10.1080/20479700.2017.1359920.

[3] Mishra, S.S. and Yadav D.K. (2009). Cost and profit analysis of Markovian queueing system with two priority classes: A computational Approach, *International Journal of Applied Mathematics and Computer Sciences,* ISSN: 1641-876X (print), 2083-8492 (online) 5:3, pp 150-156. Clarivate Analytics/Web of Science, SCI & SCOPUS, IF 1.64.

[4] Khan, M.R., and Callahan B.B. (1993). Planning laboratory staffing with a queueing model, *European Journal of Operational Research,* 67(3), 321-331.

[5] Sariyer, G., Ataman and Kiziloglu M.G. (2018). Factors affecting length of stay in the emergency department: a research from an operational viewpoint. *Int J Healthc Manag.* 2018:1–10. Available from, doi.: 20479700.2018.1489992.

[6] Green, L.V. (2006). Queueing analysis in healthcare. In: *Patient flow: reducing delay in health care delivery.* New York, Boston, MA: Springer; p. 281–308.

[7] Green, L.V. and Nguyen V. (2001). Strategies for cutting hospital beds: the impact on patient service. *Healthserv Res* 36:421-442.

[8] Green, L. (2011). Yankovic N. Identifying good nursing levels: aqueuing approach. *Oper Res.;* 59:942–955.

[9] Green, L.V. (2008). Identifying good nursing levels: a queuing approach. *Tutor Oper Res.;* 1:1-16.

[10] Erlang, A.K. (1909). The Theory of Probabilities and Telephone Conversations, *Nyt Tidsskrift for Matematik,* 20(B), 33-39.

[11] Bruin, Arnoud -M.de and Rossum, A.C. Van (2006). *Modeling the emergency cardiacin – patient flow: an application of queuing theory.* Health Care Manage science.

[12] Rawat, S., Singh, B.B., Yadav, S.K. and Mishra, S.S. (2020). Optimization of Markovian arrival and service queuing model under fuzziness, *Int. J. Agricult. Stat. Sci.* Vol. 16, No. 2, pp. 567-572, ISSN: 0973-1903, e-ISSN: 0976-3392, Scopus/Elsevier.

[13] Venkateswarlu, B. and Murty, A.V. S.N. (2016). Applications of Queuing Theory in Hospitals Using Single and Multiple Servers, *Research J. Pharm. and Tech;* 9(12):2211-2216., DOI: 10.5958/0974-360X.2016.00447.9.

[14] Boulton, J. Akhtar, N, Shuaib, A. (2016). Waiting for a stroke bed: planning stroke unit capacity using queuing theory. *Int J Healthc Manag;* 9(1):4–10.

[15] Chochran, K.J. and Bhati, A. (2006). Multi-stage stochastic methodology for whole hospital bed planning under peak loading. *Int J Ind Syst Eng.;* 1(1/2):8–35.

[16] Earlang, A.K. (1948). *The life and the works of A.K. Earlang. Copenhagen,* Denmark: Copenhagen Telephone Co.

[17] Foad, Mahdavi Pajouh and Manjunath, Kamath (2010). Applications of Queueing Models in Hospitals, Queueing Applications in Hospitals, *Proceedings of the Fifth Midwest Association for Information Systems Conference,* Moorhead, MN May 21-22.

[18] Mardiah, Fatma Poni and Basri, Mursyid Hasan (2013) The Analysis of appointment system to reduce Outpatient waiting time at Indonesia's public hospital, *Human Resource Management Research,* 3 (1):27-33.

[19] Rawat, Sandeep, Ali, S. Ahmad, Singh, Abishek, Mishra, S.S. (2020). *Artificial Neural Network Approach to Simulation and Prediction of Traffic Congestion for Morkovian Queue with Single Server,* IJASS, communicated and in process, Corres. Auth.

[20] Hall, R., Belson D., Murali P. (2006). Modeling patient flows through the healthcare system. In: Hall RW, editor. *Patient flow: reducing delay in healthcare delivery.* Vol. 1. Boston, MA: Springer, p. 1–45.

[21] Hamet, Pavel and Johanne Tremblay (2017). "Artificial intelligence in medicine." *Metabolism* 69: S36-S40.

[22] Ishan, P. Lade, Chowriwar Sandeep A and Pranay, B. Sawaitul (2013).Simulation of Queuing Analysis in hospital, *International journal of Mechanical Engineering and Robotics Research,* vol.2, No.3, ISSN 2278-0149.

[23] McClain, J.O. (1976), Bed planning using queueing theory models of hospital occupancy: A sensitive analysis, Inquiry, 13, 167-176.

[24] Preater, J. (2002). *Queue in health, Health Care Management Science,* 5, 2002, 283.

[25] Jingna, Wu, Chen Bo, Danping Wu, Wang, Jainqiang, Xiaodong Peng, Xia Xu, Optimization of Markov Queuing model in hospital bed resource allocation, *journal of healthcare engineering,* vol. 2020, article ID 6630885, 11 pages, 2020, https://doi.org/10.1155/2020/6630885.

[26] Kembe, M.M, Onah and lorkegh E.S, (2012). S,A Study of waiting and service costs of a Multi- server queuing model in specialist hospital, *International journal of scientific Technology Research,* volume 1, issue8.

[27] Kyoug, Won Cho, Seong Min Kim, Young, B.S., Moon Chae and Yong Uk Song (2017). Application of Queueing Theory to the Analysis of Changes in Outpatients' Waiting Times in Hospitals Introducing EMR, *Healthcare Informatics Research,* 23(1): 35-42, 2017, DOI: 10.4258/hir.2017.23.1.35.

[28] Mehandiratta, R. (2011). Application of Queueing Theory In Health Care, *International Journal of Computing and Business Research* 2 (2), 2229-6166.

[29] Olorunsola, S.A, Adeleke, R.A and Ogunlade, T.O (2014). Queuing theory analysis of patient flow in hospital, *IOSR Journal of Mathemtics.* e-ISSN:2278-5728, Vol (10), issue(4), pp:47-53.

[30] Peter, O. Peter & Sivasamy, R. (2019): Queueing theory techniques and its real applications to health care systems – Outpatient visits, *International Journal of Healthcare Management,* DOI: 10.1080/20479700.2019.1616890, pp 1-9.

[31] Brahma, Prasantakumar (2012). An appraisal of cost of Queuing in health sector a case study of IMS and SUM hospital, Bhubaneswar, *International Journal of Multidisciplinary Research,* Vol.2 Issue 4, ISSN2231-5780.

[32] Adeleke, R.A., Ogunwale, O.D. and Halid, O.Y. (2009), Application of Queueing Theory to Waiting Time of Out-Patients in Hospitals, *Pacific Journal of Science and Technology,* 10(2), 270-274.

[33] Rao, D.G. (1972). *Management breakthrough in Hospital Management opsearch* 9(384), 143-167. 32

[34] Mandelbaum, A., Momcilovic P and Tseytlin, Y. (2011).Queueing systems with heterogeneous servers: on fair routing of patients in emergency departments. *Manage Sci.;* 1(1):65–75.

[35] Mala and Varma S.P. (2016) Time Reduction in a Local Health Care Centre Using Queueing Theory, *IOSR Journal of Mathematics* (IOSR-JM) e-ISSN: 2278-5728, p-ISSN: 2319-765X. Volume 12, Issue 1 Ver. IV (Jan. - Feb. 2016), PP 95-100 www.iosrjournals.org DOI: 10.9790/5728-121495100.

[36] Bailey, N.T.J. (1952). A study of queues and appointment systems in hospital out-patient departments with special reference to waiting times, *Journal of Royal Statistical Society,* Netherlands, 14, 185-199.

[37] Kanna, Rajesh (2005). *Theory of Queue,* III-Edition, PHI publica-tions, Delhi.

[38] Olorunsola, S.A, Adeleke, R.A and Ogunlade, T.O (2014). Queuing theory analysis of patient flow in hospital, *IOSR Journal of Mathemtics.* e-ISSN: 2278-5728, Vol (10), issue (4), pp: 47-53.

[39] Belciug, Smaranda and Gorunescu, Florin (2015). Improving hospital bed occupancy and resource utilization through queuing modeling and evolutionary computation, *Journal of Biomedical Informatics,* Vol. 53, pp. 261-269.

[40] Taylor, S. (1994). Waiting for service: the relationship between delays and evaluations of service. *J Mark,* 58 (2):56–69.

[41] Nosek, R.A. and Wilson, J.P. (2001). Queueing theory and customer satisfaction: a review of terminology, trends and applications to a pharmacy practice, *Hospital Pharmacy,* 3(36), 275-279.

[42] Ridge, J.C. et al. (1998). Capacity planning for intensive care units. *Eur J Oper Res* 105:346-355.

[43] Agarwal, Rashmi and Singh, B. K. (2018)., An analytical study of queues in medical sector, *OPSEARCH,* volume 55, p.p. 268–287.

[44] Fomundam, S. and Herrmann, J.W. (2007). *A Survey of Queueing Theory Applications in Healthcare,* ISR Technical Report, 24. -

[45] Mustafa, Saima and Unnisa, S. (2015). A Comparison of Single Server and Multiple Server Queuing Models in Different Departments of Hospitals, *Journal of mathematics.* ISSN: 1016-2526) Vol. 47 (1) pp.73-80.

[46] De Bruin A.M., Rossum, A.C. and Visser M.C. (2007). Modeling the emergency cardiac in-patient flow: an application of queuing theory. *Health Care Manag Sci.;* 10:125–137.

[47] Agnihotri, S.R. and Taylor, P.F. (1991). Staffing a centralized appointment scheduling department in Lourdes Hospital, *Interfaces-Journal Online,* 21, 1-11.

[48] Tseytlin, Y. (2009). *Queueing systems with heterogeneous servers: on fair routing of patients in emergency departments.* Technion-Israel Institute of Technology, Faculty of Industrial Engineering and Management.

[49] Wilson, M.J. (2004). Nguyen K. *Bursting at the seams: improving patient flow to help America's emergency departments.* Washington, DC: Urgent Matters, the George Washington University Medical Center, School of Public Health and Health Services.

[50] Sharma, Arvind, Kasar, P.K. and Sharma, Richa (2014). Patient satisfaction about hospital services: a study from the outpatient department of tertiary care hospital, Jabalpur, madhya pradesh, india, *National Journal of Community Medicine* 5(2):199-203. -44.

Chapter 11

Clientele Perception and Trust on Artificial Intelligence Integrated Health Services

Andre Magpantay*
University of the Philippines, Philippines

Abstract

Artificial Intelligence is one of the latest technological innovations of the 21st century. The latest trends show its integration in different fields, one of which is in the healthcare industry. Integrations range from assisted or independent diagnosis and treatment development, patient care, health systems, and more. However, the perceptions and views of the clientele on the use of Artificial Intelligence (AI) in healthcare services remain unclear with a low trust rate. There is also a lack of research conducted on how people view and trust AI in the medical industry, mainly focusing on the diagnosis, treatment, and health systems.

Moreover, the importance of clientele perception and trust lies in the holistic and client-centered health services, which will improve the developments and applications of this technology and the overall health systems around the globe. The ethical principles on the use of AI technology in health are also a relevant consideration, especially during a time when doubts are raised on the acceptability and limits of AI technology. This chapter aims to analyze clients' perceptions of AI integrated health services through a mix of quantitative and qualitative analysis. This is achieved through a preliminary survey and an in-depth interview of chosen respondents determined through probability

* Correspondence Author's Email: andre.magpantay.14@gmail.com.

In: Industry 4.0 and Intelligent Business Analytics for Healthcare
Editors: Soumi Dutta, Vinod Kumar Shukla, Shruti Nagpal et al.
ISBN: 978-1-68507-602-3

sampling. The quantitative and qualitative data are analyzed using descriptive statistics and coded thematic analysis. Final data analysis reveals four main domains, with different subcategories and a relatively low trust rate on AI-independent services. On the other hand, it is found out that patients are more open to receiving diagnosis and treatment aided by AI as long as it is facilitated by a physician and is supportive of AI's integration in hospital systems. The resulting issues from the qualitative analysis are analyzed through different theories, including AI anxiety and AI ethical principles, in order to explain the phenomena observed. The conclusions reveal clients' perceptions and issues, which affect their decisions and behavior towards AI integrated health services.

Keywords: Artificial Intelligence, AI health services, client perception, AI integration

Introduction

The capacity of humans as the creator has peaked with the dawn and advent of Artificial Intelligence (AI). People worldwide witnessed the rise of emerging technologies like AI in different fields such as business, entertainment, education, sciences, and more. Today, one of the fields that intrigued and surprised health care providers and clients alike is applying and integrating AI in the healthcare industry. Applications include the assisted and independent diagnosis, treatment, and an overall integration in health systems. These developments gave rise to ethical issues and considerations, which is a topic of a larger debate on the limitations that need to be set in AI technology. With all these issues, one of the most important considerations is the perception and trust of the clientele. As the direct recipients of AI-integrated health care services, the clientele has had different perceptions and trust, which ranged from being open to completely avoidant of these services. However, there have only been few research studies measuring the qualitative and phenomenological beliefs, attitudes, and opinions of this population. A common root of this problem is the lack of trust in AI and awareness and knowledge of its processes. This uncertainty results in psychological and behavioral indifference towards the technology and gives rise to specific issues involving technology employment. The chapter aims to explore clientele perception and trust, which is significant to a holistic and client-centered health system and will improve the developments and applications of this technology in the overall health systems around the globe. The ethical principles on the use of AI technology in health are also considered, especially during a time when doubts are raised on the acceptability and limits of AI technology to clarify misconceptions to smoothly integrate AI in health systems. The geo-political setting is also noted as the Philippines is a developing country with limited AI services, contributing to the lack of prior knowledge and understanding of the technology in the study locale.

In this chapter, trust is defined as the belief in the reliability and openness to receive the services, while perception is the awareness, knowledge, and understanding of this technology and services. Moreover, perception is considered the contextual, ethical, and psychological foundations of the clientele regarding AI technology, and consequently, trust as its manifestation affecting the clientele's behavior. The chapter argues that trust is a function of perception. Addressing the gaps in these perceptions will improve the general view and behavior of the clientele towards AI technology in the healthcare setting. Specifically, the objective of this chapter is to determine the clientele perception and trust in AI-Integrated Health Services in terms of

1. AI-assisted Diagnosis and treatment.
2. Independent AI diagnosis and treatment.
3. AI-integrated hospital system.

The chapter also explores the general awareness and knowledge of the clientele as a contributing factor to their perceptions and the issues and concerns as reasons and results of these perceptions. The general scope of the study includes a descriptive statistic of clientele trust based on the survey of 100 consenting respondents and a phenomenological analysis of perception based on ten in-depth interviews studied through thematic coding analysis. The study is exploratory and does not relate variables such as demographics in the conclusions but explores the possible phenomena arising from perception and analysis with existing AI and ethics theories.

Background and Theories

AI Integrated Health Services

In a study by Wang and Preininger [1], the use of AI in the healthcare setting has been categorized into six major data types, which are identified as multi-omics, clinical, behavioral, environmental, and pharmaceutical research and development (R&D) data. These data types are commonly used in medical practice to provide services to patients, including diagnosis, treatment, and facility systems. The study analyzed the current literature and trends to present the current applications of AI technology in health, where it was found out that technologies have enabled the development of AI-assisted approaches, yet there are still remaining challenges in terms of more complicated functions. Meanwhile, Asan, Bayrak, and Choudhury [2] listed the significant potential applications of AI in health in areas of mining medical records, designing treatment plans, robotics mediated surgeries, medical management and supporting hospital operations, clinical data interpretation, clinical trial participation, image-based diagnosis, preliminary diagnosis, virtual nursing, and connected health care devices. Some other examples of specific tasks include closing incisions with sutures or staples for surgeries, monitoring of patient's health, physical aid, reminders to take medications, voice-command wheelchairs, and blood draws. In addition, Davenport, Hongsermeier, and Mc Cord [3] studied the integration of AI in order to improve electronic health records, which provided services such as data extraction from free text, diagnostic and predictive algorithms, data entry and clinical documentation, and clinical decision support. These applications were continuously being researched, with some medical institutions pioneering their utilization in the healthcare industry. In this study, the AI-integrated services have been categorized into three simple and defined categories that are influenced by the current ethical consideration and awareness gap of the clientele. These are:

1. AI-assisted diagnosis and treatment.
2. Independent AI diagnosis and treatment.
3. AI Integration in health and hospital systems.

Ethical Principles

There has been a call to institutionalize AI ethical principles and even pass laws that should serve as guidelines and checkpoints to ensure proper responsibility for the technology. In the last six years, private companies, research institutions, as well as the public sector have issued principles and guidelines for ethical AI. Yet, there is still a current debate on what constitutes "ethical AI' and which ethical requirements, technical standards, and best practices are needed to realize it [4]. In 2019, Morley et al. [15]; introduced a typology going to close the gap between ethical principles and practices, which can help developers apply these ethics in every stage of creation. The typology centers on the programming aspect of AI creation, mainly on Machine Learning, and findings suggest that coordination is necessary between different sectors to effectively distribute "Applied AI Ethics." The exercise of AI ethics is a matter that should be institutionalized in the AI community and society, which in turn will improve the overall acceptance of everyone on the opportunities presented by AI.

Meanwhile, Hagerty and Rubinov [6] recognized the different social impacts of AI on the geographical setting, profoundness from local cultures, and social context. Their research demonstrated that AI-driven technologies have patterns of entrenching social divides and inequalities. These patterns exist globally, suggesting that low and middle-income countries are more vulnerable to these impacts. Together with the ethical considerations, these concerns are likely to influence both the trust and perception of the population and their behavior, acceptance, and openness of these services. In East Asia, Gal [7] studied the perspectives and approaches towards AI, which dubbed the technology as "antisocial," which hinders its development and acceptance. It was found out that there need to be AI-ready societies before it is widely integrated into the world. These perceptions of AI-readiness are massively dependent on individual knowledge drawn from information found online and those portrayed, often negatively, in popular culture. In summary, the integration of AI in health increases the ethical considerations and worries as the maximum consideration on the effect of AI on human lives is at stake, resulting indirectly observable effects. The ethical concerns can be categorized as:

1. Primary safety concerns.
2. Data-privacy issues.
3. Employment concern.
4. The "doomsday" scenario often appearing to people as referenced by popular culture as AI overtaking humans, which then causes significant anxiety in advanced-level technologies.

Trust and Perception

Trust is a human belief or attitude defined based on the dimensions of benevolence, integrity, and ability [8]. It is defined in this study as the belief in the reliability and the openness to receive the services based on the dimensions of trust. The level of trust in AI has a significant impact on user's reliability [9], henceforth affecting the clientele's behavior and response to AI services. On the other hand, perception deals with the awareness, knowledge, and understanding of people. In the study, the respondents' perceptions are determined through the qualitative data in the in-depth interview.

In contrast to trust, perception is unmeasurable and grounds itself on people's wide beliefs and personal philosophies. Asan, Bayrak, and Choudhuri [2] attributed the user's perception of AI in healthcare to the AI system's ability. At the same time, a significant dimension for trust depends on the understanding of the quality of data, the mathematical problem representation, and the algorithms used in decision-making. Understanding the mechanisms and technical aspects of AI leads to the trust of creators in the technology. In simple words, "to understand is to trust"; thus, the perception of the clientele, which includes their knowledge and awareness of the technology, is significant in their trust, which then affects their behavior.

In a survey and study conducted by Bristows [10], six key findings on people's perception of AI in health were highlighted. First, the understanding of AI is determined to be broad, with only 2% thinking that it has an effect in society. This is accompanied by high expectations of both positive and negative effects. Meanwhile, it has also been found out that the younger generation is more optimistic about AI, with those aged under 35 believed in having contact with AI compared to those over 65. Some other findings include the employment concerns once AI is fully deployed, poor understanding of data privacy implications, and the belief that governments should regulate AI in all fields. These findings are significant in establishing the current concerns and gaps in the awareness of people on AI in the healthcare industry. However, the perceptions measured in this survey are based on the qualitative measurement of knowledge and awareness, which answers the questions on people's current level of perception. Meanwhile, this study focuses on answering the questions on why the clientele accepts or does not accept AI services which also explains their trust rating of the technology. These perceptions will establish and conclude the main reasons for the clientele's indifference and openness to AI-integrated health services.

Methodology

The study employed a mix of qualitative and quantitative data gathering. In quantitative and descriptive research, surveys are commonly used in health to establish persons' attitudes, opinions, or beliefs concerning health-related issues. [11] It also allows researchers to study the characteristics of the population on variables such as the utilization of healthcare services. The study employed a preliminary survey to measure the trust of the people in AI-integrated healthcare services. One hundred respondents from a specific healthcare unit determined through probability sampling, characterized by belonging to the clientele or those who have received healthcare services from the past five years, agreed to participate in the survey. The research instrument is a questionnaire measuring the trust in AI-assisted diagnosis and treatment, independent AI diagnosis and treatment, and AI integration in hospital settings. The survey aims to establish the current trust of the population in the services. The demographics of the respondents are collated, but conclusions are not drawn since the goal is to establish the phenomenon and use descriptive statistics to describe it. The results yield a description of how the population, in this case, the clientele, perceives the sensation.

Meanwhile, the study primarily employed a qualitative approach to understanding the perceptions of the clientele. Understanding the population requires studying their beliefs, desires, and intentions [12], which is achievable through qualitative research. These philosophical beliefs and intentions of the people are essential in understanding AI services in the health care setting. A phenomenological approach is used to measure the respondents' conscious experience and ideas on AI health technologies in the context of their everyday perceptions and desire. Polgar and Thomas [11] defined the approach as appropriate in the field where a system of philosophy and social science plays a vital key in understanding the human consciousness in health research. An in-depth interview with a structured and open-ended questionnaire is conducted with ten randomly selected respondents from the original survey. The questionnaire is centered on determining the knowledge, awareness, and perception of AI integrated health services and the specific processes similar to the quantitative data gathering. The interview is designed to gather data to define the phenomenon through gathering personal reasons, desires, philosophical beliefs, reservations, and uncertainties. The population's perception is treated as a product of awareness and constructed meaning from the context; thus, trust as the dependent variable is assumed as a function of perception, the independent variable.

Data Analysis

The data was analyzed and interpreted based on the different theories on AI ethics, psychological unfamiliarity, and current AI issues. A coded thematic analysis was used to observe the significant trends and information categorically given by the respondents. These categories are tallied to be interpreted as a recurring factor and highlighted in the results. Important findings best exemplified by information highlighted by the clientele are also taken into extensive consideration as substantial data for analysis. These direct quotations from the data gathering are included to present the actual qualitative data and relevant theories. After the interviews are transcribed, the themes were decided, initial domains were created and verified. Four domains were created:

1. Awareness and knowledge of AI health services
2. Perception on AI-assisted diagnosis and treatment
3. Perception on independent AI diagnosis and treatment
4. Perception on AI-integrated hospital systems

The coding process was guided by methods presented by Hill et al. [13]. The results are organized first by domain. Then, one or more category appears under each domain. The themes and subcategories are created based on trends and codes relevant to the respondent's discussion. These are collated in order to explain the characteristics of the described phenomenon under each domain. Some direct interview quotes are used in order to highlight and present the data as it is. The cross-analysis and tallying of the information by the thematic categorization and sub-categorization is presented. Hill et al. [13] suggest that the frequency of each thematic analysis should be presented and analyzed as described with words such as: Rare for single occurrence; Variant for two to four participants; Typical for five to seven; and General for eight to ten occurrences.

In the final thematic coding interpretation, the concepts and theories on AI/robot anxiety, fear of the unknown, and ethical concerns are utilized. The goal to find significant trends and similarities among the clientele's answers summarizes their ideas and perceptions on AI-integrated health services and their openness to receive them. The study analyzed the data with a focus on the significant inquiry to connect the facts gathered as a resolution to the current gap of the population in their perception of AI in terms of awareness and knowledge. Lastly, the data gathered are analyzed to draw conclusions, and significant findings on the overall phenomena experienced and explored arising issues regarding the clientele's perception, trust, and corresponding behavior in response to the AI services. The trends and the phenomena observed are presented in the synthesis of the qualitative data, results, and analysis.

Results

Preliminary Survey: Trust Rating

The quantitative research instrument surveyed the trust rating of the clientele in receiving AI health services (Figure 11.1). The results showed that 73% of the respondent's trust AI in diagnosis and treatment as assistance and aid to physicians. Meanwhile, 22% answered no, and 5% are uncertain about their opinion. On the other hand, only 12% of the respondent's trust or are willing to receive treatment and diagnosis from an independent AI technology, 85% are entirely untrusting, while 3% remain uncertain. Lastly, in terms of integrating AI in hospital systems, the respondents seemed to be more open as 82% agreed that they trust this technology, only 13% are not ready to trust it, and 5% as uncertain. The descriptive statistics show that clientele is more trusting in integrating AI in health systems, such as handling patient data, managing hospital flow and delivery, and scheduling appointments. There is also a relatively high trust rating on AI-assisted services. With only a 9% difference with the integration on health systems, which reflects that people are open to integrating AI only as an aid to healthcare providers and managing hospital delivery, in contrast with the very low trust rating on independent AI services. The clientele seemed not to trust an AI to provide services in the diagnosis and provide treatment plans without a medical practitioner's help. Bristows [10] attributed people's trust in AI to their general knowledge of its processes, with the public usually confused about what an AI is. There is also an apparent difficulty in determining the technology's safety, which accounts for the low trust ratings on independent treatments and diagnosis. The presence of a medical practitioner seems to be an essential element in the clientele's trust. Moreover, people also do not fully understand the way AI uses their data and seems to assume that data privacy issues are not a concern immediately. Thus, it accounts for a high trust rating on the integration of AI in healthcare systems.

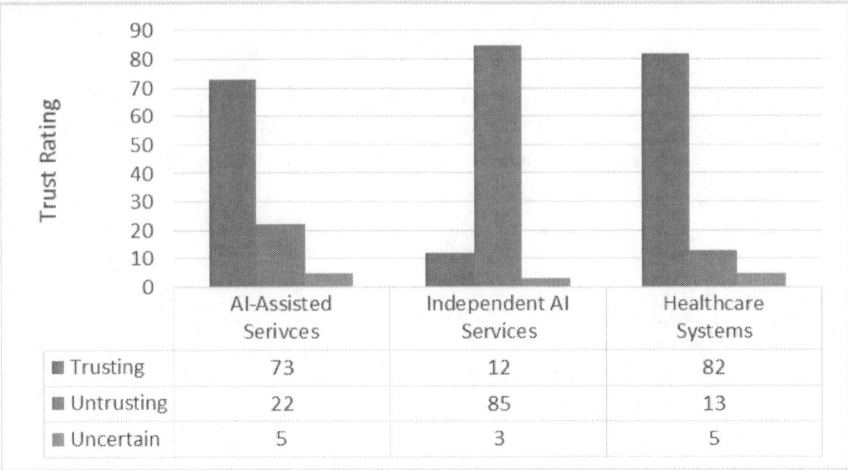

Figure 11.1. Clientele Trust Rating on AI Healthcare Services.

Qualitative Analysis: Clientele Perceptions

Awareness and Knowledge of AI Health Services

Respondents were found to be typically aware of the existence of AI-integrated health services. Seven respondents gave answers that confirm awareness. However, it should be noted that these responses do not equate to sufficient knowledge to understand the services (Table 1).

Table 1. Coded thematic analysis of awareness and knowledge of AI Health Services

Domain	Category	n	Description
Awareness and Knowledge of AI Health Services	Aware	7	Typical
	Uncertain	2	Variant
	Sufficient Knowledge	2	Variant
	Completely Unaware	1	Rare
	General Confusion	1	Rare

Therefore the concept of awareness relies on the prior knowledge that the specific technology exists and is being employed in the health care industry. One response is:

> I know that AI is used in other countries, they invented AI to improve the work of humans, and it is very helpful in the medical field. I think that they are also employing it using apps [applications]. (Respondent A, Male, 45, University Graduate).

The statement shows general awareness of Artificial Intelligence and its employment in different fields, a typical response from the clientele that demonstrates basic knowledge of the technology without the necessary comprehension of specific technologies and examples. Meanwhile, responses exhibiting sufficient knowledge appear to be variant.

> I am in the med-tech field, there is news about the use of AI in phlebotomy without the assistance of a medical technologist. It is advantageous, because it decreases errors in clinical tests, analytical, and technical aspects. (Respondent F, Female, 21, University Student).

The varied responses show the difference in understanding of the respondents on Artificial Intelligence in health. Only two respondents were able to provide an example of an integration that is consistent with verifiable facts. It is also observed among those who are uncertain that the technology is still far from reach. Their uncertainties come from their inexperience and lack of exposure to the said technology. Uncertainty also leads to a limited understanding of the technology, whereas the respondents reiterate simple examples they deem more feasible.

> I am still uncertain, I know only of apps [applications], I think they use it to call people, using the camera to find faces, calling for volunteers... (Respondent D, Female, 20, University Student).
>
> I'm not aware of any. I'm aware of artificial intelligence in general but I'm not sure if it's happening already. (Respondent I, Male, 24, University Graduate).

Lack of confidence in their knowledge of the technology usually leads to an uncertain response, whereas the respondents have usually encountered the topic in the news and social networking sites but did not profoundly engage in studying the information. The knowledge roots from occasional to frequent news on the technology usually released online, yet respondents somehow bear the idea that it is still not employable in the present. A rare answer of complete unawareness was also observed, whereas the respondent stated the lack of information on the technology's integration in the health setting.

Lastly, a confusing statement congruent with uncertainty was also given, whereas the respondent gave a mistaken example. This occurrence is rare, being only observed once.

Perception on AI-Assisted Diagnosis and Treatment

The respondents' perception regarding AI-assisted diagnosis and treatment is generally acceptable, with eight respondents saying that they will accept the technology as part of the health care industry (Table 2).

Table 2. Coded thematic analysis of perception on AI-assisted diagnosis and treatment

Domain	Category	n	Description
Perception on AI-Assisted Diagnosis and Treatment	Accepting	8	General
	Availing	5	Typical
	More Precise and Accurate	4	Varaint
	Excited/Enthusiastic	3	Variant
	Non-accepting	2	Variant

Typical responses supplement this that they are ready to avail or will avail the service in the future. Enthusiasm, meanwhile, varies, with some respondents showing their excitement to experience the technology. Some of the variant responses narrate the improvement in accuracy and precision.

> I am open. Based on my experience and knowledge, doctors are prone to human error, that's why multiple diagnoses exist together with second opinions. This can be eliminated with the help of AI and algorithm increasing precision. (Respondent C, Male, 30, University Graduate) Open, as long as the treatment is aided. The technology increases precision and accuracy. (Respondent G, Female, 47, University Graduate).

Some narrates the efficacy of AI to be employed in certain aspects especially during the current context of the COVID-19 pandemic, whilst others put trust to the AI's programming and algorithm.

> At first, I am shocked. I'm used to seeing only doctors for check-ups, to know about my current health. But I think it is a good thing, especially in the time of the pandemic, to help healthcare workers to use technology and

> lessen contact. I want to try it and I'm open, but I also have questions regarding reliability. (Respondent E, M, 27, University Student).
>
> Ok, for the treatment I think there is a protocol, as sort of a manual, it's not that worrying, because these are programmed already, AI is perfect for these. (Male, 45, University Graduate).

A common trend observed is the reiteration of the capability of AI to lessen inaccuracy and human error in diagnosis. The respondents' trust in technology, in general, is high given that the technology acts as an aid to medical professionals. The trust in programming is also mentioned as the respondent typically assign difficult works to AI involving precision and algorithmic analysis, which they tend to believe is a great improvement to the health care delivery process. Most of the respondents are also open to experience AI-aided diagnosis and treatment. However, the constant reservation will be a human health provider keeping the AI technology in check. On the other hand, variant responses include statements that the technology is still incapable and unready to be deployed in the health care industry, resulting in non-acceptance of its integration.

> No, the technology is still unready, I have not heard of anything that makes the technology reliable, I can only be sure when everyone is doing it. (Female, 20, University Student).
>
> I feel like it should not be used yet, I think that doctors are still the best fit for giving treatments and diagnosis, as such, I think it should remain that way. I don't want to use a technology that is still imperfect, who is responsible for its mistake? (Male, 24, University Graduate).

Statements that express the unreadiness of the respondents, accompanied by the belief that the technology should still be worked on, and is deemed still imperfect, gives rise to the ethical considerations on the use of AI. Such an example is the handling of responsibility in case of a mistake, as discussed by a respondent. There are also certain responses tending to question the necessity in the use of the technology, having an idea that the current systems and medical professionals are sufficient in providing care to the clientele. Two respondents share this viewpoint and are non-accepting of the need for AI in the healthcare industry.

Perception on Independent AI Diagnosis and Treatment

A general response observed amongst the participants is the unreadiness to accept and avail the concept of an independent AI giving diagnosis and treatments. 8 out of 10 respondents share the same sentiments stating various reasons are often centering on the concepts of trust, reliability, and ethical considerations. This is typically backed up by technological anxiety, which results in the clientele being scared to receive the services by the technology (Table 3).

Table 3. Coded thematic analysis of perception on independent AI diagnosis and treatment

Domain	Category	n	Description
Perception on Independent AI Diagnosis and Treatment	Not ready to accept/avail	8	General
	Anxious/Scared	6	Typical
	Possible Failures/Imperfect	3	Variant
	Lack of Empathy/Unemotional	2	Variant
	Issues on Responsibility	2	Variant
	Accepting	1	Rare
	Currently Uncertain	1	Rare

The respondents are also unaware of any services that employ the independent AI for diagnosis and treatment, with concerns being raised that the technology is new and untested. They are unwilling to be part of pioneer tastings. Examples of these responses are:

> It is new to me and I'm scared because the treatment plan was made by an AI. What if my disease becomes worse? (Respondent J, Male, 35, High School Completer).
>
> Early times, trials, if I am one of the first batch, no. I don't want to be an experimental lab rat. (Respondent B, Female, 36, High School Completer).

Meanwhile, concerns are also being raised regarding the mistakes AI can cause, its repercussions, and the entity responsible for these actions. These variant responses compare AI-integrated health utilization to other fields, reasoning that if AI fails in less critical situations, there will always be a tendency to fail when integrated into the health care setting. Questions are then raised regarding these responsibilities and who will answer in cases of malpractice.

> No, even though AI is highly learned and adaptive. There are cases outside of the health field where there are catastrophic instances where AI commits mistake, such as failure in following protocols in self-driving cars, and auto-pilot planes, in case of accidents like crash. Even though AI is adept, AI overreacts, and the programming fails. There are possibilities of small mistakes and failures… If you are dealing with human lives, this might lead to problems. It is only good when kept in check by humans. And of course, who will carry these responsibilities, in cases of mistakes and endangering lives? (Respondent C, Male, 30, University Graduate).

> No, because it can fail. Compared with people, AI mistakes cannot be easily corrected. (Respondent D, Female, 20, University Student).

> No, I would not be open specially if the technology is not fully developed yet. No, not really. Even if it is accurate, there might still be some system errors. I have issues and doubts if the technology is fully developed and I'm scared of possible failures and system errors. (Respondent F, Female, 21, University Student).

The role of human providers in healthcare as trained in empathy and patient-provider care appears to be variant and is discussed by some respondents stating that AI lacks this particular aspect important in the field of health.

> I am not open to this; the root is that we can never trust technology. The judgment of a machine (AI) is different to a person specially in healthcare. There is just no warmth and I think it will always be a bit detached. (Respondent A, Male, 45, University Graduate).

> I'm still uncertain, the good thing is that the diagnosis and the sources for this diagnosis are reliable. I think that it can lessen malpractice and false diagnosis. What is alarming is the uncertainty about the diagnosis, on how it is made and also the lack of empathy, emotional understanding, which is usually utilized by a trained person. An example will be a cancer diagnosis and how will it be said to the patient. (Respondent H, Female, 30, University Graduate).

> I think I can accept it; I just don't think it would be the same with humans. (Respondent E, Male, 27, University Student).

The observed trends lead to a general conclusion that respondents are not open to receiving treatment from an independent AI due to various reasons. The trust in the technology alone leads to more significant considerations in terms of patient care and the technology's reliability and overall development. Many patients are anxious that such technology exists and continuously reiterate that they will not accept it unless full safety is fully ensured and that the technology is widely utilized. Responses on uncertainty and full acceptance are rarely observed, each only receiving one response with reservations tackling the technology's unreliability and uncertainty.

Perception on AI-Integrated Hospital Systems

Among the three categories, the perception of the integration of artificial intelligence (Table 4) in the healthcare delivery system, such as that in a hospital setting, is generally positive. All respondents say that they accept this technological innovation. This is backed up by another eight general responses that state the benefits of the technology and how it can improve the overall system in relation to the Philippine healthcare situation.

Table 4. Coded thematic analysis of perception on AI-integrated hospital systems

Domain	Category	n	Description
Perception on AI-Integrated Hospital Systems	Accepting	10	General
	Beneficial	8	General
	Hopeful	3	Variant
	Futuristic	1	Rare

A variant response that the respondents are hopeful that the technology will be integrated was also observed. The responses are:

> It's better if AI [is employed], in information, admission of people, handling the responsibilities, it will tend to fix the crowds. (Respondent J, Male, 35, High School Completer)

> I'm happy with AI assisted health systems. It will improve patient flows specially in crowded hospitals. (Respondent G, Female, 47, University Graduate).

> Yes, this would make the workload of hospital staff easier, and the hospital flow will be better organized if it employs AI technology. (Respondent F, Female, 21, University Student).

One also compared the success of the situation to Japan's integration of the technology who also stated that the issue is if the clientele will follow the integrated system. Meanwhile, a rare response from one believes that the technology is extremely helpful yet still futuristic and far from possible.

> Based on my knowledge, I agree and support this, we all know how bad humans can handle hospital situations, there are always lapses and delays. The issue for AI is if people will follow, but this is still greatly efficient in the case of Japan. (Respondent C, Male, 30, University Graduate).
>
> For me it will greatly help the situation in the country, but I don't know if we will see it anytime soon. (Respondent D, Female, 20, University Student).

The responses did not show any knowledge and understanding regarding data privacy issues that might arise due to the system. The respondents seemed to be enthusiastic and hopeful that the technology can be utilized in order to improve the health care delivery system. Personal experiences on the lapses and problems usually encountered by the clientele in hospitals are continuously discussed. The only reservation that arises is the current impossibility that the technology will be employed. The trend also shows that the clientele is ready to assign works such as assisted triage, patient flows, room systems, and information systems to artificial intelligence, in contrast to critical functions such as diagnosis and treatment. The results give an understanding not just of people's perception of AI in hospital settings but also a rough idea of how people view the functions that can be handled by an AI and those that they perceive to be best handled and left to human providers.

The results show (Table 5) that the clientele is more accepting of AI integrations as assistance and aid to critical healthcare settings, such as diagnosis and treatment. Conversely, there is a great deal of resistance to the concept of independent AI diagnosis and treatment. The respondents are also generally trusting in the utilization of AI in the hospital setting. Nevertheless, there is still a gap in their knowledge understanding of artificial intelligence and its issues, such as data privacy security and breach. Only seven are typically aware in terms of awareness, whilst those who are sufficiently knowledgeable, uncertain, and completely unaware appear to be variant and rare. The gap in the understanding of the clientele regarding the AI-integrated services greatly affects the succeeding categories, especially in the study locale where the integration of the technology is limited, and information comes from online sources the population seldom encounters. It is a common trend that those who are aware and have sufficient knowledge tend to explain further their reasons of acceptance or non-acceptance of the technology. Nevertheless, it should be noted that prior understanding of artificial intelligence leads to a generally more accepting attitude but not directly to positive reception from the respondents in all categories. The same is true with those who are uncertain and unaware of AI in health, who mostly answered as unaccepting or uncertain of these services. The results of the qualitative analysis are also consistent with that of the quantitative survey, with the AI-assisted and AI-system receiving a relatively high trust rating of 73% and 82%, respectively, and with a generally accepting response in the coded-thematic analysis. Meanwhile, the independent AI received 12% trust in the survey and a generally unaccepting response in the qualitative analysis. The respondents discussed the issues they see during the in-depth interview appearing as variant codes in the analysis giving light to the primary reasons affecting their perception and behavior towards the technology.

Table 5. Summary of common respondent perceptions

Respondent	**Awareness (✓-Aware, O-Uncertain, X-Unaware)**	**Common Perceptions (✓-Accepting, O-Uncertain, X-Unaccepting)**		
		AI-Assisted	**Independent AI**	**Hospital Systems**
A	✓	✓	X	✓
B	✓	✓	X	✓
C	✓	✓	X	✓
D	O	X	X	✓
E	✓	✓	✓	✓
F	✓	✓	X	✓
G	✓	✓	X	✓
H	O	✓	O	✓
I	X	X	X	✓
J	✓	✓	X	✓

Some of the issues raised about artificial intelligence include (1) the aspect of mistake, fallibility, and error; (2) the issue of responsibility; and the (3) inability to convey emotions and provide care. The clientele perceives possible mistakes an AI can commit, which might affect critical cases when not kept in check by a professional medical provider. Ironically, the clientele also used the concept of human error to highlight the improvements AI can contribute, such as increased precision and accuracy while lessening human error. These two concepts lead to the desire of the clientele to ensure their safety and well-being before trusting service and lead to an informed but lacking understanding of the mechanisms and the range of services performed by artificial intelligence. The second aspect is greatly related to the first and is largely concerned with the ethical guidelines and considerations for the employability of AI. The respondents raised concerns regarding the possible mistakes an AI can commit and who will handle these responsibilities. This is further resolved by assurance and preference of the presence of a human provider, which will keep the technology in check and verify its products. Another issue raised is the inability of the technology to convey emotions and provide the classical care given by trained professionals. This concern addresses the differences in the quality of care given by the technology versus the traditional ones by medical personnel. Lastly, a general conclusion can be drawn that the clientele is more accepting of assigning AI for non-critical functions such as the management of hospital settings and as an assistant to medical professionals in comparison to completely independent treatment and diagnosis.

The use of AI alongside humans and the use of the technology in the hospital delivery setting, both of which are generally perceived by the clientele as an improvement to the healthcare settings, are widely considered by the clientele as positive. These integrations are usually said to advance tasks such as automating repetitive and well-defined functions to guide decision-making processes done by medical professionals. Asan Bayrak and Choudhuri [2] proposed the concept of “calibrated trust” dealing with the proper Human-AI trust relationship and collaboration. The proposal dealt with the deterministic and relatively predictable nature of its system in contrast with its non-deterministic nature, both of which impact the trust relationship. Different issues relevant to this trust are highlighted in order to improve human trust in technology. The purpose of the trust is greatly important in the employability of AI in the health care industry. As previously mentioned, the clientele seemed to be open to AI integrations in less-critical functions, including triage, data management, patient flow, and information systems compared with those perceived as critical such as diagnosis and treatment. They are generally not accepting that artificial intelligence can provide independent diagnosis and treatment, while a few others are entirely not accepting of AI in these critical areas. Thus, the role of trust and addressing the issues that appear is important in promoting the use of the technology to have a positive perception from the population.

The resistance to the integration of AI exhibited by the clientele is greatly related to AI-related anxiety. While usual concerns on the future of technology are heavily expressed in media, many of these are unrealistic and greatly inspired by fictional tales demonizing the technology. Johnson and Verdicchio [14] identified three factors that contribute to AI anxiety such as:

1. An exclusive focus on AI that leaves humans out of the picture.
2. Confusion about autonomy in computational entities and in humans.
3. An inaccurate conception of technological development.

These findings are significant in analyzing the perceptions of the clientele, which further proves the conclusion that they are more accepting of AI integration if it is checked and verified or used as assistance by human providers. This is further supported by Liang and Lee [15] which found out that 26% of the population experience the fear of autonomous robots and artificial intelligence (FARAI) and is deeply connected with variable demographics such as age, education, and household income. Meanwhile, the clientele's concern regarding emotional care, which is lacking in AI, is related to the general perception of the population that the technology will negatively affect international relationships in the near future [16]. Finally, concerns about the technology's novelty and "newness" are widely explained by the psychological theory of the fear of the unknown as a fundamental fear present in humans [17]. This explains the unreadiness of some respondents to experience and avail services, especially those which employ independent AI in services such as treatment and diagnosis.

Conclusion and Recommendation

The preliminary survey resulted in a relatively high trust rating of 73% on AI-assisted diagnosis and treatment and 82% on hospital setting integration. A relatively low trust rating of 12% is observed in terms of independent AI diagnosis and treatment. In the qualitative analysis of perception and awareness, seven respondents are typically aware that AI health services exist, while three respondents range from uncertainty to being completely unaware. This, in turn, affects their perception of the three defined categories, whereas those who answered as aware and knowledgeable are more accepting of the technology. Nevertheless, this group also expressed their concerns and issues about the technology, especially in independent AI integration. Conversely, those unaware of the technology are more unaccepting of its employment in assisted, and independent diagnosis and treatment yet showed support in its integration in hospital settings. General findings are usually accompanied by issues regarding the technology's integration which explains the clientele's perception. Summarizing the perception of the clientele on the three defined categories, the general responses are:

1. The utilization of Artificial Intelligence in AI-assisted diagnosis and treatment is widely accepted, receiving a general accepting response with at most eight respondents. This is accompanied by one typical and one variant response saying that they will avail the service in the future and are excited about it, respectively. Contrary, variant responses of unacceptance are observed.
2. The employment of independent AI in the same critical health function of diagnosis and treatment is widely unaccepted, receiving a general unaccepting response with at most eight respondents. This is accompanied by a typical response of anxiety with regard to receiving the said services. Meanwhile, rare accepting and uncertain responses are observed.
3. Lastly, the integration of AI on hospital systems received a general accepting response from all ten respondents. This is also accompanied by another general response saying that the technology is beneficial to the healthcare setting. A variant response from the respondents saying that they are hopeful for the technology is also observed, and a rare response that the technology is still futuristic is observed.

The general findings are explained by the common issues raised in the in-depth interview regarding the employment of AI in health care settings. These are explained by the theories on AI anxiety and human-AI trust as well as ethical considerations on explainability, safety, interpersonal relations, and responsibility. Prominent issues that arise are:

1. AI is still imperfect and is prone to making mistakes on its own. Ironically, some respondents also argued that AI is the best fit in helping human health providers avoid human errors and increase precision and accuracy. The common idea is that the integration of AI is best left as an aid and assistance to providers and hospitals. The issue centers on the clientele's need for the assurance of safety.
2. In relation to the first, the issue of responsibility was raised. The clientele seems to be concerned in cases where an AI will commit a mistake and who will be responsible for it. The general view is that if AI is employed as an aid and assistant, the human medical provider will be present to check and verify the actions and, as such, handles the responsibility for the service provided, which is significant as an ethical consideration.
3. Another common response is on the absence of emotion and care with Artificial Intelligence. The respondents argue that human health care providers are trained to give care, especially in critical cases. This is an ability that can't be taught to AI, therefore, facilitating the lack of interpersonal interaction and relationship in this service.

Lastly, it is a common trend that respondents are more accepting of AI-integrated services on less critical functions such as assisted triage, patient flows, and information systems in comparison with functions such as diagnosis and treatment. However, the clientele seemed to not be aware of issues in this particular integration, such as data privacy, which are not usually encountered by the population. The use in a hospital setting is generally perceived as more effective than independent integrations as assistance to health care providers. In lieu of this, the following recommendations are made:

1. To hospitals and health care providers, it is highly recommended that AI is employed in improving healthcare delivery systems. The use of AI in assisting medical practitioners can also be employed while addressing issues and explaining the process to clients. On the other hand, the safety and efficacy of the use of independent AI technology

should be determined, and proper awareness must be raised with the clientele and general public.

2. To AI creators and engineers, the ethical issues arising on AI as well as the concerns of the clientele, should be addressed, especially in the aspect of mistakes. The algorithms and process's explainability should be considered to ensure that the service is safe and perceived to be safe by the clientele.
3. Government institutions must also ensure that ethical considerations are addressed and bylaws are created in order to guide the use of AI technology in the healthcare field. The issue of responsibility must be addressed in the context of mistakes, errors, and malpractice. The government can also help increase the awareness of the clientele on the technology and fund research as well as integrations of the new technology in health.
4. The clientele and general public must continue to address issues and concerns on the use of AI in health being the intended recipients of these services. At the same time, proper time in order to understand these processes are needed in order to fully comprehend these services and therefore make rational decisions based on their knowledge and understanding of the technology.
5. Research can be conducted to correlate awareness and knowledge with trust and perception using experimental and quantitative techniques to statistically prove these relationships. Further qualitative research is also recommended with the use of the same in-depth interview method and coded thematic analysis or other methods such as Focused Group Discussions (FGDs), especially addressing the specific and individual categories defined in this study in order to shed light on the clientele's perception of AI technology in health and improve the community's understanding of the reasons resulting to the trust and perceptions of the clientele on AI-integrated health services.

Appendix

Respondents	Gender	Age	Educational Attainment
A	M	45	University Graduate
B	F	36	High School Completer
C	M	30	University Graduate
D	F	20	University Student
E	M	27	University Student
F	F	21	University Student
G	F	47	University Graduate
H	F	30	University Graduate
I	M	24	University Student
J	M	35	High School Completer

Figure 7. Sample Demographics of Respondent in the In-Depth Interview.

References

[1] Wang, Fei, and Anita Preininger. "AI in health: state of the art, challenges, and future directions." *Yearbook of medical informatics* 28, no. 1 (2019): 16.

[2] Asan, Onur, Alparslan Emrah Bayrak, and Avishek Choudhury. "Artificial intelligence and human trust in healthcare: focus on clinicians." *Journal of medical Internet research* 22, no. 6 (2020): e15154.

[3] Davenport, Thomas H., T. Hongsermeier, and Kimberly Alba Mc Cord. "Using AI to improve electronic health records." *Harvard Business Review* 12 (2018): 1-6.

[4] Jobin, Anna, Marcello Ienca, and Effy Vayena. "The global landscape of AI ethics guidelines." *Nature Machine Intelligence* 1, no. 9 (2019): 389-399.

[5] Morley, Jessica, Luciano Floridi, Libby Kinsey, and Anat Elhalal. "From what to how. An overview of AI ethics tools, methods and research to translate principles into practices." *arXiv preprint arXiv:1905.06876* (2019).

[6] Hagerty, Alexa, and Igor Rubinov. "Global AI ethics: a review of the social impacts and ethical implications of artificial intelligence." *arXiv preprint arXiv:1907.07892* (2019).

[7] Gal, Danit. "Perspectives and approaches in AI ethics: East Asia." *Oxford Handbook of Ethics of Artificial Intelligence, Oxford University Press, Forthcoming* (2019).

[8] Mayer, Roger C., James H. Davis, and F. David Schoorman. "An integrative model of organizational trust." *Academy of management review* 20.3 (1995): 709-734.

[9] Lee, John D., and A. Katrina. "See. 2004." "*Trust in Automation: Designing for Appropriate Reliance." In Human Factors: The Journal of the Human Factors and Ergonomics Society* 46 (2004).

[10] Bristows. "*Artificial Intelligence: Public Perception, Attitude and Trust.*" (2018).

[11] Polgar, Stephen and Shane A. Thomas. 2016. *Introduction to Research in the Health Sciences*. Elsevier.

[12] Minichiello, Victor, Rosalie Aroni, and Terrence Neville Hays. *In-depth interviewing: Principles, techniques, analysis*. Pearson Education Australia, 2008.

[13] Thompson, Barbara J., C. E. Hill, and E. Nutt Williams. "A Guide to Conducting consensual qualitative research." *The Counseling Psychologist* 25, no. 4 (1997): 517-572.

[14] Johnson, Deborah G., and Mario Verdicchio. "AI anxiety." *Journal of the Association for Information Science and Technology* 68, no. 9 (2017): 2267-2270.

[15] Liang, Yuhua, and Seungcheol Austin Lee. "Fear of autonomous robots and artificial intelligence: Evidence from national representative data with probability sampling." *International Journal of Social Robotics* 9, no. 3 (2017): 379-384.

[16] Gherheş, Vasile. "Why Are We Afraid of Artificial Intelligence (Ai)?." *European Review of Applied Sociology* 11, no. 17 (2018): 6-15.

[17] Carleton, R. Nicholas. "Fear of the unknown: One fear to rule them all?." *Journal of anxiety disorders* 41 (2016): 5-21.

Chapter 12

Leveraging Deep Learning: Early Detection and Prediction of Brain Disorders

Maha Waheed Shahzad[1,*], Aiman Siraj[2,†], Aradhana Balodi Bhardwaj[3,‡] and Vinod Kumar Shukla[4,§]

[1,3]Department of Humanities, Arts and Applied Sciences,
Amity University, Dubai, UAE
[2,4]Department of Engineering and Architecture,
Amity University, Dubai, UAE

Abstract

Neuropsychology is a structured, objective, and scientific discipline, which focuses on the brain and tries to associate various behaviors of individuals with the changes or the deficits that develop in the brain. The methods used by neuropsychologists include both experimental and scientific. Individuals are suffering from very old tremors in their hands and do not have proper motor coordination, and individuals are having tics and speech problems as a side effect of some disease they had in the past. All of these physical health conditions are associated with certain neurological problems or dysfunctions of the brain. Using neuroimaging for these dysfunctions would make it easy to identify a person's behavioral and physical health.

* Author's Email: mahas1@amitydubai.ae.
† Author's Email: aimansiraj84@gmail.com.
‡ Author's Email: abhardwaj@amityuniversity.ae.
§ Corresponding Author's Email: vinodkumarshukla@gmail.com.

In: Industry 4.0 and Intelligent Business Analytics for Healthcare
Editors: Soumi Dutta, Vinod Kumar Shukla, Shruti Nagpal et al.
ISBN: 978-1-68507-602-3

Machine learning is how the machine learns about an existing environment to evaluate or detect reoccurring patterns or behaviour around it. With this gathered information, it then proceeds to update its existing database and improve its functionalities. It is also used to predict the outcome from a given dataset. Deep learning can be defined as a state-of-the-art machine learning approach, which has shown incredible performance compared to traditional machine learning. Although deep learning techniques in medical imaging are still very recent, they have been successful in inspiring many medical professionals and radiologists as it makes imaging safer, faster, and more accessible to patients.

This chapter carefully analyses the existing literature data on the innovation and application of deep learning to detect and predict various brain disorders. This chapter highlights the different comprehensive methods used by neuropsychologists to identify deficits or cognitive impairments of the brain using neuropsychological tests. It will also develop on the techniques of neuroimaging, machine learning, and deep learning and how these can be used to detect the syndromes associated with the brain and talk about the trends in deep learning for the early prediction of these disorders.

Keywords: neuropsychology, deep learning, machine learning. neuroimaging, dysfunctions

Introduction

Neuropsychology is a unique combination of several disciplines, particularly cognitive and developmental psychology. Neuropsychology helps recognize the possible locality of the functioning of the brain by developing quantitative techniques for assessing brain damage caused. The quantitative approach to assessment in neuropsychology relies on comparing an individual's performance on standardized tests.

Individuals are suffering from very old tremors in their hands and do not have proper motor coordination, and individuals are having tics and speech problems as a side effect of some disease they had in the past. All of these physical health conditions are associated with some neurological issues or dysfunctions of the brain. Broca's region plays an important role in speech production, syntactic and semantic aspects of language. Located in the left hemisphere and posterior part of the frontal lobe, the Broca's area's regions 44 and 45 have specific phonological processes. More recent studies have concluded an interface between behavior and perception, which is to reconcile verbal and non-verbal communication between perceptual and motor functions.

Scientific advancements in neuropsychology and psychopharmacology have drastically affected the scope and role of neuropsychologists. These advancements have altered our understanding of many psychological and behavioral disorders, including autism spectrum disorder, depression; these were once thought to be environmental or functional.

Technological advancements provide researchers and practitioners with techniques to study developmental changes in the brain and to understand plasticity and reorganization. Utilizing imaging techniques makes it easier to identify the neurobiological changes in the brain, the areas of the brain that were recognized as usual or unusual.

Introduction to Deep Learning

Deep learning is regarded as a subset of machine learning, as it learns characteristics through a hierarchical learning process. These deep learning methods can be applied in various fields for the classification and prediction of diseases. Feature-based algorithm selection is used to classify these machine learning approaches in four steps; feature selection, feature extraction, and dimensional reduction. Deep learning is different from traditional machine learning; formal learning differs in how the discovered raw data is represented. Deep learning algorithms use multiple deep layers of perceptions that capture both high and low-level data representations. The use of manual engineering of the features is eliminated, enabling deep learning models to discover previously unknown patterns that can generally be linked to novel data [1].

It is a minor part of machine learning with wide applications as it can work with real-time data and function optimally. It works exactly like a brain would do and interprets and analyzes data like it to make logical decisions based on its research. You can check the accuracy of the model by comparing to the ideal one or predicting the outcomes of a system. Like machine learning, deep learning is also an AI concept and is implemented by a network of systems. Since it tries to copy or impersonate all the brain processes, it can also work with different types of data like images, texts, sounds, objects, etc. Any information that can be easily interpreted can be added to the database. It works exceptionally well with big data and other concepts as well [2].

The main factor to be noted about these systems is that they are accurate and precise in detail and are correct to the point. They are also quite fast in processing and updating the data. Hence, the hardware parts of the systems should also be suited and fit to work accordingly with such technology. These are being popularly used because the accuracy of the output data keeps on increasing each time a new set of input data is added in the system [2].

Fundamentals of Deep Learning

Figure 12.1, represents the breakdown of the types of algorithms used in machine learning research analysis and medical research [3].

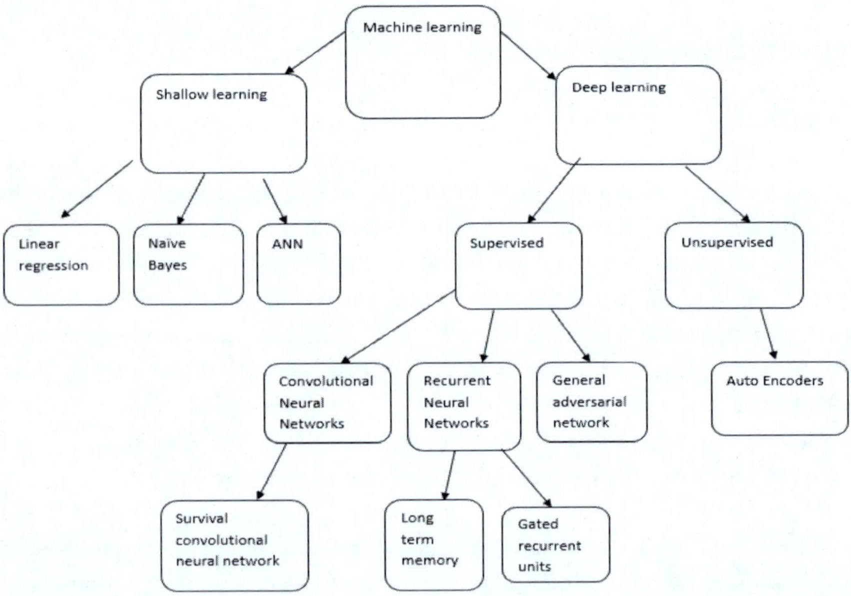

Figure 12.1. Types of algorithms used in machine learning [3].

Convolutional neural networks (CNNs) have collected a lot of attention in computers and imaging-based medical research. CNN records images across multiple layers. Specific features of the image are displayed in each layer; for example, the visual cortex can be arranged into hierarchical layers (which includes primary and secondary visual cortex and so on). The pooling layer reduces the number of features; therefore, computation makes it easier to drop out the layers and sees each of them separately. The recurrent neural network uses the gating approach to determine whether to maintain or eliminate the data from the previous elements before generating outputs. Autoencoders (AE's) are unsupervised algorithms that draw a lower-dimensional map from inputs to outputs, which help in the detection of meaningful representations of data. AEs draw abstract representations of data that include only the primary features required for the reconstruction of the input. These are also used in conjunction with the above generative adversarial strategies to learn features that can be used. These aim to generate novel data that represent graphs of the input data by latent distribution [3].

Neural Networks

These networks work by using more than one algorithm, which is used to recognize, interpret, identify and detect any type of repeated behavior or similarity in the dataset. This is exactly how our brain tries to process information. Even if the input value has changed or there is a little change in the data code, you can just update the same part. There is no need to change or redesign the whole system again. This is why it is highly flexible and popularly used. It is also really fast at identifying connections, even if the dataset is of large volume [4].

Our body has small structures called nodes that process and pass on information; in this system, the nodes are in several layers like structures and are used to exchange data. It also observes its surroundings and input data to form output values as a deep learning process. Initially, it works on sample data that would be provided to it to check the system's accuracy, but slowly, after that, it will try to collect values on its own and manipulate them. This is one of the reasons why it is so successfully implemented in AI networks [4].

Artificial Intelligence (AI)

AI is copying or trying to impersonate human intelligence by processing or evaluating information the same way as the human brain. So, machines and computers are designed to work exactly like a brain in the human body does. It is also expected to solve problems, operate, and learn exactly like it for better performance. So, the result expected is to perform and think logically and have a reason behind doing a task and do it in the best possible manner. There are multiple types and algorithms used to create such a system, and a lot of effort is put into it so that the end goal meets the user's expectation and predicts the best outcome to make things easier. These systems can also be used in predicting various types of diseases and disorders by providing consistent and non-redundant sample data [5].

Machine Learning

It's a kind of a process where the machine tries to learn from its surroundings without any human intervention. It has all the necessary codes and is programmed to do exactly what it is told by carrying out necessary procedures and processing data simultaneously at regular intervals time. Any kinds of similarities, repetitions of data values, and certain data characteristics are taken note of in the system and are used to enhance future operations and make better decisions. It could also be used to predict data and analyze it properly so that the results are foreseen. This could be great in many sectors, especially the health sector [6].

The machine takes care of both complicated and uncomplicated processes without any help. Artificial intelligence systems are bound to mark this revolutionary approach that will change the computer systems' work. The concept of data mining eases up many setbacks and brings in better solutions for such problems. If the machine can both access data and work upon it simultaneously, it would be both n opportunity and a new learning experience for it so such models can be developed in the future with an enhanced database and way better results [7].

The following are the three techniques used in the system that is proposed in this chapter. Implementation of these algorithm in dataset is been discussed in Application and result section of the same chapter.

- *Support Vector Machine Algorithm:* This algorithm uses different coordinates and creates lines between them in order to identify the relation between them by using and examining hyper-planes depending on the type of data and its relations. A method called "kernel-trick" is an unsupervised method used to classify data and manipulate it to achieve desired output quickly [7].
- *Random Forest Classifier Algorithm:* Imagine multiple decision trees working together constantly and giving out a single consistent output; that is exactly what this classifier does by combining multiple

decision trees and creating a new structure out of it so that the results are way more accurate when compared to the usual decision tree. This algorithm is a type of supervised learning where it can solve complexities but need human intervention. We are calculating a result in 'n' possible ways and taking an average of it. This increases the accuracy numerous times and increases accuracy over a period of time [7].

- *XGB Classifier Algorithm:* Extreme Gradient Boosting is an algorithm which implements such boosting machines and calculates and manipulates data in order to achieve accurate results. It also has great computability speed and high-performance features and is flexible and portable. Although the key reason why it is popular is it's computing speed but it has a lot more features apart from that [7].

Deep Learning in Neurology

The deep learning techniques mentioned above play a very important role in neurological research. Firstly, segmentation and image classification has been the main focus of deep learning development efforts in the past. The high dimensional neuroimaging data has been unfavorable to manual research and not combining the digital nature of modern imaging. Secondly, DL has been applied to fictional brain mapping correlational studies that use functional magnetic resonance imaging (fMRI), to predict seizures. Finally, the use of multiple data types for diagnostic prognostication of diseases causing risks [3].

Chella D'Andrea & Pizzella, in their paper, estimated MEG functional connectivity of different frequencies; this is described in a unified mathematical framework. In the second part of the paper, examples are given of the specific methods used for MEG data to test for visuospatial attention and working memory. The overall study results show that frequency-specific brain circuits that are partly overlapping the brain network are identified by hemodynamic-based imaging techniques, for example, fMRI. These brain circuits can be linked to behavior and anatomy, highlighting the use of MEG in neuroscience research. In conclusion, functional connectivity has advanced to a more mechanical understanding of the functions of the brain; it has further supported high-level integration tools [8].

The paper introduces the concepts of deep learning using existing literature that has used this technique to classify the deficits of the brain. The results show that deep learning can currently be a powerful tool in researching psychiatric and neurological domains. It was concluded that deep learning is designed to learn complex and abstract images through non-linear transformations; this makes it a promising idea for single-subject prediction [9].

In 2019 discussed the pathophysiology and imaging modalities of brain cancer, followed by the various computer-assisted methods used for the same. The paper also further highlights the co-morbidity of brain cancer and other brain disorders like stroke, Alzheimer's Wilson's disease, and other neurological disorders in the deep learning context [10]. Both machine learning and deep learning are concepts of artificial intelligence, which are implemented to increase the machine's knowledge by continuously analysing data and updating it in order to make better future decisions.

Application of Machine Learning and Deep Learning in the Detection and Prediction of Various Brain Disorders

Machines or computers can interpret data faster and more efficiently than us humans. This property of the computer is enhanced by machine learning as it is highly effective in detecting similarities and repetitions in the information provided and predicting the next possible value or outcome in such a scenario. Sometimes it may feel like someone may have been diagnosed with a brain disorder out of nowhere. Contrary to that, it progresses or increases with time, and the degeneration process occurs until the brain is unable to respond. Thus, early prediction can save a person with proper medication and treatment, which would lead to the betterment of the patients [6].

Machine learning can easily be used to sort out various categories of data and make sense out of it. For example, processing a data set and predicting a possible value based on that dataset. It could do the same for datasets related to neurology. Key examples of these would be a patient's MRI results, blood tests, and an overall test conducted to view his/her brain performance. The first essential step would be to classify data that would be useful based on its importance and type. Machine learning works best with numerical values such as float and int, and then after that, you can use various algorithms depending on your need or the outcome wished for [6].

Deep learning is used by processing different kinds of information using supervised or unsupervised methods to evaluate data. There are a few ways in which data can be processed by deep learning in neurology. One of them is the classification of images. This is especially done in cases of Alzheimer and similar disorders. Basically, the cognitive disabilities of the person can be detected by this process of neuroimaging. A classifier would be used to differentiate images of fine similarities and non-similarities and then predict the possible case. The seriousness of the case and the extent of damage can also be identified with the help of this method. Several brain features are looked upon closely and inspected to identify the key problem that is causing or has caused the disorder. It's also used in the case of brain hemorrhages to identify what could have possibly caused the leak [7].

Another way or step to identify the key causes is the segmentation of these images. This would help us understand the overall structure of the brain. The way it is formed, its shape, density, and any problem with thickness density or overall structure of the rain would have led to such a disorder. It could also be a case where the disorder would have led to a structural change in the brain, especially in the cases of the brain tumor. This will help us understand the exact position of the additional cells or tissues and why they could have formed there. Although the vascular-based approach is also now being considered in order to have a deeper understanding of the disorder [7].

Another main reason why deep learning is used is to prognosticate risk or predict future risks or further damages that could be caused in the coming time. A deep study of the genetics of the person is also done just in case to study the possible connection to the case. EEG output and MRI output are also used to generate information related to future risks. Also, necessary treatment can also be suggested by the use of these techniques accordingly [7].

Applications in Medical Domain

Upstream applications such as improved image quality are very important when predicting the images. It is not essential to have large sets of data rather good quality data. Besides the ethical and legal challenges, researchers find it not practical to interpret the results physiologically. Deep learning networks are like black boxes. All of the algorithms work at a higher dimension compared to what the human mind can directly visualize [11].

Medical Image Classification

The application of deep learning in the medical field involves the analysis of models to detect various deficits such as cognitive impairments and Alzheimer's disease. Earlier techniques used AEs along with a classifier to distinguish Alzheimer's disease, mild cognitive impairments, and healthy controls. Suk and Shen, with the help of stacked AE, studied the multimodal brain representation from MRI and PET and assimilated these characteristics with cerebrospinal fluid, the scores from MMSE (Mini-Mental state examination) and ADAS-Cog (Alzheimer's disease assessment scale-cognitive subscale) to train an SVM classifier. The different variations in these approaches have a gradual improvement in diagnostic performance. The old techniques were limited to 2-dimensional imaging models due to computational constraints; applications that are using newer technology can use the 3-dimensional features to view their images [3].

Medical Image Segmentation

Segmentation of the images of the brain is crucial for the accurate measurement of the regions of the brain (including thickness, shape, and volume) to quantify the changes in the structure within the brain that can occur either by nature or due to some illness. Vascular segmentation is an area of deep learning which aims to quantify brain vessel status. Livne et al. had recently run a study on blood vessel segmentation, applying a U-net model collecting data from 66 patients with cerebrovascular disease and then comparing it to the traditional vascular segmentation method [3].

Perivascular spaces (PVS) are small spaces encircling the blood vessels; stress could be a cause of the breakdown of the blood-brain barrier due to inflammation. Although PVSs have been used widely for many diseases, it isn't easy to measure these spaces even in MRI equipment with the highest resolution, as their appearance is low-contrast and tubular [3].

Classification of Brain Disorders and Functional Connectivity

Using multiple modals in research has been the main idea of deep learning, especially for illnesses such as ASD and ADHD. The diagnosis of this is dependent on non-specific symptoms such as hyperactivity and distractibility in individuals with ADHD, resulting in poor sensitivity and does not provide specific criteria for clinical diagnosis [12].

Data Reconstruction Techniques

Image Reconstruction

Deep learning is used for medical image reconstruction; this allows MRI, PET, and reduced radiations. The raw MRI image can be constructed again by performing an inverse Fourier transformation operation. Several approaches in deep learning aim to learn the mapping between sonograms and images directly. The neural network is expected to allow automatic optimization of the algorithms for the rebuilding of the image and can be technologically more efficient than classical techniques [10].

Signal Enhancement

Image reconstruction techniques could be used as image de-noising techniques. Denoising can be applied mainly for MRI, PET. Another super-resolution method consists of a combination of various images of the same type or subject, one high-resolution and the other low-resolution to balance it [10].

Cross-Modality Image Synthesis

Translation of images is used in the context of cross-modality; this allows us to generate CT. Image reconstruction, signal enhancement, and cross-modality are different alternatives of convolutional neural networks, conditional generative adversarial networks, and u-nets [10].

Proposed Framework for Early Detection and Prediction of Neurological Disorder

Our proposed framework would consist of multiple machine learning algorithms that would check a patient's details with a neurological disorder.

Suppose the patient's case turns out to be a positive value. In that case, the patient will undergo MRI and EEG scanning along with a blood test and a brain performance test which will then determine the type of disease and the seriousness of the case as the images will be classified and segmented using deep learning and the output will be predicted.

The output dataset obtained can be analyzed by machine learning, and if the result turns out to be a positive case, it can further be analyzed by deep learning imaging techniques. This will be done by using algorithms and will be accurate. Imaging analysis and simulated neural networks can be used to predict the case's seriousness, and then the images can be classified and segmented accordingly. This system will aid in the early prediction of neurological diseases, which would lead to an increase in the patient's survival rate.

Software Requirements

OS: Windows XP and above
Python IDE: python 3.x and above, Jupyter Notebook
Setup tools and pip to be installed for 3.6.x and above

Open source Python tools used are:

- Numpy – It is used to manipulate and work with matrices and arrays to make the process of dealing with them easier.
- Pandas – It is used to understand and predict information and has really high-quality performance.
- Matplotlib.pyplot – It turns the interface similar to that of MATLAB and helps to use such type of features.
- Seaborn – It is used to draw graph and statistical outputs.

Here as an example we are going to predict Alzheimer.

Parameters Used to Achieve the Output

- Subject ID of the person (Just a record value)
- Gender of the person (binary value where 1 is male and 0 is female)

- Age of the person (variable value)
- The number of visits made for checkup (variable value)
- Right handedness or left handedness (1 being right and 0 being left)
- Clinically determined dementia (1 and 0.5 being positive values and 0 is negative)
- Years of education of the person (variable value)
- Social and economic status of the person (variable value)
- A mini examination of the mental state (variable value)
- MRI Delay of the person (variable value)
- Volume of the entire brain which is normalized (0.6 – 0.8)
- The estimated sum or total of the intracranial volume (variable)
- The scaling factor value which is needed to match every atlas value. (variable value which differs for every person)

Machine Learning Application Results

Data.shape – Prints out the total number of rows and columns and describes the dataset. Next step would be to assign the group value by some variable we are using ‘y’

<table>
<tr>
<td><pre>data.shape

(373, 15)</pre></td>
<td><pre>y = data["Group"]

ax = sns.countplot(data["Group"])
target_temp = data.Group.value_counts()
print(target_temp)

0   208
1   165
Name: Group, dtype: int64</pre></td>
</tr>
<tr>
<td>Data Shape</td>
<td>Assigning Group Value</td>
</tr>
</table>

Following represents the percentage of male and female patients.

```
countFemale = len(data[data.MF == 0])
countMale = len(data[data.MF == 1])
print("Percentage of Female Patients:{:.2f}%".format((countFemale)/(len(data.MF))*100))
print("Percentage of Male Patients:{:.2f}%".format((countMale)/(len(data.MF))*100))
```

```
Percentage of Female Patients:57.10%
Percentage of Male Patients:42.90%
```

We can check for sample data of any 'n' rows using the data sample function. For example following Figure 12.2 represents the five row data as sample from the dataset.

```
data.sample(5)
```

	Subject ID	MRI ID	Group	Visit	MR Delay	M/F	Hand	Age	EDUC	SES	MMSE	eTIV	nWBV	ASF	CDR
181	182	MR1	Nondemented	1	0	F	R	63	15	2.0	28.0	1544	0.805	1.136	0.0
362	363	MR2	Nondemented	2	182	F	R	66	13	2.0	30.0	1506	0.740	1.165	0.0
221	222	MR1	Demented	1	0	M	R	70	16	1.0	25.0	1568	0.696	1.119	0.5
86	87	MR1	Demented	1	0	F	R	72	12	4.0	26.0	1453	0.777	1.208	0.5
316	317	MR1	Demented	1	0	F	R	73	12	2.0	19.0	1274	0.728	1.377	1.0

Figure 12.2. Sample Dataset.

To understand the data various techniques for the analysis can be used such as count, mean, and average to ensure data is in order. Following Figure 12.3 represent a quick sample of the analysis on these methods and its result for the sample for the analysis.

```
data.describe()
```

	Subject ID	Visit	MR Delay	Age	EDUC	SES	MMSE	eTIV	nWBV	ASF	CDR
count	373.000000	373.000000	373.000000	373.000000	373.000000	354.000000	371.000000	373.000000	373.000000	373.000000	373.000000
mean	187.000000	1.882038	595.104558	77.013405	14.597855	2.460452	27.342318	1488.128686	0.729568	1.195461	0.290885
std	107.820066	0.922843	635.485118	7.640957	2.876339	1.134005	3.683244	176.139286	0.037135	0.138092	0.374557
min	1.000000	1.000000	0.000000	60.000000	6.000000	1.000000	4.000000	1106.000000	0.644000	0.876000	0.000000
25%	94.000000	1.000000	0.000000	71.000000	12.000000	2.000000	27.000000	1357.000000	0.700000	1.099000	0.000000
50%	187.000000	2.000000	552.000000	77.000000	15.000000	2.000000	29.000000	1470.000000	0.729000	1.194000	0.000000
75%	280.000000	2.000000	873.000000	82.000000	16.000000	3.000000	30.000000	1597.000000	0.756000	1.293000	0.500000
max	373.000000	5.000000	2639.000000	98.000000	23.000000	5.000000	30.000000	2004.000000	0.837000	1.587000	2.000000

Figure 12.3. Sample tools analysis on dataset.

A *correlation matrix* (Figure 12.4) is used to detect and recognize and similarities or relations between the mentioned coefficient values and to see if they have any dependency on each other and if a variation in such values will bring a change in the dataset. It basically kind of summarizes the data and analyses it in an advanced way which could then be used for further diagnosis. We are creating one to do the same.

```
plot_correlation_map(df)
```

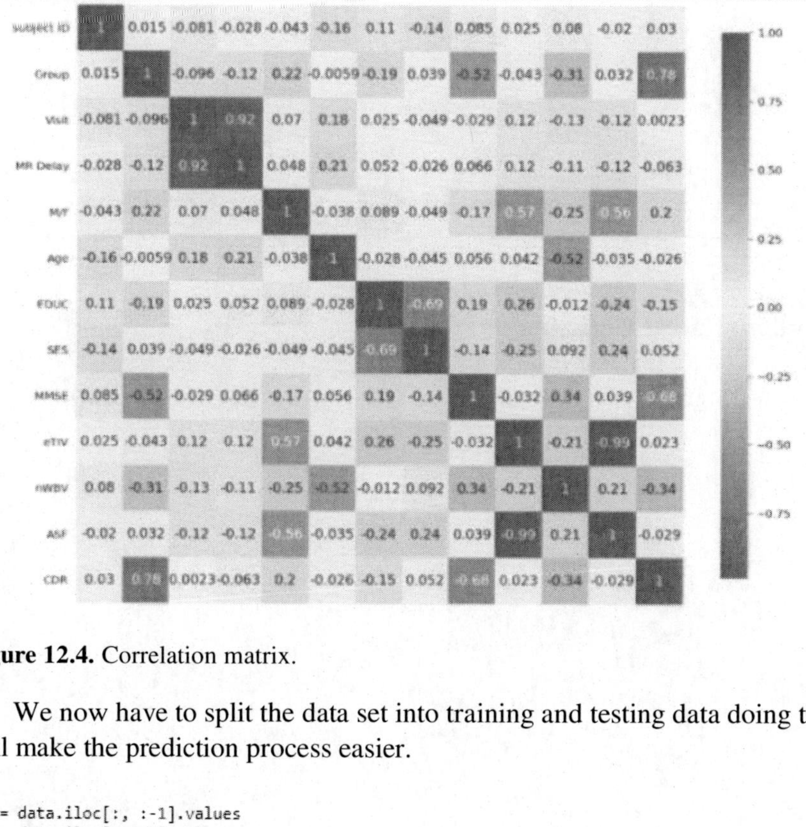

Figure 12.4. Correlation matrix.

We now have to split the data set into training and testing data doing that will make the prediction process easier.

```
X = data.iloc[:, :-1].values
y = data.iloc[:, -1].values
```

```
from sklearn.model_selection import train_test_split
x_train, x_test, y_train, y_test = train_test_split(X,y,test_size = 0.2, random_state = 1)
```

```
from sklearn.preprocessing import StandardScaler
sc = StandardScaler()
x_train = sc.fit_transform(x_train)
x_test = sc.transform(x_test)
```

Now we will individually check the accuracy of each of the three algorithms and see which one yields to be the most accurate one.

<table>
<tr><th>Support Vector Machine</th><th>XGB Classifier</th></tr>
<tr><td><pre>
print("SVM")
svm = SVC(kernel="linear", C=0.1,random_state=0)
svm.fit(X_train, y_train.ravel())
report_performance(svm)
roc_curves(svm)
accuracy(svm)
saccuracy = cross_val_score(estimator=svm,X=X_test,y=y_test.ravel(),cv=10)
print(saccuracy)
print(saccuracy.mean())
print(saccuracy.std())

SVM

Confusion Matrix:
[[46 6]
 [19 41]]

Classification Report:
              precision   recall f1-score   support

           0   0.71   0.88   0.79   52
           1   0.87   0.68   0.77   60

    accuracy   0.78   112
   macro avg   0.79   0.78   0.78   112
weighted avg   0.80   0.78   0.78   112
</pre></td><td><pre>
from xgboost import XGBClassifier
xgb= XGBClassifier(n_estimators=100)
xgb.fit(X_train,y_train.ravel())
report_performance(xgb)
roc_curves(xgb)
accuracy(xgb)
xaccuracy = cross_val_score(estimator=xgb,X=X_test,y=y_test.ravel(),cv=10)
print(xaccuracy)
print(xaccuracy.mean())
print(xaccuracy.std())

Confusion Matrix:
[[44 8]
 [11 49]]

Classification Report:
              precision   recall f1-score   support

           0   0.80   0.85   0.82   52
           1   0.86   0.82   0.84   60

    accuracy   0.83   112
   macro avg   0.83   0.83   0.83   112
weighted avg   0.83   0.83   0.83   112
</pre></td></tr>
<tr><td>Accuracy – 78%</td><td>Accuracy – 83%</td></tr>
</table>

Random Forest Classifier

It has the highest accuracy among the three algorithms which is 84%.

```
rfc=RandomForestClassifier(random_state=42)

param_grid = {
    'n_estimators': [200],
    'max_features': ['auto'],
    'max_depth' : [4,5,6,7,8],
    'criterion' :['gini']
}

CV_rfc = GridSearchCV(estimator=rfc, param_grid=param_grid, cv= 5,scoring = 'roc_auc',iid='FALSE')
CV_rfc.fit(X_train, y_train.ravel())
print("Best parameters set found on development set:")
print(CV_rfc.best_params_)
report_performance(CV_rfc)
roc_curves(CV_rfc)
accuracy(CV_rfc)
raccuracy = cross_val_score(estimator=CV_rfc,X=X_test,y=y_test.ravel(),cv=10)
print(raccuracy)
print(raccuracy.mean())
print(raccuracy.std())
```

```
Best parameters set found on development set:
{'criterion': 'gini', 'max_depth': 8, 'max_features': 'auto', 'n_estimators': 200}


Confusion Matrix:
[[45  7]
 [11 49]]


Classification Report:
              precision    recall  f1-score   support

           0       0.80      0.87      0.83        52
           1       0.88      0.82      0.84        60

    accuracy                           0.84       112
   macro avg       0.84      0.84      0.84       112
weighted avg       0.84      0.84      0.84       112
```

We can type in data to check if the algorithms can predict it. For the example we are using the Random Forest Classifier to predict as it had the highest accuracy.

```
print(rfc.predict(sc.transform([[2,538,0,1,90,18,3,27,1200,0.718,1.462,0]])))
[0]

print(rfc.predict(sc.transform([[1,0,1,1,76,16,3,21,1602,0.697,1.096,0.5]])))

[1]
```

The result predicts the target value where 1 indicates a positive patient and 0 indicates a negative patient who does not have dementia.

Deep Learning Example

The MRI data of a person is collected and processed (Figure 12.5). The data is then converted into a graph co-relation matrix (Figure 12.6). This data is then processed using the concept of neural networks where each layer is analyzed carefully and processed (Figure 12.7). A few important features are selected from the layers which could determine the output (Figure 12.8).

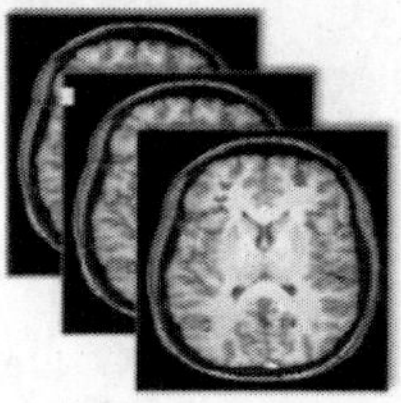

Figure 12.5. MRI Data.

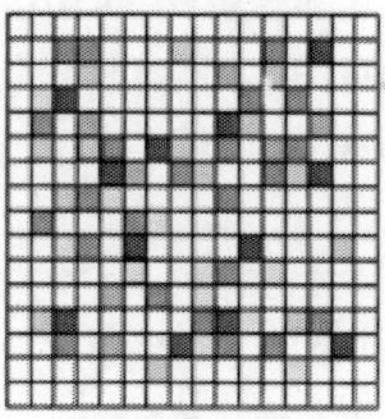

Figure 12.6. Correlation Matrix.

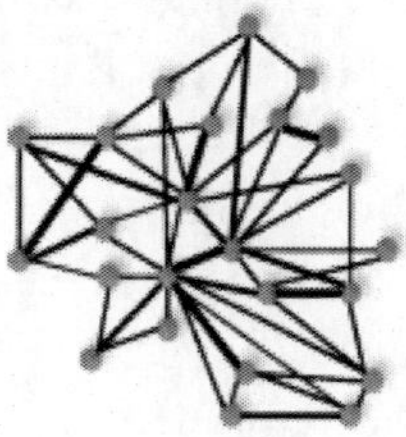

Figure 12.7. Brain Network.

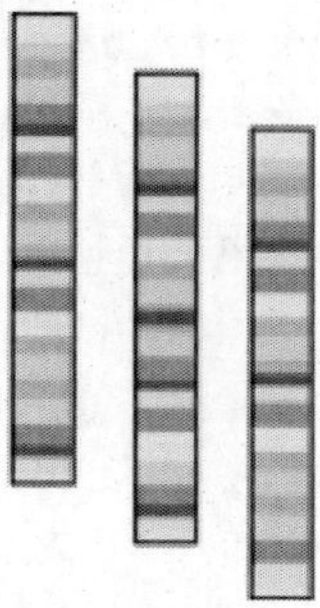

Figure 12.8. Selected Features.

Then these features are classified using deep learning techniques to obtain the output layer (Figure 12.9).

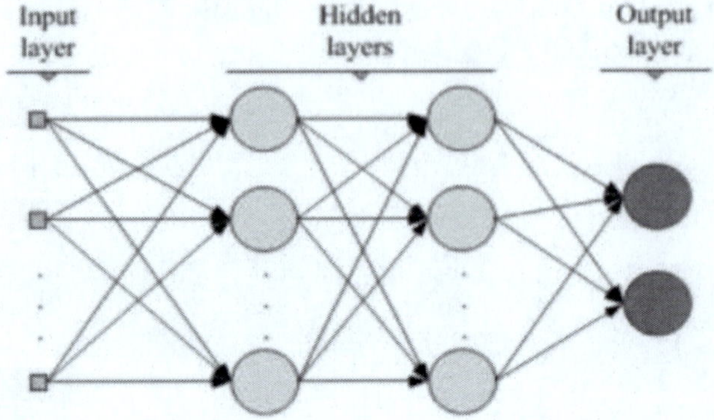

Figure 12.9. Representation of relation from various processing to output layer.

Clinical Significance

Valliani evaluated existing literature on neuro-imaging for the diagnosis and classification of Alzheimer's disease. Traditional learning approaches, deep learning, and hybrid methods have improved up to 98.8% for Alzheimer's disease classification. However, the deep learning approaches are accurate up to 96.0% for AD classification of AD. In traditional machine learning, the more complex the data, the more difficult it is to pick optimal characteristics. Deep learning can detect features that are optimal from the data automatically, without human interaction [1]. It has also discussed the challenges in involving the tools for deep learning as well as the barriers to tackle the challenges, especially in the clinical setting [3].

Shahrimnan, along with his colleagues, studied the automatic classification of healthy and control patients based on EEG activity. The comparison of the conventional artificial neural network performance indicated that classification with the vector auto-regression model is achievable with high accuracy. The CNN performed 86.9% over five fold, showing time-domain VAR features outperformed the frequency domain, partially directed coherence. In conclusion, CNN provides more feasible methods of classification in healthy and schizophrenic patients [13].

In the first part of the chapter, the authors analyzed and discussed existing literature that focuses on schizophrenia, mild cognitive impairment, AD (Alzheimer's disease), depressive disorders, ASD (autism spectrum disorder), and ADHD (attention deficit hyperactivity disorder). In the second part of this study, suggestions and common biases were discussed [14].

Future Trends

Sensors and smartphones can generate large amounts of data and represent a patient's state from time to time. The data collected by sensors can particularly be relevant to movement disorders. Other devices could be used to diagnose late-life depression and ASD (autism spectrum disorder) using RNN (recurrent neural networks) [10].

Now commonly used Genetic and genomic data in deep learning architecture, researchers have performed analysis using CNN to identify the regions responsible for autism. CNN was also developed to accurately predict amyotrophic lateral sclerosis. Genomic data has also been proven to identify 12 cancer subtypes [10].

Recent researches on automated CAD systems are prevalent mostly in epilepsy. For the diagnosis of epilepsy and seizures, EEG is used. Studies have explored the different CAD technology systems developed in about 20 years to diagnose five different neurological disorders. It concluded that there is a need to create a large standard database for neurological disorders. It also suggested that researchers should shift to machine learning-based CAD systems making the detection of disorders easier [15].

Machine learning can work efficiently with some types of processes like data interpretation and prediction. It has a unique ability to detect patterns and behaviors and use algorithms with regularly updated data. One can benefit a lot as there is barely any need to change anything. This can also be implemented with data sets of large volumes, such as the ones in healthcare. So, it can be used to detect unusual occurrences and identify areas that need to work upon so that there is optimal functionality throughout the system. This also increases the system's accuracy and speed, and implementing this on a long-term basis will yield great results [5].

Usually, when people talk about such a concept, they just think of it as a futuristic idea that could be developed rather than realizing that it is a concept that can work with real-time data at the very moment. So, it's important to find particular fields or cases in which this concept can maximize it's capabilities and give out valuable outputs. When such a technique is used there is no need to have any sort of backup as this system would take care of everything. It would have every possible kind of data which is required that no human could possibly collect on his/her own. It could predict possible treatments, medications, complications, or side effects depending on the symptoms. It would cut down the cost and help the healthcare department to come up with new solutions [5].

On the other hand, deep learning is known for its great processing speed in evaluating and manipulating data and providing an accurate platform to execute data. It has countless benefits apart from is speed, accuracy, reliability, efficiency, etc. The use of neural networks can further improve these benefits. It works exactly like a brain would do and interprets and analyzes data like it so it can make logical decisions on the basis of its research. One of its abilities is to search through huge amounts of data and check for anomalies, redundancy, and any missing data [16].

Such systems can also be used to deal with complexities and get better insights into certain situations to learn more about them. This one of the reasons why it is being noticed in the medical field. Although it is still in it's early stages of development, it has still had to bring in more results and solutions. All though what happens to it in the future will be decided by the expert. It is still important to understand that it has many potentials and can become a solution that would take care of most of the data needs and reduce the workload by a large margin [18].

AI has immense potential to work with data explicitly and can be enhanced to work with medical data and deal with complications. Especially with the concept of neurology. Their main task here is to classify data into sub-categories that will be way more helpful. When talking about the latest trends, pattern recognition is when the technique is being used to detect brain disorders. In the case of Alzheimer and other cognition-related disorders, classification is done automatically to retrieve output data, which helps identify the problems. It is also used in the case of brain tumours to predict the level of damage along with segmentation. Psychiatric disorder is a case where it is used too so that they can determine the surgical process. Machine learning is used to identify the areas which are damaged and need to be treated. Similar other neurological disorders such as epilepsy, brain strokes, seizures, and plenty others can be treated differently. Using such a system will increase the survival rate of the patient and aid in the betterment of the treatment techniques so that the healthcare system can develop tremendously [19].

Technology is playing a very important role in healthcare. Internet of things (IoT) [20], Concepts of Chabot [21], different aspects of security system in healthcare [22], along with artificial intelligence [23], are the few technologies out of many which have been successfully implemented in various domain of healthcare system along with machine learning and deep learning techniques. And collectively they are providing better result to identify and detect the disorders.

Discussion

Deep learning is a machine learning method based on an artificial neural network that includes supervised, unsupervised, and semi-supervised learning. Convolutional neural networks can be successfully applied to imaging and genetic data for numerous disorders. Recurrent neural networks showed motivating results with longitudinal research. This chapter aimed to highlight the different comprehensive methods used by neuropsychologists to identify various brain deficits and discuss the latest trends in deep learning for the early prediction and detection of these disorders. Existing literature was reviewed for this study. It was found that numerous algorithms and techniques are used for advanced medical research. Although some of these techniques have proven to be very helpful as they make the research more reliable and faster than the traditional deep learning that was done in the past, some challenges may need to be addressed.

The use of deep learning for research in the medical field is still limited to sample size and resolution [9]. The illnesses, whether physiological or psychological, could be understood better. These advanced methods help scientists see what the naked eye fails to notice. This helps see the parts of the brain from different angles with each layer to be seen separately without difficulty and provide complete transparency to the patients/clients and the practitioners. The output dataset obtained can be analyzed by machine learning, and if the result turns out to be a positive case, it can further be analyzed by deep learning imaging techniques. This will be done by using algorithms and will be accurate. Imaging analysis and simulated neural networks can be used to predict the case's seriousness, and then the images can be classified and segmented accordingly. This system will aid in the early prediction of neurological diseases, which would lead to an increase in the patient's survival rate. A similar system can also be used to predict other types of diseases too, so it has a lot of future scope.

Conclusion

The latest trends in deep learning have advanced over the years significantly and have shown auspicious results. Although neurologists and psychologists have found these advancements impacting quality research and making imaging faster, safer, and accessible, and understandable to their clients or patients [17]. These techniques are still relatively new findings and still need to be studied further in-depth.

An ideal future scenario would consist of a day-to-day environment that measures cognitive functions and activities of daily life situations and demands, detecting subtle behavioral patterns that indicate earlier cognitive decline or some neuropsychological conditions [13].

References

[1] Taeho, Jo. Nho Kwangsik & A. J. Saykin., 'deep learning in Alzeimer's disease: diagnostic classification and prognostic prediction using neuroimaging data, frontiers in aging neurosciences,' Vol 11, A 220, 2019.

[2] Rathore, H., A. K. Al-Ali, A. Mohamed, X. Du and M. Guizani, "A Novel Deep Learning Strategy for Classifying Different Attack Patterns for Deep Brain Implants," in *IEEE Access*, vol. 7, pp. 24154-24164, 2019.

[3] Valliani, A. A., D. Ranti, & E. K. Oermann, 'Deep learning and neurology: A systematic review,' *Neural Ther,* 8-351-365, 2019.

[4] Litman, E., "Computer-aided Ischemic Stroke Classification from EEG Data Using a Single-tiered Spiking Neural Network Framework," *2020 11th IEEE Annual UEMCON.*

[5] Pawar, U., D. O'Shea, S. Rea and R. O'Reilly, "Explainable AI in Healthcare," *2020 International Conference on Cyber Situational Awareness, Data Analytics and Assessment (CyberSA)*, Dublin, Ireland, 2020.

[6] Rohan, T. I., M. S. U. Yusuf, M. Islam and S. Roy, "Efficient Approach to Detect Epileptic Seizure using Machine Learning Models for Modern Healthcare System," *2020 IEEE Region 10 Symposium (TENSYMP)*, Dhaka, Bangladesh, 2020.

[7] C. S., M. S. and J. S. L., "Bag of Models based Embeddings for Assessment of Neurological disorders using Speech Intelligibility," in *IEEE Transactions on Emerging Topics in Computing*, 2020.

[8] Marzetti, L., A. Basti. F. Chella, A. D'Andrea, & V. Pizzella, 'Brain functional connectivity phase coupling of neuronal oscillations: A perspective from magnetoencephalography' *frontiers in neuroscience,* 2019.

[9] Vieira, S., W. H. L. Pinaya, & A. Mechelli, 'Using deep learning to investigate the neuroimaging correlates of psychiatric and neurological disorders:-Methods & applications,' *Neuroscience and behavioural reviews,* 2017.

[10] Burgos, N., S. Bottani, J. Faouzi, E. Thibeau-Sutre, & O. Colliot, "Deep learning in brain disorders from data processing to disease treatment," oxford university press. 2020.

[11] Bengio Y, Courville A, Vincent P. Representation learning: a review and new perspectives. *IEEE Trans Pattern Anal Mach Intell.* 2013.

[12] Shahriman, W. N. S., C. R. Phang, F. Numan, C. M. Ting, 'Classification of brain functional connectivity using convolutional neural networks' *Material science and engineering,* 2020.

[13] Zhu, G., B., Jiang, L. Tong, Y. Xie, G. Zahrachuk, & M.. Wintermark, 'Application of deep learning to neuro-imaging techniques, *Frontiers in neurology,*' 2019.

[14] Arbabshirani, M. R., S. Plis, J. Sui, & V. D. Calhoun, "Single subject prediction of brain disorders in neuroimaging;- promises and pitfalls," 2016.

[15] Raghavendra U., Acharya U. R., Adeli, H., 'Artificial intelligence techniques for automated diagnosis of neurological disorders' *European neurology,* 2019.

[16] Attallah, M. A. Sharkas. & H. Gadelkarim, 'Deep learning techniques for automatic detection of embryonic neurodevelopmental disorders,' *diagnostics,* 10, 27. 2020.

[17] Tandel, G. S., M. Biswas, O. G. Kakde., A. Tiwari, H. S. Suri., M. Turk, J. R. Laird, C. K. Asae, A. A Ankrah,., N. N. Khanna, B. K. Madhusudhan, L. Saba & J. S, Suri., A review on deep learning perspectives in brain cancer classification, cancers, 11, 111, 2019.

[18] UnaiDiaz-Orueta, Alberto Blanco-Campai, Melissa Lamar, DavidJ. Libon & Teresa Burke, Marrying past and present neuropsychology: is the future of the process-based approach technology-base?, 2020.

[19] Tyrväinen, P., M. Silvennoinen, K. Talvitie-Lamberg, A. Ala-Kitula and R. Kuoremäki, "Identifying opportunities for AI applications in healthcare — Renewing the national healthcare and social services," *2018 IEEE 6th International Conference SeGAH.*

[20] Trayush, T., R. Bathla, S. Saini and V. K. Shukla, "IoT in Healthcare: Challenges, Benefits, Applications, and Opportunities," 2021 International Conference on Advance Computing and Innovative Technologies in Engineering (ICACITE), 2021, pp. 107-111, doi: 10.1109/ICACITE51222.2021.9404583.

[21] Athota, L., V. K. Shukla, N. Pandey and A. Rana, "Chatbot for Healthcare System Using Artificial Intelligence," 2020 8th International Conference on Reliability, Infocom Technologies and Optimization (Trends and Future Directions) (ICRITO), 2020, pp. 619-622, doi: 10.1109/ICRITO48877.2020.9197833.

[22] Bhardwaj, M., N. Pandey, V. K. Shukla, A. V. Singh and N. Gupta, "Review and Analysis of Security Model in Healthcare System," 2021 9th International Conference on Reliability, Infocom Technologies and Optimization (Trends and Future Directions) (ICRITO), 2021, pp. 1-7, doi: 10.1109/ICRITO51393.2021.9596090.

[23] Shukla V. K., Wanganoo L., Tiwari N. (2022) Real-Time Alert System for Delivery Operators through Artificial Intelligence in Last-Mile Delivery. In: Garg L., Chakraborty C., Mahmoudi S., Sohmen V.S. (eds.) Healthcare Informatics for Fighting COVID-19 and Future Epidemics. EAI/Springer Innovations in Communication and Computing. Springer, Cham. https://doi.org/10.1007/978-3-030-72752-9_20.

Part 3. COVID-19, Healthcare and Technology

Chapter 13

COVID-19 Pandemic: Recovery and Death Ratio Analysis Based on Latitude Using Correlation and ANOVA

Rinkal Sardhara* **and Shanti Verma**
L. J. University,
Ahmedabad, Gujarat, India

Abstract

In March 2020, "World Health Organization" announced the COVID-19 disease outbreak as a pandemic and informed countries to take action immediately so that people's lives can be saved. Different countries have taken this disease seriously and applied locked down based on the situation. We can observe that the situation is still not in control and that the partial locked down is in some areas. Based on the situation, we have planned to do an analysis that may be helpful to decide the COVID-19 pandemic. Our earth is divided into three different temperature zones: Frigid, Temperate, and Torrid. The division is based on latitude. We have collected data from kaggle.com, which has different columns like Country name, state/province, latitude, confirmed, recovered, and death cases of COVID-19 disease and dates. We have nearly six months of data from June to December. This chapter compares variances of different zones recovery and death ratio of COVID-19 disease using one-way ANOVA. The authors have also checked the correlation between latitude and death ratio and latitude and recovered ratio.

Keywords: health care, ANOVA, COVID-19, ratio analysis, pandemic

---

* Corresponding Author's Email: rinkal.sardhara@ljinstitutes.edu.in.

In: Industry 4.0 and Intelligent Business Analytics for Healthcare
Editors: Soumi Dutta, Vinod Kumar Shukla, Shruti Nagpal et al.
ISBN: 978-1-68507-602-3

Introduction

Pandemic plays the most prominent role in technology advancement as in strict time, and the human mind makes decisions speedily for fast recovery of damage, whether economical or physical. However, it is essential to analyze the pandemic data for proper decisions. COVID-19 is the most recent infectious coronavirus disease pandemic, which started in late 2019, and its effect is still ongoing [1]. Weather plays a major role in some diseases, and it means that if the area is hot, then it might be possible that the effect of the virus is minimal. Thus, the author has collected data of different countries confirmed, recovered, and death cases of COVID-19 pandemic from the keggle.com repository. Then data categorization process has done by the authors in different temperature zones. After cleaning and organization of data, the analysis process is carried out. Mainly there are two types of analysis done by the authors. The first analysis finds a correlation between the death ratio and latitude out of the two. Another type of analysis is compared variances of different zones recovery and death ratio of COVID-19 disease using one-way ANOVA. The objectives of the analysis are:

- To find the relationship between death ratio and latitude
- To find the differences in recovery and death ratio of different temperature zones

Background

Temperature zones: Based on the Equator, our earth is divided into different temperature zones (Figure 1). The Equator forms a horizontal line that divides the earth horizontally into two equal parts: north and south. Latitude implies the geographic coordinates determining the distance of a point, north-south of the Equator. On the north side, latitude increases positively, whereas latitude has a negative value on the south side. The Equator is located at 0° latitudes. There are five different zones based on latitude. The most centred zone is the torrid temperature zone between -23.5° latitudes and 23.5° latitudes. Between latitude 23.5° to 66.5°, north temperature zone comes whereas between latitude -23.5° to -66.5°, south temperature zone comes. The north frigid and south frigid zones are located at a latitude between 66.5° to 90° and between

-66.5° to - 90° respectively. The torrid zone is known as the hot zone. A temperate zone is moderate, and a frigid zone is known as a cold zone.

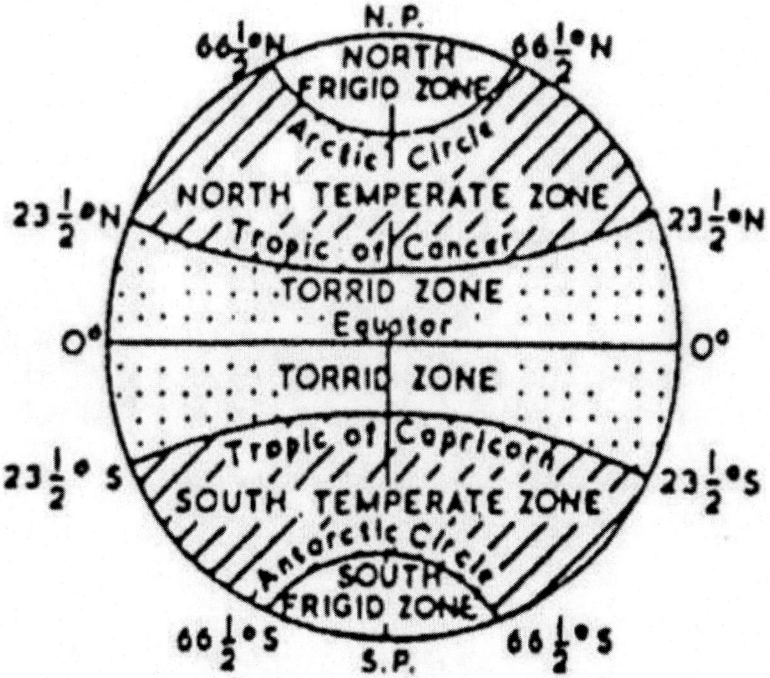

Figure 1. Different temperature Zone of earth [2].

COVID-19 Pandemic

People who have an infection of coronavirus will experience mild to moderate respiratory problems and recover without any special treatment in most cases [3]. Older people are more likely to get the infection as they also have continuous treatment for the other kind of disease at that age. The COVID-19 virus spreads mainly through droplets of saliva or expulsion from the nose when an infected individual coughs or sneezes. State or provinces of different countries worldwide have imposed lockdowns of varying degrees. Mostly, only necessary businesses are permitted to remain open. There have been a high number of confirmed cases of COVID-19, including a large number of deaths.

Technology is playing a significant role in healthcare. Internet of things (IoT) [4], Concepts of Chabot [5], different aspects of security systems in healthcare [6], along artificial intelligence [7] are the few technologies out of many which have been successfully implemented in various domains of the healthcare system.

ANOVA

Analysis of variance (ANOVA) is a group of statistical models and their related estimation actions used to analyze the variances among means. An ANOVA test is a method to determine if experiment results are weighty. ANOVA tests categorize one-way and two-way ANOVA into two types based on the independent variables. One-way ANOVA has one independent variable, whereas two-way ANOVA has two independent variables. In this chapter, the study author has used a one-way ANOVA test as a single dependent variable, latitude. The author has analyzed variation in recovered and death ratio of different temperature zone.

Research Methodology

Research methodology is the detailed techniques used to find, handpick, process, and examine information about a topic. In this section, the author has discussed different phases of the research used to analyse COVID-19 disease data.

Data Collection: There are various sources to collect data for analysis, such as data.gov.in, kaggle.com, etc. It is challenging to find data for the latitude base analysis of the covid-19 pandemic. Finally, the author has found data on kaggel.com in CSV format. Table 1 shows the different columns of the row data.

Data Cleaning: There are eight different columns in data: country name, state name, latitude, longitude, no of a confirmed case, no of the recovered case, no death case, and date. We have checked the invalid data in CSV, but fortunately, the data has no null values. In addition to that, we have also checked the value of the recover case and death case value as it should be less than the confirmed case. This way author has cleaned the data for further analysis.

Table 1. Example of data

Country/Region	Province/State	Latitude	Longitude	Confirmed	Recovered	Deaths	Date
China	Anhui	31.8257	117.2264	1			22-01-2020
China	Beijing	40.1824	116.4142	14			22-01-2020
China	Chongqing	30.0572	107.874	6			22-01-2020
China	Fujian	26.0789	117.9874	1			22-01-2020
China	Gansu	35.7518	104.2861				22-01-2020
China	Guangdong	23.3417	113.4244	26			22-01-2020
China	Guangxi	23.8298	108.7881	2			22-01-2020
China	Guizhou	26.8154	106.8748	1			22-01-2020
China	Hainan	19.1959	109.7453	4			22-01-2020
China	Hebei	37.8957	114.9042	1			22-01-2020
China	Heilongjiang	47.862	127.7615				22-01-2020
China	Henan	33.882	113.614	5			22-01-2020
Hong Kong	Hong Kong	22.3	114.2				22-01-2020
China	Hubei	30.9756	112.2707	444	28	17	22-01-2020
China	Hunan	27.6104	111.7088	4			22-01-2020
China	Inner Mongolia	44.0935	113.9448				22-01-2020
China	Jiangsu	32.9711	119.455	1			22-01-2020
China	Jiangxi	27.614	115.7221	2			22-01-2020
China	Jilin	43.6661	126.1923				22-01-2020
China	Liaoning	41.2956	122.6085	2			22-01-2020

Data Organization: The main objective of the analysis is to find the recovery and death ratio of COVID-19 cases based on different temperature zone. Temperature zones are divided based on the equator, and there are five different temperature zones. So, data are categorized into five different values: North Frigid, North Temperate, South Temperate, and Tropic. We have excluded the region south frigid as there are no COVID-19 cases detected according to data during these particular months. Table 2 shows the data with a description.

Data Visualization: This technique is one of the most popular techniques to represent the data visually, which helps anyone analyze the data more simply [8]. The author has found the ratio of recovered and death Covid-19 cases based on the month. To achieve this task author has divided the process into two phases.

Table 2. Organization of data

Field	**Description**
Country	Different countries name are there For example, India, China, etc.
Province/State	Different state or province name for example, Gujarat, Maharashtra
Latitude	Value of distance of angle between the equator and location in degree
Confirmed	Month wise total no of confirmed cases of state or province
Recovered	Month wise total no of recovered cases of state or province
Death	Month wise total no of Death cases of state or province
Month	Month of the year
Recovered ratio	It is a value of recovered / confirmed
Death ratio	It is a value of death/ confirmed
Temperature Zone	Name of the temperature zone such as North Frigid, North Temperate, South Temperate, and Tropic based on latitude value

Firstly, the sum of confirmed, recovered, and death cases have been calculated. In the next phase, to find the ratio of recovered cases, the author has divided the sum of recovered cases by the sum of confirmed cases. Similarly, to find the ratio of death cases, the sum of death cases by the sum of confirmed cases has been divided. Data visualization is carried out in this section. The following figure shows the month-wise recovered cases ratio of different temperature zones. Figure 2 shows that the North Temperate Zone has the lowest recovered rate, whereas the tropic zone has the highest recovered rate of Covid-19 cases.

The Figure 3 shows the month-wise death cases ratio of different temperature zones. It has been observed that the death ratio decreases in all other zones except the frigid north zone. The North Temperate Zone has the highest death ratio in June, while the frigid north zone has the lowest. At the end of the year 2020, i.e., in December, the death zone's death ratio is very near each other.

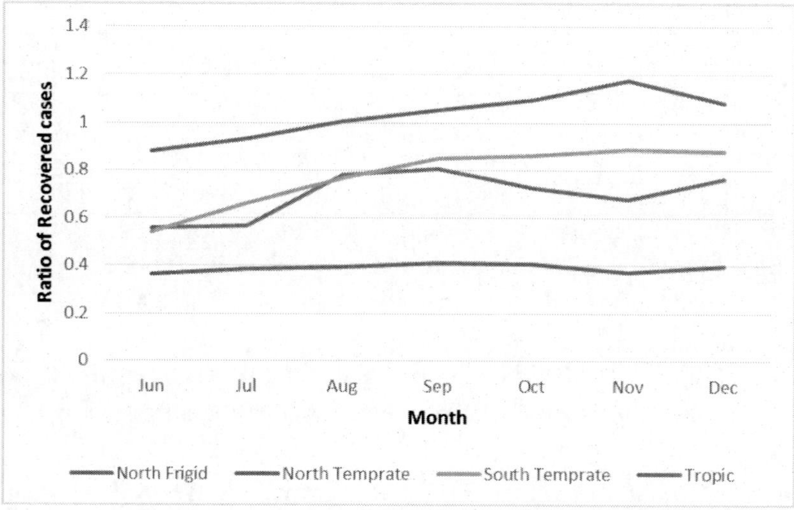

Figure 2. Temperature zone wise recovered Covid-19 cases.

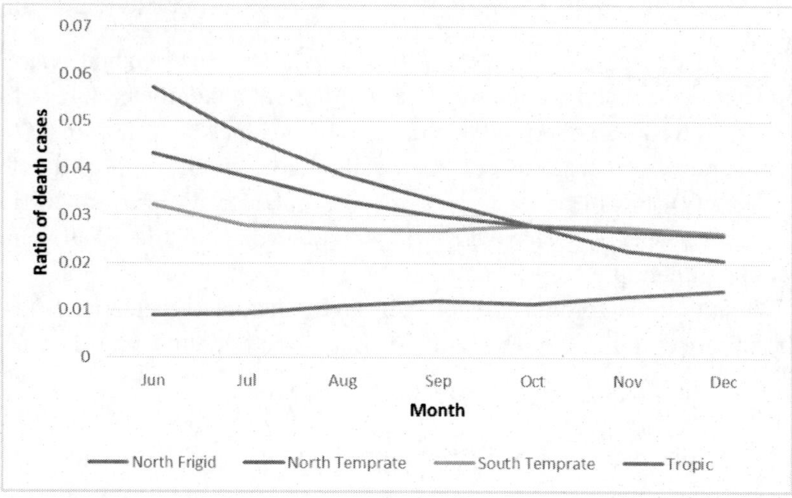

Figure 3. Temperature zone wise Covid-19 death cases.

Data Analysis: As discussed in the data visualization section author has calculated the recovered and death ratio. Table 3 represents month-wise data for the recovered ratio.

Table 3. Month wise recovered ratio of Covid-19 cases

Month	North Frigid	North Temperate	South Temperate	Tropic
Jun	0.556514758	0.364950634	0.539140226	0.87952345
Jul	0.565549439	0.387080753	0.65947405	0.92942576
Aug	0.783173845	0.396185392	0.770024874	1.00261734
Sep	0.807584857	0.412471765	0.849022293	1.04987987
Oct	0.726642706	0.406681944	0.86411901	1.09347221
Nov	0.678263846	0.373127597	0.889999585	1.17534086
Dec	0.763159788	0.399977707	0.881102453	1.08397422

Based on the data author has formed a hypothesis. The following is the hypothesis statement.

- *Null Hypothesis:* There is no significant difference between the mean of the ratio of Covid-19 recovered cases of the different temperature zones.
- *Alternate Hypothesis:* There are significant differences between the mean of the ratio of Covid-19 recovered cases of the different temperature zones.

To find the variance in mean ANOVA [9] one-way method was used. Following is the result for the hypothesis testing at a significant level of 0.05 (Table 4). It has been observed that the p-value is much smaller than 0.05. So, reject the null hypothesis and accept the alternate hypothesis. We can clearly say a significant difference between the recovered ratios of different temperature zones. Table 5 shows month-wise data for the death ratio of different temperature zones.

The author has formed a hypothesis based on data to check the difference in the variance of different temperature zones. The hypothesis for the same is:

- *Null Hypothesis:* There is no significant difference between the mean of the ratio of Covid-19 death cases of the different temperature zones.

- *Alternate Hypothesis:* There are significant differences between the mean of the ratio of Covid-19 death cases of the different temperature zones.

Table 4. ANOVA – Ratio of recovered cases

Source of Variation	SS	df	MS	F	P-value	F crit
Between Groups	1.458109	3	0.486036	50.09322	1.75105E-10	3.008787
Within Groups	0.232863	24	0.009703			
Total	1.690973	27				

Table 5. Month wise death ratio of Covid-19 cases

Month	North Frigid	North Temperate	South Temperate	Tropic
Jun	0.008982856	0.057262298	0.032290379	0.04332655
Jul	0.009271828	0.046809325	0.027895721	0.03828665
Aug	0.010864414	0.038574774	0.027131151	0.0330947
Sep	0.011965338	0.033241913	0.026997364	0.02999967
Oct	0.011369865	0.027922513	0.02799935	0.02785069
Nov	0.0129541	0.022624744	0.027503575	0.0267579
Dec	0.014132316	0.020684198	0.026296558	0.0259219

Table 6. ANOVA – Ratio of death cases

Source of Variation	SS	df	MS	F	P-value	F crit
Between Groups	0.002387	3	0.000796	14.06973	1.69E-05	3.008787
Within Groups	0.001357	24	5.65E-05			
Total	0.003744	27				

Table 6 is the result of the hypothesis testing at a significant level of 0.05. It has been observed that the p-value, 1.69E-05 is much smaller than 0.05. So, reject the null hypothesis and accept the alternate hypothesis. We can clearly say a significant difference between the death ratios of different temperature zones.

Moreover, the author has also calculated the correlation between the latitude and death cases [10]. The value of the correlation factor is -0.07, which is less than 0. So we can clearly say that latitude and ratio of death cases are negatively correlated. In other words, if latitude increases, the ratio of death cases decreases and vice versa. Moreover, the author has also found the value of correlation between latitude and recovered cases of Covid-19. The value of the correlation factor is -0.04.

Again, it is a negative correlation between the two, showing that the recovered ratio decreases if latitude increases. Suppose we move from the equator to the North Pole, the recovered and death ratios decrease.

Result and Discussion

This study performs analyses of Covid-19 cases of different temperature zones. There are two types of analysis done by the author ANOVA and Correlation. With ANOVA- one-way statistical technique, the author has checked the variance in different temperature zones' recovered and death ratios. It has been found that there is a significant difference in different temperature zones' recovered and death ratios. Table 7 represents the p-value of the recovered and death ratio of the following table.

Table 7. P-Value of recovered and death case ratio

	Recovered	**Death**
P value ($\alpha = 0.05$)	1.75105E-10	1.69E-05

The above table observed that both cases have a p-value less than 0.05, indicating rejection of the null hypothesis and acceptance of an alternate hypothesis. In other words, there is a significant difference in recovered and death ratio of different temperature zone. Using the Pearson correlation technique, the author has found a negative correlation between latitude and death case ratio and latitude and recovered case ratio. Table 8 shows the correlation value for the recovered and death case ratio.

Table 8. Correlation value of recovered and death case ratio

	Recovered ratio	**Death ratio**
Pearson correlation	-0.04	-0.07

It is visible that the recovered ratio and death ratio is negatively correlated with latitude from the above table. It means that if one decreases other one increases and vice versa.

Conclusion

Covid-19 has been the biggest pandemic in recent years. It is essential to research every aspect of this area. In this chapter, latitude-based analysis is done to find the relation between the different temperature zones recovered and the death cases ratio. Mainly authors have two objectives. The first objective is to find the variance in the recovered and death cases ratios of different temperature zones. In addition to that author has also analyzed the relationship between latitude and recovered and death case ratio. To achieve the first objective author has developed a hypothesis, and after that, they tested the hypothesis with the one-way ANOVA. Finally, it is concluded that there is a significant difference between the recovered and death case ratio of different temperature zones. Moreover, the author has used the Pearson correlation technique to find correlation factor values for the second objective. In the end, it has been observed that there is a negative correlation between the latitude and recovered ratio and latitude and death ratio. Therefore, we can say that if the value of latitude increases death case ratio decrease. This analysis is helpful in the different organizations that want to decide based on latitude related to the Covid-19 pandemic.

References

[1]. Thange U., V. K. Shukla, R. Punhani and W. Grobbelaar, *"Analyzing COVID-19 Dataset through Data Mining Tool "Orange,"* "2021 2nd International Conference on Computation, Automation and Knowledge Management (ICCAKM), 2021, pp. 198-203, doi: 10.1109/ICCAKM50778.2021.9357754.

[2]. *Diligent IAS*, [Online Accessed on June 2021] https://diligentias. com/latitudes-and-longitudes/.

[3]. Jacques Demongeot, Yannis Flet-Berliac and Hervé Seligmann: *Temperature Decreases Spread Parameters of the New Covid-19 Case Dynamics*. Biology 2020.

[4]. Trayush T., R. Bathla, S. Saini and V. K. Shukla, *"IoT in Healthcare: Challenges, Benefits, Applications, and Opportunities,"* 2021 International Conference on Advance Computing and Innovative Technologies in Engineering (ICACITE), 2021, pp. 107-111, doi: 10.1109/ICACITE51222.2021.9404583.

[5]. Athota L., V. K. Shukla, N. Pandey and A. Rana, *"Chatbot for Healthcare System Using Artificial Intelligence,"* 2020 8th International Conference on Reliability, Infocom Technologies and Optimization (Trends and Future Directions) (ICRITO), 2020, pp. 619-622, doi: 10.1109/ICRITO48877.2020.9197833.

[6]. Bhardwaj M., N. Pandey, V. K. Shukla, A. V. Singh and N. Gupta, *"Review and Analysis of Security Model in Healthcare System,"* 2021 9th International Conference on Reliability, Infocom Technologies and Optimization (Trends and Future Directions) (ICRITO), 2021, pp. 1-7, doi: 10.1109/ICRITO51393.2021.9596090.

[7]. Shukla V. K., Wanganoo L., Tiwari N. (2022) Real-Time Alert System for Delivery Operators through Artificial Intelligence in Last-Mile Delivery. In: Garg L., Chakraborty C., Mahmoudi S., Sohmen V.S. (eds) *Healthcare Informatics for Fighting COVID-19 and Future Epidemics*. EAI/Springer Innovations in Communication and Computing. Springer, Cham. https://doi.org/10.1007/978-3-030-72752-9_20.

[8]. Jhamb S., R. Gupta, V. K. Shukla, I. Mearaj and P. Agarwal, *"Understanding Complexity in Language Learning Through Data Visualization Using Python,"* 2020 International Conference on Computation, Automation and Knowledge Management (ICCAKM), 2020, pp. 268-274, doi: 10.1109/ICCAKM46823.2020.9051512.

[9]. Shanti Verma, Kalyani Patel (2017): Association between shopping habit and demographics of m-commerce user's in India using two-way ANOVA doi: 10.1109/I2CT.2017.8226090.

[10]. Rinkal Sardhara, KamalJit Lakhtaria (2019): Impact of Different Domain Inlink, Outlink and Rechability on Relevance of Web Page Using Correlation doi: 10.1109/ICCS45141.2019.9065815.

Chapter 14

Pillars of a Corruption Free Economically Strong Healthcare Industry during COVID-19: Artificial Intelligence and Global Connectivity

Kamakshi Mehta[1,*], Shikha Sharma[1,†] and Vinod Kumar Shukla[2,‡]
[1]Amity University Haryana, India
[2]Department of Engineering and Architecture, Amity University, Dubai, UAE

Abstract

COVID-19 is causing turmoil across the world's healthcare systems, aiming to contain the spread of pandemics and develop the basis for global economic productivity. A professional healthcare infrastructure would depend on the country's commitment to ethical principles, a prerequisite for effective anti-corruption governance. It serves as the creative growth accelerator for healthcare. COVID is a global threat to not all human health but also to the country's economic balance. The chapter has initiated to evaluate the relationship of the variables such as the Artificial Intelligence (AI) techniques, Global Connectivity levels, Corruption levels, and the health care systems. The research has been conducted using secondary data collected from various published online and offline sources. Our study's sample covers the various indexes

* Corresponding Author's Email: cakamakshi.edu@gmail.com.
† Corresponding Author's Email: shikhabhardwaj2008@gmail.com.
‡ Corresponding Author's Email: vinodkumarshukla@gmail.com.

In: Industry 4.0 and Intelligent Business Analytics for Healthcare
Editors: Soumi Dutta, Vinod Kumar Shukla, Shruti Nagpal et al.
ISBN: 978-1-68507-602-3

recorded by 71 countries from all over the globe. The chapter exhibits a clear and positive impact of all the variables on each other. The indexes calculated also showed that the country having a robust AI framework will have good governance resulting in an anticorruption healthcare system.

Keywords: health care, AI, GCI, CPI, corruption, COVID-19

Introduction

Its efficient health care system contributes a significant part to its economic growth. This sector is regarded as the most crucial determinant in ensuring mental and physical wellbeing. In today's healthcare sector and the medical profession, AI, algorithms, robotics, and big data are used as essential healthcare enhancements. The advent of new technologies based on big data and algorithms allows proper monitoring of medical and health trends. The health care market is expected to boom further, exhibiting a growth rate of more than 50% till the year 2025.1 Researchers and the medical fraternity have firmly believed that integrating AI techniques has helped improve the detection and prevention of diseases. Numerous studies have also evaluated the impact of AI techniques on a country's economic and health sector's growth.

Literature Review

The healthcare system's success depends on effectively leveraging financial capital, people and providing those resources promptly. It calls for a "system" that mobilizes and deploys human and management capital, manages knowledge, and supports clinicians and managers to perform their functions morally. The success of such a scheme needs to have sound governance [1]. Define good governance as "the traditions and institutions by which authority in a country is exercised." Private investors and donors are massively attracted to a less corrupt, politically stable country [2]. Many researchers have co-related more significant foreign investment with good governance [3]. Good governance has displayed a tremendous gravitational pull toward global investment, which has helped grease the economic wheels of the government

[4]. The potential investors and donors have played a significant role in the health care industry.

Artificial Intelligence (AI) is "a broad set of methods, algorithms, and technologies that make software 'smart' in a way that may seem human-like" [5]. Artificial Intelligence is the sum of varied technological and data-driven advancements and innovations [6]. The developed countries, namely Europe, the United States, and China, represent a whopping figure of 93% and above the total private investment made in AI development from 2011 to 2018. Participation in the democratic process depends on internet connectivity and data literacy [7]. Most interestingly, researchers in the biomedical fields have been actively trying to apply AI to help improve analysis and treatment outcomes and, consequently, increase the efficacy of the overall healthcare industry [8, 9, 10].

Corruption – commonly defined as the abuse of entrusted power for private gains – presents one of our time's most significant societal and political challenges [11]. Emerging in various forms, it undermines efficiencies of public institutions, widens gaps in inequalities, and thereby hinders the UN sustainable development goals [12, 13]. The ongoing COVID-19 pandemic has further exacerbated this trend, confirming previous research showing that corruption augments the adverse effects of catastrophes [14]. While vast (financial) efforts have been invested in the fight against corruption, they have shown minor signs of [15]. The advancement of digital technologies [16], particularly artificial intelligence [17], provides new hope to fight corruption more effectively. AI, defined by the EU High-Level Expert Group on Artificial Intelligence as "systems that display intelligent behaviour by analyzing their environment and taking actions – with some degree of autonomy – to achieve specific goals" [18], differs from static information and communication technologies (ICTs). AI can autonomously execute various tasks previously reserved for human actors [19]. It is already implemented in several pioneering projects and can take over anti-corruption tasks like predicting, detecting, and disclosing corruption cases [20, 21, 22].

Nevertheless, in contrast to other applications of AI to fight crime [23, 24], AI for anti-corruption is not a tool for governments to scrutinize their citizens but can be a tool for citizens to scrutinize their government. Thus, AI in the fight against corruption evokes much enthusiasm – being praised "as the next frontier in anti-corruption" [25]. At a sectoral level, several recent perception surveys of medical personnel in Latin American public hospitals provide a sense of the kinds and frequency of corruption in facilities and the likely perpetrators by profession [26]. It is argued that AI will be critical to supporting clinical and academic studies of COVID-19 and future crises [27]. AI can help us fight this virus by population screening, medical help, notification, and suggestions about infection control [28, 29, 30]. This technology can improve the planning, treatment, and reported outcomes of the COVID-19 patient, being an evidence-based medical tool.

The GCI (Global Connectivity Index) assesses the role of ICT techniques to accelerate the recovery and growth rate of the country's economy. It further highlights the measures to build a secure and robust foundation for economic growth by strengthening the GDP scores. The GCI scores of 79 countries are available online from 2015. The countries recording high GCI scores have shown high digital readiness levels, further lessening the COVID negative impact on their economies. GDP of the country showcases the economic strength of the country. Intense digitalization in countries globally well connected with higher ICT maturity has successfully mitigated the negative impact of the COVID-19 pandemic.

Objectives

- To study the impact of AI on the GDP of the respective country.
- To study the impact of the Global Connectivity Index (GCI) on the Corruption Perception Index (CPI).
- To study the interrelationship of GCI, CPI, and Health care Index (HCI).

Hypothesis

- The AI techniques do not impact the GDP levels of the respective country.
- There is no significant impact of GCI on CPI.
- There is no significant relationship between GCI, CPI, and Health care index (HCI).

Research Methodology

The empirical research evaluates four indices that evaluate the impact of AI and connectivity on the GDP and a corruption-free health care system. The data is secondary and collected from various published sources, including world bank databases. The study considered a sample of 71 countries from all the continents globally, including developed and developing economies. The first Index is the AI index, which reflects the integration of AI and Big data techniques in the country's operations in all sectors of their economy. The second Index is GCI which evaluates the level of connectivity or presence the country exhibits globally. Furthermore, the third Index is a factor that plagues every economy globally – the Corruption perception index. Last but not least, the most critical factor of our study is "The Health care index." This factor forms the base of our study as we intend to evaluate the impact of the other three variables on the health care sector's health.

Analysis and Findings

GDP-AI (Index): Artificial Intelligence Usage and Gross Domestic Product

AI techniques have deep-rooted themselves into the global economic markets. The research analyses the impact of artificial intelligence techniques on the growth acceleration of the respective country's economy. The new variable used for this study is a combination of AI index (2020) and GDP index (2019) and has been abbreviated as GDP-AI. And this has been calculated as the product of both the variables: GDP_AI = GDP*AI (Puaschunder, 2020). A cross-sectional study of 71 countries of Artificial Intelligence usage and Gross Domestic Product found that AI is significantly positively correlated with the country's GDP ($rPearson = .776$, $n = 71$, $p < .000$). AI comes from parts of the world that are perceived as less corrupt. Table 1 showcases the figures of GDP-AI (Index), and Graph 1 represents a consolidated chart showing the GDP-AI indexes.

As clearly visible from Table 1, the GDP_AI index reveals that Luxembourg followed by Switzerland tops the list and Ethiopia's lowest Index. India ranks 60th as compared to the rest of the world. The United States of America boasts of a higher index than its neighbour Canada. Similarly,

Australia ranks 8th, whereas New Zealand, its neighbour, ranks 17th on the index list.

Table 1. GDP_AI index [37, 38, 39]

Name of Country	GDP (2019)	AI (2020)	GDP_AI
Switzerland	81993.73	69.22	5675523.8
Sweden	51615.02	78.77	4065818.4
Finland	48782.79	79.24	3865450.6
Denmark	60170.34	75.62	4549961
Norway	75419.63	74.43	5613483.4
Netherlands	52331.32	75.3	3940391.2
New Zealand	42084.35	68.15	2867880.4
Luxembourg	114704.59	72.62	8329388.8
Australia	55060.33	73.58	4051173.6
United Kingdom	42330.12	81.12	3433988.5
United States of America	65297.52	85.48	5581566.5
Canada	46194.73	73.16	3379513.7
Ireland	78660.96	68.24	5368138.3
Austria	50137.66	68.23	3420892.7
Belgium	46420.66	63.14	2930861.5
France	40493.93	73.77	2987115.6
Estonia	23723.31	69.92	1658781
Spain	29600.38	68.04	2014039.3
Portugal	23252.06	63.92	1486271.6
United Arab Emirates	43103.32	72.4	3120465.1
Slovenia	25946.18	55.99	1452623
Italy	33228.24	65.39	2172827.6
Jordan	4405.49	41.76	183968.79
Chile	14896.45	53.09	790837.84
Czech Republic	23494.6	61.52	1445434.6
Lithuania	19601.89	65.02	1274593.4
Uruguay	16190.13	55.57	899604.4
Poland	15692.51	62.42	979463.52
Saudi Arabia	23139.8	56.23	1301058.3
Greece	19582.54	47.93	938649.7
Croatia	14936.1	48.62	726118.53
Oman	15343.06	52.1	799358.19
Hungary	16731.82	55.82	933936.81
China	10216.63	69.08	705764.82
Malaysia	11414.21	63.66	726662.66
Romania	12919.53	50.78	656079.55

Name of Country	GDP (2019)	AI (2020)	GDP_AI
Bulgaria	9828.15	51.42	505402.71
Belarus	6663.3	46.1	307197.9
Kuwait	32000.45	50.61	1619446.7
Argentina	9912.28	50.75	503087.95
Serbia	7411.84	53.53	396763
Thailand	7806.74	48.16	375941.48
Brazil	8717.19	47.46	413752.53
Colombia	6428.68	51.26	329546.8
Vietnam	2715.28	42.82	116278.98
Russia	11585	60.85	704912.21
Peru	6977.7	35.57	248224.55
Kazakhstan	9812.39	46.55	456806.02
Botswana	7961.33	33.27	264897.17
Morocco	3204.1	36.42	116702.75
South Africa	6001.4	48.25	289567.59
Ukraine	3659.03	48.9	178930.29
Ecuador	6183.82	32.41	200423.91
Namibia	4957.46	37.1	183901.87
Mexico	9946.03	49.36	490916.34
Egypt	3019.21	49.19	148517.75
Indonesia	4135.57	47.53	196555.34
Lebanon	7583.69	35.91	272300.14
Algeria	3973.96	33.47	132992.68
India	2099.6	55.98	117541.85
Philippines	3485.08	42.94	149663.46
Paraguay	5414.8	37.64	203813.04
Bolivia	3552.07	33.03	117324.83
Tanzania	1122.12	32.78	36780.91
Kenya	1816.55	43.66	79303.17
Bangladesh	1855.74	33	61244.98
Pakistan	1284.7	33.49	43019.53
Ethiopia	855.76	26.17	22394.41
Venezuela	2845	26.27	74738.15
Nigeria	2229.86	30.86	68822.36
Uganda	794.34	30.9	24546.73

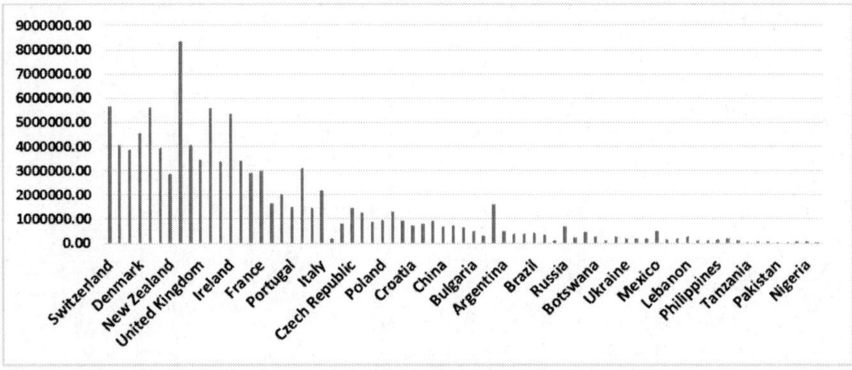

Graph 1. A consolidated chart showing the GDP-AI indexes.

Global Connectivity Index (GCI) and Corruption Perception Index (CPI)

Financial innovation and progress also bring about a simultaneous increase in frauds and corruption in the economy. The economic growth and development graph gives way to an adjacent graph of co-relating corruption and frauds. In their previous studies, researchers advocated the integration of Artificial intelligence techniques in mitigating financial losses arising from the corruption and fraudulent activities of health care industries [31, 32, 33, 34, 35]. The new variable used for this study is a combination of GCI (2020) and CPI (2019), abbreviated as GCI_CPI. And this has been calculated as the product of both the variables: GCI_CPI = GCI* CPI.

In a cross-sectional study of 71 countries' relation of GCI (2020) and CPI (2019), GCI represents the global connectivity index, which is positively supported by AI integration in the economy's communication sector, and CPI represents people's perception of corruption. The study evaluates the variables and concludes that connectivity is significantly positively related to the levels of anticorruption (*Pearson* value of $r = .843$, $n = 71$, $p < .000$). It is analyzed that the parts of the world that are more tech-savvy and well connected have fewer corruption levels. Table 1 displays the GCI_CPI Index of 71 countries around the world. It is perceived that there is an inverse relation between connectivity and anticorruption, i.e., higher the connectivity, lowers the corruption levels, and vice versa.

Table 2. GCI_CPI Indexes [37, 38, 39]

Name of Country	GCI (2020)	CPI (2019)	GCI_CPI
Switzerland	81	85	6885
Sweden	80	85	6800
Finland	76	86	6536
Denmark	77	87	6699
Norway	73	84	6132
Netherlands	75	82	6150
New Zealand	72	87	6264
Luxembourg	70	80	5600
Australia	72	77	5544
United Kingdom	75	77	5775
United States of America	87	69	6003
Canada	70	77	5390
Ireland	69	74	5106
Austria	66	77	5082
Belgium	66	75	4950
France	70	69	4830
Estonia	61	74	4514
Spain	61	62	3782
Portugal	61	62	3782
United Arab Emirates	62	71	4402
Slovenia	56	60	3360
Italy	60	53	3180
Jordan	75	48	3600
Chile	54	67	3618
Czech Republic	57	56	3192
Lithuania	58	60	3480
Uruguay	50	71	3550
Poland	51	58	2958
Saudi Arabia	53	53	2809
Greece	52	48	2496
Croatia	51	47	2397
Oman	48	52	2496
Hungary	54	44	2376
China	62	41	2542
Malaysia	53	53	2809
Romania	50	44	2200
Bulgaria	52	43	2236
Belarus	46	45	2070
Kuwait	46	40	1840
Argentina	45	45	2025

Table 2. (Continued)

Name of Country	GCI (2020)	CPI (2019)	GCI_CPI
Serbia	45	39	1755
Thailand	46	36	1656
Brazil	47	35	1645
Colombia	42	37	1554
Vietnam	41	37	1517
Russia	50	28	1400
Peru	40	36	1440
Kazakhstan	47	34	1598
Botswana	31	61	1891
Morocco	38	41	1558
South Africa	41	44	1804
Ukraine	43	30	1290
Ecuador	38	38	1444
Namibia	28	52	1456
Mexico	43	29	1247
Egypt	36	35	1260
Indonesia	39	40	1560
Lebanon	32	28	896
Algeria	32	35	1120
India	37	41	1517
Philippines	38	34	1292
Paraguay	37	28	1036
Bolivia	32	31	992
Tanzania	25	37	925
Kenya	31	28	868
Bangladesh	30	26	780
Pakistan	28	32	896
Ethiopia	23	37	851
Venezuela	35	16	560
Nigeria	27	26	702
Uganda	26	28	728

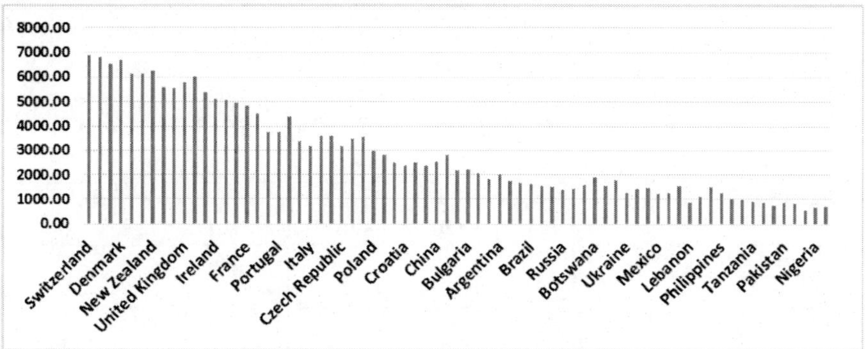

Graph 2. A consolidated chart showing the GCI_CPI indexes.

The variables are positively related, theorizing that proper integration of AI shall offer the country a corruption-free economy, which shall improve and support the country's economy in pandemic situations by enabling a corruption-free health care industry. The study concludes that a country exhibiting a higher level of a globally well-connected artificial intelligence-supported governance shall record low levels of corruption. Table 2 showcases the figures of Global Connectivity Index (GCI) and Corruption Perception Index (CPI), and Graph 2 represents a consolidated chart showing the GCI_CPI indexes.

The countries ranking high on corruption freedom and global connectivity can significantly lay a solid foundation of techniques and procedures to monitor global public health and health care systems in this volatile and insecure pandemic. An index table 1 reveals that Switzerland tops the chart in controlling corruption through an excellently connected framework supported by artificial intelligence. Sweden follows the country in topping the ranks. The African countries embed the end of the list along with Bangladesh. India occupies the 60th rank compared to 71 countries, exhibiting an undoubtedly grim situation warranting immediate and stringent remedial measures. The United States of America has proved itself a leading country compared to Australia, Canada, the United Kingdom, and many other developed countries.

Healthcare Free from Corruption Index (GCI_CPI_HCI)

The findings in the above two hypotheses have highlighted the impact and relationship between GCI and CPI as a positive and very significant one. This hypothesis intends to further analyses the impact of GCI and CPI on HCI

(2017), i.e., the impact of Global connectivity and anti-corruption on the quality level of health care services globally.

Table 3. HCI_CPI_GCI Indexes [37, 38, 39]

Name of Country	**GCI (2020)**	**CPI (2019)**	**HCI (2017)**	**Healthcare free from corruption Index**
Switzerland	81	85	91.8	632043
Sweden	80	85	90.5	615400
Finland	76	86	89.6	585625.6
Denmark	77	87	85.7	574104.3
Norway	73	84	90.5	554946
Netherlands	75	82	89.5	550425
New Zealand	72	87	86.2	539956.8
Luxembourg	70	80	89.3	500080
Australia	72	77	89.8	497851.2
United Kingdom	75	77	84.6	488565
United States of America	87	69	81.3	488043.9
Canada	70	77	87.6	472164
Ireland	69	74	88.4	451370.4
Austria	66	77	88.2	448232.4
Belgium	66	75	87.9	435105
France	70	69	87.9	424557
Estonia	61	74	81.4	367439.6
Spain	61	62	89.6	338867.2
Portugal	61	62	84.5	319579
United Arab Emirates	62	71	72.2	317824.4
Slovenia	56	60	87.4	293664
Italy	60	53	88.7	282066
Jordan	75	48	76.5	275400
Chile	54	67	76	274968
Czech Republic	57	56	84.8	270681.6
Lithuania	58	60	76.6	266568
Uruguay	50	71	72	255600
Poland	51	58	79.6	235456.8
Saudi Arabia	53	53	79.4	223034.6
Greece	52	48	87	217152
Croatia	51	47	81.6	195595.2
Oman	48	52	77.1	192441.6
Hungary	54	44	79.6	189129.6
China	62	41	74.2	188616.4
Malaysia	53	53	66.6	187079.4
Romania	50	44	74.4	163680

Name of Country	GCI (2020)	CPI (2019)	HCI (2017)	Healthcare free from corruption Index
Bulgaria	52	43	71.4	159650.4
Belarus	46	45	74.4	154008
Kuwait	46	40	82	150880
Argentina	45	45	68.4	138510
Serbia	45	39	75.4	132327
Thailand	46	36	70.8	117244.8
Brazil	47	35	64.9	106760.5
Colombia	42	37	67.8	105361.2
Vietnam	41	37	66.3	100577.1
Russia	50	28	71.7	100380
Peru	40	36	69.6	100224
Kazakhstan	47	34	61.1	97637.8
Botswana	31	61	51.1	96630.1
Morocco	38	41	61.3	95505.4
South Africa	41	44	52	93808
Ukraine	43	30	72.7	93783
Ecuador	38	38	61.2	88372.8
Namibia	28	52	53.7	78187.2
Mexico	43	29	62.6	78062.2
Egypt	36	35	61	76860
Indonesia	39	40	49.2	76752
Lebanon	32	28	80	71680
Algeria	32	35	63.7	71344
India	37	41	44.8	67961.6
Philippines	38	34	52	67184
Paraguay	37	28	60.4	62574.4
Bolivia	32	31	59.2	58726.4
Tanzania	25	37	49.9	46157.5
Kenya	31	28	48.7	42271.6
Bangladesh	30	26	51.7	40326
Pakistan	28	32	43.1	38617.6
Ethiopia	23	37	44.2	37614.2
Venezuela	35	16	64.7	36232
Nigeria	27	26	51.3	36012.6
Uganda	26	28	42.9	31231.2

The cross-sectional study of 71 countries highlights a significant positive correlation of the variables with good healthcare levels of the respective countries. The co-relation values between anti-corruption and good healthcare are significant and are positively related ($rPearson = .723$, $n = 71$, $p < .000$) and internet connectivity is also significantly positively correlated with good healthcare ($rPearson = .854$, $n = 79$, $p < .000$). AI comes from parts of the world perceived as less corrupt and features better public healthcare. Healthcare free from anti-corruption Index has been calculated as follows: GCI*CPI*HCI. Table 3 showcases the healthcare figures free from the anti-corruption Index, and Graph 3 represents a consolidated chart showing the HCI_CPI_GCI indexes.

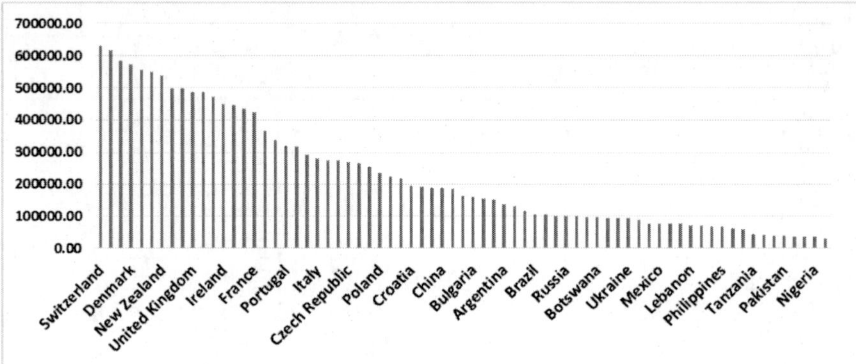

Graph 3. A consolidated chart showing the HCI_CPI_GCI indexes.

An analysis of the table shows that the countries which are well connected with extensive use of artificial intelligence ensure to a great extent a corruption-free health care system. Again, the results support the previous hypothesis showing that countries like Switzerland and Sweden top the charts in this Index and all our previous analyses. Australia leads the United Kingdom, Canada, and even the USA, indicating a high corruption-free health care industry level. The African continent has ensured its last place in every chart, indicating a low level of AI leading to a low level of GCI and a highly corruption-infested health care system. India has succeeded in maintaining itself on the 60th rank exhibiting a health care system that calls for more extraordinary efforts to eradicate corruption decaying not only the industry but also the economy of the country.

Conclusion

The developed countries that have made their mark in providing excellent global connectivity through intensely integrated Artificial Intelligence techniques have also topped the charts in providing good, corruption-free health care infrastructure to their citizens. These indices can prove to be the strongest ever pillars of an anticorruption health care structure [36]. The chapter concludes four indices, namely GDP, GCI, AI, and HCI, as the essential framework pillars ensure effective AI integration into all sectors. And this leads to a globally well-connected economy which further enhances the GDP by ensuring a low corrupted leadership in the respective country. These countries who have gained the highest ranking in the comparative charts can light the path for a better and robust economy for other developing and underdeveloped countries of the world.

Practical Implications

The torrential impact of COVID-19, which is terrorizing the countries globally, is not ready to slow down. It is the pace of destroying the global economies. The pandemic has had its worst impact on the health care sector. In the current digitally activated scenario, it is witnessed that AI technologies have fostered the economy innovatively beyond imagination. The study recommends that AI techniques be called upon in the international health care sector to monitor and minimize the crisis risk in the management of the health care industry. Big data techniques and digitalization have red-carpeted the way for an innovative digital health care system, which is also the need of the hour in this pandemic. These new technologies allow monitoring large-scale medical trends and measuring individual risks based on big data-driven estimations.

References

[1] Kaufman, D. and A. Kraay. 2003. *Governance and Growth: Causality in which way? – Evidence for the World, in brief.*" Washington, D.C.: World Bank

[2] Kaufman, D, A. Kraay and M. Maztruzzi. 2005. "*Governance Matters III: Governance Indicators for 1996-2002.*" Washington, D.C.: World Bank.

[3] Ryterman, J., J. Hellman and G. Jones et al., 2000. "Corruption in Russia: Interim Report." *World Bank*. Mimeo (June) Processed.

[4] Kaufmann, D., and S.-J. Wei. 1999. "*Does "Grease Money" Speed Up the Wheels of Commerce?*" NBER Working Papers 7093. National Bureau of Economic Research, Inc.

[5] Robertson, D. J., Noyes, E., Dowsett, A. J., Jenkins, R., & Burton, A. M. (2016). Face recognition by metropolitan police super-recognizers. *PloS one*, 11(2), e0150036.
[6] Dowell, R. (2018). Fundamental protections for non-biological intelligence or: How we learn to stop worrying and love our robot Brethren. *Minn. JL Sci. & Tech.*, 19, 305.
[7] Beerbaum, D., Piechocki, M., & Puaschunder, J. M. (2019). Measuring Accounting Reporting Complexity with customized extensions XBRL–A Behavioral Economics approach. *Journal of Applied Research in the Digital Economy* (JADE), 1(3).
[8] Yu KH, Beam AL, Kohane IS. Artificial intelligence in healthcare. *Nat Biomed Eng* 2018;2(10):719–31.
[9] Mamoshina P, Vieira A, Putin E, Zhavoronkov A. Applications of deep learning in biomedicine. *Mol Pharm* 2016;13(5):1445–54.
[10] Peng Y, Zhang Y, Wang L. Artificial intelligence in biomedical engineering and informatics: an introduction and review. *Artif Intell Med* 2010;48(2–3):71–3.
[11] Fisman, R., & Golden, M. A. (2017). *Corruption: What everyone needs to know.* Oxford University Press.
[12] Rothstein, B., & Varraich, A. (2017). *Making sense of corruption*. Cambridge University Press.
[13] Mungiu-Pippidi, A., & Heywood, P. M. (Eds.). (2020). *A research agenda for studies of corruption.* Edward Elgar Publishing.
[14] Ambraseys, N., & Bilham, R. (2011). Corruption kills. *Nature*, 469(7329), 153-155.
[15] Mungiu-Pippidi, A., & Johnston, M. (Eds.). (2017). *Transitions to good governance: creating virtuous circles of anti-corruption*. Edward Elgar Publishing.
[16] Mattoni, A. (2020). Practicing Media—Mediating Practice| A Media-in-Practices Approach to Investigate the Nexus Between Digital Media and Activists' Daily Political Engagement. *International Journal of Communication*, 14, 18.
[17] Aarvik, P. (2019). Artificial Intelligence–a promising anti-corruption tool in development settings. *U4 Anti-Corruption Resource Centre.*
[18] Ala-Pietilä, N. (2019). *Risk factors for surgical site infection after cesarean delivery*.
[19] Rahwan, I., Cebrian, M., Obradovich, N., Bongard, J., Bonnefon, J. F., Breazeal, C., ... & Wellman, M. (2019). *Machine behavior. Nature*, 568(7753), 477-486.
[20] López-Iturriaga, F. J., & Sanz, I. P. (2018). Predicting public corruption with neural networks: An analysis of Spanish provinces. *Social Indicators Research*, 140(3), 975-998.
[21] Martins, A. M., Guimaraes, C., & dos Santos, M. N. (2018). Innovation and Impact from a Brazilian Perspective. *Sustainable Innovation and Impact.*
[22] Lima, M. S. M., & Delen, D. (2020). Predicting and explaining corruption across countries: A machine learning approach. *Government Information Quarterly*, 37(1), 101407.
[23] Ryman-Tubb, N. F., Krause, P., & Garn, W. (2018). What an Artificial Intelligence and machine learning research impact payment card fraud detection: A survey and industry benchmark. *Engineering Applications of Artificial Intelligence*, 76, 130-157.

[24] Crawford, J. (2019). *Brownlie's principles of public international law.* Oxford University Press, USA.

[25] Miller, H., Petheram, A., & Martinho-Truswell, E. (2018). Want to get serious about artificial intelligence? *You will need an AI strategy.*

[26] Di Tella, R. and Savedoff, W. D. (eds.). 2001. *Diagnosis Corruption.* Washington, DC: Inter-American Development Bank.

[27] Browning, L., Colling, R., Rakha, E., Rajpoot, N., Rittscher, J., James, J. A., ... & Verrill, C. (2020). Digital pathology and artificial intelligence will be key to supporting clinical and academic cellular pathology through COVID-19 and future crises: the PathLAKE Consortium perspective. *Journal of clinical pathology.*

[28] Haleem A, Javaid M, Vaishya. Effects of COVID 19 pandemic in daily life. *CurrMed Res Pract* 2020. https://doi.org/10.1016/j.cmrp. 2020.03.011.

[29] Bai HX, Hsieh B, Xiong Z, Halsey K, Choi JW, Tran TM, Pan I, Shi LB, Wang DC, Mei J, Jiang XL. Performance of radiologists in differentiating COVID-19 from viral pneumonia on chest CT. *Radiology* 2020. https://doi.org/10.1148/radiol.2020200823.

[30] Hu Z, Ge Q, Jin L, Xiong M. *Artificial intelligence forecasting of COVID-19 in China.* arXiv preprint arXiv:2002.07112. 2020 Feb 17.

[31] Campos, J. E., & Pradhan, S. (Eds.). (2007). The many faces of corruption: tracking vulnerabilities at the sector level. *World Bank Publications.*

[32] Escresa, L., & Picci, L. (2017). A new cross-national measure of corruption. *The World Bank Economic Review*, 31(1), 196-219.

[33] Mungiu-Pippidi, A., & Dadašov, R. (2016). Measuring control of corruption by a new index of public integrity. *European Journal on Criminal Policy and Research*, 22(3), 415-438.

[34] Rose-Ackerman, S., & Palifka, B. J. (2016). *Corruption and government: Causes, consequences, and reform.* Cambridge university press.

[35] Rose-Ackerman, S. (2021). Corruption and COVID-19. EUNOMÍA. *Revista en Cultura de la Legalidad*, (20), 16-36.

[36] Beerbaum, D., & Puaschunder, J. M. (2019). A behavioral economics approach to digitalization: The case of a principles-based taxonomy. In *Intergenerational Governance and Leadership in the Corporate World: Emerging Research and Opportunities* (pp. 107-122). IGI Global.

[37] *Consultancy.in*, [Online Accessed on May 2021] https://www. consultancy.in/.

[38] *World Bank*, World Bank Data, [Online Accessed on May 2021], https://data.worldbank.org/.

[39] *Global Connectivity Index*, "Shaping the New Normal with Intelligent Connectivity," [Online Accessed on May 2021] https:// www.huawei.com/minisite/gci/en/index.html.

Chapter 15

Analyzing COVID-19 and Other Pandemics through Human-Computer Interaction

Dulini Ratnayake[1,*], Vinod Kumar Shukla[2,†] and Ruchika Bathla[3,‡]

[1,2]Department of Engineering and Architecture,
Amity University, Dubai, UAE
[3]Amity Institute of Information Technology,
Amity University, India

Abstract

Human-Computer Interaction (HCI) has swiftly made its way into the spotlight as an emerging branch of computer science and is gaining more importance with the passing day. It is quick to understand that technological inventions are used only if the users can take enough value out of them. This chapter of the interactions and associations between the users and the machines is the essence of HCI. Human-computer interactions become even more vital when the result of such interactions can be lifesaving. This is the case regarding global pandemics that often leave society in dismay and mayhem. The numerous challenges posed by pandemic outbreaks can be complex, and there is a growing need for new insights and novel methods to tackle these life-threatening circumstances. HCI is believed to be a growing discipline that, if used appropriately, can do wonders when faced with dangerous circumstances. When looking at the numerous pandemics over the years, it becomes clear that the success in response to each of them appears to

* Corresponding Author's Email: duliniR@amitydubai.ae.
† Corresponding Author's Email: vinodkumarshukla@gmail.com.
‡ Corresponding Author's Email: bathla.ruchika@gmail.com.

In: Industry 4.0 and Intelligent Business Analytics for Healthcare
Editors: Soumi Dutta, Vinod Kumar Shukla, Shruti Nagpal et al.
ISBN: 978-1-68507-602-3

directly correlate to how well humans take value out of the latest technologies. The greater the ease with which each groundbreaking technical development can be handled, the greater the success is in tackling the outbreak. Ranging from the Severe Acute Respiratory Syndrome (SARS) at the very beginning of the decade to the current COVID-19 pandemic, many changes are seen to have come into light with regards to how we have evolved in our interaction with technology. The role played by HCI and its association with pandemics become clear as we investigate the numerous developments in the field over the years with each passing pandemic. This report provides an insight into how humankind has interacted with technology over the years to mitigate catastrophic global viral outbreaks and discusses the primary technologies used during each of the major pandemics while highlighting how HCI played a role in the success of each of them.

Keywords: HCI, Technology, Pandemics, COVID 19, Artificial Intelligence

Introduction

A relatively younger discipline of computer science, Human-Computer Interactions (HCI), is seen as a fusion of computer science and cognitive psychology [1]. The chapter throws light on the interaction between human users and computer systems [2]. It embodies the studies of software engineering, natural language processing, artificial intelligence and links it with the findings of sociology, linguistics, ergonomics to strike the perfect understanding between the two intelligent systems: the machine and the human [3].

The discipline has gained much popularity today, vastly due to the increased access of computers to all population segments, not limiting to high skilled professional computer uses. The accurate adaptation of HCI has made it possible for almost any individual to now interact with a computer system after a few learning steps [3]. The rise in usability translates into the ubiquitous use of computer systems making its reach far and wide. So, it is evident that these systems and the role of HCI make an appearance when faced with significant circumstances in managing them [4]. One such situation happens to be global pandemics. *Pandemics* are atrocities that have shaken humankind from the dawn of time and continue to do so. However, the way these pandemics are dealt with over time has drastically improved. It would not be wrong to say that HCI has a significant role in mitigating the effects of pandemics alongside advancements in medicine and technology. The way information and data are provided and perceived by individuals significantly impact the outcome of a pandemic. HCI directly affects optimizing this link between the two parties, making it a powerful tool. This chapter focuses on the role of HCI in the face of global pandemics, including the current pandemic, COVID-19, to analyze what impact it had or has in the control and mitigation of these unfavourable circumstances. It hopes to bring out the prominent role HCI has to play alongside the technology as it often tends to go unnoticed.

Challenges Posed by Pandemics

Pandemics have terrorized civilizations since time immemorial. A *pandemic* is a novel disease that affects multiple continents, causing damage to all spheres of life [5]. The most dangerous aspect of any pandemic is its quick transmission and spread, which is the fundamental cause of concern that vilifies any disease as a pandemic. Living in a globalized world with increased travel, tracking and managing the spread of any disease is a grave task. Proper modes of contact tracing in the initial stages of the onset of a pandemic can significantly affect how well it can be controlled, making it one of the primary challenges [6].

Following up is the need for proper diagnostics tools with data record management. Diagnosis on its own can be a tedious task, but diagnosis without proper record entries and management can be devastating [6]. Lack of an appropriate system of information flow between diagnosis centres, research centres, and government bodies is vital for tracking the disease and staying on top of any developments in the pathogens causing it, which can help in treatment production and in placing regulations in affected areas.

Next, the toll taken on an individual during a crisis can be overly challenging. Misinformation can damage both individual mental health and the world economy. Regulatory agencies need to ensure verified information is available to people with efforts to take down fake news that can cause mass hysteria. The widespread misinformation can lead to a lack of order taking away control and peace, which are key components in the response for any pandemic [7]. Lastly, another major issue regarding any pandemic is sustaining the flow of life. With limitations on movements, the signature of most pandemics, daily routines, citizen mobility, commodity flow, or any other social requirements considerably dwindle. A complete restriction of all movements can severely harm the economy and human morale. A carefully designed process for collaboration between all sectors within a country and even the world becomes a vital issue in an outbreak control plan [7].

Numerous methods have been put in place to ensure these challenges are tackled in the best possible way by governments around the globe when faced with a pandemic. However, the effectiveness of the methodologies used varies greatly. Technology has taken centre stage in the battle against pandemic challenges. Effective HCI models are the backbone that supports these novel inventions, genuinely making them valuable assets. Quite often, the importance of HCI gets hindered in the face of the technology itself, eclipsing the value HCI brings to make these innovations a success. It is essential to see the part played by HCI to analyze further how to improve on them, thus improving the overall technology in overcoming the challenges mentioned above of pandemics.

Role of HCI In Pandemics

Technology has revolutionized our ability to tackle and manage the mass spread of outbreaks. Compared to 20th-century pandemics such as the 1918 pandemic (H1N1 Virus) or the "Spanish flu" that took over 50 million lives in just one year [8], the 21st-century pandemics are seen to be dealt with in a better way. The critical difference between the two cases is none other than the technological advancements. There is technology, HCI, as individuals take value out of technology only if they can understand how to interact and extract usage. Numerous technological advancements supported by interaction models in medical research, medical facilities, government bodies, mobility, supply chain, socialization and daily tasks have positively impacted the preparedness and response to global pandemics in the present age. The chapters that follow examine several 21st-century pandemics and the role of HCI in combating them. The current research highlighting these trends is also used to complement the discussion of these pandemics, highlighting the importance of HCI in each case.

Severe Acute Respiratory Syndrome (SARS) -2003

SARS, a viral respiratory disease caused by the coronavirus, was first detected in China, 2003 and was seen to spread across North America, Asia, Europe and South America [9]. It was the first pandemic of the twenty-first century, and the importance of travel in the disease's spread was evident at the time. With the pandemic came a stream of new technologies to help mitigate the dire situation at hand. Many technological and human collaborations led to a reasonably successful approach towards dealing with the circumstances faced.

The Healthcare link is one of the early examples of the involvement of HCI in the domain of healthcare in relation to an outbreak. It is a program that promises the detection of SARS even prior to the occurrence of symptoms. It can deliver on this promise through data aggregation from a mass of patients wherein each patient is requested to log their temperature and travel history via phone or internet. Physicians then review the data to alert concerned bodies of any unusual occurrences. Another platform that closely resembles the previous is MedDay that urges patients to enter health information to a portal via smartphones, which would then be transmitted to disease centres for processing. Such platforms act as early warning systems and help inpatient monitoring and tracking. Though in its rudimentary forms, they show the power a direct human-machine collaboration can have. The simple and straightforward interfaces provided by the platform make more and more individuals use it and thus add value to the overall process [10].

In addition to tracking and alert systems, another sphere in which the SARS pandemic saw HCI is worldwide collaboration platforms. Over nine countries and 11 laboratories took part in SARS diagnosis research projects. Special secure websites and email platforms were created through which all available research data were published such that all involved parties were supported in their research and developments [10].

Another exciting trend observed during the pandemic was the role played by online vendors and their platforms for the first time. Especially in Hong Kong, where the infection rates were high, most consumers turned to online platforms to purchase even the smallest product in hopes of mitigating the viral infections [11]. Many local suppliers thus were encouraged to create simple yet engaging online portals for their products to empower the consumers to carry on with their natural consumer patterns. The platforms thus created saw a significant spike in consumer engagements. For instance, Park'N Shop, a popular online platform in Hong Kong, saw a 161% rise in its online audience, [11] indicative of the popularity and success of the outlets. Such platforms also supported saving the plummeting economy of the pandemic-stricken countries and keeping the needs of the general population met. It becomes clear that such tools were only possible due to the marriage of high technology with simplistic designs for its quick and convenient usage, which is the role fulfilled by the discipline of HCI.

(H1N1) Influenza -2009

First detected in the United States, H1N1 influenza was unlike its predecessors. The virus was a unique amalgamation of influenza genes and was a combination of viruses found on birds, pigs and humans. It soon got coined with the term Swine Flu due to its point of origin [12]. The novelty of the virus imposed many challenges adding to the already existing hurdles of mass outbreaks.

As the outbreak was in the era after the launch of some major social media platforms, the manner of response to it saw new trends. One of the most popular and innovative applications was found to be Twitter informatics [13]. As the platform is accessible to any individual, a large influx of information and misinformation was observed. Twitter was seen as a mode to sample a large population. In comparison to the SARS epidemic that required dedicated platforms for individuals to enter data regarding their health status, Twitter acted more so as an all in one platform. Its familiarity among the users and ease with which they can share and access data made it a trendy hub of informatics. Thus, the massive data sets collected were transformed into a tracking and predictive tool for the outbreak [14]. A data set of 3 million tweets with the term "Flu" was observed during the peak phase of the H1N1 pandemic with people self-diagnosing [13]. Such data could then be processed to identify further research and precautionary measures patterns.

Ebola Virus Disease (EVD) – 2013

Transmitted predominantly by fruit bats, the Ebola virus disease (EVD) was one of the deathliest pandemics of the 21st century, with an average mortality rate of 50%. With the first outbreaks in the villages of central Africa, the virus soon made its way to neighbouring countries [15]. During the phase of Ebola, several technologies were modified and used as the backbone of the response and mitigation system. Maps for geolocation services, real-time surveillance and tracking, information services, big data analytics and logistical support via numerous platforms marked a new approach towards pandemic mitigation efforts.

mHero is an open-source mobile communication platform that allows informing, contacting, and surveying frontline workers on training, data, and laboratory tests to provide the highest quality services to the infected even if world-class practitioners are unable to be present at the site physically. The platform was intertwined with government institutes to increase effectiveness [16].

New computer outlets were made available for temperature tracking in real-time through a simple to read dashboard that indicated critical cases in red and the normal in green. GIS or Geographic information systems were used for live updates and thus to carry out follow-ups. The system commonly used to carry out the above was mTrac [17], which included real-time surveillance and alerts through SMS. This approach was taken as it was something the general population was already familiar with and was believed to reduce the learning curves associated with a novel design, thus increasing user engagement. mTrac provided free SMS support to alert the public of Ebola cases, collaborated with the Ministry of Health (MoH) and the District Health Teams (DHTs) to get the latest updates and disseminate the data to the concerned parties to gain the most value [16].

The most popular chat application, WhatsApp, was incorporated in the fight against the outbreak. BBC created WhatsApp Ebola, an information service on the already known application that provides texts, audio, video and images to provide the newest data on the developing cases [18]. As WhatsApp is the most widely used application for communication in the region, it only made sense to extend the same to combat the virus.

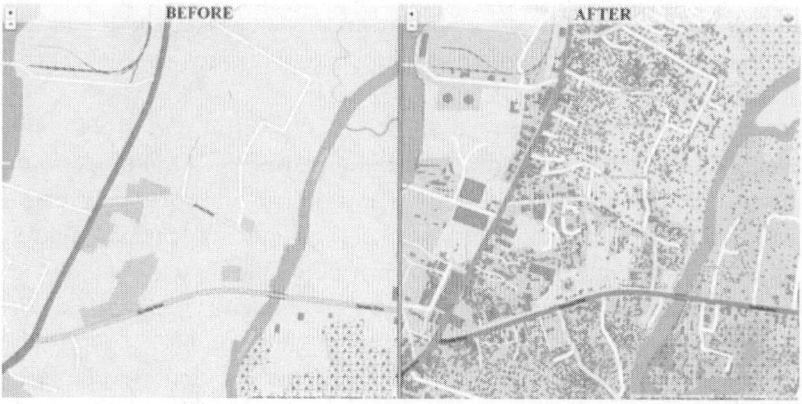

Figure 15.1. OpenStreetMap before and after being mapped by volunteers for active EVD cases [16].

In addition to information services platforms, the Ebola outbreak also saw the rise of several map-based tracking systems. HealthMap [19] and OpenStreetMap (Figure 15.1) [16] were two popular platforms used at the time. The former uses online sources and aggregates data for real-time surveillance and monitoring and is available both as an app and as a website. The latter includes the support of volunteers to build maps targeting the infected locations to give a clearer look based on satellite images.

The most novel approach used in the fight of the outbreak comes from big data and the use of IBM's Watson supercomputer. The staggering computing power of Watson was used to identify trends in the virus spread to help restrict it, the study of its mutation and pathology and the studies for a possible vaccine to eradicate the virus for good [16].

COVID 19 -2019

A respiratory illness caused by the “severe acute respiratory syndrome coronavirus 2 (SARS-CoV-2)” was first detected in Wuhan, China, and is the largest pandemic noted to date with 220 countries affected [20]. Living in a time where everything is digitized and human-computer interactions are much more frequent than any other human interaction, there is no doubt of the vital role played by HCI during this pandemic. Several new technological trends are seen to come into light during this pandemic and include the roles played by Artificial Intelligence (AI), Big Data, Internet of Things (IoT), Virtual Reality (VR) and robotics. Among others are advanced forms of telemedicinal platforms and information services, all-surpassing the previously set standards to tackle the pandemic at hand.

Artificial intelligence is seen to be very powerful due to its ability to enhance the capabilities of already existing platforms. AI is used mainly in research optimization, contract tracing algorithms, and robots' development for sterilization and cleaning purposes [21]. Fake news detection algorithms in association with social media giants are put in place to track and restrict the flow of any damaging information through the Internet [22]. In association with IoT and big data, AI has also given rise to platforms that support symptom detection. Disease spread analysis, contact tracing and development of containment strategies and regulations. One example of an AI model that revolutionized the pandemic diagnosis is XGBoost [23], a classifier cable of categorizing patient blood samples as general, moderate or high risk making it also possible to change the course of treatment depending on the specific case at hand. Contract tracing is commonly done through AI-based fever detection and facial recognition, and online data analysis via big data to ensure proper precautionary measures. The security personnel commonly uses similar platforms at crowded locations to carry out necessary actions if the required protocols are not met. The relative ease with which the platform can be interpreted by a commoner who does not necessarily need to understand the underlying algorithms speaks to how well the interface designs are put in place to make the most value out of even the most complex systems.

When almost the entire world is quarantined and forced into their homes, the popularity of a new range of platforms was getting popular. With businesses and schools forced to go online, many new business platforms came into being, and these were supported by cloud computing and virtual reality (VR). Cloud computing provides any user with the required computing resources ranging from storage, servers etc., for a flexible yet stable infrastructure. Common cloud-based platforms that are at an all-time high right now include Zoom, MS Teams, and Netflix, which have helped normalize life amidst a pandemic. These platforms also incorporate elements of VR to bring a sense of interactiveness, such as video conference calls, real-time collaborations via interactive whiteboards and other simulation tools. Additionally, cloud services such as Google Cloud, Amazon Web Services, and Microsoft Azure have completely simplified the ability of any business to go online via its pay per use portals [21].

Patients with intermediate symptoms of the virus were advised to self-quarantine with checkups done via telehealth services to decrease the mounting burden on hospitals so that the severe cases may be given greater attention. Telemedicine involves patients getting checked via real-time communication systems over a phone or a computer. It is carried out by either remotely located specialists or notable chatbots governed by complex algorithms. Such systems are available anywhere, reduce the travel time of patients and doctors, reduce any further exposure to the virus, and handle a more significant number of patients than an in-person checkup. The online self-checker named “Clara” deployed by the US Center for Disease Control and Prevention (CDC) has been a robust platform that supports many people concerned with showcasing specific symptoms. There was a 50% increase in the demand for such telehealth services in the US and the UK, which was met by many interactive platforms such as Doctolib by General Atlantic, Germany’s Compugroup, France’s Qare, UK’s Push Doctor, among many others. Doctolib, for instance, showcased a 40% rise in usage, showing that more and more people preferred video consultations via computer interactions rather than in-person checkups [22].

One more significant change in the fight for pandemics, as seen during COVID-19, is the roles taken up by autonomous drones and robots. Combined with IoT and AI, these units can carry out numerous tasks ranging from population control and regulation, disinfection, symptom checkers and product delivery [21]. The Chinese company CloudMinds created and donated over six different types of robots to assist in security and cleaning. A hospital in Wuhan was completely staffed with robots for tasks such as temperature checks, meal delivery, and disinfection to reduce the burden on the healthcare workers. Unique robots were also deployed to support conference call services for doctors and patients [22]. Additionally, germ-killing bots for aeroplane sanitization such as GermFalcon created by Honeywell too are used by international airports with hopes to control the outbreak. These robots or drones are powered by a combination of complex technologies ranging from sensors, IoT, AI and 3D printing. However, its popularity is high due to the designer's ability to layout the human interaction side of things with relative ease. For instance, GermFalcon may be used by any airline crew member following a small training, increasing its usability.

Result

The above discussion throws light on the numerous developments made over the past decade in response to pandemic outbreaks with regards to the role of technology and HCI. Compared to the SARS viral outbreak of 2003, the growth in the responsiveness and interaction of humans with numerous technologies seen in the present COVID-19 pandemic is quite drastic. The chapter presented here solidifies the importance of the need to bring about simplified approaches to highly technical applications. More and more people can be involved in their utilization and accelerate the containment and recovery process. The chapter establishes the importance of HCI in pandemic response as it could often be eclipsed by the technology they try to support. The research provides evidence as to how great interaction models should go hand in hand with the upcoming technologies to provide the maximum benefit to the masses.

Conclusion

Over the years, many deadly infectious pandemics have emerged to surface, disrupting the lives of millions across the globe. With each outbreak came a new challenge that humanity collectively tried to overcome. Many technologies made their way to the centre stage to respond to such deathly pandemics. Each of these novel technologies only succeeded due to the role of HCI in making complex technologies user friendly and appealing to the general population as pandemics affect the masses than a few. As shown in this report, the technologies used got advanced with each pandemic through time. However, the effort needed to be put by humans in its interactions with the platforms remained relatively simple, if not even simplified. Inventors found ways to incorporate the most familiar aspects of technology with novel designs such as social media and smartphones to bring the most out of these platforms. All designs are minimalistic with a minimum learning curve, making these platforms to be adopted by the public with ease and then making them the norm. Thus, the report concludes that technology indeed plays a significant role in the fight against pandemics. However, the component of HCI makes it a success, making the general public adopt the use of complex systems via simplified computer interactions. As a result, such designs will have even more power, bringing us one step closer to combating deadly pandemics through collaboration and creativity.

References

[1] Collazos, C., T. Granollers and C. Rusu, "A Survey of Human-Computer Interaction into the Computer Science Curricula in Iberoamerica," in *2011 Eighth International Conference on Information Technology: New Generations*, 2011.

[2] Wen F. and L. Song, "The Human-computer Interaction Design and Research of Virtual Experiment," in *2014 Sixth International Conference on Intelligent Human-Machine Systems and Cybernetics*, 2014.

[3] Pan, C. "Human-computer interaction system design and implementation in network," in *2010 2nd International Conference on Computer Engineering and Technology*, 2010.

[4] Yun, Y., D. Ma and M. Yang, "Human–computer interaction-based Decision Support System with Applications Data Mining," *Future Generation Computer Systems,* vol. 114, p. 285–289, 2021.

[5] Krishna Reddy, R. "Smart technologies for fighting pandemics: The techno- and human- driven approaches in controlling the virus transmission," *Government Information Quarterly,* 2020.

[6] Madhav, N., B. Oppenheim, M. Gallivan, P. Mulembakani, E. Rubin and N. Wolfe, "Pandemics: Risks, Impacts, and Mitigation," *Disease Control*

Priorities: Improving Health and Reducing Poverty, vol. 3, p. Chapter 17, 2017.

[7] Ghita, M., M. khadija, B. Siham, B. Mariam and M. Hicham, "Digitalization against the new outbreak," in *2020 Fourth World Conference on Smart Trends in Systems, Security and Sustainability*, 2020.

[8] Centers for Disease Control and Prevention, National Center for Immunization and Respiratory Diseases (NCIRD), "Past Pandemics -1918 Pandemic (H1N1 virus)," Centre for Disease Control and Prevention, 20 03 2018. [Online]. Available: https://www.cdc.gov/flu/ pandemic-resources/1918-pandemic-h1n1.html. [Accessed 22 11 2020].

[9] National Center for Immunization and Respiratory Diseases, Division of Viral Diseases, "Severe Acute Respiratory Syndrome (SARS)," Severe Acute Respiratory Syndrome (SARS), 06 12 2017. [Online]. Available: https://www.cdc.gov/sars/. [Accessed 22 11 2020].

[10] Eysenbach, G. "SARS and Population Health Technology," *Journal for Medical Internet Research,* 2003.

[11] Forster P. and Y. Tang, "The Role of Online Shopping and Fulfillment in the Hong Kong SARS Crisis," in *Proceedings of the 38th Hawaii International Conference on System Sciences - 2005*, 2005.

[12] Centers for Disease Control and Prevention, National Center for Immunization and Respiratory Diseases (NCIRD), "2009 H1N1 Pandemic (H1N1pdm09 virus)," 11 06 2019. [Online]. Available: https://www.cdc.gov/flu/pandemic-resources/2009-h1n1-pandemic.html. [Accessed 23 11 2020].

[13] Szomszor, M., P. Kostkova and C. St Louis, "Twitter Informatics: Tracking and Understanding Public Reaction during the 2009 Swine Flu Pandemic," in *2011 IEEE/WIC/ACM International Conferences on Web Intelligence and Intelligent Agent Technology*, 2011.

[14] Lamos, V., T. Bie and N. Cristianini, "Flu Detectot- Tracking Epidemics on Twitter," in *European Conference on Machine Learning and Principles and Practices of Knowledge Discovery in Databases*, 2010.

[15] World Health Organization, "Ebola Virus Diseas," [Online]. Available: https://www.who.int/news-room/fact-sheets/detail/ebola-virus-disease. [Accessed 23 11 2020].

[16] The United States Agency for International Development's (USAID), "Technical Brief: Use of Technology in the Ebola Response in West Africa," The United States Agency for International Development's (USAID), 2014.

[17] Dr. Musinguzi, D. *mHealth Working group email excerpt from UNICEF/Uganda, Health Systems Strengthening,,* 2014.

[18] BBC, "BBC launches WhatsApp Ebola service," 16 10 2014. [Online]. Available: https://www.bbc.com/news/world-africa-29573964?print=true. [Accessed 24 11 2020].

[19] HealthMap, "HealthMap," 2014. [Online]. Available: https:// healthmap.org/ebola/#timeline. [Accessed 24 11 2020].

[20] World Health Organization, "Coronavirus," 2020. [Online]. Available: https://www.who.int/emergencies/diseases/novel-coronavirus-2019. [Accessed 23 11 2020].

[21] Javaid, M., A. Haleem, R. Vaishya, S. Bahl, R. Suman and A. Vaish, "Industry 4.0 technologies and their applications in fighting COVID-19 Pandemic," *Diabetes & Metabolic Syndrome: Clinical Research & Reviews 14,* pp. 419- 422, 2020.

[22] Kritikos, M. "Ten technologies to fight coronavirus," European Parliamentary Research Service, 2020.

[23] Lalmuanawma, S., J. Hussain and L. Chhakchhuak, "Applications of Machine Learning and Artificial Intelligence for COVID-19 (SARS-CoV-2) pandemic: A review," Chaos, Solitons and Fractals, 2020.

Chapter 16

Electronic Health Records and Challenges in Human Computer Interaction

Pooja Lohit[1,*], Vinod Kumar Shukla[1,†] and Anjuli Chaubey[2,‡]

[1]Department of Engineering and Architecture,
Amity University, Dubai, UAE
[2]Dr. Harisingh Gour University, Madhya Pradesh, India

Abstract

As healthcare facilities embrace digitalization, electronic health records (EHRs) have proven to be extremely beneficial. By storing patients' records and data digitally, the scope for human error reduces greatly and improves its reliability, security, mobility, and storage. There are three domains through which this can be achieved, namely, health information exchange (HIE), computerized physician order entry (CPOE), and clinical decision support (CDS). Despite the innumerable benefits, there are challenges faced in the arena of human-computer interaction (HCI) with respect to the usability of EHRs. These have been categorized into five groups: the display of information, cognitive overload, navigation, workflow, and functionality. The use of EHRs often disrupts the workflow of a healthcare facility, wherein a fraction of the time is lost in the documentation of reports. This needs to be avoided. Also, the use of CDS during a patient's visit must be aligned with the facility's workflow. Lastly, in the case of functionality, there are four concerns being raised:

* Corresponding Author's Email: poojal@amitydubai.ae.
† Corresponding Author's Email: vinodkumarshukla@gmail.com.
‡ Corresponding Author's Email: anjuli17.83@gmail.com.

In: Industry 4.0 and Intelligent Business Analytics for Healthcare
Editors: Soumi Dutta, Vinod Kumar Shukla, Shruti Nagpal et al.
ISBN: 978-1-68507-602-3

collaboration, error prevention, privacy and security, and availability of the sources of information. It can be beneficial for an EHR to offer better collaborative options so that healthcare facilities and pharmacies can collaborate for the welfare of the patients. This ability manages the following functions: storage, messenger, orchestrator, and monitor, which ensures better collaborative characteristics of an EHR. Error prevention can prove to be very useful in a healthcare facility that provides a highly interruptive environment prone to erroneous data entry. In such cases, it is beneficial to indicate anomalous data to prevent further impediments. Privacy and security are integral to the functioning of EHRs, and at the same time, pose a risk to the HCI in terms of EHRs. In recent times, many attacks have been noticed that have led to the loss or theft of data. As one's health is intimate information, protecting it from malicious intent must be prioritized. Lastly, the availability of the sources of information ensures higher credibility for further use. The chapter sums up the need for EHRs and their benefits, followed by the challenges in human-computer interaction affecting their usability and lack of adoption by healthcare facilities.

Keywords: human computer Interaction, electronic health records, healthcare, pandemic

Introduction

An electronic health record (EHR) can digitally store documents and information about patients in real-time and ensure that all the data is secure and accessible upon appropriate authorization. As the data is digitized, it is more reliable, and there is less scope for human error. Simultaneously, it allows remote access, as the data is not localized to one specific device. This enables more efficient storage and access of patients' data. It can contain a wide array of data ranging from medications, patient's medical history, diagnoses, treatment plans, results from laboratory tests to radiology images. With such rich access to information, doctors can make better predictions about the patients' health [1]. The advantages of an EHR are numerous but can be broadly categorized into three areas (Figure 16.1): health information exchange (HIE), computerized physician order entry (CPOE), and clinical decision support (CDS).

CDS enables a deeper, enhanced predictive analysis of a patient's health based on their previous records, which may not be noticed manually. It can flag potential drawbacks of a prescribed drug or the possibility of a triggered allergic reaction.

CPOE enables the user to register orders electronically. This makes ordering from a pharmacy much easier as the pharmacist does not have to seek clarification regarding any order. It also reduces the scope for potential confusion due to illegible writing. It also eliminates the involvement of the patients in the process, which is helpful as the patients are typically unaware of the details of the drugs they are prescribed.

HIE enables the seamless and fast movement of patient records from one facility to another. This is highly valuable as a patient's data can be accessed from any facility quickly in times of emergencies [2]. To sum up, EHRs can prove beneficial to an institution due to their ease of storage and migration, higher security, more accessible access, better readability, and greater accuracy.

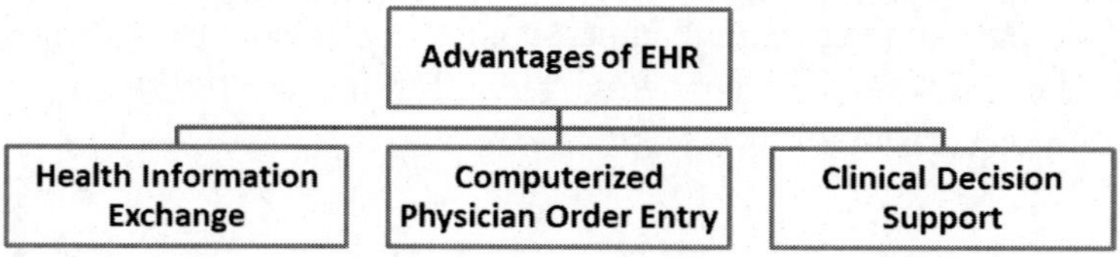

Figure 16.1. Advantages of HER.

Challenges of Electronic Health Records

Despite the innumerable benefits of EHRs, they are not fully adopted by India's healthcare facilities. The display of information plays a major role in the entering and retrieval of data as well as the process of coordinating and communicating the same. The poor display might indicate missing data or poorly presented data, usually as a result of an inadequately designed interface. Cognitive overload is caused by the presence of multiple sets of data, graphs, and reports being displayed to the user at once, or on the other hand, by the inadequate amount of data being displayed at once, both of which add excess pressure on one's cognitive abilities to recollect and correlate information. The navigation within the system is integral to its usability as the user often needs to switch between multiple windows to gain useful insights. It gets cumbersome if the navigation between the most visited windows is weakly designed, causing wastage of time. The Government of India has initiated multiple standards that enable facilities to adopt EHRs, but there is still a long way to achieve this. One such standard was initiated by the Ministry of Health and Family Welfare in 2013 that went through further amendments in 2016. This laid out a set of guidelines for the uniform and appropriate creation and maintenance of EHRs. Other initiatives such as an act called digital health information in healthcare security (DISHA) and the establishment of the national e-health authority of India (Neha) have still been unable to digitize healthcare in the country. The reason behind this points to the potential human-computer interaction issues that arise while dealing with EHRs. In [3], we understand that data scientists cannot infer much information from the EHRs due to a number of discrepancies that arise due to the physicians being unable to understand how to interact with the system. A poorly designed interface leads to wastage of time and risks to a patients' diagnosis [4]. Suppose the system is not devised in a manner that is easy for a healthcare professional to interact with. It leads to a lack of motivation among the users to adopt this technology and may avoid its usage altogether. By addressing each of the potential human-computer interaction concerns, we can perfect the digitization of patients' records, thus enabling more reliable healthcare services to all [5].

Addressing the Challenges

We can arrive at several potential human-computer interaction risks while using an EHR by assessing a few case studies that have been observed in the past. This issue was approached qualitatively, and a number of case studies were studied. Multiple reports, papers, and articles were examined to categorize the different kinds of HCI issues that EHRs pose. Each category is described with supporting case studies and implications. There are five categories that the potential risks have been categorized into, with their own set of sub-categories. These have been discussed in detail. The human-computer interaction risks related to EHRs can be categorized into five main domains (Figure 16.2).

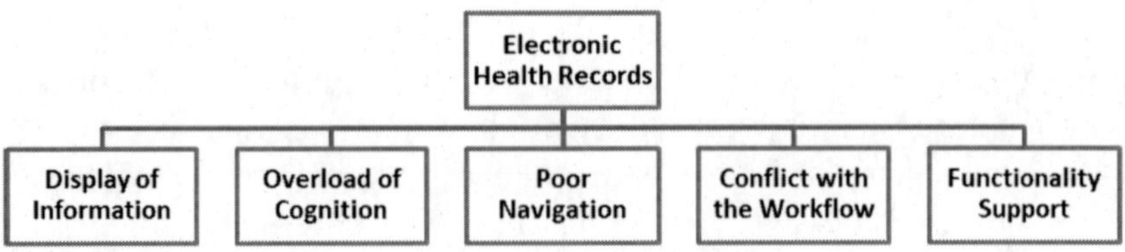

Figure 16.2. Electronic Health Record and its category.

Display of Information

Here, the data is either not easily visible or presented in confusing ways. One case study relevant to this concern needed a drug to be administered to a patient only if the blood pressure level was above a certain level. This added note was visible to the pharmacist but not the nurse resulting in the nurse administering the drug to the patient even though the blood pressure level was below the threshold level, resulting in complications. Another case study to support this is an EHR that measured weight in pounds but did not display that information and led to the healthcare professional assuming it to be in kilograms and administering an overdose of a drug that was not necessary in the first place [6]. Concerning how data is displayed on the screen, there could be interaction issues in mainly two areas: first, entering and retrieving data, and secondly, communicating and coordinating the data. When it comes to the first case, there are a number of concerns:

1. It is important to have an interface that can be worked with even in a highly interruptive environment, which is expected of a healthcare facility. In most cases, professionals are multi-tasking and end up clicking on items around the desired option due to their improper positioning and the disruptive environment around them that demands a large amount of their focus.
2. The interface very often requires an elaborate process of data entry, which becomes time-consuming.
3. There is a need to switch between multiple windows to record different kinds of graphs and data, which is not ideal. This is not a problem with paper records as all the different data points would be available on the same page [7].
4. The EHRs marking more than the necessary input data points as compulsory for the data to be ‘complete’ acts as an added disadvantage.

These concerns make the process of entering and retrieving data tedious and faulty [8]. In the second case, it is usually observed that the system cannot account for the discrepancies that arise in the communication and coordination of data. In one such case, medication was administered to a patient thrice a day but soon was discontinued. Before this, one dose was already provided to the patient, but the system did not allow the nurse to enter this as it was not supposed to be administered at all. Another issue that needs to be addressed is when certain medications need to be given before the physician can approve of it due to the urgent nature of it. The interface becomes very rigid in such cases and does not allow for any flexibility [9].

Overload of Cognition

As mentioned before, healthcare professionals deal with a highly interruptive environment that requires a lot of cognition and focus. During this time, as discussed in the previous section, poor display affects the accuracy of the data input by the users. At the same time, the amount of cognitive load that is involved in the process also affects the precision of the entered data. Cognitive load can be described as the amount of memory and information a human brain can hold and process at a time. It can also be seen to recall and recollect information from memory during a task [10]. This leads to an overload in the case of a healthcare professional as they must record every piece of information into the EHR while physically catering to the patient to ensure a fast response and at the same time recall information from memory to correlate and identify the issue at hand [11].

The problem that an EHR poses is that it only acts as a record of data, which becomes an additional task for the professional rather than helping them in collaborating or communicating.

It is often observed that a nurse cannot recognize important and urgent pieces of information on the system due to a number of such messages being displayed, leading to a cognition overload. The cause for such an overload arises from the usage of unnecessary alerts, cluttered templates, multiple charts with many data points, and data that is only useful for billing and not patient diagnosis [12].

According to a study, physicians spend about half a day and an additional two hours at home working with an EHR resulting in an overload of information and ultimately burnout [13]. A study that was conducted concluded that with the increase in the amount of task load, the ability to analyze data became harder for physicians [14]. Thus, it is important to minimize the amount of cognitive overload associated with EHRs to help the healthcare professionals and ultimately the patients in better treatment and diagnosis [15].

Poor Navigation

The usability of EHRs plays an integral role in the diagnosis and treatment of patients at healthcare facilities. According to research, poor usability is caused by an interface that is not user-centric. Its navigation decides a major portion of the usability of an interface. As mentioned before, patients' details are usually spread out in multiple graphs on numerous windows containing various data points. The users are expected to infer from the data by navigating through all the multiple windows themselves. As only one screen is visible at a time, the user is expected to hold most of the data they collect from the various graphs in their memory for them to be able to correlate it with the data being displayed on the screen. This leads to cognitive overload, as discussed in the previous section. As a result, the healthcare professional might have to revisit windows multiple times, leading to wastage of time, reduced efficiency, and more potential for errors [16].

In [17], research was conducted on the navigation patterns of healthcare professionals while using EHRs. They concluded that there existed inter-user but not a lot of intra-user variation in the navigation patterns. It is important to have a structured framework concerning navigation within a page and from one page to another. Navigation plays a major role in retrieving information from large sets of records as well [18]. The search option provided by EHRs often fails to assist the user in navigating through the numerous reports. The search can only enable access to specific parts of reports, withholding intricate details that the users must search for themselves. This situation hampers a brisk review of the most significant realities, conceivably negatively impacting the nature of clinical choices. For quite a while, issue records or analysis records in clinical records have been key data sources since they contain an attractive determination of the most pertinent data things, separated, and summed up by doctors [19]. At the same time, it is required to develop a system that is more seamless for healthcare workers to correlate data with previous patients who have undergone similar conditions and navigate through them. There is also a growing need for temporal queries and deep analyses regarding all the data collected [20]. This can help reduce the number of complex tasks a healthcare worker/professional must undertake in a day's work, avoiding cognitive overload and a better response to patients' diagnosis and treatment.

Conflict with the Workflow

An EHR can benefit a healthcare facility but can affect the temporal workload [21]. This suggests that the order in which operations are done in a healthcare facility upon the arrival of a patient has changed EHRs do not account for any dynamic operations. At the same time, the time being spent on the process of documentation has also increased considerably in the previous years. With numerous data points to be entered, records to be documented that have to be at par with the facility's workflow lead to the physicians' burnout.

In [22], a comparison was performed between the workload upon the use of EHRs and without their use and the amount of documentation done by the healthcare professionals. They concluded that there was a change in the tasks that occurred after the review with the patients. Upon using EHRs, documentation and clinical review took up a major portion of the operations that occurred during the treatment.

The integration of EHRs into ambulatory care is essential to the process of digitizing healthcare. However, studies have shown that clinicians are still hesitant of doing so due to its potential ability to change the workflow pattern and their productivity as a result [23]. The workflow usually consists of recording the patient's history, examining and surveying them, developing treatment plans, providing training, prescribing the required drug, ordering strategies and lab tests, and finally following up with the patients. With such an intricate set of tasks lined up in the workflow for every patient, it is understandable if the workers are reluctant to adopt EHRs, which may hinder the flow of tasks.

This is observed in pediatric care as well. Workflow risks that are usually faced are: signing in to numerous frameworks independently, broad control of consoles to enter data, the number of clicks engaged with prescription requesting measures, trouble in handling orders, troubles in swapping between screens to enter and recover data, understanding drug profile plan, number of alerts and messages, trouble seeing patient names on the screen, and missing free content section and other functionalities [24]. One way that healthcare workers cope with this is by having a workaround, which is a procedure that is usually not recommended or in the protocol in order to deal with the situation. One such workaround is the process of copying and pasting information to reduce the time taken for the task. For example, around 25% of reports included in patients' documentation included information copied from previous reports [25].

Assessed the situation at hand and analyzed if the use of EHRs impacted the workflow, and concluded that there was a considerable decrease in the productivity upon their use. This issue points to the human-computer interaction and the problems that workers face while dealing with the interface, causing more wastage of time and hence, less productivity [26].

Functionality Support

Gaps in the functionality provided by an EHR can hinder human-computer interaction and lead to a number of issues in the healthcare domain. The first concern is in regard to the option of collaboration offered by EHRs, due to their capability to store patients' information. EHRs can behave as a catalyst to improve the communication and collaboration between public health departments and primary healthcare providers. EHRs can be used to track communicable diseases and chronic diseases. In Covid-19, EHRs could be used to track the ones affected by the virus and increase surveillance for primary healthcare providers. For this to be efficient, it is required for EHRs to be effectively coordinated [27]. In [28], a system was developed for better collaboration and communication between healthcare providers and pharmacies to offer a better follow-up to patients suffering from diabetes and hypertension using EHRs. According to [29], a collaboration between EHRs falls under four main categories: repository, messenger, orchestrator, and monitor. The repository that is the ability of EHRs to hold all data is responsible for EHR-to-EHR communication as well as HIE. The orchestrator is responsible for ensuring the right worker is engages at the right time with the patient, driving the workflow accurately. The monitor assesses the gaps and improvements required.

Messenger is the ability of EHRs to transfer as well as assist in the communication between healthcare providers and members, which could be achieved through flags, messages, pop-ups, or paging. There have been hindrances in the way that the process of collaboration has previously taken place in the context of an EHR.

The second concern is with respect to the privacy and security concerns related to EHRs. There have not been many policy changes with respect to how privacy is looked at with respect to EHRs [30]. There have been instances of theft or loss of important data. It is ideal to have the patients gain access to their EHRs, but this opens new risks. There is a worry about unauthorized access being provided to patients' EHRs. A patient's EHR may be divided and available from more than one destination, especially with a more collaborative system. These frameworks could make the exposure of data to unapproved people or organizations, which could easily mishandle the data [31].

The third concern is error prevention. It is essential for EHRs to alert the users during the entry of suspicious or anomalous medical entries to avoid further complications [32]. A dynamic CDS coupled with a system to avoid prescribing errors can reduce the number of anomalies created in communicating the medication to the patient by the pharmacy [33]. An error is very easy to occur in the setup of a healthcare facility due to the highly interruptive environment that exists there, as mentioned in the previous sections. Therefore, the system needs to be able to recognize these errors and provide feedback or alerts when a set of information that does not correlate to the existing records or data points is entered.

The fourth concern is the availability of the source of information. Physicians need to have access to the source of information so that they can cross-check and ensure its credibility. A piece of information or a data point, if it seems irregular to the healthcare professional, can be checked accurately if the source of information is present as well. As EHRs hold patients' data for years, it can get challenging for physicians to trust old data if the source is not current. In certain situations, when the physician requires a large amount of data to be conclusive, it is ideal for them to have access to a large database of the patient's medical history. However, such large amounts of data may prove futile if they are not credible [34].

Conclusion

To conclude, EHRs show great promise in the process of digitizing healthcare. But numerous human-computer interaction risks pose challenges in its adoption. These affect not only the usability but also the diagnosis of patients. To solve these issues, it is advantageous to design an interface that allows for better display by presenting all the necessary information and ensuring the screen is not too cluttered. The framework must be consistent, and the updating, communicating, and coordinating of data must be prompt. Necessary steps must be taken to avoid the cognitive load on the users, either through the design or the implementation of EHRs. The navigation through the most commonly used windows must be seamless and easier to access. To implement better collaboration, the process of monitoring, orchestrating, collecting, and communicating data must be done efficiently. The data stored can undergo encryption and other security measures to not be prone to losses or thefts. To prevent errors, an alert system must be designed to avoid potential risks. Lastly, the sources of information must be made available to the users so that the data shown is credible and can be trusted for further diagnosis. By implementing the above-mentioned solutions coupled with others that solve the major human-computer interaction risks in EHRs, we can take a step forwards towards digitalizing healthcare and offering better services to patients and at the same time encouraging healthcare workers to adopt and use them.

References

[1] Menachemi, T. H. C. Nir, "Benefits and drawbacks of electronic health record systems," *Risk Management and Healthcare Policy,* vol. 4, pp. 47-55, 2011.

[2] Wadhwa, M. "*Electronic Health Records in India,*" March 2020. [Online]. Available: https://csd.columbia.edu/sites/default/files/content/docs/ICT%20India/Papers/ICT_India_Working_Paper_25.pdf. [Accessed 24 November 2020].

[3] Bologva, E. V., Prokusheva, D. I., Krikunov, A. V., Zvartau, N. E., & Kovalchuk, S. V. (2016). Human-computer interaction in electronic medical records: From the perspectives of physicians and data scientists. *Procedia Computer Science, 100,* 915-920.

[4] Clarke, M. A., Steege, L. M., Moore, J. L., Belden, J. L., Koopman, R. J., & Kim, M. S. (2013, July). Addressing human computer interaction issues of electronic health record in clinical encounters. In *International Conference of Design, User Experience, and Usability* (pp. 381-390). Springer, Berlin, Heidelberg.

[5] Sittig, D. F., Murphy, D. R., Smith, M. W., Russo, E., Wright, A., & Singh, H. (2015). Graphical display of diagnostic test results in electronic health records: a comparison of 8 systems. *Journal of the American Medical Informatics Association, 22*(4), 900-904.

[6] Mulkey, M. "*Poor Usability of Electronic Health Records Can Lead to Drug Errors, Jeopardizing Pediatric Patients,*" PEW, 24 April 2019. [Online]. Available: https://www.pewtrusts.org/en/research-and-analysis/issue-briefs/2019/04/poor-usability-of-electronic-health-records-can-lead-to-drug-errors-jeopardizing-pediatric-patients. [Accessed 24 November 2020].

[7] Collins, R. F. Rhonda DNP, "Clinician Cognitive Overload and Its Implications for Nurse Leaders," *Nurse Leader,* vol. 18, no. 1, pp. 44-47, 2020.

[8] Cimino, J. J. "Putting the "why" in "EHR": capturing and coding clinical cognition," *Journal of the American Medical Informatics Association,* vol. 26, no. 11, p. 1379–1384, 2019.

[9] Sinsky, C., Colligan, L., Li, L., Prgomet, M., Reynolds, S., Goeders, L., & Blike, G. (2016). Allocation of physician time in ambulatory practice: a time and motion study in 4 specialties. *Annals of internal medicine, 165*(11), 753-760.

[10] Nijor, Sohn, Eric Gokcen, and Nimit Lad. "Patient safety issues from information overload in electronic medical records: A systematic review." (2020).

[11] Ahmed, A., Chandra, S., Herasevich, V., Gajic, O., & Pickering, B. W. (2011). The effect of two different electronic health record user interfaces on intensive care provider task load, errors of cognition, and performance. *Critical care medicine*, *39*(7), 1626-1634.

[12] Shirts, B. H., Salama, J. S., Aronson, S. J., Chung, W. K., Gray, S. W., Hindorff, L. A., ... & Overby, C. L. (2015). CSER and eMERGE: current and potential state of the display of genetic information in the electronic health record. *Journal of the American Medical Informatics Association*, *22*(6), 1231-1242.

[13] Zhang, M. F. Jiajie, "TURF: Toward a unified framework of EHR usability," *Journal of Biomedical Informatics,* vol. 44, no. 6, pp. 1056-1067, 2011.

[14] Koopman, R. J., Steege, L. M. B., Moore, J. L., Clarke, M. A., Canfield, S. M., Kim, M. S., & Belden, J. L. (2015). Physician information needs and electronic health records (EHRs): time to reengineer the clinic note. *The Journal of the American Board of Family Medicine*, *28*(3), 316-323.

[15] Roman, L. C., Ancker, J. S., Johnson, S. B., & Senathirajah, Y. (2017). Navigation in the electronic health record: a review of the safety and usability literature. *Journal of biomedical informatics*, *67*, 69-79.

[16] Coleman, C., Gotz, D., Eaker, S., James, E., Bice, T., Carson, S., & Khairat, S. (2021). Analysing EHR navigation patterns and digital workflows among physicians during ICU pre-rounds. *Health Information Management Journal*, *50*(3), 107-117.

[17] Kreuzthaler, M., Pfeifer, B., Vera Ramos, J. A. et al. EHR problem list clustering for improved topic-space navigation. *BMC Med Inform Decis Mak* 19, 72 (2019). https://doi.org/10.1186/s12911-019-0789-9.

[18] Duncan, B. J., Kaufman, D. R., Zheng, L., Grando, A., Furniss, S. K., Poterack, K. A., ... & Doebbeling, B. N. (2020). A micro-analytic approach to understanding electronic health record navigation paths. *Journal of Biomedical Informatics*, *110*, 103566.

[19] K. W. C. P. &. B. S. Taowei David Wang, "Extracting Insights from Electronic Health Records: Case Studies, a Visual Analytics Process Model, and Design Recommendations," *Journal of Medical Systems,* vol. 35, p. 1135–1152, 2011.

[20] Denton, C. A., Soni, H. C., Kannampallil, T. G., Serrichio, A., Shapiro, J. S., Traub, S. J., & Patel, V. L. (2018). Emergency physicians' perceived influence of EHR use on clinical workflow and performance metrics. *Applied clinical informatics*, *9*(03), 725-733.

[21] Carayon, P., Wetterneck, T. B., Alyousef, B., Brown, R. L., Cartmill, R. S., McGuire, K., ... & Wood, K. E. (2015). Impact of electronic health record technology on the work and workflow of physicians in the intensive care unit. *International journal of medical informatics*, *84*(8), 578-594.

[22] Bowens, F. M., Frye, P. A., & Jones, W. A. (2010). Health information technology: integration of clinical workflow into meaningful use of electronic health records. *Perspectives in Health Information Management/AHIMA, American Health Information Management Association*, *7*(Fall).

[23] Lowry, S. Z., Ramaiah, M., Patterson, E. S., Brick, D., Gurses, A. P., Ozok, A., ... & Gibbons, M. C. (2014, June). Integrating electronic health records into clinical workflow: an application of human factors modeling methods to ambulatory care. In *Proceedings of the International Symposium on Human Factors and Ergonomics in Health Care* (Vol. 3, No. 1, pp. 170-177). Sage CA: Los Angeles, CA: SAGE Publications.

[24] Fleming, N. S., Becker, E. R., Culler, S. D., Cheng, D., McCorkle, R., Graca, B. D., & Ballard, D. J. (2014). The impact of electronic health records on workflow and financial measures in primary care practices. *Health services research*, *49*(1pt2), 405-420.

[25] Häyrinen, K., Saranto, K., & Nykänen, P. (2008). Definition, structure, content, use and impacts of electronic health records: a review of the research literature. *International journal of medical informatics*, *77*(5), 291-304.

[26] Barrett, K. K. S. Ashley K. "Making Electronic Health Records (EHRs) Work: Informal Talk and Workarounds in Healthcare Organizations," *Health Communications,* vol. 32, no. 8, pp. 1004-1013, 2017.

[27] Calman, N., Hauser, D., Lurio, J., Wu, W. Y., & Pichardo, M. (2012). Strengthening public health and primary care collaboration through electronic health records. *American journal of public health*, *102*(11), e13-e18.

[28] Renfro, C. P., Ferreri, S., Barber, T. G., & Foley, S. (2018). Development of a communication strategy to increase interprofessional collaboration in the outpatient setting. *Pharmacy*, *6*(1), 4.

[29] Chase, D. A., Ash, J. S., Cohen, D. J., Hall, J., Olson, G. M., & Dorr, D. A. (2014). The EHR's roles in collaboration between providers: A qualitative study. In *AMIA Annual Symposium Proceedings* (Vol. 2014, p. 1718). American Medical Informatics Association.

[30] Fernández-Alemán, J. L., Señor, I. C., Lozoya, P. Á. O., & Toval, A. (2013). Security and privacy in electronic health records: A systematic literature review. *Journal of biomedical informatics*, *46*(3), 541-562.

[31] Adebayo Omotosho, J. E. "A Criticism of the Current Security, Privacy and Accountability Issues in Electronic Health Records," *International Journal of Applied Information Systems (IJAIS),* vol. 7, no. 8, pp. 11-18, 2014.

[32] Gai, K., Qiu, M., Chen, L. C., & Liu, M. (2015, August). Electronic health record error prevention approach using ontology in big data. In *2015 IEEE 17th International Conference on High Performance Computing and Communications, 2015 IEEE 7th International Symposium on Cyberspace Safety and Security, and 2015 IEEE 12th International Conference on Embedded Software and Systems* (pp. 752-757). IEEE.

[33] Burlison, J. D., McDaniel, R. B., Baker, D. K., Hasan, M., Robertson, J. J., Howard, S. C., & Hoffman, J. M. (2018). Using EHR data to detect prescribing errors in rapidly discontinued medication orders. *Applied clinical informatics*, *9*(01), 082-088.

[34] Clarke, M. A., Belden, J. L., Koopman, R. J., Steege, L. M., Moore, J. L., Canfield, S. M., & Kim, M. S. (2013). Information needs and information-seeking behaviour analysis of primary care physicians and nurses: a literature review. *Health Information & Libraries Journal*, *30*(3), 178-190.

Chapter 17

A Novel Model to Anticipate Transparency in COVID-19 Records of India Using Blockchain

Shanti Verma* **and Rinkal Sardhara**
L. J. University, Ahmedabad, Gujarat, India

Abstract

COVID-19 pandemic was announced by the "World Health Organization" in March 2020. There are many developments done in modern healthcare systems to handle this pandemic. Blockchain is a modern technology used in healthcare systems to provide transparency in resource allocation, deployments, and several recovered, dead, and affected people from COVID-19 Blockchain technology for financial and non-financial sectors. As we know that falsification in the number of COVID-19 records of different countries has enormously increased, the current health care systems cannot provide integrity and authenticity. Thus, developing a blockchain-based model to provide non-volatility of information received from authenticated organizations like WHO is required. In this chapter, we have proposed a blockchain-based model to anticipate transparency of COVID-19 records through smart contract and web services to track new and recovered cases of COVID-19, which are obtained from trusted sources. Results verify that the proposed model is economical and ensures the integrity of the data.

Keywords: blockchain, healthcare, COVID-19, pandemic, technology

* Corresponding Author's Email: shanti.verma@ljinstitutes.edu.in.

In: Industry 4.0 and Intelligent Business Analytics for Healthcare
Editors: Soumi Dutta, Vinod Kumar Shukla, Shruti Nagpal et al.
ISBN: 978-1-68507-602-3

Introduction

COVID-19 pandemic plays the most significant role in technology expansion. COVID-19 virus is a part of the coronavirus ribonucleic acid virus family [1] that has provoked a worldwide pandemic. As this virus is straightforward to spread, it impacts society's healthcare system and intensities. We see in this pandemic that how developed countries and developing countries both faced difficulties with handling recovery and death rates. So countries need to make advancements in their healthcare systems [2], [3]. To improve the efficiency of any healthcare system, accuracy and transparency in datasets are required. However, the existing technologies cannot provide trustable datasets about the COVID-19 pandemic. The source of COVID-19 datasets is hospitals and clinical laboratories, but the datasets are not authentic because the technologies used to store and monitor these datasets are not trustworthy.

Therefore, it is required to use pioneering technologies like machine learning, deep learning, and blockchain to battle disasters. In this chapter, the authors proposed to use blockchain technologies to provide accuracy and transparency in COVID-19 datasets. Blockchain is a decentralized technology that uses cryptographic tools to provide transparency. The blockchain records are stored in the ledger by the cryptographic method, and it is traceable and tamper-free. [4] This technology is cryptographically secured, transparent, auditable, and provides data integrity without any third party, which creates interest in research areas [5], [6], [7]. It did not grow as it should have grown because of its technical and legal limitations. Some limitations are limited scalability, high latency, storage constraints, limited consensus mechanisms, lack of governance, high energy consumption, inadequate tooling, and the threat of Quantum computing [8].

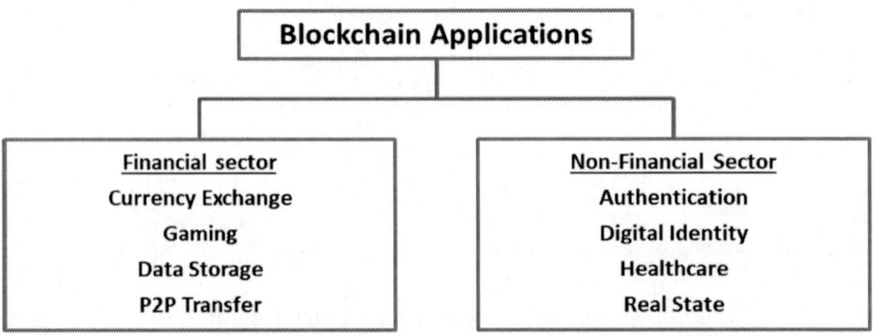

Figure 1. Application of blockchain.

Nowadays, Blockchain technologies have been implemented in many domains. Figure 1 shows the applications of blockchain in financial and non-financial sectors. We can use blockchain technologies in several ways to tackle the COVID-19 pandemic. It can be used to abridge transparency in supply and demand of vaccination, donation tracking, and fundraising, and also act as a trusted information provider.

This chapter proposes a novel model to focus on authentication and confidentiality in collecting and reporting COVID-19 datasets. These data may be collected from several trusted sources such as WHO, the National health portal of India (NHP), and the "Aagogya-setu" Application. As all these data centres are worked for centralized database architecture, there are chances of compromising data security in authentication, integrity, and confidentiality. Hence there is a need to propose a model, which can prevent hacking from cyber criminals based on blockchain technology. The residue of this chapter is organized as follows:

Section II talks about the COVID-19 pandemic and explains the benefit of blockchain technologies in handling this kind of data. Section III provides the detailed three-layer model based on blockchain technology to anticipate transparency in COVID-19 records. Section IV results and discussion on the proposed model. Furthermore, Section V presents the conclusion of our work.

Background

COVID-19 Pandemic: People who have an infection of coronavirus will experience mild to moderate respiratory problems, and it is recovered without any special treatment in most cases. Old-age people already struggling with other health problems are more prone to get infected with this infection [9]. The COVID-19 virus spreads mainly through droplets of saliva or expulsion from the nose when an infected individual coughs or sneezes. COVID-19 pandemic was announced by the "World Health Organization" in March 2020 [10]. As a result, states or provinces of different countries worldwide have imposed lockdowns of varying degrees. Some include total movement control, while others have imposed limits based on time. Mostly, only necessary businesses are permitted to remain open.

There are three vaccines: Pfizer, Modena, Oxford-AstraZeneca are now available to prevent COVID-19 disease. During the last stages of COVID-19 in India, where senior citizens received this vaccine. Figure 2 summarized the three levels of patients diagnosed with COVID-19 with symptoms, oxygen level, and preventive measures.

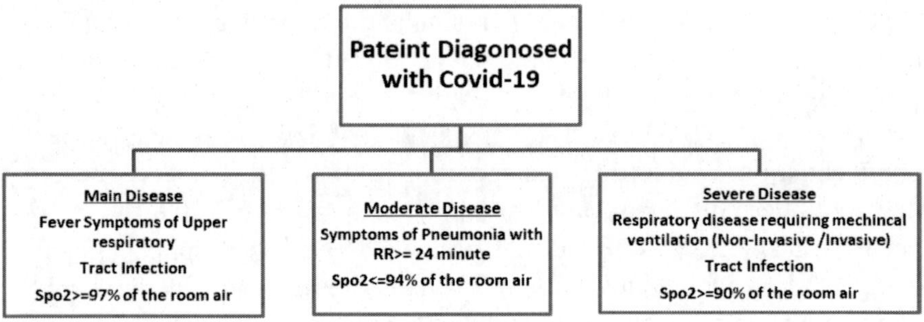

Figure2. Classification of patients diagnosed with COVID-19.

Blockchain Technology:Blockchain is a community ledger database that holds the encrypted ledger. According to IBM, blockchain is a decentralized ledger that stores or provides the process for record-keeping and tracking in a network. It keeps the details of all properties or things and their transactions over the web. Each transaction is encrypted using cryptographic functions, and then all these transactions are stored in a block. As a result, these blocks are connected together via cryptography so that anyone can make no additional modifications. The whole process created an immutable and unforfeited record of the transaction [11].

There are many characteristics of blockchain which made its application apart from cryptocurrency. These are transparency, decentralization, immutability, and consensus-driven, etc. Blockchain technology includes many profits, such as fewer intermediaries and censorship resistance. On the other hand, when blockchain technology was proposed, it was initially implemented only in the financial sector. Still, its advanced features like decentralization and transparency grab attention in the non-financial sector.

The main features of Blockchain (Figure 3), like decentralized access, auditability, security, disintermediation, and programmability, are more favourable. Blockchain solutions also have many potential business features like improving profitability and quality, increasing transparency using a distributed ledger, and reinventing products and processes.

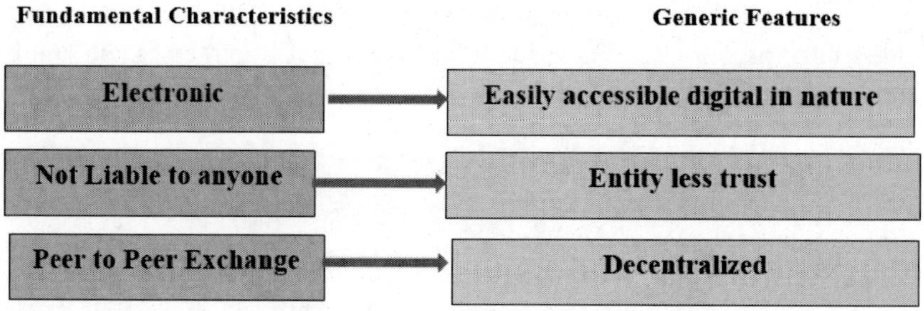

Figure 3. Features of blockchain.

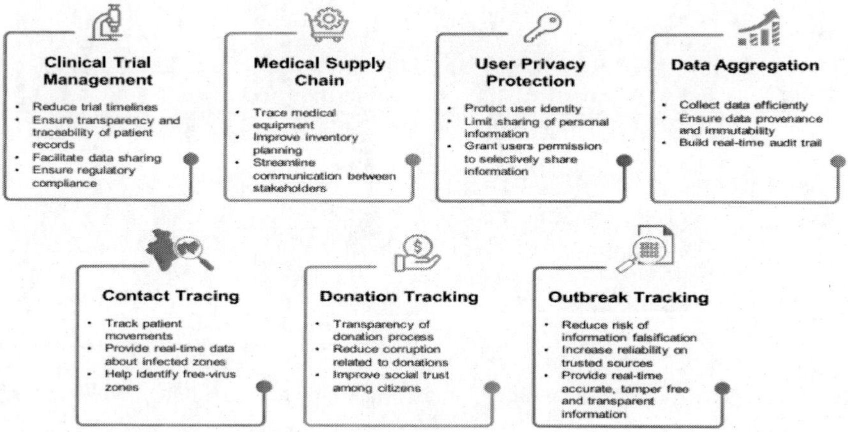

Figure 4. Blockchain based use cases of COVID-19.

With the help of Blockchain technology, it is possible to solve the problem related to the outbreak, which happened due to the COVID-19 pandemic. This technology can play a vital role in healthcare and its management and help track, trace, supply chain, logistics with proper authenticity [12]. The potential uses cases are summarized in Figure 4.

Proposed Blockchain Based Model to Anticipate Transparency

We propose a blockchain-based model (Figure 5) to provide transparency and integrity in COVID-19 records. Here records mean the number of patients affected, recovered, and deaths with COVID-19 disease. The proposed model uses data from WHO, NHP, and "Aarogya-setu" etc. The proposed model is divided into three layers: Frontend for users, Smart contracts, Data sources, and trusted database.

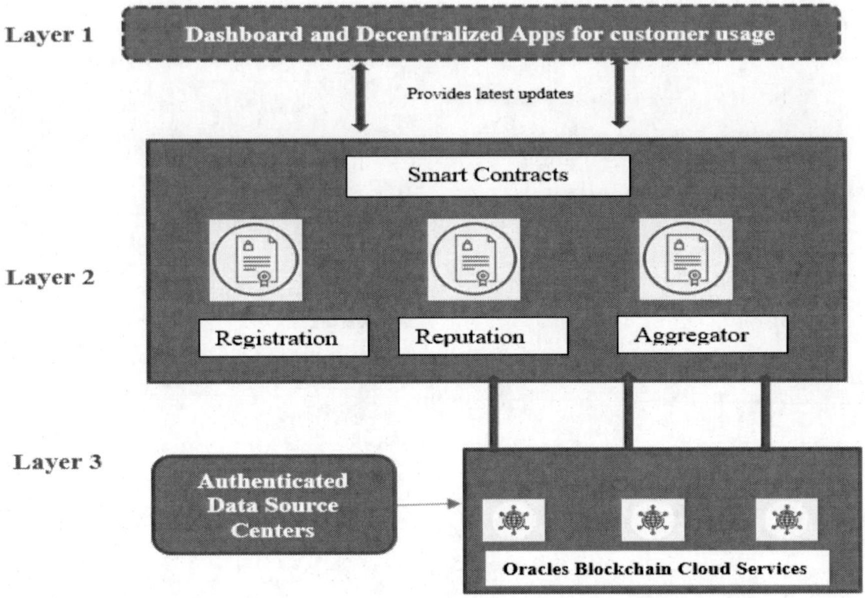

Figure 5. Proposed blockchain based model to anticipate transparency in COVID-19 datasets.

Layer 1: Dashboard and Dapps: In Figure 5, layer 1 is used by users/customers who want to access information about several confirmed/recovered/death COVID-19 cases using real-time data access with smart contract. This dashboard provides information about COVID-19 records, which are stored as smart contracts in a decentralized environment, so chances of changes in these datasets by intruder/hacker are nill. So the information is up to date and authentic.

Layer 2: Smart Contracts: This layer is the hidden layer from the user and will store three types of smart contracts. These smart contracts are registration, reputation, and aggregator. To develop these contracts, we can use public blockchain like *Ethereum*. Smart contracts are executed the terms of agreements by two parties automatically also verify transaction without involvement of the third party. Registration smart contract will include information of parties involved in transactions and web sources that provide real-time datasets of COVID-19.

*Reputation*is a trust score. A reputation system should give several data points to be used differently by different applications to determine an appropriate reputation for the given task. For example, when signing up for an Uber-like service, proving that you have a great history with such services should provide you with a better starting point, even a discount? In our proposed model, we can calculate reputation score from evaluating trusted web sources to retrieve datasets and assign that score on an oracles blockchain cloud services.

The total reputation score of oracles is dependent on the reputation score given by the user and the credibility of web sources. Reputation score depends on the trustworthiness of oracles. Can we use some threshold value to check total reputation score will calculate or not? If the trustworthiness of oracles cloud services is more than the defined threshold value, the total reputation score is calculated as equation 1:

$$\mathbf{Trep(X)} = \frac{rep(X)*T}{4*AF} \tag{1}$$

If the trustworthiness of oracles cloud services are less than defined threshold value, total reputation score is calculated as equation 2.

$$\mathbf{Trep(X)} = \frac{rep(X)*T}{4*(10-AF)} \qquad 2)$$

where Trep(X) represents the total reputation of oracles cloud services and X is the address of oracles. rep(X) denotes the reputation score of the trusted web source, and AF is the adjustment factor that shows the harsh and lenient behaviour with nodes having incorrect values. T represents the trustworthiness of oracles which is calculated as in equation 3.

$$T = \mathbf{T_{oracles}} - \mathbf{T_{smartcontract}} \tag{3}$$

where $T_{oracles}$ is the trustworthiness value of oracles and $T_{smartcontract}$ is the trustworthiness value of smart contract.

We require *Aggregator smart contract* to get real-time updates and send updates to front end users. This contract will filter updates based on the reputation score of oracles. If the reputation score is more than defined, threshold updates are sent to the frontend user and if fewer updates are dropped and not sent to the frontend user.

Layer 3: Oracles Blockchain Cloud Services: This layer acts as a third party used to build and run smart contracts and maintain a tamper-proof distributed ledger. It provides external information as they are unable to fetch their own. They use web APIs of external sources like WHO, NHP and "Aarogya setu" to fetch every 60 students and send it to oracles. Oracles use this information and feed it into smart contact to execute it. We cannot believe in one piece of information, so multiple information is passed into oracles to improve accuracy. In this manner, we can handle single point failure errors and trust only one source.

Result and Discussion

Our proposed model to anticipate transparency in COVID-19 records in India is a three-layer model. It provides real-time updates about several confirmed, recovered, and deaths cases. Using this method, we can make data management cost and security of customer data. Whenever smart contract is executed, the customer has to pay a gas fee in the Ethereum platform. The gas fee is paid in ether (ETH), Ethereum currency. The minimum required gas for the primary transaction is 21,000 gas. As ETH value is changed frequently, researchers analyze that the customer's maximum cost will not exceed 5 USD. So we can conclude that the proposed model is feasible and reassures cost saving.

We want to analyze basic security properties using CIA (confidentiality, integrity, and authorization) in the proposed model. Our proposed model ensures that the information added into the new block is trustable and valid with the help of miners. Moreover, after adding information into the block, it is challenging to change the hash of that block, so our model assures the integrity of records. We also know that all the information stored in the block is encrypted with a secure encryption algorithm, so our model also assures confidentiality. In our proposed model, a smart registration contract assures that all the customers are registered first to interact with the smart aggregator contract. Hence the proposed model ensures authorization and authenticity controls.

Conclusion

We here proposed a model to provide validation and transparency in COVID-19 records. This model uses data from various sources and reduces data modification and data hacking chances. The proposed model is for the healthcare system and can be used in any industry where data validation and transparency are needed. Here we also analyze cost and security for the proposed model and found it is feasible to use. In future work, we will try to develop smart contracts and make the system use of customers.

References

[1] Ambika, M., and K. Latha. "Intelligence Based Recommendation System for Healthcare: a Patient centred Framework." In *CAASR International Conference on Innovative Engineering and Technologies*. 2015.

[2] Trayush, T. R. Bathla, S. Saini and V. K. Shukla, "IoT in Healthcare: Challenges, Benefits, Applications, and Opportunities," 2021 *International Conference on Advance Computing and Innovative Technologies in Engineering (ICACITE)*, 2021, pp. 107-111, doi: 10.1109/ICACITE51222.2021.9404583.

[3] Athota, L. V. K. Shukla, N. Pandey and A. Rana, "Chatbot for Healthcare System Using Artificial Intelligence," *2020 8th International Conference on Reliability, Infocom Technologies and Optimization (Trends and Future Directions) (ICRITO), 2020*, pp. 619-622, doi: 10.1109/ICRITO48877.2020.9197833.

[4] Madhavan, Subha, Lisa Bastarache, Jeffrey S. Brown, Atul J. Butte, David A. Dorr, Peter J. Embi, Charles P. Friedman et al. "Use of electronic health records to support a public health response to the COVID-19 pandemic in the United States: a perspective from 15 academic medical centers."*Journal of the American Medical Informatics Association* 28, no. 2 (2021): 393-401.

[5] Anwar, S. V. K. Shukla, S. S. Rao, B. K. Sharma and P. Sharma, "Framework for Financial Auditing Process Through Blockchain Technology, using Identity Based Cryptography," *2019 Sixth HCT Information Technology Trends* (ITT), 2019, pp. 099-103, doi: 10.1109/ITT48889.2019.9075120.

[6] Wanganoo, L. B. Prasad Panda, R. Tripathi and V. Kumar Shukla, "Harnessing Smart Integration: Blockchain-Enabled B2C Reverse Supply Chain," *2021 International Conference on Computational Intelligence and Knowledge Economy (ICCIKE), 2021*, pp. 261-266, doi: 10.1109/ICCIKE51210.2021.9410677.

[7] Gupta, R. V. K. Shukla, S. S. Rao, S. Anwar, P. Sharma and R. Bathla, "Enhancing Privacy through "Smart Contract" using Blockchain-based Dynamic Access Control," *2020 International Conference on Computation, Automation and Knowledge Management (ICCAKM),* 2020, pp. 338-343, doi: 10.1109/ICCAKM46823.2020.9051521.

[8] Alam, Tanweer. "Blockchain-Enabled Mobile Healthcare System Architecture for the Real-Time Monitoring of the COVID-19 Patients." *Available at SSRN 3772643* (2021).

[9] Thange, U. V. K. Shukla, R. Punhani and W. Grobbelaar, "Analyzing COVID-19 Dataset through Data Mining Tool "Orange"," 2021 *2nd International Conference on Computation, Automation and Knowledge Management (ICCAKM), 2021*, pp. 198-203, doi: 10.1109/ICCAKM50778.2021.9357754.

[10] Lee, Brian, Brandi Dupervil, Nicholas P. Deputy, Wil Duck, Stephen Soroka, Lyndsay Bottichio, Benjamin Silk et al. "Protecting Privacy and Transforming COVID-19 Case Surveillance Datasets for Public Use."*arXiv preprint arXiv:2101.05093 (2021).*

[11] Gupta, Mansi, and Vimal Kumar. "Revealing the Demonstration of Blockchain and Implementing Scope in COVID-19 Outbreak." *EAI Endorsed Transactions on Scalable Information Systems*8, no. 29 (2021): e2.

[12] Kondilis, Elias, Dimitris Papamichail, Valentina Gallo, and Alexis Benos. "COVID-19 data gaps and lack of transparency undermine pandemic response."*Journal of public health (Oxford, England)*(2021).

Chapter 18

Applications and Implementation of Contactless Hand Sanitizer Using Proximity Sensor

Syeda Fizza Nuzhat Zaidi[1], Vinod Kumar Shukla[1,*], Ashok Chopra[2] and Archana Singh[3]

[1]Department of Engineering Architecture and Interior Design,
Amity University, Dubai, UAE
[2]Department of Management and Commerce,
Amity University, Dubai, UAE
[3]Department of IT, Amity University, Uttar Pradesh, Noida

Abstract

In a recent global pandemic, Covid-19 has affected every individual across the globe. People everywhere have tried to develop brand new inventions and safety solutions to protect themselves and others from this virus. Mandatory guidelines are put forward in every country, including malls, offices, universities, schools, supermarkets, grocery stores, government buildings, areas of tourism, etc. After months of lockdown and conversion of all jobs and education branches to stay at home jobs and online modes of education, the world is finally getting used to the pandemic and is coming up with ways to cope with the new normal. There are a number of precautionary rules followed by everyone such as wearing a mask at all times, using hand sanitizer after using public facilities and touching anything which is not owned by oneself, not giving handshakes as a form of greeting anymore, going out lesser and only when its essential and maintaining social distance at all times and everywhere. This chapter concentrates on applying and implementing

[*] Corresponding Author's Email: vinodkumarshukla@gmail.com.

In: Industry 4.0 and Intelligent Business Analytics for Healthcare
Editors: Soumi Dutta, Vinod Kumar Shukla, Shruti Nagpal et al.
ISBN: 978-1-68507-602-3

contactless hand sanitizers using proximity sensors, transistors, dc water pumps, resistors, silicon or airline tube, battery holder, etc. The disposal machine can be any container, which can be cleaned and large enough to allow easy functioning and placement of the circuit, and the materials can be bought online and in stores worldwide. Many companies have used different types of complicated circuit based contactless hand sanitizing machines with the help of sensors since the beginning of this pandemic. However, now it is becoming easier to make these, and at once, own expertise, and the circuits used have become more integrated, thus requiring no expert help and a hefty budget.

Keywords: contact less sanitizer, pandemic, Covid-19, healthcare, proximity sensor

Introduction

Covid-19 is a highly infectious disease caused by a newly discovered virus known as the coronavirus. It has been spreading rapidly, and either the virus or the effects it has had on society affect everyone [1]. It has become a global concern because it has spread to every nation. According to the world health organization (WHO), most people infected with the COVID-19 virus will experience mild to moderate respiratory illness and recover without requiring special treatment. Older people with underlying medical problems like cardiovascular disease, diabetes, chronic respiratory disease, and cancer are more likely to develop serious illnesses [2]. It is essential to make sure that you keep yourself safe even if you do not fall into these categories, so you do not end up unknowingly spreading it to someone who falls into this category but gets affected by your actions. In this time of crisis, We must all look after each other and ensure that we do not end up harming someone else, be it our relatives, friends, colleagues, classmates, or even a stranger. With the rise of novel Coronavirus or COVID-19, health-based chatbots were designed in providing personal medical care. As there has been an increase in patients globally due to the virus spread, governments were facing a tough time providing various health equipment, staff, and resources to other clinics and health centres. Chatbots were also made, which helped reduce the burden of the healthcare industry. Hence, specific COVID-19 virtual assistants were made with unified applications to assist during the pandemic. For example, the World Health Organization (WHO) launched an application in seven languages to protect the general public from virus infections. Similarly, countries like Germany developed a "fight COVID messenger bot" application. The SAJIDA Foundation of Bangladesh's developed a bot with detailed information on protective measures and a symptom checker. Arogya Setu app by the Indian government has also helped create awareness of COVID-19 [3] [4].

Use and Importance of Technology during Pandemic Time

Technology has taken over our lives, which has been very helpful, particularly during the pandemic. The use of technology before the pandemic was mainly for leisure and for time to pass. It was when we needed a break from work or reality in general. We would watch TV for entertainment and play games on our mobile phones when we needed a break from the hectic work life or school life. It was always an alternative to our reality and our way of getting some alone time and peace of mind.

However, technology is no longer just an escape from work life or school life; it is our connection to work-life and school life during this global pandemic [5]. It is our only way of keeping in touch with others and keeping track of our social and work life. The mobile phones we used for fun, and playing games are now used to keep track of news channels and find out how many new cases are there every day. The laptops we used only to watch movies when we needed a break from work is now used to connect with teachers, colleagues, etc. to have work meetings and have an online class. The Computers we used for fun are now being used to submit assignments and meet due dates for an online school or meet deadlines for work. The TV we used to watch for entertainment is now always switched to the World News channels to keep track of the pandemic updates. Various apps are now used globally for professional use, such as Whatsapp, Amazon, Microsoft Teams, Microsoft Office, Zoom, Google Meet, Outlook, Gmail, Telegram, Instagram, Adobe, Twitter, Linkedin, etc.

The work that used to be done outside is now all done from home through various apps. The pandemic has led to the shutdown of numerous businesses worldwide but has led to the rise in countless online businesses and stores. Engineers and construction workers have been affected negatively by the pandemic because they cannot be done using just technology. However, the entrepreneurs such as social media influencers, YouTubers, musicians, video editors, etc. have hugely benefitted from this pandemic due to technology and social media business. To look at the use of technology during the pandemic as a whole, We can say that the same laptops we used to switch on to take a break from work life and reality are now the ones we switch off to take a break from work life and enjoy reality.

The best way to prevent ourselves from getting coronavirus is by washing our hands frequently, by drinking a lot of water, by wearing a face mask every time you step out of your home even if it is for just a small task, by using sanitizers every time you go somewhere and after you touch something outside, by taking a shower after coming back home from outside even if you went out only for a short time, by social distancing and making sure that you only step out of home when it is a need and not all the time, by making sure you go to places that are sanitized properly and ensure your safety as well as safety for others around you, by keeping a distance from everyone every time you go out and making sure you don't come in physical contact with anyone, by greeting only by words and not shaking hands with anyone you meet to make sure germs are not spread when you get in contact with someone, by taking the vaccine which is now available for everyone, by making sure you only go to places with limited amount of people and if you go to someone's home then they have limited amount of people and follow the rules given for a get together during the pandemic by the safety and health organizations.

Need and Consumption of Sanitizer Worldwide

Sanitizers have always been a way to keep our hands clean and have always been used. However, with the onset of the pandemic, the demand for sanitizers has increased rapidly, and now every person owns at least three different sets of sanitizers be it for home use or outside use. This has led to extremely high production of sanitizers, and as demand increases, the price also increases. Thus, making sanitizers one of the highest on-demand products globally during the pandemic.

Sanitizers have also been integrated with technology just like everything else and are now automatic contactless hand sanitizers are available. This makes the use of sanitizers even safer since there will not be any contact with the device and thus reduce the spread of germs and the virus even more. Instead of using globally produced automatic hand sanitizers, which can be expensive for daily use, people have creatively started experimenting with creating more affordable sanitizers which can solve the purpose. Figure 18.1 shows the increase in demand for health and safety products during the pandemic. The highest demand, as it can be seen, is for Hand Sanitizers which can be in any form: Gel, Foam, Alcohol-free, Alcohol-based, etc.

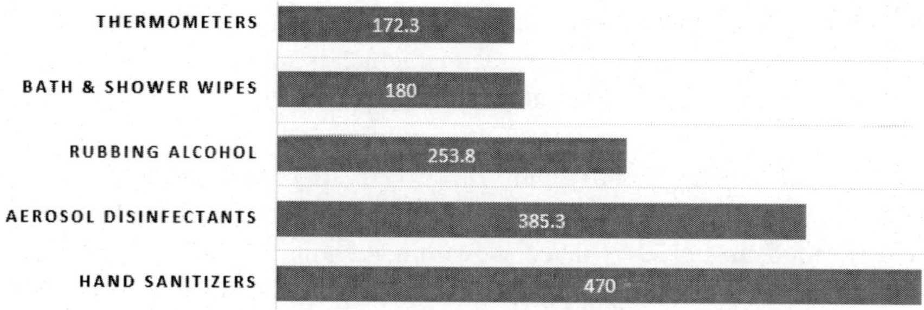

Figure 18.1. Health and safety products demand (March 2020) [6].

The most demanded health and safety products are:

- Hand sanitizer: +470%
- Aerosol disinfectants: +385.3%
- Rubbing alcohol: +253.8%
- Bath & shower wipes: +180%
- Thermometers: +172.3%

Due to the increasing demand for hand sanitizers, every company has started producing and marketing them, and it has become of global demand. There are hand sanitizer disposals present at every public place, such as institutions, universities, hospitals, offices, schools, malls, tourism areas, etc. The issue here is that most of these places have hand sanitizer disposals that use contact of the hand with the disposal machine to get the sanitizer into the user's hand. This could cause more of a problem than a solution because every individual will have contact with the particular disposal system. One of these or more than one of these users could be covid-19 positive, thus affecting the other users. Thus, there comes a need for contactless hand sanitizers to ensure the safety of the users and ensure there is no safety concern with using the disposal systems. Many public facilities have hence started using contactless hand sanitizers to reduce the risk for the users. This has led to increased demand for sensor-based hand sanitizer disposal systems to be contactless and safer to use in this rapidly increasing pandemic.

Proximity sensors are one of the most successful sensors in various fields, and now in the consumer electronic market, they are also getting trendy [7]. Various types of proximity sensors are available and can be used based on the application and need of the project/prototype [8]. This chapter puts forward the application of proximity IR sensors into making an automatic device that is contactless and useful in this pandemic, which is spread out worldwide.

Infrared proximity sensors are also getting very popular due to their ease of use and price affordability. The infrared sensor sends various infrared signals, which helps identify the objects. An IR-based proximity sensor's working is done by object detection based method. In this type of detection, every second an object is detected within the Line of sight of the sensor working on IR. There will be a reflection using a signal in the direction of the infrared sensor. This type of reflected signal is often known as an echo signal [9].

Suppose we use a proximity sensor that works on IR and is used for a working model for automatic contactless detection. The presence of the hand when it comes near the sensor to get hand sanitizer from the dispenser will disturb or block the Line of Sight of the IR signal, which will then give an echo signal. This shows an object detected that over here is a hand and will trigger the 6V DC water pump attached inside the dispenser to release the sanitizer from the tube or nozzle into the person's hand without them having to make any contact. Similarly, the absence of an object or hand over here will not give out an echo based signal. This shows that there is no need for the sanitizer to come out, and hence only limited sanitizer or alcohol solution will come out whenever needed. Thus, using this method, proximity-based sensors working on IR is used to find out the presence of a hand to release sanitizer, thus making the device automatic and contactless.

Hardware Requirement

Infrared Sensor

The sensor used in this project research is a proximity infrared sensor, which can be used for obstacle detection and avoidance. The module light of this sensor is easily adaptable for any surroundings and the working voltage to be used here is to be above 3.3V and below 5V. This sensor has two IR or infrared transmitting and a tube for receiving. The range of its effectiveness is from 2-80 cm.

TIP32C or BD140 Transistor

The transistor used here is TIP32C transistor and can also be substituted by BD140 transistor. This transistor is of PNP type and is famously used in most electric circuits. This transistor can handle current of 1.5A or in terms of mA, it can handle current of 1500 mA. The TIP32C transistor has a silicon Epitaxial-base and is a PNP power transistor in a plastic package. This can be used for different applications involved with switching and is used in medium power linear.

1k Resistor

The resistor is used to reduce or resist the flow of current. The value of the resistance is represented or expressed as the number of ohms. Hence, here 1k resistor is being used as it has the value of 1,000 ohms.

18650 Double Battery Holder

The battery holder required here should hold two 18650 batteries in it to provide the necessary power for dispensing the sanitizer from the contactless hand sanitizer dispenser.

6V Water Pump

The water pump used here is a DC water pump of 3-6V and is 120 L/H ultra-quiet and is micro horizontal and is submersible in water. The operating current is 130-220 mA, with a hydraulic head of 40-110 cm, flow of can be above 80L/H and should be up to maximum 120 L/H and the power can range from 0.4 to maximum 1.5W. The pump used here is non self-priming pump.

Aquarium Tube

The aquarium tube required here can be of up to 15 cm and should fit the 6V water pump insertion area for pump entirely without leaving any gap so there will not be any loose ends. It can be an airline tube pipe or a silicone hosepipe.

18650 Batteries

There are two 18650 batteries required here. The 18650 batteries are lithium-ion batteries and can be used in multiple appliances such as flashlights, laptops, vaporizers, cameras, electrical devices, etc. The 18650 describes their size which means they are 18 mm by 65 mm.

Coffee Jar

The jar should be cleaned thoroughly and dried before being used here. This jar will be used as the dispenser for the contactless hand sanitizer and should be big enough to let the 6V water pump be inside it to function the contactless sanitizer dispenser circuit.

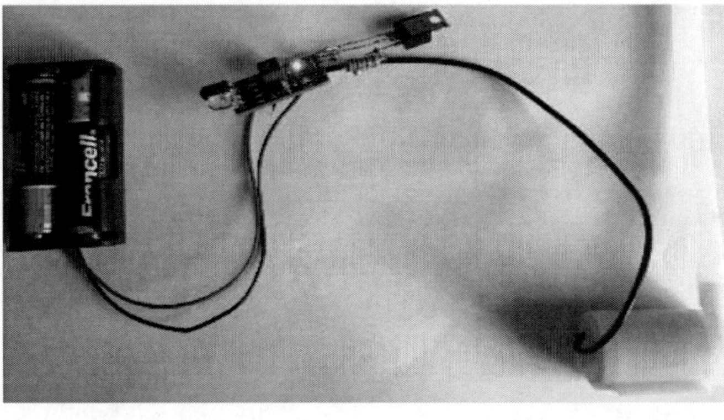

Figure 18.2. Circuit diagram for contactless hand sanitizer disposal machine [10].

Circuit Diagram: Sensor Based Contactless Hand Sanitizer

The above circuit diagram (Figure 18.2) is the base circuit followed for this chapter. The proximity sensor's OUT (output terminal) is connected to one end of the 1k resistor. The GND (ground terminal) is connected to the 6V DC water pump terminal and is extended to the battery holder/USB cable. The proximity sensor's Voltage Common Collector (VCC) terminal is connected to the battery holder/USB cable. It is extended to the TIP32C PNP transistor. The other end of the resistor is connected to the TIP32C PNP transistor. The C terminal of the TIP32C PNP transistor is connected to the latter connection of the 6V DC water pump. This connection is set up using a soldering iron to make sure the devices are not spoilt in connecting, and the circuit is set up so that there is no chance of short-circuiting. The circuit is then checked for faults to avoid and correct any failure before setting it up on the dispenser device. It is essential to make sure that there are no loose connections because it can lead to failure of proper functioning of the device and can slow down the model's performance. The batteries used should be new so they can be long lasting.

The complete circuit is then attached to the coffee jar or any dispenser device used. The airline tube or the silicone pipe tube is then connected to the 6V DC water pump and fixed properly, ensuring no air gap between the tube and the 6V DC water pump. The 18650 lithium-ion batteries are placed into the battery holder. It is then tested for faults again. Once working successfully, the sanitizer is added into the dispenser, and the battery holder is switched on so the device can begin working correctly and be of use.

Placement of the Circuit

The resistor and transistor used here are shown in the following image, where the resistor is of 1k or 1000 ohm. The transistor follows the PNP circuit system and should be connected in the method shown in the circuit diagram (Figure 18.3).

The sensor used here is a proximity infrared or IR sensor and can be seen below (Figure 18.4). It contains two LEDs and is used for object detection. Infrared sensors or IR based proximity sensors usually will have a silicone TFT made from polycrystalline or, in other words, diodes are known as photodiodes. These might also contain silicon-based TFT's made from monocrystalline or a nanocrystalline. The proximity sensors that use infrared or IR-based procedures may also contain semiconductors and are not made from silicon and can still be used to make these types of sensors [11]. The proximity sensors, which are of our knowledge or knowledge, have a refined or tuned type of circuit, including a capacitor and a coil. Their impedance will change whenever an object or obstruction approaches them and thus results in a signal which lets us know that there is an obstruction to the proximity-based infrared or IR sensor [12].

The connection was checked thoroughly for faults and placed within the container used as the dispenser for contactless automatic hand sanitizer. This was then rechecked to ensure the circuit did not have any loose connection and would not have any short-circuiting. The model is shown below (Figure 18.5) after placing the circuit on the container.

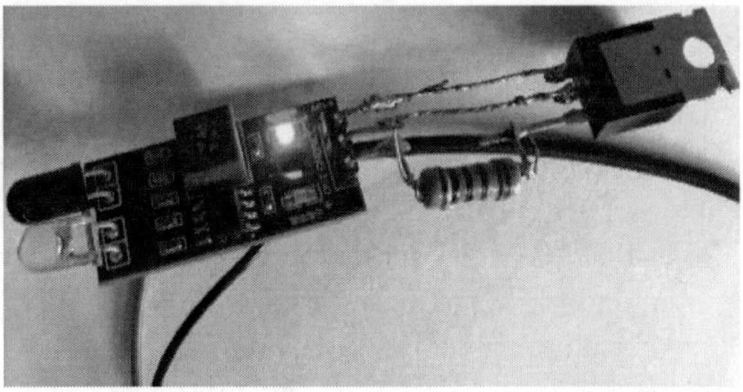

Figure 18.3. Resistor, transistor and sensor used for the contactless sanitizer.

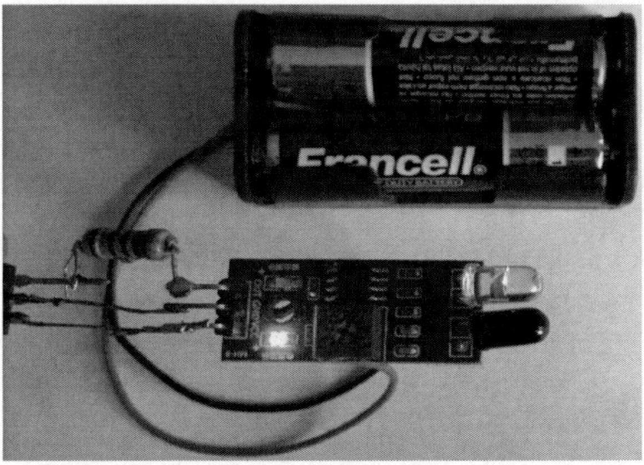

Figure 18.4. Proximity infrared sensor connection.

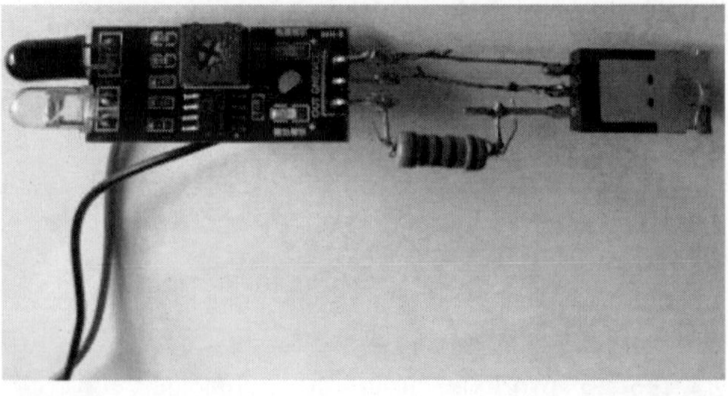

Figure 18.5. Placement of circuit.

Testing of Infrared Proximity Sensor

The infrared light, also known as IR light, is based on the principles of optics in physics. The IR proximity sensors work by applying a specific voltage to a pair of IR LEDs, also known as Light Emitting Diodes. These will, in turn, emit infrared or IR light. If the object is nearby or close by, the reflected light will be stronger than when the object is farther away from the sensor.

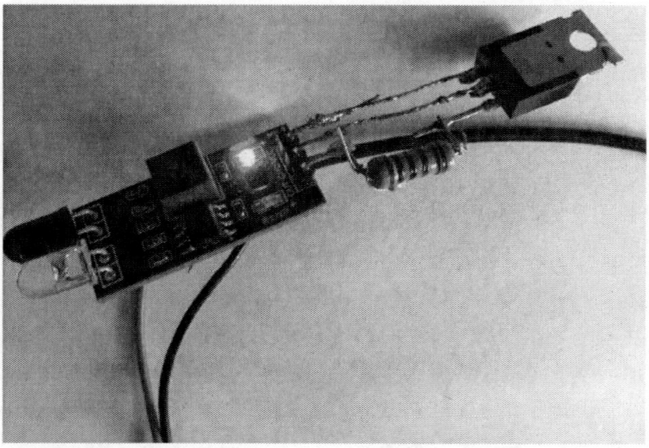

Figure 18.6. Testing sensor lights.

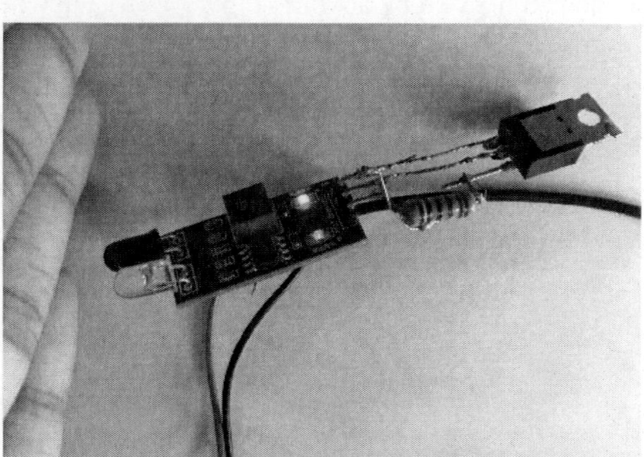

Figure 18.7. Testing of sensor lights on object proximity.

The testing should be done to ensure the IR/Infrared proximity sensor is working correctly and that the Light Emitting diodes are working properly.

This testing can be done by setting up the connection for the circuit diagram and then testing the sensor by bringing an object or your hand closer to the sensor (Figure 18.6 and Figure 18.7). If the light is emitted, the sensor works and can be used in the circuit for the model.

The sensor lights up and is working correctly, which shows the circuit is connected properly and has no loose connections in any set devices. The circuit is then stuck to the container device and is put so that it is presentable and does not lead to a short circuit, especially when used, which could cause a shock to the person using it.

Result and Understanding

The Sanitizer or Isopropyl 70% solution Alcohol is added into the dispenser, and the dispenser is closed safely and tightly to make sure the dispenser is safe. The circuit is then switched on, and the hand is put under the sensor. The IR LED lights up and activates the circuit when the hand is put under the sensor, sending signals to the 6V DC water pump through the 1k or 1,000-ohm resistor. This, in turn, activates motion in the 6V DC water pump, and this generates a motion, which lets the sanitizer come out through the attached airline tube or silicone tube nozzle. Thus, it becomes an automatic contactless hand sanitizer and can be used by anyone (Figure 18.8), anywhere and at any time, making sure that anyone who uses it will be safe and will be protected.

Figure 18.8. Automatic contactless hand sanitizer – final working prototype.

Conclusion

The global pandemic, Novel Coronavirus or covid-19, has now become the new normal and everyone has to adjust to this new lifestyle in whatever way possible till the end of this pandemic which is hard to control and will not come to an end anytime soon despite the release of the new vaccine. This results in people worldwide trying to come up with new inventions and solutions to get over this pandemic and be able to survive this pandemic in whatever circumstances possible. There are so many prototypes and ideas that people from all over the world have come up with, and it is only a matter of time that someone else comes up with much more accessible solutions to the porotypes put forward by these people [13]. The contactless automatic hand sanitizer dispenser is also one such idea which was first a highly complex prototype because it used Arduino sensors and similar prototypes. This has been reduced to simple and much more integrated prototypes so people can make it themselves in a cost-effective and expert free help manner. This project was thus aimed at coming up with a solution using a circuit with minimal cost and devices and using sensors that can be found easily.

References

[1] Thange, U; Shukla, VK; Punhani, R; Grobbelaar, W. "Analyzing COVID-19 Dataset through Data Mining Tool "Orange"," *2021 2nd International Conference on Computation, Automation and Knowledge Management (ICCAKM)*, 2021, pp. 198-203, doi: 10.1109/ICCAKM50778.2021.9357754.

[2] Coronavirus disease (COVID-19), *WHO*, [Online: Accessed on 20.05.2021] https://www.who.int/health-topics/coronavirus#tab=tab_1.

[3] Battineni, G; Chintalapudi, N; Amenta, F. AI Chatbot Design during an Epidemic Like the Novel Coronavirus. In *Healthcare*, 2020, June, (Vol. 8, No. 2, p. 154). Multidisciplinary Digital Publishing Institute.

[4] Athota, L; Shukla, VK; Pandey, N; Rana, A. "Chatbot for Healthcare System Using Artificial Intelligence," 2020 8th International Conference on Reliability, *Infocom Technologies and Optimization (Trends and Future Directions) (ICRITO)*, 2020, pp. 619-622, doi: 10.1109/ICRITO48877.2020.9197833.

[5] Java, S; Mohammed, H; Bhardwaj, A; Shukla, V. Education 4.0 and Web 3.0 Applications in Enhancing Learning Management System: Post-Lockdown Analysis in COVID-19 Pandemic. In S. Kautish, D. Singh, Z. Polkowski, A. Mayura & M. Jeyanthi (Ed.), *Knowledge Management and Web 3.0: Next Generation Business Models*, (2021), (pp. 85-110). Berlin, Boston: De Gruyter. https://doi.org/10.1515/9783110722789-006.

[6] CAMILA DOMONOSKE AND AVIE SCHNEIDERMAR, "Here's What's Been Flying Off Store Shelves" [Online: Accessed on 20.05.2021] https://www.northcountrypublicradio.org/news/npr/ 816404689/spiking-demand-for-sanitizer-canned-goods-leaves-stores-struggling-to-keep-up.

[7] Siraj, A; Shukla, VK. "Framework for Personalized Car Parking System Using Proximity Sensor," *2020 8th International Conference on Reliability, Infocom Technologies and Optimization (Trends and Future Directions) (ICRITO)*, 2020, pp. 198-202, doi: 10.1109/ICRITO48877.2020.9197853.

[8] Wu, J. *"Improvement of IR Proximity Sensor Based on Digital Simulation Mixed Subtraction Circuit"*, 30, December 2013.

[9] Mamta, B; Umair, MQ; Faisal, KS. "*Performance Analysis of Proximity and Light Sensors for Smart Parking*", 2016.

[10] ASCAS, "DIY Automatic Alcohol Dispenser (No Arduino Needed)", [Online: Accessed on 20.05.2021] https:// www.instructables.com/DIY-Automatic-Alcohol-Dispenser-No-Arduino-Needed/.

[11] Willem, DB; Steven, B; Stephen, EH; Shahram, I. "Infrared sensor integrated in a touch panel", 2013.

[12] Ken, H; Phillipe, P; Oliver, F. "Proximity sensor and method for operating a proximity sensor", 2004.

[13] Banani, T; Amit, A. *"Review Paper on New Technology Based Nanoscale Transistor"*, March 2016.

About the Editors

Dr. Soumi Dutta is an Associate Professor and Assistant HOD of Department of Computer Application at the Institute of Engineering & Management, India. She has completed her PhD from the Department of CST, IIEST, Shibpur. She received her B.Tech. in IT and her M.Tech. in CSE securing 1st position(Gold medalist), both from Techno India Group. Her research interests include Data Mining, Information Retrieval, Online Social Media Analysis, Micro-Blog Summarization, Spam Filtering Sentiment Analysis, and Clustering of Micro-Blogging Data. She was the editor of CIPR2019, IEMIS2018 Springer Conference for 3 volumes and 2 special issue volumes in IJWLTT, IEMIS 2020 and CIPR 2020. She is a TPC member in various international conferences such as SEAHF, DSMLA, ARIAM, and CIPR. She is a peer reviewer of different international journals such as *Journal of King Saud University, Computer and Information Sciences*, Springer, Elsevier etc. She is a member of several technical functional bodies such as IEEE, MACUL, SDIWC, ISOC, ICSES, and IEEE WIE. She has published several papers in reputed journals and conferences. She has recently published 2 patents on "System and Method for Solar Powered Washing Machine for Industrial Purposes" and "Sensor Based Artificial Limb for Physically Challenged People".

Email: soumi.dutta@iemcal.com

Dr. Vinod Kumar Shukla (*and Contributor to Chapters 1, 4, 9, 12, 14, 15, 16, 18*) is currently working with Amity University, Dubai, UAE as Associate Professor and Head of Academics in the School of Engineering Architecture Interior Design. He has more than 14 years of experience. He has completed his PhD, in the field of "Semantic Web and Ontology". He is an active member of IEEE. He has published many research papers in various reputed journals/conferences. He has also completed "General Management Programme" from Indian Institute of Management Ahmedabad (IIM-A). He is also a certified Network Trainer CCNI (Cisco Certified Network Trainer). He has conducted many training programs, including a training program for the employees of Delhi Transco Limited (D.T.L), Indian postal department in Megdoot Bhawan, Delhi, and Directorate General Resettlement (DGR) as an Inter Service Organization functioning directly under the Ministry of Defence (D.G.R). He has also written a case study on "Online Retail in UAE: Driven to Grow" and "Modi's Visit to UAE: Uncovering New Areas of Cooperation" which are hosted by European Case Clearing House (ECCH), the case center, UK.

He received the "Inquisitive Award", in Unanimity 2020, organized and hosted by Amity University Dubai, UAE. He has been awarded the Star Supporter Award 2019, which was presented by Manzil Center, Sharjah, UAE. Her Highness Sheikha Chaica S. Al Qassimi and Dr. Ayesha Saeed Husaini, Director, Al Manzil Center, Sharjah, UAE, handed over the "Appreciation Certificate and Star Supporter Award 2019" to Amity University Dubai received by Vinod kumar Shukla for the continuous support to community engagement and volunteerism. And he has received Memento for Amity University Dubai, from Mrs. Gloria Gangte, Deputy Chief of Mission, Embassy of India, Sultnate of Oman for Guidance Seminar 2016.

Email: Vshukla@amityuniversity.ae
Orcid ID: 0000-0002-1143-0992

Dr. Shruti Nagpal is Assistant Professor in the Computer Science department of Worcester State University, Massachusetts, USA.

She is an experienced academician with a presence in Academics for the last 12 years, with a prior demonstrated history of working in the IT industry for 5 years. Her varied skill set includes not only Business Analytical Skills and end-to-end ERP Implementations, but also teaching Databases, Programming Languages, and Management courses. Her teaching pedagogies include active learning techniques like Flipped classroom, and Process Oriented Guided Inquiry Learning (POGIL). She is a strong research-oriented educational professional with publications and/or presentations in International Journals and/or Conferences.

Email: Shruti.nagpal@gmail.com snagpal@worcester.edu

Dr. Niranjanamurthy M is Assistant Professor, Department of Computer Applications, M. S. Ramaiah Institute of Technology, Bangalore, Karnataka. He earned his PhD in Computer Science at JJTU, Rajasthan (2016), his MPhil-Computer Science at VMU, Salem (2009), and his Master's in Computer Applications at Visvesvaraiah Technological University, Belgaum, Karnataka (2007). He received a BCA from Kuvempu University 2004 with University 5th Rank. He has 10 years of teaching experience and 2 years of industry experience as a Software Engineer. He has published 4 books in Scholars Press Germany and has 1 book under process in CRC press. He is a Series Editor in CRC Press and Wiley SP. He has published 54 research papers in various National / International Conferences and Reputed International Journals. He has filed 12 Patents, 2 of which were granted. Currently he is guiding 4 PhD research scholars in the area of Data Science, Edge Computing, ML, and Networking. He is working as a reviewer in 22 International Journals. He received the Best Research journal reviewer award 2 times. He received the Young Researcher award, Computer Science Engineering, Global Outreach Education Awards in 2018. He worked as a National/ International PhD examiner. He conducted various National Level workshops and Delivered Lectures. He has conducted National and International Conferences. He is a member of various societies such as IAENG, INSC, and IEEE. His areas of interest are Data Science, ML, Augmented and Virtual Reality, Edge Computing, E-Commerce and M-Commerce related to Industry Internal tool enhancement, Software Testing, Software Engineering, Web Services, Web-Technologies, Cloud Computing, Big data analytics, and Networking.

Email: niruhsd@gmail.com

About the Contributors

S. Ahmad Ali is a Professor in the Department of Mathematics & Computer Science, Babu Banarasi Das University. He is a PhD in Mathematics from the University of Kanpur and is a Fellow of Institute of Mathematics and Applications, U.K. He has published thirty seven research papers and authored three text books on undergraduate mathematics. He is on the Editorial Boards of a number of Indian and foreign journals. He has attended, presented his work and delivered invited talks in more than fifty universities in India and abroad. He is associated with many professional bodies and currently an executive council member of Indian Mathematical Society and Bharat Ganita Parishad.

Ms. Ruchika Bathla is pursuing a PhD (Information Technology) from Amity University, Uttar Pradesh. She is working as Assistant Professor in Amity Institute of Information Technology, Amity University, Noida. She has done MCA from Kurukshetra University. She has more than 16 years of teaching experience.

She has authored a book and also published several research papers in various National & International conferences. She is life time member of Computer Society of India. She has published many chapters and also filed 4 patents and 2 copyrights which is an outcome of her passion and determination for research. Her research area includes Recommender Systems, Machine Learning, Data Mining and Big Data Analytics.

Dr. Fatima Beena is the Dean of Business Department & Associate Professor at American College of Dubai, UAE. A PhD in Commerce having a vast experience of 20 years in teaching and academic administration.

Recipient of several awards for her contribution in Academics & Research. Recipient of SHE Awards UAE, Amity Young Researcher Award, 2020, "Best Woman Performer in Academic Leadership Award (Overseas)" at International Inspirational Women Awards (IIWA) 2020, and 3-times best faculty award among couple of others. In her career span of 20 years, she has authored several research papers for National & International level journals. She has been very active for social causes and has been participating in several drives along with the robin hood army. She is also the Founder & Director of a Sec 25 Company- Social Research & Human Development Foundation.

She has published book chapters in Scopus indexed books and Research papers in Scopus and ABDC listed journals. Along with training and skilling professionals in the area of Consumer Behavior & Behavioral Finance.

Dr. Aradhana Balodi Bhardwaj is the Program Head-Psychology at Amity University Dubai. She has completed her Masters and Masters in Philosophy in Psychology. Her PhD Topic is Cognitive Behavior Intervention for Generalized Anxiety Disorder Patients. She has 18 years of experience in teaching, research and counselling post her masters. Over the years, she has taught courses like Experimental Psychology, Applied Positive Psychology, Science of wellbeing, Human skills development, School counselling and various Behavioral Science courses and guided students in their project works. She is gold medalist in the Diploma of Clinical Psychology and Diploma of Guidance and Counseling. Dr. Aradhana has published many research papers in international journals and has presented papers in conferences. She has also written case studies on "Ministry of Happiness: Can Dubai Become the World's Happiest City" and "Can the UAE Address Issues Related to Genetic Disorders?" which are hosted by European Case Clearing House (ECCH), the case center, UK.Her research interests are in the area of Positive Psychology, Sports Psychology and Mental health. She has participated in many Career

Fairs, workshops faculty development programs, Women Empowerment Programs, exhibitions, summer schools programs and Health fairs.

Dr. Anjuli Chaubey completed her PhD from Dr. Harisingh Gour University, India. She has published many research paper in reputed journal and conferences. Her research area is comprised of agriculture, agrochemicals, crops, fertilizers, genetic engineering, greenhouses, humidity sensors, irrigation, learning (artificial intelligence), moisture, organic farming, pH, soil testing. Currently she is exploring the area of Artificial Intelligence and its multi-dimensional role related to Industry 4.0 technologies.

Dr. Ashok Chopra is a highly skilled, accomplished and experienced Senior Academician in Teaching, and Training & Development, with strong learning acumen. Demonstrated research success with multiple published articles/papers, books and book chapters. Expert in creating effective environments for applied learning, which accommodates students'/trainees' diverse cultural and educational backgrounds, experiences, and individual learning styles. Have more than 24 years of international industry experience at senior and leadership positions; Entrepreneurial experience of more than 10 years and more than 12 years of experience in as academician and corporate trainer. A perfect blend of academia, industry and entrepreneurship.

Core skills as academician include ensuring program and course curricula are current, relevant and reflective of best practices within a professional/program discipline. Further defining, evaluating, and validating learning outcomes for courses and programs. Creating learning environments that accommodate students' diversity in cultures, education, experiences, and learning styles. Designing appropriate strategies and methods for facilitating and assessing student learning that are invitational and reflective of best practices in teaching. Developing methods to assess student performance consistent with the learning outcomes of the course, and metrics that address multiple learning styles. Producing multi-media materials, alternative delivery strategies, and incorporating a variety of educational technologies into the learning process. Communicating, ensuring that students are aware of course, program learning outcomes, learning strategies and evaluation techniques; providing individual tutoring, and academic counselling as per student needs.

Mr. Mark Eugine Z. Francisco is a Psychology graduate and holds Masters of Arts in Applied Psychology from Amity University Dubai. He is a licensed teacher in the Philippines and an Applied Behavior Analysis (ABA) Therapist accredited by Behavior Analyst Certification Board (BACB). He is highly experienced professional with over 8 years of diversified work experience of which over 6 years have been in the Counseling and Special Education Needs in the academe. Also, he is passionately inclined in academic and case writing about current trends and pop culture.

He is currently practicing his certification as Registered Behavior Technician (RBT) that provides one-to-one therapy session to a child with Autism Spectrum Disorder (ASD). Mr. Mark is driven to upskill his ABA career by pursuing a higher degree as Board Certified Behavior Analyst and later be a Behavior Analyst.

Dr. Shaurya Gupta is currently working in the capacity of Assistant Professor (Selection Grade) with University of Petroleum and Energy Studies, Dehradun, Uttarakhand, India. Prior to this he has worked with Amity University, Rajasthan, India in the same capacity. He has completed his PhD (IT) from Amity University, Rajasthan. He has done M.Tech (CS) from Jagannath University Jaipur and has over 11 years of experience in Teaching, Administration, Liaison & Coordination, Student Management and Research & Analysis. He has published various research papers in reputed research journals and attended many National and International conferences. His areas of interest are Delay Tolerant Network, Wireless Sensor Network, Ad Hoc Network, IOT and Machine Learning. Apart from research, he is involved in academics by means of preparing exercises, questionnaires and assignments for students at various levels and setting & marking assignments and tests, assessing students work for internally assessed components of qualifications for both UG and PG level.

ORCID ID: 0000-0001-8774-2688

Carol Hargreaves (Assoc Prof): Director of Data Analytics Consulting Centre, Department of Statistics and Applied Probability, Department of Mathematics, Faculty of Science, National University of Singapore: https://www.stat.nus.edu.sg/consulting/data-analytics-consulting-centre/, carol.hargreaves@nus.edu.sg (E): www.stat.nus.edu.sg (W), Company Registration No: 200604346E:
https://www.linkedin.com/in/carolhargreaves/

Farhana Hussain Altaf Hussain graduated from Amity University in Dubai with a bachelor's degree in Information Technology. Her prior experiences have evolved her to be more professional, providing the necessary understanding to deal with the complex method of decision-making.

She believes she has the capacity to operate in diverse work environments with different clients and achieve amazing results utilizing her strong technical skills/credentials and talents that may help both a company and her by enabling her to push her limitations to work harder each time. She is excited to be challenged in-order to master and enhance her IT skills.

Kush Kalra (Sharda University) is a law graduate and writer from India. He has written a total of thirty one books on law and is a Limca Book Record Holder for most books published on law in a year. He is the recipient of National Youth Award by Ministry of Youth Affairs and Sports and has attained the Gold Standard of Duke of Edinburgh Award. He has written many articles which are published in national and international journals of repute. He believes that education can bring big difference to improve our lives. He also believes in Justice Krishna Iyer sayings "Something was dead in all of us, what was dead is hope and positivity".

ORCID ID: 0000-0002-6044-0273

Dr. Pradeep Kulshrestha, Professor (Sharda University) has been awarded an Honorary Doctorate (Law) by National American University, South Dakota, USA and also received a merit scholarship from the Government of Uttar Pradesh. He has published 'Constitutional Law of India and 'Law of Tort for the law students and his academic works 'Criminal Justice in India Maladies, Challenges and Recourse has been published by Lambert, Germany. He has also been extended the privilege of reviewing 'Legal Aspects of Business, Oxford, Delhi, 2011, 'Mercantile Law Tata McGraw Hill, Delhi, 2012 Albuquerque Daniel, Legal Aspects of Business, Oxford, Delhi, 2012.

Pooja Lohit is a highly motivated Electronics and Telecommunication undergraduate from Amity University Dubai. Currently working as a Sales Account Manager at Beta Information Technology, Dubai. Pooja has worked on three projects so far comprising of an 'Automatic Plant Watering System,' 'Internet of Things (IoT) based Fire Alert and Evacuation System,' and an 'Image Processing and Machine Learning based Waste Segregation System.' She was privileged to be trained as an intern at Beta Information Technology, Dubai during which she demonstrated extensive knowledge in the field of Server Virtualization, Hyper-convergence, Data Networking, and Cloud Computing solutions. As a result of her proclivity towards research, she has had her paper on 'Analysis of Machine Learning Algorithms in Smart Manufacturing' published in the IEEE's 8th International Conference on Reliability, Infocom Technologies and Optimization (ICRITO) 2020.

Andre O. Magpantay is an interdisciplinary scholar of the arts, sciences, and humanities. He graduated with a diploma in Special Health Sciences from the De La Salle Medical and Health Sciences Institute. He studied biology and is currently pursuing a degree in Art Studies (Interdisciplinary) in the University of the Philippines - Diliman, with concentrations on New Media, Emerging Technologies (AI, VR, AR), Popular Culture, and East Asian Studies. He also holds a part-time research position from the same university.

He received various trainings in emerging technologies and Artificial Intelligence (AI) from IBM, deeplearning.ai, CertNexus, Reaktor and university-authorized specializations from the University of Helsinki, and Yonsei University. He also received AMA PRA Category 1 Credits of Healthcare-related courses from the Harvard Medical School. His research interest includes the interplay of health with the arts and humanities and the integration of new media and emerging technologies in medicine. He also works with various organizations for environmental conservation and received various international and national awards for leadership and the environment.

https://orcid.org/0000-0002-0366-1133.

CA. Kamakshi Mehta is an Assistant Professor at Amity University, Haryana, India, with an experience of 23 years. She has completed her CA from ICAI in 1998 and her Master's degree in commerce from Mahatma Gandhi University, Meghalaya. At present she is pursuing her doctorate from JNU, Rajasthan. She has also qualified her NET in Commerce in the year 2019. She has secured 8th Rank in BCom (Hons) from Guwahati University 1994. She has presented papers at various international and national conferences and published research papers in the journals of repute. Her research interests include Forensic Audit, Frauds, NPA, Banks, Sustainability.

Orcid ID: 0000-0002-3709-2338

S. S. Mishra is a Professor in the Department of Mathematics and Statistics (Centre of Excellence), Dr. Rammanohar Lohia Avadh University, Ayodhya, UP, India. He received his degree of MSc in Mathematics with specialization in Statistics in year 1987, and earned his degrees of PhD in Mathematics and DSc in O.R. in years 1992 and 2008 respectively. He is widely travelled in several countries for his academic pursuits including Ethiopia, Switzerland, Romania (thrice), the USA, Germany, Thailand, Nepal, and Mauritius. He received best research paper award in 2010 which was jointly given by DGBA Maryland and University of Maryland Eastern Shore, USA. He is a reviewer and a member of several prestigious academic bodies. He has received several national and international awards and fellowships. Recently, he received a most coveted award of SHIKSHAK SHREE for his significant contribution to mathematics which was conferred by Government of Uttar Pradesh, India in 2019. He has so far published 107 papers, two books, supervised three research projects and 12 PhDs, and delivered more than 50 talks/lectures in the fields of O.R. and Computing.

Dr. Sana Moid is a professional with more than a decade of experience in Academics, Training and consulting. She is currently working with Amity Business School, Amity University Uttar Pradesh, Lucknow Campus as an Assistant Professor in area of Finance. Her research interest areas are in Behavioral Finance, Menal Accounting, Women Entrepreneurship, Women Issues, Service Quality, Social Innovation and this srongly reflects in her expertise. She has been key resource person for institition of emiminent importance in India in the area of Behavioural Finance. Her workshop on Financial Planing with goverment universities in India has been acknowledged as effective and engaging. She is also reviewer for several prestigeous publishing houses like Emerald, Sage and IGI. She is currently working on National Commission for Women Funded Project as Co-Principal Investigator.

She has published two edited books (Scopus listed) and has published several research papers and book chapters in Scopus and ABDC listed journals. Has been recognized for her work from policy framing bodies under the aegis of Government of India.

Dr. Saktipada Nanda did his post graduation in Mathematics from Calcutta University and was awarded PhD (Science) from Jadavpur University. Dr. Saktipada Nanda currently works at the Department of Electronics & Communication Engineering, Institute of Engineering & Management, Kolkata, India. His domain of research are associated with Mathematical Modelling, Blood flow in the constricted human artery and vein and in the study of Brain injury problems. He has published more than 30 research papers in various Journals. He has written 11 volumes on Mathematics and Statistics published by reputed publishers in India and abroad. He is the author of a few Book Chapters placed in book volumes. He chaired national and international conferences and was Keynote Speaker in some of them. Many MTech, MPhil students are doing their project work under his direct supervision. He is guiding PhD scholars leading to Doctorate degree. His name is accepted as Reviewer of reputed Journals. He was the Project Supervisor of UGC sponsored project.

Dr. Saktipada Nanda is the Managing Editor of *Journal of Mathematical Sciences & Computational Mathematics (JMSCM)*, published from Smart Society, USA [ISSN: 2688-8300 (Print), 2644-3368 (Online)], He is still active in teaching U.G. and P.G. engineering students and in research activities.

Sibashis Nanda, founder and CEO of Rapidense Solutions, has over two decades of data management experience. He is a software developer by profession and a Mathematics & English teacher by passion. Sibashis is a prolific academic writer with 20+ internationally available academic books on varied subjects as Mathematics, Reading Comprehension and Thinking Skills. Along with managing Rapidesnse solutions, Sibashis runs a Sydney, Australia based tutoring company - Learnikx Education.

Simra Fathima Nazim, is a self-motivated Electronics and Telecommunication engineering graduate from Amity University Dubai. She is highly interested in IoT and automation technologies and looking forward to work towards smart industry developments. She is performance-driven individual with a passion to learn new things and eagerness to accept challenges while gaining experience from them. As a Port digitalization intern at SIMPORT AB, Sweden, she was able to explore the "State of the Art" Digitalization technologies in order to provide solutions to make ports smarter and participated in the *Portathon Baltic 2020, International port technology hackathon* and secured a position in the top three winners. She had worked on a major project Smart Glasses: A visual assistant for the blind, a project aimed to help the blind be aware of their surrounding by using computer vision to recognize objects, faces, texts while measuring distance from them to avoid obstacles and work on speech commands. She had also worked on other IoT based projects such as Biometric based Smart Attendance, Deep Learning methods in Image Processing for plant disease classification and a group project IoT based Fire Evacuation system which received a certificate and medal at Skyline University Innovation competition 2019 for showcasing a promising project prototype.

Dulini Ratnayake, graduated from Amity University Dubai, majoring in B.Tech. Electronics and Telecommunications Engineering. Dulini is passionate about the conscious use of technology in tackling present-day issues and has a growing interest in finding innovative engineering solutions for the improvement and development of sustainable forms of living. She has co-authored a paper on "Analysis of Machine Learning Algorithms in Smart Manufacturing" published at ICRITO'2020 and has carried out research and authored papers on the transmission of data through visible light, the use of blockchain technology to strengthen the security issues of the Internet of Things amongst others. She also has worked on the development of an IoT-guided fire evacuation system and her latest efforts are being focused on prototyping an Unmanned Surface Vessel (USV) for the detection and remediation of mid-ocean oil spills using IoT and computer vision. Dulini is continuing to pursue her interest in sustainability and innovation with her latest internship at OrionTEK Innovations, contributing to the development of sustainable engineering solutions for a better way of life.

Sandeep Rawat is a PhD research scholar in the Department of Mathematics and Computer Science, Babu Banarsi Das University, Lucknow, UP, India. In 2010, he received his MSc degree in Mathematics with specialization in Statistics from the Department of Mathematics and Statistics (Centre of Excellence), Dr. Rammanohar Lohia Avadh University, Ayodhya, UP, India. He has two years research experience as a Junior Research Fellow (JRF) and one year as a Senior Research Fellow (SRF) under NBHM research project funded by the Department of Atomic Energy, Mumbai, Govt. of India during 2013-2016 which was run at the Department of Mathematics and Statistics (Centre of Excellence), Dr. Rammanohar Lohia Avadh University Ayodhya. He has so far published seven research papers of national and international repute and participated and presented nine national and international conferences/ workshops.

Dr. Yasmeen Shamsi Rizvi is a PhD in Management from Amity University Uttar Pradesh, Noida, MBA in HRM and Marketing, and M.Sc. in Biochemistry from Aligarh Muslim University, India. She is also certified by Rice University, USA; Johns Hopkins University, USA; University of Minnesota, USA; University of Toronto, Canada; Rutgers University, USA; Indian Institute of Management Bangalore: IIT Roorkee.

Dr. Yasmeen has over 20 years of experience in teaching in MBA and Post Graduate Management Programmes at premier institutes such as Indian Institute of Management, Lucknow; CMS-Jamia Millia Islamia, New Delhi; Amity Business School, Noida. She has headed the Training and Engagement function at Max Saket Super Speciality Hospital, New Delhi. Presently she is Assistant Professor at Centre for Management Studies, Jamia Millia Islamia, Central University, New Delhi and teaches subjects in HRM and OB specialization area. She has published numerous research papers and case studies in reputed journals and conference proceedings and has presented papers in many national and international conferences.

ORCID ID is 0000-0002-7850-049X

Dr. Sonakshi Ruhela is currently serving as the Associate Registrar at Amity University Dubai. She has previosuly served as the Head of Academics- Humanities, Arts and Applied Sciences & Program Director- Psychology and Behavioral Science at Amity University Dubai. She is the author of the Book- "Counseling Interventions for Millennials," published in 9 languages by Lambert Publications (2020). She has over 11 years of full-time experience in Undergraduate and Post graduate teaching, mentorship and research. She is the Recipient of the People Choice Award for Excellence in Mental Health at The Worlds Health Awards (2021); Great Indian Women Leader, Category- Education Award by GIWA, golden signature awards (2021); Middle East Women Leaders Award, World Women Leadership Congress & Awards (2020); Academic Leadership Award, GISR Foundation (2019); Best Paper presentation award at the International Conference on Current Practices & Future Trends in Media Communication (2019) and Outstanding achievement for Autism Awareness award by Child Early Intervention and Medical Centre and Maharat Learning center (2018). She has conducted Trainings for Sharjah Tourism, Dubai Electricity and Water Authorities (DEWA), Paramilitary trainings (India), Prison Inmates Training (Tihar Jail- India), Higher College of Technology, Dubai and several schools and corporates in India and UAE.

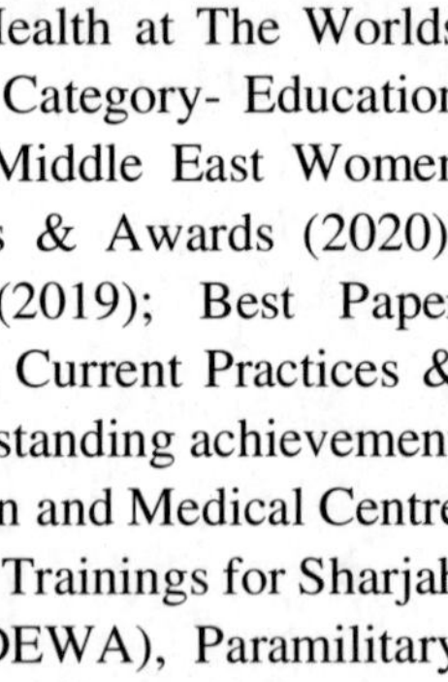

Sonia Saini is working as Assistant Professor in Amity Institute of Information Technology, Amity University, Noida since 2006. She has more than 18 years of teaching experience.

She is pursuing PhD (Computer Science and Engineering) from Birla Institute of Technology (BIT), Mesra, Ranchi, India. She has also submitted her thesis in December, 2020. She has done M. Tech. (IT) from Punjabi University, Patiala. She has filed four patents and 1 copyright. She has also published 25 research papers in various international conferences and journals. Her research areas include Data Mining, Big Data Analytics, and Healthcare Analytics.

Dr. Rinkal Sardhara is a passionate researcher and academician, with excellent academic track record and experience across diverse computer subjects. She is working as an Assistant Professor in L. J. University since last 11 years. Her area of interest is Data Mining, Data Structures, Data Science, Search Engine Optimization, Machine learning and Programming Languages.

Dr. Komal Saxena, PhD in (CS & IT) MCA. LL.B, has over 20+ years of rich indigenous experience (3 years in Corporate and 17+ years in Academics) presently working in Amity Institute of Information Technology, Amity University, Noida since last 15+ years. Her Research areas of interest are Cyber Security, AI, IOT, Big Data Analytics, ERP, SCM, and CRM. She is a member of Computer Society. She acts as a reviewer for many journals such as IEEE Access She has published more than 20 papers in Scopus indexed conferences, Journals and UGC journals. She also has filed 9 Patents and wrote 2 chapters for Wireless Communication Publisher Taylor Francis. She has also communicated 2 more chapters in willey's publication.

Orcid ID: https://orcid.org/0000-0001-5070-8355

Ms. Maha Waheed Shahzad completed her BA (Hons) Applied Psychology from Amity University, Dubai, UAE. Due to her developing interest in Neuropsychology, she interned under the mentorship of a Neuropsychologist at Mindease Psychological services and wellness center. She has also worked as an intern with Auracle wellness Centre Dubai. She had participated as a poster presenter in the CPFTMP-2019. Maha has coordinated events at university such as

World Mental Health Day, Environment Day, and Autism awareness day. She has participated in many community outreach events and activities outside university.

Dr. Hibah Shata, a dentist from the Kingdom of Saudi Arabia holds a master's degree from the University of London and a fellow of the Royal College of Surgeons in Ireland. She holds a degree in Business Administration from Dubai University, and a Certified Quality Evaluator certified by the European Society for Quality Management. Member of the Committee for Advocacy of People of Determination in the Human Rights Department of the Community Development Authority, founder and executive director of several medical and educational centers, the Early Medical Intervention Center for Children, the Child Learning and Enrichment Medical Center, Maharat Learning Center and Maharat Arabia Learning Center in Riyadh, the Kingdom Saudi Arabia, and established the first integration center at the International School of Creative Science.

Dr. Nitin Shankar is a professional with more than 14 years of diverse experience in academics, Banking and consulting. Currently associated with Amity Business School, Amity University Uttar Pradesh, Lucknow Campus as an Assistant Professor in area of Finance. Prior to this he was associated with ICICI Bank ltd, handling forex and trade. This interest area of 'Foreign Exchange Risk Management' was carried forward in his PhD work. He has carried forward his passion of Project management from his first professional stint with Genpact by mentoring and engaging with NGO's and start-ups for finding resolutions and structuring processes. His research interests are in foreign exchange risk management, Behavioral Finance, Strategy and integration of aforesaid with upcoming technology.

He has published book chapters in Scopus indexed books and Research papers in Scopus and ABDC listed journals. Along with training and skilling rural youth in the area Banking and Financial services.

Dr. Kanta Prasad Sharma has a rich experience of more than 13 years as an innovative academician. Dr. Sharma has PhD in Information Technology from Amity University Master from UPTU (Uttar Pradesh Technical University) Lucknow, India. At present, he is working as an Assistant Professor in Computer Science & Application at University Institute of Computing, Chandigarh University-India. He has published 15+ research papers with SCI; SCOPUS indexing international Journals and Conference Proceedings and is also a Member of ACM; Computer Society of India, IEEE. He has been engaged as faculty guide for more than 15 undergraduate and graduate students and also supervising PhD. research scholars in the field of IOT, navigation and communication, Wireless Sensor Networks, Finger control technology. He is also a member of the Reviewer & Editorial Board of more than 5 International and National Journals and TPC member of more than 10 international & National conferences. He has received the best research paper award in international conferences at Dubai & delivered more than 15 Expert Talk on latest technology at National & International platforms. He is presently the editor of Smart IoT for Research and Industry; EAI/Springer Innovations in Communication and Computing; Series (Springer Nature), Evolving Networking Technologies: Developments and Future Directions (Wiley); Guest Editor in multimedia under springer & CMC (SCI) journals Special Issue.

ORCID ID: orcid.org/0000-0003-3976-5839

Dr. Shikha Sharma received her B.Com (Hons.) degree from the University of Delhi in 2008, the M.B.A. degree from Maharishi Dayanand University (Rohtak) in 2010, and the PhD degree from Amity University, Haryana in 2020. From 2010 to 2013, she worked as a Lecturer in KIIT College. She is currently an Assistant Professor in the Department of Commerce at AMITY University, Haryana. Her research interests includes sustainable Tourism, Masstige Marketing, Work Life Balance, Consumer Attitude and Behavior. She has professional membership of Indian Commerce Association.

Orcid ID: 0000-0002-2710-8447.

Dr. Archana Singh, having experience of more than 20 years in Academic and IT Industry. Presently, she is working as a Professor, Department of IT, Amity University, Uttar Pradesh, Noida. Her research area interests include Data Sciences, Machine Learning, Artificial Intelligence, ICT, Business Intelligence, Data Analytics, Big Data, and its applications. She has more than 50+ research papers including a few SCI indexed Journals and 20+ in Scopus Indexed Journals like ACM, Springer, Elsevier, Wiley, and others. Dr. Singh has reviewed many articles of International Journal and Conferences and regular reviewer of International Journal of Retail and Consumer Services (Elsevier) journal and has been recognized for the same. Dr. Singh has delivered several invited talks on Pattern Recognition, Deep Learning and Machine Learning.

She is a guest editor for special issue of *Inderscience Journal* and Editor of SAGE publications and recently added Taylor and Francis book on "ICT and Data Sciences". She has extensively contributed for several IT Meets, Panel Discussions and Faculty Development Programs. She is NPTEL certified of many courses related with Data Sciences. She is a member of I.E.T.E, New Delhi. She has been guiding many Engineering graduates, Postgraduates and PhD scholars.

Ms. Aiman Siraj interests area are software development and cyber security. One of her greatest abilities is that she learns quickly and tries implementing new solutions which work well. Aiman has done several research papers – some of related to IoT and data science. Aiman has also learned networking and routing principles. Aiman is passionate about working and always eager to connect with others. Her specialties include learning new skills and programming languages, problem solving and domain driven design. So far, Aiman have tried mastering C, C++, MySQL, Java, Linux, R, HTML, PHP, Python and networking skills.

Dr. Amit Verma is Academic Director at HTMi Switzerland Dubai, and he has 16 + years of experience in the Academic and Tourism industry. He has 12 years of experience in the Higher Education industry in India, Singapore, Uzbekistan, and UAE. He has worked with Amity University Dubai, Skyline University Sharjah, Management Development Institute of Singapore, Uzbekistan, SIBMR Lucknow University, and has been the visiting lecturer for Bangor and Sunderland University UK. He has extensive experience in Airlines, Hotels, Destination Management Companies, and Online Travel companies like Austrian Airlines, TAJ Hotel, Crown Plaza, Make my trip, and Carlson Wagonlit Travel respectively. His latest academic qualification is Executive-GMP, a General Management Program from IIM-Ahmedabad.

Dr. Amit Verma has contributed to the Emiratization plan effectively in Dubai and managed the project of the Ajman Tour guide Training program and initiated the Tour guide license framework in the capacity of Head of Department in Skyline University. He has been instrumental in the publication of development initiatives of Fujairah in coordination with the Fujairah Tourism & Antiquities Authority. He has achieved awards for successful administration of several training programs like the IATA Top performer Award, ACCA Gold status award.

He is an active researcher with a keen interest in Technological Innovation in the Tourism industry and presented more than 20+ papers focusing on Cultural Tourism, Smart cities, Robotics, Artificial Intelligence, Virtual Reality, IoT, and other innovation-based solutions of the Tourism and Hospitality Industry. He has written a book chapter focused on Diversity and Inclusion and Blockchain and is an editor of an upcoming book AI in service Industry by Nova Science Publishers, USA.

Dr. Shanti Verma is a passionate researcher and academician. She is working as an Assistant Professor in L.J. Institute of computer Applications and having 15+ years of teaching experience. Her areas of interests are Machine Learning, Network Security, Data Science and Programming Languages.

She had published and presented sixteen research papers in international reputable journals and conferences, such as ACM/Springer/IEEE. You can find her papers with citation at:https://www.researchgate. net/profile/Shanti_Verma.

Orcid Id: https://orcid.org/0000-0001-5336-923X

Dr. Sonali Vyas is serving as an academician and researcher for approximately a decade. Currently, she is working as Assistant Professor (Selection Grade) in the School of Computer Science at University of Petroleum and Energy Studies, Uttarakhand. She is a professional member of CSI, IEEE, ACM-India, IFERP, IAENG, ISOC, SCRS and IJERT. She has been awarded as "Best Academician of the Year Award (Female)" in "Global Education and Corporate Leadership Awards (GECL-2018)." Her research interest includes Database Virtualization, Data Mining, and Big Data Analytics. She has authored the ample number of research papers, articles and chapters in refereed journals/conference proceedings and books. She authored a book on "Smart Health Systems", Springer. She is an editor of *"Pervasive Computing: A Networking Perspective and Future Directions", Springer Nature and "Smart Farming Technologies for Sustainable Agricultural Development, IGI Global."* She acted as a guest editor in a special issue of Machine Learning and Software Systems in *"Journal of Statistics & Management Systems (JSMS)" (Thomson Reuters).* She is also a member of Editorial Board and Reviewer Board in many referred National and International journals. She has also been a member of Organizing Committee, National Advisory Board and Technical Program Committee at many International and National conferences. She has also Chaired Sessions in various reputed International and National Conferences.

ORCID ID: 0000-003-2348-3394

Ms. Leena Wanganoo brings in a total of about 26 years of corporate and academic experience. In her 18 years of Corporate experience, she has worked with Fortune 500 companies like John Deere, India, and DHL Danzas, Dubai in Senior Management roles. She started her career in International Marketing and later shifted to Supply Chain management for Engineering and Industrial Goods.

Her passion for preparing the next generation for industry readiness led her to join academics after a stint as a corporate trainer, where she shares her hands-on experiences with students. She is also pursuing her PhD in Supply Chain and Logistics from the University of Petroleum and Energy, Dehradun.

Dr Sufian Zaheer, MBBS, MD (Pathology) is Professor at Vardhman Mahavir Medical College and Safdarjung Hospital, New Delhi, India. He has 13 years teaching experience, teaching undergraduate, diploma and post-graduate medical students. He teaches and trains student in Pathology by innovative ways like problem-based learning, clinical scenario, online teaching methodology, etc.

He has published numerous research papers, review articles, editorials, case series and case reports in reputed journals and conference proceedings and has presented papers in many national and international conferences.

ORCID ID is 0000-0002-8044-4327.

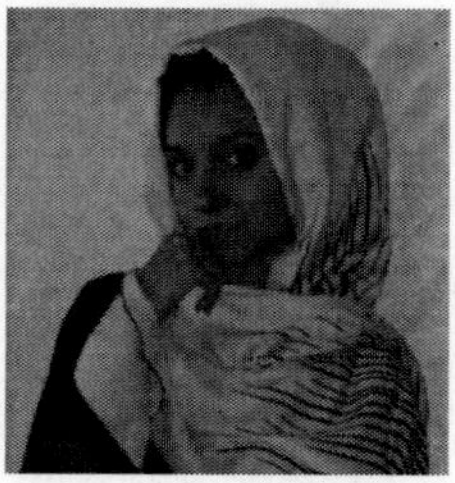

Syeda Fizza Nuzhat Zaidi, graduated with a Bachelor of Science in Information Technology from Amity University, Dubai. Her paper on "Redefining Home Automation System using Voice Recognition System" has been published online and was presented by her in IEMIS 2020 International Conference. She was also one of the top 6 finalists for EUREKA 2020 competition and Dubai SME conference. She also took part in Gulf Medical University for her noted project "Solar Powered Wheelchair" which was also submitted for EXPO 2020 qualifications. Apart from being known for her wall murals and artwork, she has also been part of organizing various International Events such as "Women in Aviation 2021", "Global Airport Leaders Forum Conference" hosted by Dubai Airport Show and was also credited with a special bonus for her exceptional hardwork in the "WETEX SOLAR EVENT 2020" by DEWA. She also has various certificates such as "Google Garage" certificate, "Memorial Education Excellence Award 2016", etc.

Index

A

AI health services, 190, 196, 197, 198, 209
AI integration, 190, 192, 195, 205, 207, 208, 209, 260, 267
AI literacy, 118
AI training, 118
ANOVA, vi, 241, 242, 244, 248, 249, 250, 251, 252
arterial segment, 92, 93, 104, 106
Atificial Intelligence (AI), ix, 12, 22, 23, 24, 26, 30, 31, 32, 35, 41, 45, 79, 117, 118, 119, 120, 121, 122, 123, 124, 125, 126, 127, 129, 130, 131, 132, 133, 137, 138, 139, 140, 142, 143, 144, 172, 174, 189, 190, 191, 192, 193, 194, 195, 196, 197, 198, 199, 200, 201, 202, 203, 204, 205, 206, 207, 208, 209, 210, 211, 212, 213, 217, 219, 234, 236, 237, 253, 254, 255, 256, 257, 258, 259, 260, 263, 266, 267, 269, 278, 280, 321, 333, 339, 343

B

bitcoin mining, v, 49, 50, 52, 55, 58, 59, 61, 62, 63, 64, 68
blockchain, vii, 11, 13, 14, 31, 50, 51, 52, 53, 54, 55, 56, 57, 58, 60, 61, 63, 65, 66, 67, 68, 299, 300, 301, 302, 303, 304, 305, 307, 308, 336, 343
brain injury, 92, 93, 95, 96, 97, 98, 99, 102, 115

C

client perception, 190
clinical application, 126
Cloud computing, 279
clustering, 56, 181, 296
CMC, 341
CNN, 218, 232, 233
coding, 32, 191, 196, 295
cognition, 234, 290, 295, 296
cognitive abilities, 287
cognitive function, 236
cognitive impairment, 216, 224, 232
cognitive load, 290, 294
cognitive process, 118
cognitive psychology, 178, 272
communication, ix, 25, 32, 47, 74, 75, 77, 78, 82, 125, 140, 143, 217, 255, 260, 277, 279, 289, 293, 297
communication skills, 77, 78
communication systems, 279
communication technologies, 47, 255
contact less sanitizer, 310
coronavirus (COVID 19), 17, 20, 25, 26, 27, 92, 93, 96, 113, 242, 243, 269, 272, 274, 278, 283, 300, 301, 310, 312, 321
corruption, 253, 254, 255, 256, 257, 260, 263, 264, 265, 266, 267, 268, 269
Corruption Perception Index (CPI), 254, 256, 260, 261, 262, 263, 264, 265, 266

D

data mining, vi, 41, 145, 146, 147, 156, 157, 168, 169, 220, 251, 281, 307, 321, 323, 327, 339, 344
data processing, 22, 236
data set, 10, 25, 113, 114, 129, 139, 142, 165, 182, 222, 229, 233, 276
data structure, 55
data transfer, 50

database, 121, 157, 160, 216, 217, 220, 233, 294, 301, 302, 304
decentralized distributed ledger, 50
decision trees, 146, 147, 159, 160, 165, 181, 220
decision-making process, 159, 207
deep learning, vi, 124, 132, 145, 146, 160, 161, 162, 166, 167, 169, 215, 216, 217, 218, 219, 221, 222, 223, 224, 225, 226, 231, 232, 233, 234, 235, 236, 237, 268, 300, 336, 342
digital healthcare, 118, 127
digital technologies, 255
disease, 4, 8, 16, 17, 18, 19, 20, 23, 24, 25, 26, 27, 31, 34, 43, 46, 75, 87, 93, 104, 107, 112, 113, 119, 120, 122, 124, 138, 145, 146, 148, 151, 152, 153, 154, 155, 156, 161, 166, 168, 169, 202, 215, 216, 222, 224, 226, 232, 236, 241, 242, 243, 244, 273, 274, 275, 276, 278, 279, 281, 282, 301, 303, 310, 321, 336
doctor(s), 9, 28, 31, 34, 38, 40, 43, 45, 52, 56, 118, 121, 122, 123, 127, 138, 139, 140, 142, 143, 147, 153, 173, 174, 181, 200, 201, 279, 280, 286, 291
dysfunctions, 92, 215, 216

E

electronic health records, vii, 47, 122, 127, 132, 140, 192, 212, 285, 286, 287, 295, 296, 297, 307
emerging technologies, 23, 28, 29, 30, 32, 50, 190, 333
evolutionary computation, 173, 187

F

financial, 40, 44, 50, 254, 255, 260, 297, 299, 301, 302
financial sector, 299, 301, 302
foreign exchange, 340
foreign investment, 254

G

Global Connectivity Index (GCI), 254, 256, 257, 260, 261, 262, 263, 264, 265, 266, 267, 269
Google, 9, 123, 279, 311, 345
Gross Domestic Product (GDP), 256, 257, 258, 259, 260, 267

H

Health 4.0, 8, 30, 35, 38, 45, 46
health care, vi, 29, 30, 31, 32, 33, 34, 35, 36, 37, 39, 41, 42, 43, 44, 45, 46, 47, 52, 93, 118, 121, 124, 125, 126, 133, 143, 144, 171, 172, 173, 174, 181, 184, 185, 186, 187, 190, 192, 195, 198, 200, 201, 202, 205, 207, 209, 210, 241, 253, 254, 255, 257, 260, 263,264, 266, 267, 297, 299
Health Care Index (HCI), 3, 4, 5, 8, 9, 10, 11, 12, 13, 14, 256, 263, 264, 265, 266, 267, 271, 272, 274, 275, 278, 280, 281, 285, 288
health care system, vi, 44, 171, 172, 173, 174, 181, 184, 186, 253, 254, 257, 263, 266, 267, 299
health emergencies, 16
health inclusion, v, 29, 30, 34, 38, 41, 45
health services, 8, 139, 174, 189, 190, 194, 195, 196, 197, 198, 209, 211
healthcare professional, vi, 8, 9, 13, 117, 118, 119, 121, 141, 288, 289, 290, 291, 292, 294
human computer interface (HCI), v, 3, 4, 5, 8, 9, 10, 11, 12, 13, 14, 256, 263, 264, 265, 266, 267, 271, 272, 274, 275, 278, 280, 281, 285, 288
human rheological system, 92, 93, 96, 111

I

inclusion, 34, 38, 72, 85, 94, 96, 102, 343
Industry 4.0, iii, v, ix, 1, 3, 4, 6, 7, 9, 29, 30, 31, 34, 35, 36, 37, 38, 41, 46, 47, 72, 83, 283, 329
information technology, 125, 126, 296
infrastructure, 7, 19, 20, 25, 33, 39, 41, 139, 173, 253, 267, 279
integration, 7, 16, 23, 30, 35, 37, 109, 111, 126, 127, 129, 131, 132, 189, 190, 192, 193, 195, 197, 199, 201, 204, 205, 206, 208, 209, 210, 221, 257, 260, 263, 267, 292, 296, 333, 340

J

Java, 321, 342

L

learning, 22, 72, 77, 78, 79, 82, 94, 119, 122, 123, 124, 126, 133, 134, 143, 146, 147, 157, 158, 160, 167, 177, 181, 216, 217, 220, 221, 222, 223, 225, 232, 233, 234, 235, 236, 237, 272, 277, 281, 325, 329, 339, 342
learning environment, 79, 329
learning process, 217, 330
learning technologies, 72

M

machine learning, vi, 22, 117, 119, 128, 135, 143, 144, 145, 146, 147, 157, 159, 160, 161, 163, 166, 167, 168, 169, 193, 216, 217, 218, 220, 222, 225, 226, 227, 232, 233, 234, 235, 236, 268, 282, 283, 300, 327, 330, 332, 336, 342, 343, 344
mathematical models, v, 91, 92, 93, 94, 95, 96, 97, 98, 102, 104, 105, 112, 114
medical education, 39, 117, 118, 125, 126, 127, 128, 129, 131, 132, 133

N

Narayana Health, v, 29, 30, 34, 38, 41, 43, 45
Neural Network Model, 169
neural networks, 22, 119, 146, 161, 162, 166, 177, 218, 219, 225, 226, 231, 233, 234, 235, 236, 268
neurodiverse, v, 71, 72, 73, 74, 76, 77, 78, 80, 82, 83, 84, 85, 86, 87, 88, 89
neuropsychology, 215, 216, 217, 237, 339
non-Newtonian fluid model, 93

O

operations, 5, 7, 8, 16, 20, 32, 43, 44, 52, 64, 145, 171, 172, 192, 220, 257, 292
operations research, 171, 172

P

pandemic, v, vi, ix, 15, 16, 18, 19, 20, 21, 22, 23, 25, 27, 28, 32, 37, 44, 118, 200, 241, 242, 243, 244, 251, 255, 256, 263, 267, 269, 271, 273, 274, 275, 276, 278, 279, 280, 281, 282, 283, 286, 299, 300, 301, 303, 307, 308, 309, 310, 311, 312, 313, 314, 321
patient, ix, 3, 4, 6, 8, 9, 10, 11, 12, 13, 14, 31, 32, 34, 35, 36, 37, 38, 40, 41, 42, 43, 44, 45, 46, 50, 52, 56, 67, 111, 118, 119, 120, 121, 122, 123, 124, 127, 129, 131, 132, 137, 138, 139, 140, 143, 146, 147, 148, 155, 161, 166, 173, 174, 175, 177, 179, 180, 181, 184, 185, 186, 187, 188, 189, 192, 197, 203, 204, 205, 207, 210, 222, 225, 226, 231, 233, 234, 235, 256, 275, 278, 285, 286, 287, 289, 290, 292, 293, 294, 296, 307
patient care, 6, 41, 118, 120, 122, 129, 131, 137, 189, 204
performance measures, 172, 174, 175, 184
physicians, 8, 36, 38, 49, 50, 56, 119, 121, 122, 123, 124, 125, 126, 127, 130, 133,

142, 197, 288, 290, 292, 294, 295, 296, 298
proximity sensor, vii, 309, 310, 313, 314, 316, 317, 319, 322
public administration, 20, 21, 22
public health, ix, 16, 23, 49, 124, 263, 266, 293, 297, 307, 308

Q

queueing models, 171, 172, 173, 184, 186
queuing theory, 185, 187

R

ratio analysis, vi, 241
rheological parameters, 93, 95, 104, 108
robotics, ix, 4, 35, 126, 137, 192, 254, 278

S

SARS-CoV, 16, 22, 25, 26, 278, 283
science, 15, 22, 27, 31, 66, 79, 88, 89, 92, 95, 96, 104, 118, 122, 125, 126, 128, 132, 138, 144, 171, 172, 177, 185, 186, 187, 195, 213, 236, 271, 272, 281, 295, 325, 327, 328, 331, 335, 337, 338, 339, 340, 341, 342, 343, 344, 345
security, 8, 11, 35, 52, 53, 58, 65, 66, 67, 205, 234, 244, 278, 280, 285, 287, 288, 293, 295, 301, 302, 306, 307, 336, 342
servers, 175, 183, 187, 279
smart contract, 50, 52, 67, 299, 304, 305, 306, 307
soft-skills training, 118, 125
software, 3, 7, 30, 31, 50, 52, 54, 56, 62, 63, 64, 77, 78, 87, 126, 141, 255, 272, 342

T

techniques, 22, 25, 32, 54, 93, 97, 138, 140, 146, 153, 156, 157, 168, 171, 172, 173, 186, 213, 216, 217, 220, 221, 223, 224, 225, 226, 228, 231, 234, 235, 236, 237, 244, 246, 253, 254, 256, 257, 260, 263, 266, 267, 325, 330
technology(ies), v, vi, ix, 3, 4, 5, 7, 8, 9, 11, 13, 14, 26, 28, 30, 31, 35, 37, 40, 41, 42, 44, 50, 51, 55, 57, 59, 61, 67, 68, 71, 77, 78, 79, 83, 88, 92, 96, 119, 123, 125, 126, 128, 130, 131, 133, 137, 138, 139, 141, 145, 147, 156, 169, 186, 187, 189, 190, 191, 192,193, 194, 197, 198, 199, 200, 201, 202, 203, 204, 205, 206, 207, 208, 209, 210, 211, 213, 218, 224, 233, 234, 237, 239, 242, 244, 256, 271, 272, 274, 275, 280, 281, 282, 288, 296, 299, 300, 301, 302, 303, 307, 311, 312, 322, 325, 327, 331, 332, 336, 338, 339, 340, 341, 345

U

urban administration, 16
urban control centers, v, 15, 16

V

vocational training, v, 71, 72, 81

W

web, 6, 56, 60, 138, 299, 302, 304, 305, 306
workflow, 130, 285, 292, 293, 296, 297
workforce, 74, 76, 80, 82, 83, 84, 85, 86, 87, 88, 129, 131
workload, 205, 234, 292
workplace, 80, 82, 83, 84, 85, 89
World Health Organization (WHO) , 28, 49, 104, 119, 131, 299, 301, 304, 306, 310, 321